LEARNING TO FORGET

LEARNING TO FORGET

Schooling and Family Life in New Haven's Working Class, 1870–1940

Stephen Lassonde

Yale University Press
New Haven and London

Published with the assistance of the Frederick W. Hilles Publications Fund of Yale University. *Cau*

Set in Galliard type by Achorn Graphic Services.

Printed in the United States of America by Sheridan Books, Ann Arbor, Michigan.

ISBN 0-300-07396-8

Library of Congress Control Number: 2004117580

A catalogue record for this book is available from the British Library.

The paper in this book meets the guidelines for permanence and durability of the Committee on Production Guidelines for Book Longevity of the Council on Library Resources.

10 9 8 7 6 5 4 3 2 1

TO MY PARENTS, PAT AND MERT LASSONDE,
AND TO MY CHILDREN, ALEX AND
JONATHAN LASSONDE

CONTENTS

Preface   IX

Introduction   1

1 Immigrants and Immigrant Neighborhoods:
   Economic and Residential Change in New Haven,
   1850–1930   13

2 Learning and Earning: Schooling, Juvenile Employment,
   and the Early Life Course in Late-Nineteenth-Century
   New Haven   24

3 The Painful Contrast: Italian Immigrant Children at Home
   and at School   53

4 Hands to Mouths: The Changing Economy of Giving and
   Taking in Italian Immigrant Families   81

5 From Courtship to Dating: The Marriage Market,
   Schooling, and the Family Economy   103

6 The Landscape of Ambition: Geography, Ethnicity,
   and Class in Children's School Experiences   122

7 "Too Good for That": Effort and Opportunity in the "New"
   High School   155

Conclusion: Elm City's Youth   189

Notes   197

Bibliography   259

Index   291

PREFACE

If, as Dickens biographer Peter Ackroyd once observed, "family ties and early childhood are the two most boring elements in anyone's life," then I am doomed, it seems, to a life of tedium. For unlike Ackroyd, I find irresistible the minutiae of children's dealings with parents and kin. When one looks closely at patterns emerging from these relationships, they reveal much about our culture. Moreover, since so much of children's lives in the twentieth century have been spent in schools, children's experiences in school and parents' regard for formal education have made me wonder, further, how the lives of children have come to be so closely associated with school, how schooling has shaped children, and how some children have managed to evade its iron impositions.

When I reflect on how I came to be a historian of childhood and education, the cause is now transparent in the way that the meaning of a dream is rendered by assembling and examining its shards. The triangulation of parents, children, and schools began to occupy me, I imagine, from the moment I first sat in one of those tan metal desks in first grade and continued to dwell in my thoughts through high school—eleven years and nine schools later. I grew up in an air force family, and we moved every three or four years until I was sixteen. The schools I attended were parochial, public, urban, suburban, and military. They were in the American South, the northern Midwest, and the Pacific Northwest, as well as overseas. In one school our desks were arranged in a series of squares to make a large rectangle; in another, we were assigned seats according to how competently we diagrammed sentences. In one school a classmate was suspended because he had failed to bring a sharpened no. 2 pencil to our science test; in another, students threw elbows and shoved other children to the cafeteria floor to be the first in line at lunch. In one grade I was told by my teacher that the mathematics I had learned up to that point had all been useless. Two grades later, in yet another school, I was told that I was too advanced in math to find an appropriate placement, so wouldn't I rather work in the cafeteria as a dishwasher for two dollars an hour during the period my math class met? One school was composed entirely of the children of military personnel, and two schools later I was part of the federal government's effort to desegregate an all-African-American junior high school in the heart of Montgomery, Alabama.

How these schools were organized and how each differed from the one before it was certainly not the intellectual puzzle it would later become for me. As I passed through each school, it was hard for me to know whether the social kaleidoscope I encountered in each new class was a function of my promotion to a higher grade or if other forces were at work. What changed little from school to school, I now see, was the unyielding structure each school imposed on my sense of time. Significantly, the school day delineated family time at either end of the day, and the school day itself was parsed by bells. This regulation of time contrasted with the way I experienced time outside of school and the school's regimen, where time seemed to stretch on forever. We children took for granted the rules, customs, and expectations of the school and the adults who embodied them for us, just as we accepted as *natural* the ways of our own families, as explained to us and modeled by our parents every day. Each—schools and parents—in their implementation of daily routine, in effect, their attitudes toward time, represented a different "face" of authority: one explicit and "rational," the other implied and intuitive, one finite and "crisp," the other infinite and supple. Yet, these lived qualities deeply inform the way I think as a historian, about how people (though tender in age) and institutions (which as children we thought had existed forever) form themselves to and around one another and how they change over time.

I owe many people thanks for their contributions to this book. Foremost, my parents, Pat and Mert Lassonde, who have lived and loved through so many changes of their own as well as through the changes I have experienced over the years. They have given everything to me that parents could, and so much more than any son might rightfully expect. I only hope they know how profoundly I appreciate their support, their love, and their pride in me and how much I love them. My own sons, Alex and Jonathan, in turn, are a source of intense pride and happiness to me. I hope that they, too, understand how much they mean to me and how they have sustained me in writing this book.

My professional historical interest in children and schooling began under the inspired guidance of John Modell, whose intellectual enthusiasms are impossible to keep at arm's length. He and I approach the content of the past differently, but we care deeply about the same things. I humbly thank him for standing by me in so many ways, but most of all for believing in my ability to find my way through the thickets of historical inquiry, as well as through the thickets of life, with all its commitments and uncertainties.

John Demos was my mentor in graduate school and the spiritual "father" of this book in the sense of offering, through the example of his work, a posture toward historical materials and their interpretation that I can only ever hope to approach through mindful, if imperfect, emulation. I am ever in awe of the power and elegance of his prose—an appreciation that deepens with every attempt I make to put thought into words, and words onto paper.

Nancy Cott first suggested that I make this a *local* study. In retrospect this seems such an obvious decision that it is now hard to conceive how it could ever have been otherwise. Her criticism has been invaluable at every stage, and her talent for getting to the bottom of complicated intellectual tangles has more than once put me back on the right path. David Montgomery, in his quiet forthrightness, challenged me to think hard about the meaning of social class in American family life. To the extent I have succeeded, it has been because he prods us all to consider how working people *think* about their lives and ambitions. Judith Smith graciously helped me in the early stages of my research and writing with insights accumulated during her own study of Italians in Providence,

Rhode Island. Lizabeth Cohen gave me unsurpassed assistance in thinking about potential sources for this study. Had it not been for her resourceful suggestions, the mountain of dissertations on New Haven social life sitting in the vaults of Sterling Memorial Library might have escaped my notice.

Paula Fass has championed my work and excerpted part of it in her own book, *Childhood in America*. But my deepest thanks to her are reserved for involving me as an associate editor on her encyclopedia, *Children and Childhood*, which provided a perspective that was both longer and broader than a case study permits. The view afforded surely made this a better book than it otherwise would have been. Jean-Christophe Agnew has been a constant source of encouragement, an exemplary teacher, and an acute critical presence since my days in his classroom. Richard Brodhead, whose own interest in the history of education and family life has touched mine from time to time, exemplifies for me the fruitfulness and intelligence of interdisciplinary scholarship at its best. Thanks to Peter Stearns for his interest in and editorial touch on an earlier version of chapter 2, which appeared in the *Journal of Social History*. Thanks, also, to Richard Altenbaugh and Bruce Nelson for their criticism of excerpts that make up portions of the book's middle chapters, which were published as an article in *History of Education Quarterly*. Douglas Rae offered extremely useful (and timely) comments on the display of schooling and population data throughout the book and made it much better as a result. I also thank him for giving me permission to use material of mine that appeared in his book, *City*, in an altered form in my Introduction.

William Kessen and Edith MacMullen kept this book alive in my mind at times when my desire to finish it was dulled by more pressing obligations. Bill, especially, was critically helpful at the crossroads between dissertation and book manuscript. His insistent view of life and history as intertwined—of the inseparability of present and past—constantly reminded me of the importance of recovering the attitudes of the people who grew up in New Haven early in the twentieth century, before their stories faded forever. Edie, a wonderful conversationalist, energetic debater, model teacher, and cherished friend, has been the dearest of companions in my study of the history of education.

Gladys Topkis took an eager interest in the manuscript in its earliest stages and was absolutely instrumental in turning it into a book. Donald Cohen, renowned child psychiatrist and director of the Yale Child Study Center, furnished crucial support in getting this book into print. In my gratitude to him I join legions of colleagues who mourn his passing. Erin Carter of Yale University Press breathed new life into this project after I had been away from it for too long. She inspired me to "bring it home," and for that I owe her an enormous debt of thanks.

A number of friends and colleagues read all or parts of the manuscript. Glenn Wallach patiently listened to me talk my way through each of these chapters on long strolls up Prospect Street hill and over quick cups of coffee at Willoughby's—before I even knew they were chapters. Glenn's friendship and uncomplaining support redefined the meaning of dependability. Susan L. Neitlich, who so kindly shared materials from her interviews with the Lender family, read, criticized, and edited several of the manuscript's chapters and offered not only her keen insights into family and local history but also her warm, steady support throughout each stage of the writing and revisions. Her husband, Matthew Broder, also lent his critical eye to a few of the chapters, offering unstinting encouragement and friendship. My good friend David Posner read the entire manuscript and helped me master spreadsheets and graph-making software. His discerning eye both improved my prose and helped me to avoid some egregious errors. But even more than that, his wit and friendship sustained me through the last several months of writing.

Christopher Sterba, fellow historian of New Haven's Italians, read parts of the book and offered innumerable helpful citations and background sources. His openness and generosity are a model of scholarly cooperation. Another fellow traveler, Anthony Riccio, ethnographer, historian and photographer, read the manuscript with the fierce interest of a local expert on the city's Italian migration. I am delighted to thank him for his commentaries and enthusiastic support. Rhonda Vegliante read the manuscript from cover to cover and pointed out a number of typographical errors. I thank her for her assistance, her interest in the subject, and her gentle friendship. Avni Gupta accumulated a mound of information on the evolving ethnic composition of New Haven's schools during the first half of the twentieth century. I thank her for completing this work with such diligence and cheerfulness. Reuben Grinberg came through in a pinch to get the manuscript, and particularly the graphs, into publishable form. I am especially grateful to him for his willingness, more than once, to put aside whatever he was doing to lend his expert hand.

My teaching colleagues, Doug Rae, Alan Plattus, and Cynthia Farrar, have continually recast the way I have thought about aspects of schooling and family life in New Haven ever since we began teaching a history and policy course together in 1996. Each time we teach it, it seems, our perspectives on the city's past, collectively and individually, are shifted by bumping up against one another's new discoveries. I want to thank them for reteaching me about New Haven's history as we have taught hundreds of students the lessons we have learned together.

A few of my colleagues in the Yale College Dean's Office deserve special mention: Joe Gordon has tutored me in the arts of deaning since my arrival in 1993. I treasure his friendship, which has been a very special source of comfort to me for a decade now. Mark Schenker, whose humor and camaraderie are priceless, has helped me "keep my eye on the ball" in my decanal duties. And Susan Rieger, now of Columbia University, has been a wise and faithful friend throughout the time this book was being revised. William and Betsy Sledge have been my partners in running Calhoun College for the past nine years. I want to express my gratitude to them for making our time here so brimming over with fun, laughter, collegiality, and purposefulness. Colleen Esposito, my administrative assistant, devoted many hours to the typing of this manuscript. But more than that, her high spirits, helpfulness, and friendship have made it such a pleasure to come to work every day.

Thank you to the Lender family for allowing me to use transcripts from oral histories conducted by Susan Neitlich. Their family history offered a beautiful counterpoint to my findings on New Haven's Italians during the same period and went far toward filling in the silences of the past with their vivid recollections. Jeremy Brecher taught me how to conduct oral histories with sensitivity and imagination. Thank you to the Greater New Haven Labor History Association and its past president, Debbie Elkin, for providing dozens of women and men to interview, for archiving my interviews, and for sharing those of my colleagues in our attempt to document the history of garment workers in New Haven during the Great

Depression. And most thanks, of course, to the men and women of New Haven who so willingly shared their time and stories with us.

Thank you to librarians and archivists at the Research Library of the Balch Institute for Ethnic Studies in Philadelphia, the Labor-Management Documentation Center of the New York State School of Industrial and Labor Relations at Cornell University, the Whitney Library of the New Haven Colony Historical Society, the Immigration History Research Center at the University of Minnesota (and my former teacher Rudolph Vecoli, the center's founder and director), the Rockefeller Archive Center of Rockefeller University, the Franklin D. Roosevelt Library in Hyde Park, New York, as well as Manuscripts and Archives at the University of Connecticut–Storrs. Very special thanks go to Judith Schiff, William Massa, and Diane Kaplan, archivists at Manuscripts and Archives at Sterling Memorial Library, Yale University, who have been so resourceful in assisting my research for this book. Three people at Yale University Press who assisted in the production of this book in its final stages deserve special mention. Amy Smith Bell, a superb editor, smoothed out lines of prose that had become snarled during my many attempts to "get it right." Veteran editor Laura Jones Dooley met my excitement at seeing the book come alive with grace and enthusiasm. Late in the day, Michael O'Malley cheerfully adopted this manuscript and gave it all the attention I could have hoped for. As an engaged reader he offered crucial advice on tone and content and supervised its completion.

It would have been impossible to have researched and written this book without the financial support of several institutional contributors. I was most fortunate to receive a handsome National Research Service Award Training Fellowship from the National Institute for Mental Health (5F31-MHO 9943-03). This fellowship afforded extensive travel to archives, the recording of oral histories, and time to complete my research and write a good portion of the dissertation. A Spencer Dissertation Fellowship allowed me to complete the central chapters of this work and inclined my thinking toward schooling in a way I had not originally anticipated. The American Italian Memorial Scholarship enabled me to conduct more oral histories. Two other awards supported work that bridged the period between the formulation of my project and the initial stages of research: the Josephine de Kármán Fellowship and the Paul C. Gignilliat Fellowship in the Humanities. I am indebted to each of these programs for critical early support. I thank the Graduate School of Yale University for its University Fellowship, which paid my tuition during the first four years of graduate training. Last, I am very grateful to the Whitney Humanities Center's Hilles Publication Fund for providing a grant to reduce significantly the publication costs of this book.

INTRODUCTION

To none was there available reliable lore or reserves of knowledge and
experience to draw upon in gaining control over the environment: parents
no less than children faced the world afresh. In terms of mere effectiveness,
in fact, the young—less bound by prescriptive memories, more adaptable,
more vigorous—stood often at advantage. Learning faster, they came to
see the world more familiarly, to concede more readily to unexpected
necessities, to sense more accurately the phasing of a new life. They and not
their parents became the effective guides to a new world and they thereby
gained a strange, anomalous authority difficult to accommodate within the
ancient structure of family life.
—Bernard Bailyn, *Education in the Forming of American Society*

In 1932, Vittorio Racca, researcher and interpreter for a child
health study sponsored by the Rockefeller Foundation, was dispatched to
investigate the role of family life in the welfare of Italian immigrant
schoolchildren in New Haven. "John [Barone], now 55," reported Racca
that March, "is a barber, but does not have his own shop. . . . He has
seven children, some of them home, but what they earn they mostly keep
to themselves. 'It is the American way; you cannot do a thing with your
children in America. All you can do is have them arrested.' Here he
stops," wrote Racca, "meaning in his heart, 'Only a tiger could do that.'"[1]
Racca's report illuminates a host of tensions in twentieth-century working-class parent-child relations: foremost, this father's embittered resignation at his inability to command his children's obedience, his dismay at

their defiant "American ways," and his speculative if halting appeal to an impersonal, antagonistic authority to uphold what he believes to be his rightful claim to his children's wages. The distance between Barone's desire to compel his children's compliance and his despair at what seems the only effective means of securing it is a measure of his bewilderment in a time of profound social change.[2]

On the face of it, this is a familiar theme in the history of immigration and ethnicity in the United States—an account of intergenerational conflict and acculturation.[3] In the eyes of immigrant parents like Barone, such restiveness in one's own children flowed plainly from the alien moral order of the new land they inhabited. Appalled as they were by the way Americans appeared to indulge their children, immigrant parents were unsurprised nonetheless. Why should the folkways of the Americans whose houses they rented, whose churches they filled, and whose schools their children crowded into offer the solace of familiarity any more than the perplexity of canned vegetables or prepared poultry sold at the corner store?

Still, a deeper story lies beneath Barone's vexation. It is a narrative not simply of straining ethnic consciousness and generational rift but of incipient individualism in the rising generation, a reversal of income flows between parents and children, and a resetting of the lines of authority. Although it is in the immigrant saga where the features of this story emerge most vividly, the changing tone of parent-child relations characterized the experience of *most* of the U.S. working class during the early twentieth century. It is, in part, a tale of economic change that penetrated to the heart of relations between parents and children and raised the sentimental regard for children in working-class families to new heights. Rising wages due to the successes of the American labor movement, the institution of the "five-dollar day" on the Ford assembly lines, the restriction of immigrant labor following the outbreak of war in Europe in 1914, and increased demand for labor in response to U.S. involvement in that conflict by 1917 each contributed to enhanced standards of living and the establishment of the ideal of the "breadwinner wage" in working-class households.[4] The breadwinner wage, uneven in its realization to be sure, eventually obviated juvenile earnings, allowing children's sentimental value to rise as their earning potential fell, creating what one scholar has called the "priceless" child.[5] A generation of "priceless" children, those born between the wars and who came of age during and after World War II, would themselves, in turn, fashion "child-centered" families—more privatized, nucleated, self-sufficient, consumerist, and, above all, more attuned to the individual needs and desires of their children than even their own parents had been, or could have afforded.[6]

The conception of working-class childhood promoted by this changing economy of relations between parents and children—one nurtured in the bosom of middle-class households since the mid-nineteenth century—was carried forward by schooling as well. Indeed, John C. Caldwell has argued that schooling first sowed the seeds of revolution in the moral economy of working-class family relations.[7] For everywhere that mass education has been instituted, he has written, it has meddled with the "family system of morality," an ethos that "enjoins children to work hard, demand little, and respect the authority of the old."[8] This family system of morality furnished the psychological and moral rationale of the family wage economy, which "operates best with many workers and a unified commitment to the interests of the family group as a whole."[9] By daily exposing children of the working class to habits and attitudes that promoted middle-class values such as punctuality, regularity, individualism, and meritocracy, schooling retarded the development of family morality. And schooling, not affluence, Caldwell has asserted, reversed the direction of wealth flows between generations: no matter how apparent the link between economy and sentiment, the shifting moral ground of the family wage economy owed more to a crisis of faith than to an abundance of bread—a crisis induced by the incursion of schooling into the lives of working-class children.

Caldwell's insight suggests that historians of family life, who have directed only faint attention to the influence of education on family relations, would do well to contemplate the affects of school attendance on working-class children's changing economic and emotional worth. For schooling determined when young people could enter the working world. Moreover, Caldwell has argued, schooling was instrumental in cultivating attitudes antithetical to familism by competing for the loyalties of children. Educated children import the authority of the school into their homes, challenging the ways and words of their parents. Schooling placed parents in fear of alienating the educated child, who was both less likely to be dependent on family employment and less disposed to respect the prerogatives of elders. Consequently, children ceased to regard responsibilities to parents as the sole source of their commitments and came instead to consider their own needs as preeminent.[10]

Two considerations nag at Caldwell's bold claims for schooling's impact, however. First, we know that working-class children's enthusiasm for schooling varied considerably when compulsory attendance laws were coming to be widely enforced. Second, the mere *fact* of schooling, arguably, was insufficient to reverse the flow of wealth between children and parents. As David Levine has observed, Caldwell obscures the fundamental material reality that sentimental ideas toward children turned on the capacity of families to afford them in the first place. In Levine's view, the beginning of the end of the family wage economy (and of the family system of morality in its turn) demanded at the very least a rise in the working-class standard of living from its abysmal state during the latter half of the nineteenth century as well as the widespread establishment of the breadwinner wage, which in the United States occurred roughly during the first half of the twentieth century.[11] Neither of these conditions was met in the Northeast until well *after* the enforcement of compulsory school attendance. Levine is thus rightfully skeptical that working-class children were easily moved by the tone and content of their school lessons to embrace the ethos of schooling over parents' objections. He believes more readily in the hold of the "antischool world" on working-class children than in the schools' ability to pry children loose from the sphere of parental influence.[12]

A further difficulty lies in Caldwell's implicitly Lockean view of the child as a blank slate.[13] Even very young children are not empty vessels into which knowledge, aptitudes, habits, beliefs, and dispositions can be poured. If this were true, there would not be a crisis in public education each generation: every child would learn with comparable ease, would be equipped with similar tools for success and individual striving. Learning is a process of give-and-take, and what children take from schooling depends not only on their natural, individual abilities but on their environment as well—the relative support or opposition of their parents and siblings to education, who their teachers and fellow students are, and where their school is located.[14] Even while recognizing the truth in Caldwell's observation that schooling presented challenges to parents' values that were both overt and subtle, I share Levine's skepticism over the ineluctable power of education to alter parent-child relations. A better barometer of change than sheer exposure to schooling is the increased tendency of working-class youths to remain in school beyond the age of compulsory attendance.[15] For the impact of schooling on parent-child relations is not the dichotomous proposition Caldwell supposes it to be but rather an incremental one. Schooling, once established, introduces changes by degree, and over time incremental change can be transformative. The eventual voluntary extension of schooling during the early decades of the twentieth century was just such a change and one with enormous and unforeseen consequences. Chiefly, it ensured the possibility of progressively recombining the relative influences of parents, teachers, and peers as children moved through the public schools.[16]

In part, the geography of class and ethnicity in the United States at the beginning of the twentieth century mitigated the potential transformative power of schooling on parent-child relations. In New Haven, as in most cities of the industrial Northeast and Midwest during the early twentieth century, children were sent to schools in their own neighborhoods, which were often relatively homogeneous ethnically, racially, and socioeconomically.[17] Even though ethnic and religious differences among students were a source of tension and at times bitter conflict, the similarities among immigrant working-class children often bound them to the very "antischool world" that Caldwell believes they inevitably abandoned. This antischool world, often engendered by a deeply felt commitment to family and kin, was nested in communities of ethnic fellow-feeling, work, and worship, which assisted children in their resistance to the school's ideology.[18] As long as schooling at the elementary level occurred in the neighborhoods where children played and parents, siblings, and kin toiled, all was relatively familiar. The school, then, while foreign and for some even objectionable, was not necessarily the irritant of ineluctable change assumed by Caldwell.

As children rose through the educational hierarchy, however, they moved successively outward from their own neighborhoods. With the initiation, in the second decade of the twentieth century, of a curriculum more suited to the interests of non-college-bound students and the decline of youth jobs after World War I, more children from more varied backgrounds were promoted out of the familiar confines of their neighborhood elementary schools and into junior high schools many blocks away from home. The pyramidal design of city school systems like New Haven's combined with geography to separate children physically from their families and communities more distinctly than had been the case during children's elementary years. By 1930 New Haven's public school system consisted of fifty-four elementary schools at its base, each with small enrollments; four junior high schools with comparatively large enrollments; and two high schools at its apex, Commercial and Hillhouse (the city's academic high school), each boasting enormous pupil populations.[19] The four junior high schools were built during the 1920s to accommodate the growing numbers of teens electing to continue their schooling, and these were necessarily at some distance from the neighborhood elementary schools that fed them. The junior high schools were instituted with the aim of creating an easier transition to the city's high schools. By 1930 a wide majority of young people attended either Commercial or Hillhouse.[20] Both high schools were located downtown on the perimeter of Yale University.

Schooling created a physical sphere of relations with others from beyond the neighborhood world and illuminated models of American or middle-class life that offered proximate alternatives to the worldview of the children they served. But the schools were colonizers in part, foreign bodies within the communities they inhabited. This relationship was reversed, however, when children completed sixth grade. The remoteness of Hillhouse and Commercial high schools from the elementary schools and the junior high schools that fed them required most students to journey past the businesses and municipal establishments of downtown New Haven. The walk to school visually reinforced the perception of civic authority as something foreign and grounded outside of young people's own neighborhoods. Whether they were journeyed to by foot or by streetcar, the city high schools were interwoven into the fabric of New Haven's other grand civic institutions: City Hall, Center Church, the municipal court house, the public library, Chapel Street's department stores, Broadway's retailers, the ancient New Haven Green itself, and of course, neighbor and wealthy collegiate cousin Yale University. New Haven's neighborhoods, in their scaled-down familiarity, stood in shrunken contrast to the granite ambitions of this old Yankee city.[21] And although the sensation of being culturally at sea was deepest and most daunting to the children of immigrants, it was palpable nonetheless to all but the very few whose forebears had been the merchants, industrialists, and civic leaders of Old New Haven. The high schools, then, offered young people both a glimmering prospect of individual success and upward mobility on one hand and the fearsome possibility of failure and continued marginality on the other.

During adolescence young people are developmentally most open to exploring alternative, competing values that call their own parents' principles and designs for living into question.[22] For the first time in American history, during the 1920s and 1930s, most sixteen-year-olds were in school rather than in the workforce; and although schooling was critical to the spread of the sentimental regard for children, the middle-class values borne by the schools were as likely to be encountered by adolescents *outside* the classroom—on the walk to school, in the school yard, and in extracurricular and school-related social activities—as *in* it.[23] Exposure to peers of other class and ethnic backgrounds posed different modes of relating to authority, of expressing affection, love, and loyalty, and of organizing commitments to family and kin. Such encounters could drive a wedge into relations between parents and children in a way that could not have occurred among children at earlier developmental stages.

Moreover, from the end of the nineteenth century (when schooling became universal but ended for the majority of children between grades six and eight) until the 1930s (when all children were required to enter high school), the great majority of young people satisfied the legal minimum of compulsory schooling without ever leaving their parents' neighborhoods. The convergence of extended schooling and adolescence, which combined to produce a full-blown youth culture by the 1930s, was leavened by the rise of mass media during the same period—motion pictures, radio, and advertising—which celebrated and drew attention to this dynamic new social phenomenon. Therefore, while young people could make choices about their schooling, jobs, friends, and future spouses and still appear to conform to the spirit of familism, reciprocity, and filial piety, these choices often admitted aspirations that rendered children's ability to respond to family need less flexible and obscured their own consequences. Only in time did the significance of remaining in school, aspiring to a white-collar job, or moving out of one's parents' neighborhood emerge to fashion a way of life that made responsiveness to parents, siblings, and kin an increasingly remote and unrealistic prospect.

Historians have tended to study separately families and schools—the two most powerful socializers of children in the twentieth century—even though there are patent advantages to a stereoscopic view that brings both into focus simultaneously. Why is this? It is easily forgotten that it was only in the twentieth century that schools came to occupy, fully, the majority of children's time. The bulk of historiography on working-class family life then is understandably concerned with the struggle to earn daily bread, the changing forms of family structure, and the ideology of family relations. With equal parochialism, the historians of education have focused on the emergence of schooling as an institution—the major trend of the twentieth century to be certain, but one cultivated at the expense of a better understanding of the social experience of children's development. Critics of education in postwar America, from policy-makers to the public, are as apt to blame "the family" as the public schools for the changing fortunes of popular education.[24] Still, scholars have been slow to see the relationship between families and schools as a dialectic that shapes, reshapes, and shapes again the one to the structures and rhythms of the other.[25] The outcome of this relationship by the mid-twentieth century was the acceptance among the U.S. working class of the sentimentalized child and the recognition of childhood as a "sacred space" for the child's development in preparation for adult responsibilities.

This story is about the dialectic between schools and working-class families as they sought to define the significance of age and its relation to parents' and children's dependence on, and obligations to, one another. The experience of many ethnic groups would serve to illustrate this important social and cultural change during the twentieth century, but in this book I focus on the experiences of Italian immigrants and their children in New Haven. Italian immigrant children were the largest group among the generation of children that entered the city's school system during its period of greatest expansion and curricular change. When New Haven's population peaked in 1920, Italian immigrants and their children comprised 25 percent of the city's total population. Overall, four out of ten children in the public schools were of Italian descent, so they were crudely "representative" of the pupil population in the way that social historians tend to think about the experiences and circumstances of the ordinary person. But their representativeness merits qualification: having come from the most rural provinces of Europe and drawn as they were to a city with a large proportion of semiskilled and unskilled industrial jobs, Italian immigrants found work at the lowest rungs of New Haven's occupational ladder. Thus, even though Italian immigrant children constituted the majority of a diverse pupil population, socioeconomically they were not strictly representative of the city's average pupil, since their families were typically larger, their housing was more crowded, and their household incomes were smaller than the mean for the city's working class. But even more important from the perspective of New Haven's educators, the attitudes of Italian immigrant parents generally were resistant if not outright hostile to schooling; and because their children represented a plurality of New Haven's pupil population, they posed the school system's profoundest challenge.

At one end of a spectrum of attitudes toward schooling in turn-of-the-century America, the experience of Italian immigrants dramatizes the interplay of the family economy and schooling in an era that witnessed the end of children's significant contributions to family earnings. New Haven's Italian immigrants were, sociologically, a well-studied group whose voices have been recorded in rich detail, offering keen and otherwise unrecoverable insight into the ambitions, struggles, and commitments that defined the bonds and boundaries of working-class family life in the early twentieth century. And yet some formidable obstacles lay in the path of the historian who tries to reconstruct the changing meaning of family life and the impact of schooling on parent-child relations among Italian immigrants. Although historians have long recognized the importance of studying the relationship between families and schools, there are still no examples in the literature to follow. The historical record itself, moreover, is abundant and evocative in some decades, spare and unyielding in others. I have employed the evidence at hand, using oral histories in particular to interrogate my sources, to guide my questions, and to understand the logic of everyday life among a people whose ways were often perceived as marginal to the tenor and thinking of those around them.

Social historians tend to explain changes in schoolchildren's experiences over time as organized by schools. Although this is understandable, it dictates an undue emphasis, from my perspective, on schooling as an institution. An institutional focus too often drives the narrative of change, negating our understanding of the importance of the relationship between families and schools and ultimately distorting our picture of how children's lives have been shaped by this dynamic. What we lose is the opportunity to comprehend the history of education "in the broadest sense," as outlined by Bernard Bailyn and Lawrence Cremin more than forty years ago.[26]

Schooling, as these historians have urged us to understand, is an intervention into the lives of children and their parents. New Haven's fathers determined shortly after founding the town in 1638 that such an intervention was necessary to perpetuate the convictions of their pious community. New Haven's first immigrants were conservative Puritans, who in looking to settle in the New World, purposely skirted the Massachusetts Bay settlement, whose colonists' bland religiosity they found uncomely.[27] Like the separatist founders of the Plymouth colony, who worried about spiritual malaise among family heads down through the generations, New Haven's founders believed that where faithless parents failed their children morally, civic statute must compensate. Thus in 1641 the town's leaders ordered the construction of a schoolhouse and an allowance for a schoolmaster "to be paid out of the town's stock." Justification for this unusual expenditure was recorded "for the better training of youth in this town, that through God's blessing they may be fitted for public service hereafter, either in church or commonweal."[28] In 1656 the New Haven Code compelled instruction in reading by parents to children and masters to servants so that they may "attain at least so much as to be able duly to read the Scriptures, and other good and profitable printed Books in the English tongue, being their native language, and in some competent measure, to understand the main grounds and principles of Christian Religion necessary to salvation."[29]

As town grew into city and colony into state, the port of New Haven prospered and its population became more religiously, ethnically, and socially complex. A variety of schools were formed to spread literacy and furnish the rudiments of citizenship in the new republic for the children of parents too poor to afford them schooling. By the second quarter of the nineteenth century the common school found eager supporters across the state. Although the common school had many antecedents, effective schooling of large numbers of children was pioneered by the "Lancasterian" or "monitorial" system, which employed a method of mentoring by older "scholars" in training their younger peers.[30] The result was that a great number of children in one large room could be successively educated at a much reduced cost. A Lancasterian school was established in New Haven in 1823 and quickly replicated in Hartford and nearby Guilford.[31] Yet by midcentury the arrival of great numbers of immigrants of little means, speaking different languages and adhering to different religious convictions, began to pose a stiff challenge to the cultural homogeneity of the city's social order. The small number of schools devoted to the education of children of all social ranks could no longer do the work required to remedy the perceived negligence, intemperance, ignorance, and dysfunction of family life among the city's new peoples.[32]

This book begins with the establishment of public schools in New Haven in the 1850s, examining the effort to attract then compel all children to attend school, and it ends on the eve of World War II, when high school graduation attained the status of a norm in American society. Over the course of this period, the impact of schooling on relations between parents and children deepened as the middle-class ideal of sentimental childhood spread and took root in a very diverse American working class. The school was the primary vehicle of this change, but it was the elaboration of a system of schooling for all children and its physical location beyond the child's neighborhood that drew working-class boys and girls into contact with their middle-class peers who embodied the very cultural ideals espoused by the schools.

An irony, however, sprang from the success of universal schooling in eroding the authority of the "anti-school world" of family morality. As familism gave way to the ethos of extended schooling and strangers increasingly assumed responsibility for socializing adolescents, a budding youth culture—unofficial and at times antischool—arose to compete for the attention of young people just as the great majority of teens were under the collaborative supervision of nonfamily adults for the first time in the history of human society. Working-class parents who delivered their children to the schools relinquished control over them at two successive removes: first, to the official culture of American middle-class society as expressed in the curriculum and authority of the schools; and second, to the "unofficial" society of the peer group and its participation in an emerging national youth culture.[33] In either instance—whether native-born or immigrant—working-class youths were "learning to forget": in New Haven's schools and in the nascent teen world that coincided with their own coming of age, they were *un*learning the very lessons their parents had taught them about the connection of their needs and aspirations to their commitments to others.

1

IMMIGRANTS AND IMMIGRANT NEIGHBORHOODS: ECONOMIC AND RESIDENTIAL CHANGE IN NEW HAVEN, 1850–1930

The citizens of New Haven are familiar with the fact that the city is growing . . . but many of them fail to realize how rapid and how profound these changes are likely to be in the near future. . . . Many of those now living will see the completion of the process by which it is being transformed from the pleasant little New England college town of the middle nineteenth century, with a population of relatively independent, individualistic and self-sufficing householders, into the widespread urban metropolis of the twentieth century, the citizens of which will be wholly dependent upon joint action for a very large proportion of the good things of civic life.
—Cass Gilbert and Frederick Law Olmstead, "Report of the New Haven Civic Improvement Commission"

After the 1840s the composition of New Haven's neighborhoods changed almost continuously and kaleidoscopically. As the city's economy shifted from maritime and mercantile pursuits early in the nineteenth century to an industrial manufacturing base and the economic fortunes of its parts prospered, declined, and revived, property changed hands cyclically and routinely. The same pattern was repeated throughout the city in areas wherever manufacturing grew up under the stimulus of industrial capitalism: residential districts developed by the merchant class fell out of favor or were sold off piecemeal for industrial or commercial uses and, often, eventually working-class occupancy. The new economy transformed New Haven's neighborhoods in every direction: on Howard Avenue at the city's south end; to the north in Newhallville, where an early New Haven carriage factory flourished; and later, on the blocks surrounding the mammoth Winchester factory, along Oak Street and Legion Avenue; and around Wooster Square. One-family homes built by prosperous industrialists or more modest shopkeepers were eventually tendered to skilled workers and shop foremen as the upper and middle classes moved, by the end of the nineteenth century, toward the city's outer reaches or up Prospect Street or Whitney and Whalley Avenues. Many of the residences they left behind were partitioned and leased to fetch as much rent as the market would bear with the influx of rural and immigrant families into New Haven. Tenements as well as two- and three-family houses sprang up in parts of the city where industry attracted labor, followed by a demand for inexpensive housing.[1]

At the turn of the twentieth century, the arrival of tens of thousands of people from Eastern and Southern Europe swelled New Haven's population. Between 1890 and 1920 the city's population nearly doubled, expanding from 86,000 to 162,000, largely as a result of the mass migration across the Atlantic to North and South America.[2] And although New Haven's increase from midcentury to 1890 had been even more dramatic, quadrupling between 1830 and 1890, the provenance of immigrants to the city as it reached industrial maturity was decidedly non-Protestant and non-English speaking (see fig. 1.1).

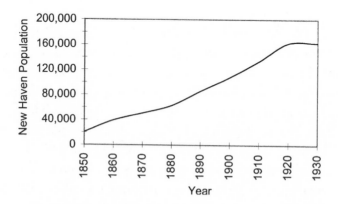

Fig. 1.1 Growth of New Haven population, 1850–1930. *Sources:* New Haven, *Annual Reports,* 1857–1930; Wrinn, "Development of the Public School System"; New Haven, *New Haven's Schools,* 16–23

Immigrants stepping off trains they had boarded in New York for New Haven could journey a mile and a half west, northwest, or south and find themselves surrounded by speakers of Croatian, German, Polish, Russian, Serbian, Slovak, and Yiddish, as well as the dialects of most of the regions of Italy. In clusters of settlements around the city they molded a multitude of communities out of the convulsive sprawl of iron, brick, grime, and soot they came to inhabit.[3] In shanties, tenements, "deep lots," and cold-water flats German and Irish immigrants at mid-century were followed by Italians, Poles, Russian and Polish Jews, and "Slavs" from the 1880s to World War I. Each group in its turn sought to reconstruct the web of relations that had furnished whatever measure of security and comfort they had relied upon in the ancient towns from which they had emigrated.[4]

The primary area of settlement for every immigrant group in New Haven since the mid-nineteenth century was the "Hill" district, which extends from the city's railroad terminal westward across Oak Street and Legion Avenue to the West River, where it juts sharply south toward City Point—New Haven harbor's western reach.[5] Home to Union Station, the hinge of the New York, New Haven, and Hartford Railroad, the Hill's proximity to the city's major point of embarkation made its neighborhoods the likeliest first stop for peoples new to the city and its environs. German and Irish immigrants came before the rail. Indeed, Irish labor made later immigration and industrial expansion possible. Irish immigrant workers excavated the state's south-central section of the Farmington Canal with picks and shovels during the mid-1820s.[6] After the canal failed, Irish workers were harnessed once again to construct the railroad beds, lay the track, and build the yards that linked the trains they carried to a vast continental network, a feat that signaled the birth during the 1840s and 1850s of the United States as a future industrial giant.[7]

Although the Irish outnumbered all other immigrants until 1900, Italians were the largest (and poorest) of New Haven's new peoples by the time immigration effectively ceased in 1924. Two sections within the Hill's teeming triangle of people, commerce, and industry—the lower Hill and Oak Street—received many of the early Italian immigrants. The first Italians to take up residency in New Haven were from the northern and central provinces of Italy but prominently from the Marches, which lay just north and east of Rome.[8] These "Marchigiani" settled in the southeastern section of the Hill toward the rail yards and the harbor in an area more prosperous than the Italian settlements that followed. Here a greater proportion of New Haven's Italians owned their own homes, and among them resided the community's most skilled craftsmen and earliest professionals.

Until the 1880s there were still relatively few Italians in the city. During that decade, however, a large group from Benevento, approaching about five hundred in all, had been drawn to New Haven to lay the expansion of railroad track between New York and New Haven.[9] This group settled in the lower Hill, which also became home to compatriots from Caserta and Avellino—neighboring cities in Campania, the region around Naples. They moved in among lingering Irish immigrants and the first of the city's growing Russian Jewish population. This furnished the first influx of southerners to New Haven and foreshadowed a migration that would transform the city's complexion over the next three decades.

Before 1900 young Italian male migrant workers ("birds of passage" as they were known in the United States, because they returned to Italy's shores as frequently as they arrived in New York) were but a trickle of the immigrants arriving in New Haven in search of work after 1900.[10] They sought to escape worsening economic conditions in southern Italy, many in the hope of returning to their native land one day, secure or even prosperous. This migratory pattern was not new, of course. The attempt to supplement family earnings by journeying abroad for work had proceeded for centuries across the length of Italy (though with greater effect in the North than in the South), but it was not until the end of the nineteenth century that the search for seasonal employment reached beyond the sphere of European labor markets.[11]

Improvements in the Atlantic passage made possible by the steamship after 1870 reduced the travel time from Europe to the Americas from as much as six weeks to as little as seven days by 1890. This improvement was not simply a matter of enhancing the convenience of passage either. It greatly increased the volume of transatlantic migration by drastically diminishing the danger of the spread of disease, which often flourished on long oceanic voyages. Moreover, the number of passengers who could be accommodated was enlarged by the introduction of mammoth vessels at century's end, as well as by the expansion of steamship fleets.[12] Add to this the sponsorship of workers' passage by industries hungry for European labor and almost overnight the more remunerative labor markets of North America were placed within easy reach of Europe's traditional population of migratory workers and the growing pool of laborers displaced by the "creative destruction" of industrial capitalism.[13]

Cheap, rapid travel between Europe and America made the phenomenon of "return migration" increasingly possible, and Italian immigrants exploited the abbreviated ocean transit in greater numbers than any other European immigrant group after the turn of the century. Nonetheless, like every immigrant group that preceded them, the longer Italians remained in the Americas the more likely they were to attract family and kin who would seek work in the same factories and shelter in the same neighborhoods, partially reconstituting in North and South American cities the southern Italian villages from which they had come. From 1900 to the outbreak of World War I, rates of outmigration from parts of the Italian peninsula below Naples (including Sicily) ranged from 50 percent to as much as 100 percent. Since one of two emigrants came back in the same year, in some villages half of everyone left and returned only to leave again in the same calendar year.[14]

The very conditions that inspired emigrants' departure for the Americas persisted from 1880 to 1920, "pushing" others out of Italy to join their kin in Argentina, Brazil, or the United States.[15] Agricultural productivity, especially in the remote mountain hamlets of Italy, where the bulk of southern emigrants came from, continued to spiral downward, causing the meager wealth of small landholders to deteriorate, edging subsistence into desperation and flight. What is more, Italian immigrants in America unwittingly exacerbated the problem: On one hand, their reports home of abundant work and high wages in the United States raised the sights of kin and countrymen, swelling the annual tides of migratory labor that flooded American ports of entry. On the other hand, by sending part of their income home (the major portion of earnings in many cases), they triggered an inflationary trend that progressively devalued Italy's currency over the period, worsening the poverty of the poor and lowering the standard of living of everyone who was not a steady beneficiary of these birds of passage. By the turn of the century Italian immigration was in full swing, and the Italians arriving in the Americas were no longer just young men, but young and old women, fathers and mothers of men in search of work, as well as cousins, brothers, sisters, uncles, aunts, and grandparents. The familial character of twentieth-century Italian immigration bespoke another change: while the pattern of return migration continued, increasingly immigrants from the South came to the United States to stay.[16]

Although the Italians of the lower Hill thought themselves superior to those who arrived at the turn of the century and after, it was Oak Street that attracted the greatest number of arrivals and was soon the Hill's most dense, vital section. This was especially so by the early twentieth century, when Oak Street and its offshoot, Legion Avenue, came to be dominated by the butcher shops, junk stores, green grocers, bakeries, synagogues, and tenements of New Haven's Russian Jews.[17] After 1900 New Haven's Italian immigrants came almost exclusively from the South rather than from northern and central Italy—from Abruzzi, Apulia, Basilicata, Calabria, and Campania—from Naples down to the toe of the Italian peninsula and Sicily. As much as possible, these peoples clustered on blocks whose residents spoke the same dialect and had come from the very villages that they themselves had abandoned to find work in the United States. As Italians and Russian Jews moved into the Hill, the more affluent Irish moved out—to Westville, along upper State Street, and in large numbers to Fair Haven across the Mill River, due east of the downtown area. Yet the attempt to reconstitute the social fabric of the Italian village met with only fleeting success, it seems, for the Hill was not as geographically delimiting as the other major area of Italian settlement, Wooster Square.

The Wooster Square settlement was a compact mixture of residences, small businesses, factories, and warehouses huddled around an English-style city park, which had been laid out in 1825 and named for a locally renowned hero of the American War of Independence.[18] Two of its borders were formed by the first railroad constructed in Connecticut. Framed on the west by tracks that looped the edge of downtown heading north to Hartford, the rails jogged east on their way out of New Haven, defining the square's northern edge before meeting up with the Mill River, whose left bank collaborates to make the district's third side as it meanders south to the flats of the city harbor. Wooster Square sprang up as a new settlement just east of the city's historic nine squares, aiming to capitalize on its location at the nexus of New Haven's cresting maritime commerce and the next wave of economic prosperity, which would come, it was believed, with the construction of the Farmington Canal.[19] The canal skirted the square's western flank but was soon annulled by the coming of the railroad, which literally dispossessed the canal of the channel that had been carved out for it. No matter that the square's founders were utterly mistaken in their speculations on the canal's role in New Haven's future. The railroad accomplished in a stroke the purposes of the city's industrial pioneers by permanently uniting New Haven's deep water port with the New England hinterlands and beyond. Rail was superior both in its carrying capacity and in its independence from the natural but arbitrary advantages of water power.[20]

Before locomotion, the canal was seen as the cheapest and most efficient means of connecting up sites of production formerly stunted by their lack of access to water power and relative distance from river shipping. But hundreds of local railroad companies sprouted up throughout the Northeast during the mid-nineteenth century, both outstripping the canals' capacity to move cargo and negating whatever competitive obstacles nature had inserted between maker and market.[21] One of these companies—the New York, New Haven, and Hartford line—became a behemoth. Gathering up dozens of local railroad companies between the 1870s and the turn of the century, it created one vast system of rails along the coast of southern New England and reached north, penetrating deep into its interior.

Wooster Square, whose stately houses gazed out upon the Long Island Sound, sat at the center of this the dynamic juncture of New Haven's rail and shipping terminals. By the mid-nineteenth century it had become home to many of New Haven's emerging industrial titans, but as its merchant- and manufacturer-residents prospered before and after the Civil War, they gradually deserted the square to build the mansions that now adorn Prospect Street, stretching from Grove Street Cemetery a mile and a half to the north.[22] As they moved out, many of their homes were transformed into tenements and flats to shelter the crowds of laborers who came to work in the area's nearby workshops, factories, and warehouses.

Although the Italian settlement in Wooster Square took longer to develop than the Hill "colony," the first child of Italian immigrants to be born in New Haven arrived in the square in 1861. By the beginning of the new century, Wooster Square had become thickly peopled not only by Italians—from Almalfi, Atrani, Salerno, and Scafati—but by Irish, Poles, Lithuanians, a small contingent of French wood workers and blacksmiths who toiled in the booming carriage industry, Hispanic immigrants of unknown origin, and African Americans whose forebears had lived in the Elm City since the eighteenth century.[23] Wooster Square lay at the heart of the Tenth Ward, which, with its neighbors the Twelfth and Eleventh, formed a gnarl of factories, warehouses, and tenements that made it the city's most densely inhabited area. Despite this rich blend of immigrants from across the European continent, however, only two decades into the 1900s the neighborhood around the park would become overwhelmingly Italian: whereas in 1908, 54 percent of its residents had been born in Italy or were of Italian parentage, by 1930, 84 percent of the population in the three wards surrounding Wooster Square were of Italian origin; fewer than 10 percent were of native-born, white parentage; and 3 percent were Polish. While, in part, the concentration of Italians was realized by immigration and natural increase, during the 1920s the area's total population decreased as many non-Italians moved out, effectively increasing the ratio of Italians in the district, especially in Ward Twelve. At the start of the decade, New Haven possessed one of the highest fractions of Italian immigrants per capita in the United States; within this population Ward Ten contained the densest concentration of Italian-born heads of household. Italians and their children totaled 41,858—one-quarter of the city's entire population.[24]

The 1930s marked the end of a century-long period of commercial and industrial growth in New Haven. Much of this growth occurred in this very section of the city where the amount of land devoted to business and industry was four times the city average. Eighteen percent of all the city's businesses, 46 percent of its manufacturing, and 42 percent of its wholesalers were located in these three wards alone, which comprised a mere 5 percent of the city's total land area. By the beginning of the Great Depression, the Wooster Square area and its neighboring wards remained the city's most densely populated and industrial district. A social survey conducted in the early years of the Great Depression found that the area also housed the city's poorest residents. Sixty percent of the gainfully employed people living in this part of the city were semi-skilled or unskilled workers (as compared with an average of 38 percent for the rest of New Haven). One-third of the area's families were on relief during the worst years of the Depression, and three-quarters of all its residents had had some contact with one or more social agencies. Crowding and poverty were borne out by other social statistics as well. Whereas 64 percent of New Haven's residents lived in single-family houses in 1931, 26 percent were in two-family dwellings, and 11 percent resided in buildings that housed three or more families. Wards Ten through Twelve housed 49 percent of its residents in single-family homes, 25 percent in two-family units, and 24 percent in multifamily dwellings.[25] The average rent in Wards Ten through Twelve was $20 per month, as compared with an average of $36 elsewhere in New Haven, and the median value of homes was $8,000, three thousand dollars below the city median. Most revealing was that the number of families per habitable acre was a swollen thirteen, as compared with a city average of five.[26] Seventy percent of the families in this area earned incomes of less than $1,000 per month (compared with the city ratio of 40 percent), and mean family size was 4.31 for these wards, 3.45 for the city.[27] Finally, the age of the population of the Wooster Square area was markedly younger as well: whereas 62 percent of New Haven families had no children under the age of ten, for this area almost half of all families (48 percent) had children under ten; and the percentage of families in Wards Ten through Twelve with three or more children under ten was 18.5 percent, as compared with the city average of 8.3 percent.[28]

Unlike the Irish, who quickly converted their numerical preponderance into political hegemony in New Haven (and indeed, across the urban industrial landscape of the United States), regional pride, jealousy, suspicion, and devotion to the home village—the fabled *campanalismo* of the *contadini*—bred social divisiveness and political apathy.[29] *Campanalismo* refers to the phenomenon of intense local identity among Italian immigrants which derived from a sense of devotion to their villages of origin in the southern peninsula and Sicily. The term refers specifically to the village and its surrounding countryside, encompassing a distance no farther than one could hear the ringing of church bells from the town's center.[30] By 1930, fully fifty years after the immigration from Italy had begun in earnest, there were still eighty Italian ethnic societies in New Haven, each arising to sustain the sense of loyalty and affection that these people felt for their villages in their homeland. In addition to annual *festas,* which paid homage to their home village's patron saints, and the foundation of "national" parishes, which participated in the recognition of each region's and village's traditions, there were innumerable social clubs for young men that facilitated a larger sense of belonging to culturally distinct ways of life. This phenomenon, however conducive to sustaining the web of mutual expectation among Italian immigrant neighbors, spelled disaster politically for the larger ethnic community. Even with overwhelming numerical superiority by 1920, the city's Italian immigrants failed to muster sufficient electoral clout to elect a mayor from their own group until the mid-1940s, a full generation later. Between their deep-seated suspicion of politicians and civil servants—an impulse reinforced by profound inexperience with the democratic political process—and rivalries that had carried over from their homeland, Italians took significantly longer than the city's other immigrant groups to assert their political will.[31] Token recognition of the strength of the Italian immigrant population was granted in the form of school buildings whose names honored great figures in Italian history, like Dante and Columbus, but the schools themselves were administered and staffed almost exclusively by Yankees and Irish Americans. Only a handful of Italian Americans had been hired as teachers even by the end of World War II, when the presence of this group could no longer be denied and the city's first Italian-American mayor wrested the power of patronage from Mayor Murphy, installing Italian Americans in the civil service positions so long monopolized by New Haven's Irish-American population.[32]

The period beginning in 1850 and ending in 1930 marked the rise and culmination of New Haven's industrial and economic expansion, immigration, and population growth. These decades also coincided with the institution of a free, citywide system of public schools, which by 1900 was considered one of the premier urban school districts in the United States. Crowning the New Haven schools was one of the most highly regarded public high schools in the nation, Hillhouse High School. Yet the implementation of mass schooling and the goal of keeping all young people in school through high school were aims accomplished because a new view of children and childhood was championed during the same period. This perspective, which held revolutionary implications for the operation of working-class families, was forged out of compulsory school attendance laws and the legal imposition of middle-class conceptions of how children were to be prepared for adulthood.

2

LEARNING AND EARNING: SCHOOLING, JUVENILE EMPLOYMENT, AND THE EARLY LIFE COURSE IN LATE-NINETEENTH-CENTURY NEW HAVEN

As New Haven becomes more and more a manufacturing community, we add to our stable and permanent population . . . [others] . . . who, saving nothing when work is plenty and prices remunerative, become dependent upon . . . charity the moment the factories diminish the hours of work and the numbers they employ. . . . The heedlessness and shiftlessness of . . . [these parents] . . . extends to their children, and makes it almost impossible for [them] to become amenable to the rules and requirements of efficient public schools.

—New Haven, New Haven Board of Education, *Annual Report,* 1874

From the middle to the end of the nineteenth century in New Haven, the use of children's time came under increased scrutiny. The passage and enforcement of compulsory education laws during this period, which greatly expanded the proportion of children under the schools' supervision, reformulated children's utility and imposed a roughly uniform course of socialization upon all children.[1] Thus, children's time in two senses had become an object of intense social concern: the inculcation in children of an appreciation for the value of time itself, and the creation of an institutional basis for childhood— a time of life—as a period of formal preparation for adulthood. This reformulation of children's utility was but another face of the now familiar and much broader cultural movement toward the sentimentalization of children and childhood.[2] This chapter traces the evolution

of institutional initiatives to standardize the early life course and explores the extent and forms of resistance to their implementation by
working-class families in New Haven over the latter half of the nineteenth century.[3]

From 1850 to 1900 middle- and working-class parents held distinct
views of the usefulness of formalized learning and differed accordingly in
their use of the schools. These differences derived not only from the
demands of the working-class family wage economy but from divergent
notions about the significance of the process of emergence into adulthood as well. For middle-class boys and girls the transition to adulthood
was becoming more articulated than in working-class families, though
not as pronounced as it would become. Childhood in the urban middle-
class perspective was a protected, increasingly precious, and celebrated
stage of life.[4] Schooling embodied and reinforced middle-class parental
attitudes toward children and youths, particularly in its regard for the
span of time before adulthood as years of formal preparation and semi-
autonomy.[5] Accordingly, the training to be obtained in primary and
grammar school was thought to inhere as much in attitudes as in
the acquisition of skills fundamental to future employment. Schooling
was to furnish, according to Mary P. Ryan, a programmatic "social base
for boyhood."[6] The expansion of public schooling and the implementation of compulsory education broadened this social base, not merely for
boyhood but for childhood, as middle-class girls and then working-class
youngsters were gathered into the schools.

To many working-class parents, however, schooling appeared as a kind
of idleness incongruous with the organizing principle of family life in the
nineteenth century—what John Modell, Frank F. Furstenberg Jr., and
Theodore Hershberg have called "timeliness."[7] Timeliness, they say,
"consisted of helpful response in times of trouble." And for many families
of the working class during the latter half of the nineteenth century, times
were often troubled—by layoffs, strikes, short time (fewer hours work
per week than usual), protracted unemployment, sickness, disability, and
death. Indeed, such troubled times required not merely that assistance be
flexibly responsive but that such responsiveness be built into the ways in
which families managed their resources. Apart from parents' esteem for
the value of reading, writing, and arithmetic, schooling—with its own

and distinctly alien sense of time and productivity—did not figure easily into the tacit, mutual understanding of family roles and obligations.

Schooling, then, would ultimately introduce into the family wage economy a powerful new element in the socialization of children, for schooling defined and regulated childhood and youth as discrete, sequenced phases of preparation for adulthood.[8] By 1900 the minimum age of school-leaving had been raised to fourteen throughout the Northeast, extending by statute the nonworking, and thus "child," status of youth across the social structure. In effect, the state sponsored a middle-class version of the early life course that not only militated against the requirements of the working-class family wage economy but also challenged parents' ideas about the pedagogical function of juvenile labor. Yet the story of the gradual reining-in of the school-age population as well as the story of the institutionalization of an emerging middle-class life course with its emphasis on abstract time over responsiveness to family need was much less certain and more tumultuous than appears in the long perspective of the historiography of education in the United States.

Educators during the mid-nineteenth century had grave doubts about the commitment of working-class parents to their children's schooling that was matched by a concern—to them equally worrisome—to attract the children of the middle class to the public schools. Efforts to address each of these problems locally had several results: the "grading" of New Haven's common schools and the creation of a citywide public school system during the 1850s; the establishment of an annual census to identify "school-age" children later in the same decade; the state's passage of a compulsory education law in 1872; the development of a statewide system of enforcement of compulsory schooling between 1880 and 1900; and, finally, in the complementary implementation of a program of child-worker certification by the state board of education in 1911. But historians' attention to educators' success in herding children into the public schools by the end of the nineteenth century has overshadowed the consequent rearrangement of fundamental understandings of age and obligation between working-class parents and children.

Because the sentimentalized child was first cradled in the middle class, historians have necessarily concentrated on the middle-class experience to reconstruct the origins of "sacred" childhood.[9] Yet the achievement of mass schooling, by definition, meant that the children of working-class parents were to be corralled into the schools, and the response of wage-earning families has received scant attention. Indeed, on the question of how children's lengthening stay in school affected working-class parents' perceptions of the relationship of age to obligation in their children, there is nothing in the scholarship. While some historians have documented steadily rising levels of grade attainment from the mid-nineteenth century on, none have linked the role of compulsory schooling to the establishment of a standardized early life course, its effect on the family wage economy, and the rise of the sentimentalized child in the working class.[10] Careful examination of local school reports during the second half of the nineteenth century, however, offer a revealing glimpse of working-class parents' resistance to the imposition of a standardized early life course. Moreover, local documents also show that although authorities' expectations of increased levels of popular schooling rose continually during the period, the attitudes of working-class parents toward education were often fractious and thus defy easy correlation to the steady climb of grade attainment among children nationally. Continued adherence to the principle of timeliness by working-class parents, in opposition to the institutionalization of sentimentalized childhood, characterized the attendance behavior of many working-class children until the end of the century.

The expansion of popular schooling in New Haven may be divided into two distinct periods after midcentury: 1852 to 1871 saw the conversion of loosely organized, ungraded common schools into a citywide system of graded public grammar schools; and 1872 to 1911 marked the passage of a compulsory education law and the development of the means to enforce it, including a rising concern with absenteeism, withdrawal rates, truancy, vagrancy, and juvenile labor—all of which were brought under control by the end of the century.[11] While the philosophical bases of grading and compulsory school attendance were complicated by egalitarian and elitist aims, the effect of grading and compulsory education was to universalize the early life course. The mechanisms for accomplishing this were by-products, however, rather than the ultimate aim of grading and compulsory education. Yet because the standardizing effect of these mechanisms on the transition to adulthood evolved over the whole period and were overlapping, it will be necessary at points to cast both forward and backward in time to render their significance for the survival of timeliness as an organizing force in working-class family life.

In 1851 almost four thousand children were enrolled in New Haven schools. Although total registration amounted to almost 78 percent of the city's school-age population[12]—an extraordinarily large ratio for the time—in fact, actual attendance was much lower. In the city's common schools average daily attendance was well under two-thirds of total registration.[13] A narrow majority, 2,041 children, were attending the city's private and parochial schools, but this was to change beginning the following year.[14] In 1852 city school officials argued that the patronage of New Haven's middle-class parents was essential to establishing broad-based support for a publicly financed school system. They urged, in turn, that the creation of graded schools was the only means of improving schools that were widely perceived as a kind of "public charity."[15] While opponents of a graded system had argued repeatedly that sorting children by age and achievement was anti-egalitarian, school officials countered successfully that grading—by raising the quality of instruction to standardized, graduated levels and thereby winning the "moral support of the community"—was the only certain path to ensuring that "the children of the rich and poor will occupy contiguous desks, to the common benefit of both classes and of society at large."[16]

According to reports by educator Henry Barnard in the *Connecticut Common School Journal,* New Haven had captured the vital center soon after the first of its common schools, Webster, was graded. After visiting the reorganized school in 1854, Barnard observed that its establishment had elicited applications "so numerous that the [school society] committee are put to their wits' end to know what to do. . . . Parents who had before thought the public schools unfit for their children are now hastening to withdraw their children from the private schools and place them in the people's school—the common school."[17] By 1857, when a publicly financed and unified city school system began to operate, three graded schools were in existence and the remaining five "white" schools were slated for grading.[18] While Barnard's national renown as an authority on popular education made him a potent advocate of graded public schools, his assessment of the depth of demand for public education is probably a better gauge of middle-class enthusiasm than a guide to general opinion.

For as New Haven educators were to discover, enlarging the enrollment of a rapidly expanding and increasingly socially stratified, ethnically diverse population presented a number of problems, the resolution of which were often tangled in contradiction. If the faith of middle-class parents was vital to securing necessary fiscal support, as Barnard proclaimed, the true test of efficacy in a public system lay in the ability of the schools to enroll and retain both middle- *and* working-class children.[19] This tension—between a demand for low-cost schools that would prepare middle-class youths for entry-level, white-collar employment and the desire to offer practical training to working-class youths while withholding increasing numbers of them from the labor market for lengthening periods of time—characterized every effort to reform New Haven's public schools from 1852 until the end of the Great Depression.

Almost as soon as the first of these aims had been realized, New Haven educators turned their attention to the second, seeking to amplify the social mission of the newly formed public school system. Whereas the common school had been, in the superintendent's own estimation, an unapologetic mechanism for social control, by the 1860s the schools' stance toward the children of the city's working class was loftier and more generous: "The old feeling that a public provision for Common school education was mainly designed to secure the community from the danger and disgrace of a population, any part of which should be wholly uneducated," he reflected in 1862, "has given place to the newer idea, that its proper end is to furnish a thorough elementary education to all youth of the community, irrespective of parental wealth or parental negligence."[20] Yet this "newer idea" set into motion a logic rooted in that "old feeling," and the institutional linchpin in this philosophical shift was an insistence upon faithful attendance.

As long as the common schools were ungraded, episodic absence and even casual attendance—though detrimental to individual progress— were not institutionally disruptive. For example, tolerated, if not condoned, in the era before graded schools was the kind of periodic, discreet reliance on child labor by parents that elicited the matter-of-fact observation in 1852 that attendance in one of the city's subdistricts was annually hampered by the withdrawal of children during the winter season "to help in the family industry of oyster opening."[21] No doubt this kind of seasonal absence was understood in terms comparable to the familiar withdrawal of farm children from rural schools during spring planting season and the autumn harvest. Poor attendance at midcentury was not confined to working-class schoolchildren, however. It prevailed throughout city schools and was attributed by school visitors to the "extreme indulgence of parents who seemed heedless of the injurious effects upon their own offspring."[22] Among the effects of the general laxity toward attendance, school visitors in the same year enumerated the following: "'few of the Schools were commenced at the same time'; 'children were permitted to leave one school and go to another, as whim or fancy dictated, thus breaking down all government and subordination'; 'children were permitted to go from the Schools of one District to those of another, without sufficient reason'; and finally, 'there was little or no discipline exercised over tardy or truant scholars.'"[23]

In the era of the ungraded common school, the individual, internalized sense of a schedule—an age-based timetable of skill acquisition, information mastery, and cognitive development—did not drive the system of promotion, nor did it reflect upon the schools' efficacy. Grading achieved both. The schools' effectiveness in promoting groups of children through a standardized curriculum became the gauge of success in the effort to routinize graduated training for their pupils. Grading assumed a rough degree of continuity in personnel from one achievement level to the next and in effect created the peer group.[24] In turn, the peer group operated as a social expression of the individual's internalized sense of a schedule. This developmental schedule, which became more highly articulated after the turn of the century—with the passion for standardized intelligence and achievement testing and the preoccupation with age-grade tables and "retardation"—had its origins in graded public schooling.[25]

As grading was phased in during the 1850s and 1860s, pupils competed with one another for admission to the reorganized schools. This enabled the school district, for the first time, to penalize students for inadequate attendance, and indeed the board of education soon authorized the suspension of pupils who had accumulated more than ten unexcused absences over a term. In practice, however, the penalty was ineffective. Almost yearly in the period before compulsory schooling, the lack of regard for regular attendance and punctuality were evidenced in the *Annual Report.* For even as the public schools added greater numbers of middle-class youngsters to their rolls, absenteeism and tardiness continued to nag: "If children are frequently late in their attendance," the superintendent complained in 1864, "it is because their parents attach a greater importance to something else than to school. Nothing is more common than excuses of this nature—to attend a circus, a menagerie, a fair, or a pic-nic, to go on an errand, to go out of town, to receive music lessons, to attend dancing school, to prepare for a party or, more common than all, an excuse without any reason whatever being assigned."[26]

Although nettled by the low esteem in which many parents held the use of their children's time, school officials were more disturbed by the intractability of parents whose material needs required children's participation in the family economy. Paradox was the price paid for grading the public schools. Increasingly, the city schools served two very different groups of children: those who carried excuses from parents asking teachers to pardon their child's absence to attend a picnic or dancing school and those whose parents asked no pardon at all. The more attractive the public school became for the middle class and the more educators pressed for universal elementary education, the wider the chasm became that separated children of the middle and working classes within the rooms of city schools. Grading the common schools was operationally at odds with the rhythms and demands of the working-class family wage economy—a consideration educators only vaguely understood. Although mindful that poverty prevented an indefinite number of children from enrolling in the schools or if enrolled, precipitated their withdrawal, educators often blamed parents for their poverty even as they occasionally recognized the impersonal causes of individual financial misfortune. In prosperous years parents of working children were deemed greedy and exploitative. During depressions family reliance on child labor was said to testify to parents' lack of foresight and self-discipline.

At least since the mid-nineteenth century in the United States war and depression have been two of the most powerful levers on schooling and juvenile employment. Indeed, during the Civil War a booming economy drew many of New Haven's children out of school and into the workforce. As pupils interrupted their schooling to work, absences mounted, followed by suspensions and withdrawals. By 1864 the superintendent was forced to concede that the school board's suspension policy had been unrealistically rigid, since its intent had been to encourage punctuality and attendance short of pushing children out of the schools. Absolute enforcement of the rule, he concluded, "had been found to involve occasional hardship to the children of very poor parents. . . . The extreme poverty which exists in cities, furnishes frequent illustration of the difficulty with which a strict rule of this kind can be complied with," for the unintended effect of suspension was that it might "do great injustice to the least fortunate among us" and turn children into the streets, who but for "the exercise of a little good sense and feeling . . . [could] . . . be saved as useful members of society."[27]

Yet the line between "extreme poverty" and the kind of chronic privation that caused parents to rely on their children's labor was ordinarily visible to school officials only in extraordinary times. Just a decade later, one year into what would become a lengthy economic depression, the same school official remarked that the industrial character of New Haven's economy was attracting greater numbers of people dependent upon waged work but who had little will or conception of how to set aside savings in flush times to sustain them through periodic economic downturns. Their children, he charged, shared this cast of mind and were thus, by extension, equally given to evade the "rules and regulations of efficient public schools."[28] Throughout the 1860s withdrawal rates at several of the city's schools exceeded 50 percent of enrollment. Overall, close to 30 percent of children enrolled at any time during the year eventually withdrew. Parents of working children sincerely wanted them to be educated, the superintendent urged, "only their desire is so feeble that it is useless to expect from them much beyond a passive acquiescence in what others may do for their children."[29] School officials' frustration at enforcing attendance in the face of such high withdrawal rates undoubtedly drew them closer to the conviction that attendance must be compulsory if a public graded school system were to succeed.

By 1871, in anticipation of a state-sponsored compulsory education law, New Haven authorities began to consider creating a truant school to house the habitually absent and, in the superintendent's words, the "roving, idle, mischievous boys out of whom in time come the chief recruits to the criminal classes of society."[30] The mandate of compulsory educa-tion—at once coercive and altruistic, invasive and disinterested, fearful and idealistic—triangulated the interests of society, the child, and his or her parents. Suspended between desires equally sincere—to form a liter-ate and numerate citizenry, and to confine and supervise the unruly prog-eny of the "dangerous classes"—New Haven's civic leaders and educators juggled what were often conflicting philosophical and pedagogical ends, so deeply ambivalent were they over the implications of coercing parents to send their children to school. On one hand, they regarded relations between parents and children and the parent's authority as "more sacred than human law" and reasoned, moreover, that the preservation of per-sonal and parental rights constituted the "foundation of a free govern-ment." On the other hand, the "natural" authority of parents could abrade the civil right of children (as defined by the state) to receive "ade-quate instruction," in which case it was held that the state's authority superseded that of the parent.[31] As city school officials approached endorsing compulsory schooling, however, they persuaded themselves that the state possessed a firmer conception of the child's best interests than parents in the grip of poverty.

In 1872 the Connecticut General Assembly passed a compulsory educa-tion law requiring all children between the ages of eight and fourteen to attend school for three months of the year, six weeks of which were to be consecutive.[32] Enforcement of the statute would necessarily draw increas-ing numbers of "ignorant and vicious" children into city classrooms, New Haven's superintendent allowed, presenting a "practical difficulty" in fulfilling the mission of the public schools. "Two theories of public education are in constant tension," he observed, "One theory . . . is that [our public schools] . . . are specially and emphatically designed for the benefit of those who would otherwise grow up ignorant and vicious. . . . The other theory is, that the good of the great body of children is chiefly to be consulted, and that everything that detracts from the general good . . . should be removed, so that even fastidious parents may find nothing of which to complain."[33] The purpose of public schooling, he concluded, must be to embrace both ends without compromising either.

Nevertheless, the reconciliation of these two objects, it seems, was not to be obstructed so much by the school district's "fastidious parents" as by those whose children were potentially "ignorant and vicious"—a problem that the superintendent felt was becoming increasingly acute. While the relationship of the authority of the state to that of the parent, he admitted, was still confused and "far from being settled. . . . Every year it has become more apparent . . . that parents [of unschooled children] to a considerable extent are insensible to the wrong they are permitting to be inflicted upon their offspring."[34] Behind the shield of parental authority two perils to the child were sheltered, in his estimation: parental "cupidity and carelessness" and "the excessive and growing demand for the cheapest possible labor" by employers.[35] However, whereas it was granted that employers were driven by market forces to purchase labor at its lowest price, parents of unenrolled children were perceived as deviant, ignorant, or both in depriving their own of a "fair elementary education."[36]

In the wake of the establishment of compulsory education, the former philosophical uneasiness over coerced schooling yielded to concern for the *utility* of children—the use of children's time. Schooling had implicitly—and traditionally—concerned itself with occupying children's time in ways that educators considered productive. Thus, the novelty of this particular conception of utility lay in its formalism: it demanded not that children be materially useful and responsive to family need but that they learn to be *not idle*—to be routinely concerned with organizing and exploiting time. Schooling as a term of preparation for adulthood then was to socialize children to value time for its own sake. This vision was projected both within the schools (to organize children's school-day routines) and also without (to define legitimate and illegitimate juvenile activities). Whereas formerly the schools lacked the apparatus to enforce registration, attendance, and punctuality, with the creation of truant schools and an array of legal tools to punish absenteeism and nonregistration, the activities of unschooled children could be scrutinized and brought under control.

In this new regime children could only lawfully be "in school" or "at work." Every alternative in between was illegitimate and testified to the official contention that parents, either in ignorance or selfish defiance, did not observe the necessity of supervising their children and structuring their time. In part this contention derived rather mechanically from the enforcement of compulsory education and the operation of a graded school system, but it had a philosophical foundation too, which again reflected the somewhat contradictory missions of public schooling. While the notion of utility had roots deep in the Anglo-American past, it was also inspired by nascent middle-class patterns of child-rearing, which coalesced in the northeastern United States during the 1830s and 1840s.[37] The petit-bourgeois family, Ryan has argued, imprinted on its children "values . . . [such as] . . . honesty, industry, frugality, temperance, and preeminently, self-control." Middle-class mothers, she asserts, "conspired to equip children with sensitive consciences . . . a kind of portable parent," she says, "that could stay with the child long after he left his mother's side and journeyed beyond the private sphere out into the streets and into the public world."[38] Middle-class children were the first to be submitted to the contrived regimen of a value system necessitated by the enforced idleness of sentimentalized childhood.

Complementary to this mode of socialization was an organization of the school day, which was now also directed at the *other* public of the public schools: future workers. In 1869 New Haven's superintendent of schools had implemented a detailed course of study designed to consolidate the advances achieved by grading.[39] This first step was followed in 1875 by a second, more elaborate plan, specifying "what exercises were required, and the number of minutes to be devoted to each, through the day, in order to secure steady and uniform employment to both teachers and pupils. No teacher was at liberty to omit any exercises, nor introduce any other not named in the program. Instruction in Morals and Manners was likewise included among the duties of the teachers."[40]

Historians of labor in the industrial era have made much of the application to factory work of values like punctuality, obedience to authority, discipline, and reliability. They have looked at efforts to induce workers to internalize the apprehension of time, to inure workers first to labor timed by the clock and then, in E. P. Thompson's phrase, to feel a "sense of conflict between labor and 'passing the time of day,'" and finally to regard such whiling away of time as "wasteful and lacking in urgency."[41] In tandem, historians of U.S. education have roundly documented a movement by educators in the late nineteenth and early twentieth centuries to imbue working-class (and increasingly non-English-speaking immigrant) children with such "workmanlike traits."[42]

As children's utility was recast within the schools and manifest in the minute regimentation of the school day, the same impulse—a growing concern to mold and scrutinize children's activities—led to the definition of truancy and vagrancy as social problems (that is, as categories of deviance relative to school enrollment and attendance). In turn, the creation of these categories prompted an empirical accounting for children's whereabouts and activities within the city school district, as well as a concern for juvenile "idleness." In 1873 the superintendent calculated that some 41 percent of the city's elementary school-age children were "daily outside of the rooms of the public schools, throughout the year"— a number "still too large for a city provided with the educational facilities furnished by New Haven."[43] Girls formed a disproportionate number of the unschooled in the city: 524 more girls lived in the city's school district than could be found at school or certified as working, it was reported. Commenting upon the variety of ways in which these girls were thought to have occupied themselves, the superintendent noted that "the number of young girls employed in stores, and at light mechanical work in shops, is known to be large . . . [and that] not a few parents . . . keep their children at home to assist in the work of the family, or send them out to light domestic service." Whether girls unaccounted for were being kept at home or unlawfully employed is unclear. What is clear is that whether girls were at home, at work, or in school, no one appeared to notice.[44]

Boys, on the other hand, seem to have presented a vague social nuisance. Once school and civic officials adopted a unified vision of children's utility, youngsters whose activities fit uneasily into either of the sanctioned uses of their time—school or work—were viewed with decreasing tolerance: "The children most difficult to reach," commented the superintendent on the resistance of groups of children to the city's efforts to enforce the attendance law, "are those who find occasional employment in the shops and who make this an excuse for entire non-attendance at school. They lounge around the factories, and are ever ready with the excuse that they are going to have a job next week. They are not employed, they are not at school; they are simply ready for a short job, and for quarreling, fighting, and a long play spell."[45] Unlike girls, boys—when unoccupied or unregistered—were regarded as "naturally" given to "roam in the streets." If the city's unschooled girls were "sufferers" in the estimation of city officials for want of formal education, New Haven's vagrant and truant population was, in the words of the superintendent, an "army of boys . . . who found a pleasant excitement during school hours in watching the arrival and departure of the trains, or fishing from the wharves and docks, or playing ball in the outskirts of the city, or hanging around stables, or perching upon fences near the school houses."[46]

Apart from the "worthy" children of the working poor who aided parents in furnishing food, clothing, and shelter, then, was this group of "neglected, untaught [and] vagrant" children. Beyond the watchful eyes of parents, teachers, and employers they formed a "street school," the superintendent cautioned, "preparing to become criminals hereafter to scourge the community and fill out prisons."[47] He might have called it a boys' school, so exclusive was the contempt reserved for the male half of the city's unenrolled and nonattending youth. No doubt some portion of these boys did take the low road of vandalism and crime to reform school. As Joseph F. Kett has noted, with the intensification of city growth in the United States from the 1830s on, a parallel rise in juvenile delinquency occurred so that increasingly reform schools were turned into "dumping grounds for teenage felons and troublemakers. . . . high schools for the lower classes, with a concentration of inmates between 14 and 17."[48]

Yet the establishment of "ungraded classes"[49] in New Haven during the 1870s was undertaken as a more hopeful, intermediate institutional alternative to housing the city's truants among the hardened, older inmates of the reform school at nearby Meriden. The ungraded classes— "truant schools"—in effect initially provided a mechanism for dealing with youths whose unoccupied time might eventually land them in trouble. Moreover, in officials' eyes truant schools had the added virtue of imparting a proper appreciation for the use of time. Some boys, offered the superintendent, "gladly embraced" the ungraded classroom, as the "opportunity thus offered to improve them" otherwise would have been "wasted while waiting for work." While school officials eventually concluded that segregating the city's entire population of truants in one or two buildings had simply reinforced their distaste for schooling, at first it was seen as a workable means of disciplining pupils whose irregular attendance was considered so disruptive to the conduct of the graded classrooms.[50]

Truants would gain increased attention as the end of the century neared and the city enlarged its staff of school census-takers and added a second truant officer. Certainly some portion of truant youngsters simply rebelled against the rigor and confinement of school or employment, but it is likely, too, that some other part of this group were casual workers who trod a path between school and work as family need required. Although truancy declined markedly as the century turned, evidence of youths' lingering persistence in this pattern can be found in the large numbers of students kept back for lack of progress in the course of study during the 1890s.[51] These so-called laggards filled the lower grades of the elementary schools, biding their time until they reached legal working age, forsaking the classroom periodically as the opportunity to earn beckoned.[52]

A seminal motive for compulsory schooling in Connecticut seems to have been a deepening concern with the "roving, idle, mischievous boys" whose presence on city streets rose numerically if not in proportion to the doubling of New Haven's population between 1870 and 1900. Although the ratio of school-age children in the city not in school declined slowly during this period, their numbers increased absolutely. Moreover, this increase was magnified by the influx of Italian immigrants, whose children were increasingly to supplant Irish and Yankee working-class children in the juvenile workforce. A notorious and well-publicized incident during the early years of New Haven's Italian settlement undoubtedly deepened whatever prejudicial impressions city officials had formed of the immigrant population that would eventually outnumber all others in the city: In 1873 three Italian *padroni* were arrested in New Haven under an anti-slave-labor law for controlling the services of a group of boy "musicians" and bootblacks. The boys, it seems, had been sold to these "slave masters" by their parents for a period of four to five years. According to an account of the incident in the local press, each boy's parents received about twenty dollars a year from the arrangement. Further, it was stipulated that the parents would absorb any medical expenses incurred on the child's behalf and forfeit all wages, as well as pay a fine of eighty dollars should the child run away during his term of service. The incident caught the eye of the superintendent of schools, who remarked in his report for that year that its occurrence was "suggestive of causes which keep children from school and in the ignorance of barbarism." In this sobering if sensationalist vein, he proceeded to point out that it "is not the foreign taskmaster alone who brings with him his little victims, and compels them to perform menial services in the shadow of the school-house. . . . Parents have been found so debased and besotted as to keep their own children from school, and . . . for the small pittance a child can earn, are willing to sacrifice the future welfare of their offspring to secure it."[53]

Hugh Cunningham has observed of England during the same years that it was not an overwhelming sense of pity for the welfare of working children that inspired compulsory schooling in that country, but rather "concern to structure the time of the idle . . . for, in the long term, it was the unemployment of children as much as their exploitation within labour which was a matter of concern to those in authority."[54] Similarly, in Connecticut a rising desire to structure and monitor the use of children's time underlay the establishment of universal elementary schooling during the late nineteenth century.

One class's social problem is often another's bread and butter: truancy and vagrancy emblematized an entire range of behaviors between work and school. Much of the "idleness" uncovered among the city's children as school officials began to press the truancy law, then, was a consequence of interrupted employment. Regardless of whether a child participated partially or fully in the sphere of wage-earning or alternated between school and work, underemployment and unemployment punctuated the experience of all who entered the most marginal of nineteenth-century labor markets—the juvenile labor market.[55]

Indeed, work shortages were as much a fact of life for minors as for adults in nineteenth-century America.[56] High levels of child underemployment and unemployment were symptomatic of the general abundance of labor that characterized the growth of cities in the era of industrialization, a problem compounded by the frequency of financial panics spawned by fits of economic expansion and contraction.[57] In the hierarchy of wage-earning workers, children and youths were lowest and most expendable. Alexander Keyssar has found that although the "incidence of joblessness during depressions was always checkered, erratic, variegated," falling differently on different groups in different depressions, workers younger than age twenty were the unhappy exception, consistently suffering the highest rates of unemployment in economic downturns.[58] The Panic of 1873 caused not only widespread unemployment but a long-term depression of wages as well—a deficit from which workers would only begin to recover by the end of the century. And, of course, there were two intervening depressions (1882–85 and 1893–96). In fact, between 1870 and 1900 sixteen years were depression years. Consequently, the standard of living of the U.S. working class relative to the middle and upper classes declined significantly during this period.[59]

Still, the economic reverses of the late nineteenth century were not the only threats to juvenile employment: young workers were as vulnerable to wage rate cutting and peer competition as their adult counterparts in the labor market. As one labor observer commented, "As the boy of ten will work for half the price that the boy of fifteen expects, the small boy who should be at school gets the job, while the large boy thinks something should be done to check excessive competition."[60] Again, to cite a parallel example in mid-nineteenth-century England, wide regional variation in employment levels and in employability characterized juvenile labor with the onset of industrialization.[61] Although some communities in certain areas compelled schooling through age fourteen, in most of England during the nineteenth century the employability of children turned on factors ranging from the extensiveness of factory work (associated with cities) to the degree and kind of agricultural production conducted in more agrarian provinces. Both gender and age determined the amount and type of work available to children. Generally, in industrial towns and in cities, children younger than ten (and within this group, especially girls) found little work, while children fourteen and older were commonly employed. In addition, there was less work in winter than in summer.[62] New Haven, the most populous city in one of the most industrialized states in the nation during the late nineteenth century, apparently offered circumstances for juvenile employment after the Civil War comparable to those described by Cunningham and Neil J. Smelser for England's industrial cities.

Although the dimensions of child employment and joblessness in Connecticut are difficult to gauge for the nineteenth century, Cunningham has noted that the seasonal nature of much of child labor would also appear to apply to employment conditions for juveniles in New Haven.[63] Typically, historians have contrasted the seasonality of rural child labor with the steadier employment of urban youths.[64] The contrast, however, distorts the difference. In part, this distortion stems from the comparison of rural and urban school enrollment rates. Rural children typically enrolled in higher proportions than urban youths but attended school less regularly than urban pupils. This fact is often associated with the seasonal demand for child labor in agriculture and the readiness to allow children to withdraw from school temporarily while remaining officially enrolled.[65] Urban youths, forced to choose between work and school, chose work in greater proportions than did rural children (that is, child agricultural workers did not *have* to choose but routinely enrolled in school *and* worked). Therefore, many urban youths counted neither as "in school" nor "at work" were actually working, though episodically, when work was available or as their families required. Many industries had periods of intensive activity requiring numerous casual laborers, often children, followed by slack times in which the hours of the regular workforce were reduced and casual labor was laid off entirely.[66] Most industries routinely had peak times lasting from two to three months once or even twice a year, followed by periods of predictable slackening. While production peaks and valleys varied by industry, factories generally reached their annual troughs between December and February.[67] Coincidentally, the annual school census was conducted in New Haven precisely when employment for "secondary" workers—like children— was at low ebb. Although this factor had slight bearing on the total number of children enrolling in New Haven's schools, it helps to explain the large fraction of unenrolled children whose status was recorded as neither "in school" nor "at work."

Within this group, in addition, some portion of working children may have been unaccounted for by the school census-takers (again, difficult to estimate), since they labored for and were paid by their fathers rather than by an employer, as one worker reported: "I receive two different prices for day work. . . . The higher rate is paid me for work which requires more skill. . . . My son, when he works by the piece is simply working for me, on work I do by the piece, although he has some other work he does by the piece. . . . My son receives 15 cents per hour, when he works for the company."[68] This practice, working for a parent at a discounted or unremunerated rate, was a vestige of the early phase of factory production. Although this man's son was serving a form of apprenticeship under his father and may in fact have appeared on the rolls of the employed, it takes little imagination to picture children working for parents in this way, who thus evaded enumeration of any kind by census-takers.[69]

An agent of the New Haven Board of Education in the 1870s attributed the failure of enforcement to the complicity of manufacturers willing to look the other way while work was jobbed out to the lowest bidder, often a "subletter" employing child workers: "The actual employer of the boy is often not the manufacturer or his responsible agent. Contractors engage to do certain kinds of work at a given price, and they employ whom they please. Naturally the contractor is desirous of doing his work as cheaply as possible . . . When complaint is made to the manufacturer, that boys are employed in his factory contrary to law, he says that he does not employ any boys, and cannot control the action of his contractors."[70]

Parents, according to official accounts, were only too willing to deceive, or even to threaten, employers in the hope of obtaining work for their children—pressuring them to hire unschooled children or forgo the services of all other family members.[71] Even much later, well into the twentieth century with the subsequent passage of child labor legislation, enforcement was notoriously difficult and particularly so during depressions. For while most children were pushed into the schools for lack of opportunity, the most desperate among them—those whose older relations were chronically unemployed, crippled, or infirm—remained in the workforce with the consent of "benevolent" employers.[72]

Although enrollment levels climbed from 1850 on and the duration of schooling for children across class converged, actual attendance from the mid-nineteenth century until the 1890s was less impressive and diluted the significance of both school-going and school-leaving for children whose families required material assistance. In the 1871–72 school year, for instance, 881 juveniles between the ages of five and fifteen, just 8 percent of the school-age population, were reported by parents to school census-takers as being "at work," yet the schools' effectiveness in their own estimation was being compromised by the nominal participation of a sizable group of registered casual attendees. "Of those whose names are enrolled members," the superintendent observed, "some are present only a few days or a few weeks of the entire year; so that if we find the difference between the average number belonging and the whole number enrolled, it will appear that about fifteen percent of the latter are merely nominal attendants, coming and going; seldom remaining long enough anywhere to gain much good; more frequently proving detrimental to every room they enter."[73] His concern on this score was justified as the gap between total enrollment and average enrollment by the early 1870s widened after eight years of rough correspondence.[74] From 1873 to 1893 the broad disparity between total and average enrollments continued. Despite a steady and impressive overall growth in total registration during these two decades, total and average registration diverged from between 21 percent to 34 percent annually (see fig. 2.1).

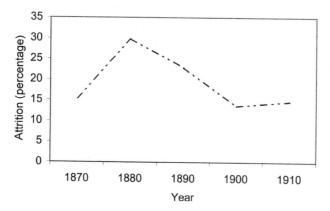

Fig. 2.1 Annual attrition of New Haven public schoolchildren, 1870–1900. *Sources:* New Haven, *Annual Reports,* 1857–1935; New Haven, *New Haven's Schools,* 16–23

Other indicators similarly point to attendance problems until the turn of the century.[75] Of even greater concern, however, were the large numbers of students who withdrew from the schools during the year. Unfortunately, statistics for this group were recorded for just seven years (1870–76), but they are highly revealing nonetheless. In 1870, just two years before the start of compulsory schooling, 3,196 children withdrew from the public schools. This group comprised almost half of all registered public school children in that year. In 1873 the situation appeared only a little better, considering that compulsory attendance had just gone into effect: one-third of those enrolled at the year's beginning had left before the schools let out for the summer. Three years later 3,866 children (again, more than a third of those registered) withdrew, and almost as many, 3,577, had not registered in any school that year.[76]

Despite wide recognition of employment as an alternative to schooling in this period, the enumeration of children employed was sporadic. From 1850 to 1900 the number of school-age children officially counted as being "at work" was recorded only six times. Still, these figures yield some notable contrasts. The first four entries cover the years 1866–76. During this period the proportion of children officially "at work" to the total population of school-age children ranged from 7 percent to 15 percent. By contrast, in 1890 parents reported just 307 children as working (225 in 1891), which was fewer than 2 percent of all school-age children in New Haven in that year. Because school officials no longer recorded the number of children withdrawing annually after 1876, it is impossible to know if the number of withdrawers moved downward with the decline in children "at work."

If children unaccounted for were in fact the under- and unemployed, truants (numbered among the city's registered schoolchildren) formed another significant if nebulous group whose activities shuttled between school and casual employment. If the experience of the Great Depression (the first period for which there are detailed statistics on juvenile unemployment) provides any index of the relative severity of juvenile unemployment during previous economic crises, then a good deal of truancy and vagrancy may be accounted for by the mounting economic woes of the 1870s and 1880s. As I have already mentioned, the number of truancy cases spiked during the 1870s, reaching a high of 1,810 in 1876 (nearly one-quarter of average enrollment in that year), retreated during the 1880s, and ascended again during the depression of 1893 through 1896. As much as any other group among children younger than fourteen, their school-going hinged on the availability of work. During depressions they seem to have been steadier in attendance. When the economy rebounded, however, they stepped out to work. Thus in 1880, for example, as the Panic of 1873 receded, the superintendent complained that "progress had been slowed" that year by the "withdrawal of scholars to engage in employments which the increase in business activity created. Many pupils have been tempted to leave school temporarily, and on their return have found themselves behind in their classes."[77] In his report the following year, he noted the tendency of many children, excused from school because of some "family contagion," to extend their absence. "In many cases," he surmised, "it was quite obvious that the child quite enjoyed a little vacation thus obtained and was in no special haste to return to the school." Yet "too often," the superintendent concluded, "parents were not unwilling to prolong the time when some little service could be performed, or small earnings secured. Thus the tendency to undervalue the importance of regular attendance increased in the mind of both parent and pupil."[78]

In 1890 an agent of the state board of education was sent to ascertain the degree of parental compliance with the compulsory attendance statute in the city that was home to one-ninth of the state's school-age children. During his brief stay he discovered 147 cases of "neglect" in New Haven, resulting in 12 prosecutions.[79] This initiated a more systematic campaign by the city board of education to apprehend truant youths, producing official annual counts approaching a thousand wayward youngsters during the middle years of the decade (see fig. 2.2).[80] Thus, although the scale of juvenile employment in New Haven was not comparable to that of the mill towns of northern New England earlier in the century, the diversity of the city's industrial and commercial base seems to have enabled juveniles to find work when necessary or desirable in the many small shops and factories that sprang up during New Haven's golden age of economic expansion. Yet, again, the work itself was often temporary or broken by both predictable and unanticipated layoffs.

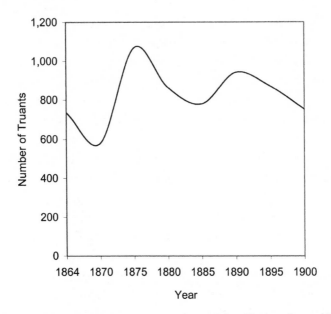

Fig. 2.2 Truancy in New Haven, 1864–1900. *Source:* New Haven, *Annual Reports,* 1864–1900

School-leaving, the measurement of which historically has been made possible by U.S. federal censuses since 1840, has served as a convenient index of the length of children's formal preparation for adulthood—the point of departure for a series of transitions leading to family formation. But school-leaving for working-class youngsters represented a more superficial than meaningful passage into the workforce. Census-derived statistics on the enrollment status of children during the nineteenth century can tell us only the point at which a child had *finally* left school. They are silent on the most familiar feature of working-class school-going children: episodic withdrawal from school in response to family need. Indeed, in the context of family obligations, compulsory schooling was inconsistent with the outlook of working-class parents and youths— an outlook reflected not simply by the "in-school" or "at-work" status registered in the federal censuses, but rather in a more heterogeneous set of responses that included irregular attendance, nonenrollment, nonattendance, and part-time and episodic employment, in addition to enrollment and full-time employment. The persistence of these behaviors—

even as the enforcement of compulsory schooling threatened them—signifies family strategies that incorporated a notion of the early life course distinct from that prescribed by the law and practiced by the children of middle-class families in New Haven. It was a conception of childhood and youth that *interpolated* learning and earning. If the hallmark of childhood is dependence, then "youth" for many children of working-class parents began where opportunity to work first presented itself. Therefore, *employability* in good measure set the perimeter between childhood and youth in the family wage economy.

Employability, from one side, was constituted by the demand for labor and by constraints on this demand stemming from the enforcement of compulsory schooling. From the other side, childhood as a dependent status in working-class families was bounded by the child's developing mental and physical capacities, a sense of mutual obligation between parents and children, and the interplay of family need with the opportunity to earn income. While the earnings of a male breadwinner determined the kind and degree of demands placed upon children, so too did a child's gender, birth order, and the family's procession through the family cycle.[81] Whatever form children's contributions took, the *lesson* of their labors also figured into parental regard for the purpose of children's work: the collective nature of effort within the family group and the cultivation of responsiveness to family needs were the principal objects of their instruction in life's enduring values.

Officially, of course, the "working age" was set by statute at fourteen, but school authorities recognized that the lower end of the working-age threshold was around eleven: "Few children can earn anything before they are eleven," remarked the superintendent in 1871, for "up to the period when a child's time has a money value, many motives act upon both child and parent . . . to induce a tolerably regular attendance. It is so convenient for . . . [extremely poor] mothers to get rid of children for a few hours daily, that very little urgency is . . . needed to induce them to send their offspring to school."[82] If the tone of this assessment sounds unduly skeptical, it was nonetheless not far off the mark. Although the "warehousing" function of public schools has long been acknowledged in the historiography of U.S. education, there is little doubt that many parents were anxious to take advantage of the schools' services so long as they did not restrict children's earning potential at inopportune moments.

As the child was transformed into a potential earner, school, by occupying time that might be spent by the child working or looking for work, deprived the family of needed or desired income. Every month beyond the age of compulsory school attendance invited parents to weigh the value of school against the cost of nonemployment. As the child became employable, time spent in school proved a liability. This much becomes evident when we examine the decided drift of children out of the schools in the months after age thirteen. "Up to about twelve years old the public schools may count upon nearly undiminished numbers," observed the superintendent in 1870. "From twelve to thirteen a small percentage drop off. From thirteen to fourteen a very large number leave, and when a boy is fourteen, few parents in straitened circumstances will continue him at school if he can earn from three to five dollars a week by easy labor."[83] Even this portrait fails to convey how variable attrition and sensitive juvenile employment were to swings in the economy. In 1866, for instance, almost 10 percent of children enrolled in the schools at age nine had left by age ten. The proportion of ten-year-olds leaving by age eleven rose to about 17 percent, and those leaving between ages twelve and thirteen constituted almost one-third of those who had been in the public schools at age nine. In 1873, on the other hand, the schools retained their hold on each age cohort up to years thirteen and fourteen, at which point enrollment (as indicated earlier) fell precipitously. While it is tempting to attribute this newfound persistence to the compulsory education law, we find that three years later, as the economy continued its long slumber, the former pattern reasserted itself and the schools lost on average from 5 percent to 10 percent of each age cohort between the ages of nine and fourteen.

The effectiveness of compulsory education after the turn of the century, however, is evident in the continuation rates of New Haven's schoolchildren at two intervals thirty years apart. In 1878, 7 percent of children between the ages of ten and eleven left school. By age twelve, 18 percent of those who had been enrolled at age ten had exited, and by age thirteen fully 36 percent had left school. In 1908, however, virtually no children left school until the age of fourteen, after which point attrition accelerated rapidly.[84]

While the degree of reliance by parents on children's earnings ranged from routine to episodic, monthly reports solicited from an array of Connecticut workers in 1887 suggest just how unremarkable were parents' expectations that children would help redress family expenditures.[85] Among those who reported sending children out to work, debt, the difficulty of "cornering the necessaries of life," and inadequate clothing, in particular, were mentioned most often as sources of anguish and embarrassment. Most in this group also stressed the significance of children's income to family subsistence or to the provision of whatever small margin of comfort workers had achieved. Almost without exception workers with or without children complained of slack time, unemployment, and declining rates for piecework as the most nagging problems of the 1870s and 1880s. Typical was a tinsmith's description of the clash between impersonal economic forces and the vagaries of family life: "If I had always had steady work, I could have managed to live on my wages, but . . . slack time, sickness, death, and trouble was the cause of my being deeply in debt, from which condition I could never have extricated myself but for the help of my sons. About three years ago my wages were reduced ten per cent, a new baby was born, and I was factorized. I am still compelled to buy on credit. . . . I hope that in the near future, with the assistance of my boys, I will be able to pay cash for what I purchase."[86]

Several of the accounts combine expressions of pride, anxiety, and shame over the struggle to balance family hands to mouths. "By strict economy and sobriety I have saved a little even when my pay was small," declared a laborer, but he adds with a note of caution, "My girls' work is precarious lately." A brass finisher said, "Our expenses in some months are more than [reported here] . . . but we manage to put aside $4.00 a week that my boy earns and live on what my wife and I earn monthly."[87] A saddler, pointing to lost time, was ensnared by debt, shame, and hurt: "I got into debt . . . [and] . . . have made myself and family miserable on account of it. . . . When I have a spare dollar I pay it out to reduce the principal, though my wife and family are not even dressed decently enough to take the air in the streets, or to go to church or social gatherings. It is hard to keep my children decently covered to attend school. . . . I can stand it as far as I am concerned, but it is painful to me to see my family deprived of decent clothing, and confined and shut up in the house like prisoners in jail."[88] All of the reports resound with the judgment that conditions beyond the individual's control had constrained the options available to many working-class families to deal with unsteady work and poor pay. Still, there are occasional and revealing glimpses of how they thought about the narrow choices that confronted them: "You will see that I have two boys old enough to work," said a watchman, "but I will not let them work for fifty cents a day so long as I can take care of them."[89]

Most striking in this worker's testimony is the recognition of some socially recognized age level (here unspecified) at which boys would earn their keep, that as family breadwinner he chose to purchase his sons' idleness, and that he held a notion of the worth of his sons' labor that caused him to spare them and himself the quiet humiliation of sending them out to work at any price. Rather than subverting the lesson of family collectivity, perhaps he regarded withholding their labor as an *embellishment:* teaching his sons the importance of maintaining self-respect in the sale of one's labor. This too was a lesson to be learned in the world of work. But notice, as well, that he says *nothing* of school. There is no direct and necessary link in his mind between work and school. He does not even offer in defense of his decision a desire to keep his boys in school instead. Finally, in all of this there is a terse mingling of sentiment and calculation that belies the way historians usually approach family decision-making—a combination that is key to understanding the dynamics of working-class family life during the latter half of the nineteenth century.[90]

Even though most working-class parents did not send their children out to work as soon as the market permitted, the fact that a significant minority did indicates that for many families formalized learning and juvenile "dependency" were contingent upon family need. In all of this we can glimpse a conception of the life course in working-class families differing from that of the middle class—and the schools. Although enrollment levels climbed impressively from 1850 on, and while the average duration of schooling across class converged as well, actual attendance from the mid-nineteenth century until the 1890s was distinctly less impressive. For throughout this period children of working-class parents continued to drift in and out of the workforce in response to family need. This reduces the salience of school-*going* as a frame for children's socialization and dilutes the significance of school-*leaving* as a threshold between childhood and youth in the U.S. working class until the very end of the nineteenth century. In this light the enforced idleness of working-class school-age children assumes a certain literalness that was not lost on parents. If we were to formulate something like a working-class conception of youth as a period of preparation for the responsibilities of a working-class adulthood from 1850 to 1900, a complementary conception of "training" might consist precisely of the kind of movement into and out of the workforce that occurred—the type of training that inculcated a proper sense of responsibility to family as well as an appropriate responsiveness to wage-earning opportunity. Thus training for working-class sons and daughters was, properly, preparation for a lifetime of getting a living.

At the beginning of the twentieth century, the demand for child labor declined precipitously. Mechanization in many branches of industry and the advent of Taylorism not only led to the de-skilling of highly trained adult male workers but reduced the number of unskilled, menial tasks that traditionally underlay juvenile employment.[91] In effect, compulsory schooling had initiated the "enclosure" of the juvenile labor market in Connecticut after the turn of the century—a campaign to constrict the employment of children and youths and to defer their entry into the workforce.[92]

By 1900 it took no Thomas Gradgrinds to exhort children to abstain from the "wonder, idleness and folly" of the passing circus, or even the more mundane temptations of rail yards, stables, ball fields, schoolhouse fences, and wharves. Significantly, school-leaving and workforce entry defined the boundary between childhood and youth in a meaningful way for the first time, since mechanisms like child accounting, grading, standardized testing, and the apprehension of truant children had finally been made to work together effectively. Childhood then, as a discrete phase of dependence and socialization, was progressively an institutionally mediated stage of life as greater numbers of children entered the classroom, were exposed to an increasingly standardized curriculum, and remained in school until age fourteen.[93] Even if the conception of children's utility championed in late-nineteenth-century classrooms was not "gladly embraced" by children who formerly would have been responding in timely fashion to the demands of family need, structurally at least the upper threshold of childhood was regulated as this early life course stage became an increasingly similar experience for children of the middle- and working-classes by the century's end.

3

THE PAINFUL CONTRAST: ITALIAN IMMIGRANT CHILDREN AT HOME AND AT SCHOOL

School is a kind of castor oil America forces the younger generation to swallow, but it will not influence their lives in the least.
—Vittorio Racca, "Selected Family Histories" (Tranquilli family)

As schooling defined the border between childhood and youth, it also assumed a share in many of the chores once performed primarily by families, such as socializing children, instilling moral principles, teaching vocational skills, and furnishing the rudiments of citizenship. The school's influence over the shape of children's lives appeared to come directly at parents' expense; and because so many parents were immigrants whose exposure to schooling in Europe had been minimal and whose folkways clashed so with what their children were learning in school, the perceived power of the schools to put their stamp upon children was exaggerated beyond its true impact. Even though it could be conceded that schools were better equipped than parents to teach children how to read, write, and cipher, instruction undertaken by the schools in other realms clearly intruded upon more closely guarded and intimate aspects of family conduct. This caused a further blurring of the "rightful" and respective functions of families and schools. Matters such as discipline, decorum, religion, and the appropriate expression of sentiment were as integral to nineteenth-century American pedagogy as the "three R's."[1] For instance, although the schools avoided explicit promotion of any one religious denomination, passages of the Bible

were daily read aloud in the schools that reflected the Protestant pre-
dilection for the Old Testament over Catholics' leanings toward the
New Testament.[2] Similarly, a growing aversion to corporal punishment
within the northern, urban middle class was exercised in administrators'
admonitions to city school teachers, even though corporal punishment
continued to typify disciplinary practices inside many classrooms and
among the city's working-class families through much of the following
century.[3]

Other factors that affected the school's ability to assume functions
once performed by families were hampered or furthered by the politics
of public education and this varied enormously from city to city.
Officials in Boston, for example, actively discouraged poor and immigrant children from attending school by expressing openly their contempt for them and consigning immigrant children to the city's most
inferior facilities, whereas in Chicago an aggressive parochial school system created a competitive rival to the public schools that spurred attendance among immigrant children across the board.[4] These outcomes,
which David W. Galenson has called "neighborhood effects"—the idea
that the efficacy of schooling is influenced by forces at the neighborhood level—complicate conventional arguments that attempt to explain
ethnic, racial, or socioeconomic differences in educational attainment.
Neither of the influences described by Galenson in Chicago or Boston
appear to have operated in New Haven. From the very establishment of
public schooling, the city dedicated itself to distributing resources
uniformly throughout the district, "so that no advantage should be
enjoyed by the children in one neighborhood over those in another."[5]
Moreover, no viable parochial school alternative existed until the mid-
1930s, so the stimulus to school attendance present early in Chicago's
history was absent in New Haven for almost a century. Still, Galenson
underscores the variability of neighborhood ecologies in nurturing or
neglecting the schools and the children who attend them. He rightly
advocates a closer examination of the "cultural geography" of schooling: the interplay of ethnicity, race, socioeconomic status, and the interaction of schools with other community institutions. The social
composition, social cohesiveness, and continuity of families and institutions within neighborhoods appear to have had real consequences for

children's school experiences, though retrieving their content and gauging their meaning becomes increasingly difficult as they recede into the past.[6]

As families slowly yielded their authority to form children in some significant respects, the importance of the *relationship* between families and schools loomed ever larger. A kind of Weberian specialization of societal function appeared to be at work as a division of labor emerged between families and schools. It would take many years to sort out which aptitudes were best developed and by whom, since their responsibilities overlapped so extensively. Moreover, the history of schooling and school reform documents the contested nature of this relationship. Calls for the reform of public education alternate between attacks on "the family" and criticisms of the school: either the schools are failing society by inadequately educating its children or the erosion of family life requires intervention by the schools to compensate for what parents fail to provide their children in the way of morality, ethics, and cognitive and social skills. By the beginning of the twentieth century, public schools, whatever their shortcomings, possessed overweening confidence in their ability to equip children with the skills necessary to become informed and active citizens and to succeed in a rapidly changing industrial economy. But they simultaneously trampled on the traditional rights of parents to cultivate in their children conduct and attitudes most dear to them. Neighborhoods presumably mediated between families and schools, furnishing a social ecosystem that brought the imperatives of family life into rough alignment with the structure and aims of schooling. The neighborhood functioned tacitly as a court of public opinion that rationalized deviations from the schools' demands on one hand, while sanctioning the school as an arena for the implementation and practice of social order on the other. The tone of this mediating influence, however, depended very much on the socioeconomic and ethnic composition of the city's neighborhoods as well as a variety of other factors. Whether a neighborhood was predominantly middle class and Yankee, German American, or Irish American—or working class, immigrant, and Italian American, Russian American, Polish American, or African American— greatly affected the way children encountered one another and learned from their teachers. Whether parents and siblings supported pupils' efforts in school and whether they reinforced at home the lessons their children learned in the classroom seems to have made a difference not only to their attendance and achievement but how they viewed themselves and their prospects as well.

New Haven's immigrants brought with them from the cities, towns, and villages they had left behind a wide range of attitudes toward schooling. Yet more than other immigrants in New Haven, southern Italians strained under the forced reorganization of work within the family group necessitated by their compliance with Connecticut's compulsory schooling laws. Because schooling grated so against their conception of what children owed their parents, because Italian peasants customarily relied on their children's earnings to meet expenses, and because schooling in the United States addressed subjects that appeared to usurp the rights of parents to inculcate in their children their own moral principles, they objected strenuously to these laws. Because the children of Italian-born parents comprised such a large share of the city's school-age population, they were the subject of scores of social investigations by city and state agencies, by school visitors and social workers, by sociologists, economists, psychologists, and educators, creating a vivid account of their accommodation to New Haven's factories, churches, schools, and neighborhoods.[7] Scattered among these interviews, statistics, and reports, Italians' grievances against schooling and Americans' attitudes toward children can be found in abundance. Assembled they offer a rare and tantalizing view of the impact of schooling on the economy and psychology of working-class family life. Other groups of course also bridled at schooling, if to lesser degrees, and still others embraced the opportunity presented by free public schooling to improve the occupational prospects of their children. But in the example of New Haven's Italians, the clash of school and family crisply illustrates the extent to which institutions and constructions that are accepted today as natural and necessary—like school, childhood, and adolescence—are rendered strange through strangers' eyes. It is upon this group, therefore, that we fasten our attention.

Southern Italians were profoundly skeptical about what education had to offer their children. Partly this owed to their own inexperience with schooling and partly to its irrelevance to the economy of their existence in their home villages in Abruzzi, Apulia, Basilicata, Calabria, and Campania. Rates of illiteracy in these regions ranged from 70 percent to 90 percent during the period of heaviest emigration. The most highly educated among them had attained enough education to be able to read, write, add, and subtract. More training than this, it was commonly believed, was neither necessary nor desirable for a people who for centuries made their livelihoods by harvesting the fruits of the soil and the sea.[8]

In New Haven, as elsewhere, Italian immigrant parents had a reputation for being both indifferent to their children's performance in school and fixated on their pecuniary worth. Their children were considered uninterested and undistinguished in academic subjects. Compared with the parents of children of other ethnic groups of similar socioeconomic status in the city, Italian immigrant parents were deemed antagonistic and reportedly regarded teachers' inquiries about their children as intrusive and superfluous. In-depth case studies of pupils' family circumstances in New Haven's poorest and most densely populated Italian neighborhood revealed a general "lack of contact" with the schools on the part of Italian parents in particular. Although the parents of children of other ethnic groups exhibited a range of contact, on the whole it was observed that they had much more interaction with the schools than Italians did.[9] What educators in the public schools comprehended through their own encounters with the children of Italian immigrants was documented by a multitude of surveys throughout the period of heaviest immigration, ranging from the massive 1911 "Dillingham Report," to a variety of narrowly focused studies comparing the performance of children of different nationalities on standardized cognition tests throughout the 1920s and 1930s.[10]

In the wake of the success of IQ testing during World War I, a wave of tests were developed to measure children's abilities across an array of cognitive functions. Early proponents of standardized testing equated poor performance with the apparent genetic inferiority of Southern and Eastern Europeans.[11] Slavs and Italians in particular were singled out for their consistently low scores, which were attributed by testers and social scientists to hereditary mental deficiencies in these "races." By the late 1920s, however, the eugenicist interpretation of standardized test performance had retreated somewhat as test theorists recognized the importance of the acquisition of English language skills to positive performance on standardized tests. The persistent use of languages other than English in children's homes was viewed increasingly as a nagging cause of underachievement among low-scoring groups like Italians and Slavs. Nationally, Italian immigrants in the United States were noted for the slowness with which they relinquished the use of their native speech. This was due no doubt to the tendency of so many Italians to repatriate, but it was also attributable to the fact that they formed so significant a segment of the immigrant population wherever they lived in the United States. Surrounded as they were by speakers of their own dialects, they often had little need to learn English. And because most cared little about their children's achievement in school, they did not insist on the use of English at home, as was characteristic of other immigrants who placed greater emphasis on schooling as a path to upward social mobility.[12]

By the 1900s New Haven school officials were already alive to the potential "threat" posed by the introduction of so many non-English-speaking children into the district. During the early 1890s, after a decade in which the city's school-age population had increased by one-third, the superintendent of schools complained about the ignorance and illiteracy of foreign-born parents and their disregard of school laws. New Haven's population, he said, which was "increasing and promiscuous . . . containing a large foreign element," had recently witnessed an "influx . . . [of] . . . people who were ignorant of our institutions, laws, language, people who had not been accustomed to send their children to school in the country from whence they came and who seemed to care but little for their education, especially in the English language."[13] By 1908 the board of education had conducted its first full census of pupil "nationality," and in 1915 it initiated an annual survey of the public schools' ethnic composition, organized by school and subdistrict.[14] It is not clear whether New Haven's educators read or were aware of the findings of the Dillingham Report, so it is impossible to know if it influenced their opinions. But the report would have presented few surprises to the city's teachers and principals in any case: Italian immigrant parents, characteristically, were barely literate and had had little schooling; their children left school as early as was legally possible; a comparatively high proportion of them were

"over-aged" for their grade in school; and Italian immigrant children figured among the city's most frequent offenders of truancy and juvenile
delinquency.[15] Each of these findings was documented in the Dillingham
Report for other cities. Probably some small measure of comfort could
be taken from the fact that these same features characterized Italian
immigrant children throughout the United States. But the combined
effect of such consistent findings across the nation cast the Italian immigrant child as the problem child of American education from the turn of
the century until the Great Depression.

What were the consequences of Italian children's comparative underachievement for immigrant families? Joel Perlmann has shown decisively
the long-term economic significance of early school-leaving for these
children: intergenerational upward social mobility was slower for Italian
immigrants than for any other white subgroup in the United States during the first third of the twentieth century.[16] Still unknown, however, is
what children's performance expressed about the role of schooling in the
southern Italian immigrant family economy. In short, how were compulsory education and extended schooling understood by Italian immigrant
parents as secondary education became the average experience? How did
these parents respond to the constraints imposed upon the economic and
emotional organization of their family life? How did the changing educational aspirations of their children reconfigure this matrix? The answers
to these questions lie in four interrelated areas: (1) traditional attitudes
toward schooling that had been cultivated among southern Italians for
generations before they migrated to the Americas; (2) views of children
and an understanding of age that dramatically diverged from what they
experienced in the United States; (3) a conception of family life characterized by clearly demarcated gender roles and a hierarchical organization of
responsibility and authority; and (4) an emphasis on the functioning of
the household more as an economic collective than as a site for the cultivation and expression of sentiment.[17] These elements combined in ways
that betray the artifice of examining them separately. But for the sake of
understanding their roles in shaping the response of Italian immigrants to
the unraveling of family wage economy, I examine them in parts—as if
they could be understood discretely. The remainder of this chapter
reviews the nature of southern Italians' experiences and conceptions of

education before they came to the United States and how this informed their response to their children's schooling in New Haven. We also look at Italian immigrants' ideas about childhood and adolescence, which strongly affected their attitudes about schooling and the operation of the family wage economy. In Chapter 4 we explore the influence of Italian immigrant children's experiences in changing their views of the function and purposes of family life.

From the perspective of Italian immigrant parents, the consignment of daughters and sons to school—and thus to a state of suspended childhood—threatened not only to create family hardship but also to teach their children the *wrong* lessons about their obligations to others. In this respect, Italian immigrant parents at the turn of the century differed little from their working-class predecessors in the United States, many of whom had resisted the introduction and enforcement of compulsory schooling from the 1870s to the end of the century. But whereas compulsory education and the legal apparatus that supported it were phased in gradually over the latter half of the nineteenth century in Connecticut, immigrant families arriving after 1900 encountered a highly integrated system of enforcement. It was a system that mobilized and coordinated the efforts of state and city educators, civic officials, employers, local police, truant officers, and judiciary to commit children to school until age fourteen. Immigrant families, then, confronted a compression of all the social, legal, and cultural imperatives that had swirled around public education for more than three decades. Given the *contadino*'s limited exposure to schooling in southern Italy, he could only have experienced the demands of the local schools as yet another manifestation of his cultural separateness—as the consequence of ethnic differences that marked off the host culture in which he dwelt as alien and hostile.[18]

Here was a challenge to the contadini's most basic understanding of human relations, involving heretofore unquestioned elements of power and sentiment in family life: the respect of children for their parents' authority, the prerogatives of age and male privilege, and most generally a sense of devotion to parental welfare as the center of a child's concerns. Thus, the characteristic expression of astonishment by Italian immigrant parents at the length of schooling required in the United States encapsulated two basic reactions: the disturbing priority given to children in American society (and its implicit dangers), and the state's role in imposing and maintaining what Italian parents regarded as an insidious "dependence" of children on their parents. Both notions betokened a reversal of the order of things that immigrants found deeply perplexing.

Leonard Covello, a high school principal in New York City and a prominent educator of immigrant children during the first half of the twentieth century, was an early proponent of the idea that understanding an immigrant group's "Old World traits" was key to comprehending the behavior and attitudes of immigrant parents and their children in the United States.[19] Covello devoted a significant portion of his doctoral thesis to the worldviews, customs, and daily practices of the southern Italian peasants whose children attended the schools of East Harlem.[20] Covello is the best known and certainly most perceptive contemporaneous student of Italian immigrants' attitudes toward schooling during the early decades of the twentieth century.[21] In addition to his fine-grained sociological studies of Italian immigrant family life and education, he effectively plumbed his own experience as a child to explain the psychological rift that he felt characterized parent-child relations in many other immigrant families. Highly sensitive to the social and psychological dynamics of immigrant families, Covello was able to pose questions that went to the core of Italian immigrants' attitudes toward schooling. His book *The Heart Is the Teacher*, is an especially penetrating personal account of his own journey from immigrant child to preeminent educator of immigrant children.[22]

Covello's work combined to yield a rich, multitextured, and highly nuanced analysis of education and family life in immigrant America. Moreover, he developed an authentic and compassionate critical voice even as he strained to establish an authoritative, intellectual distance between himself and his lifelong subject, the immigrant school child in the United States.[23] His published observations of southern Italian peasant family life, his manuscript notes, and the scores of unpublished interviews that he and his students at New York University conducted with East Harlem's contadini are an incomparable guide to the role of schooling in southern Italian family life. Much of what follows in this chapter is based upon his observations, qualified wherever possible by the experience of New Haven's Italians to amplify and extend the implications of his insights.

Covello observed that the contadino experienced the cultivation of any intellectual interests in his children as a direct threat to his whole way of life. Since the possibility in Italy of a peasant's son or daughter becoming anything *but* a peasant was remote, there seemed no point in schooling the child. Any education that did not directly translate into some vocation or income was considered superfluous. This pertained not only to the role of formal learning for his children but to realms that affected his own livelihood as well. Even the acquisition of information about agricultural innovations that might assist him on a daily basis or improve his productivity was viewed with suspicion. Covello quoted a familiar proverb that succinctly captures the profound skepticism among contadini of things new and untested: "He who leaves the old way for the new, knows what he leaves but knows not what he will find."[24]

Covello stressed the significance of peasant society as an oral culture: wisdom, it was believed, could be found not in books but in the collective representations of the aged and respected family members. Elders with a reputation for reciting folk sayings that were passed from generation to generation, he points out, were revered not for their "personal wisdom but solely because of their mnemonic faculties." These elders possessed the ability to repeat innumerable proverbs faithfully and to relate them to personal experiences, which both animated them and bore witness to the truths they embodied. The most common underlying themes of such folk wisdom, according to Covello, were loyalty to the larger group rather than individual interest, the cultivation of humility over the kind of ambitiousness aroused by schooling, and the "dread consequences" of going against the wishes of one's parents. Anything beyond the teaching of basic skills in school that did not reinforce filial piety was considered superfluous, dangerous, and, ultimately, immoral. To be well educated in the contadino sense of the term meant to have "absorbed the codes of etiquette, manners, and behavior norms . . . appropriate for all occasions in . . . familial or communal life."[25]

In southern Italy, in particular, popular education was discouraged, and the schools themselves were held in disdain by the upper classes. For the children of contadini who did attend school, learning rarely extended beyond reading, writing, and arithmetic. Covello presented the account of "Alfano" as typical: "I went for two years to school. I wouldn't say two full years because many times the teacher excused [us to] help my father in his work. I know how to write and to read, a little of each. But I hardly believe I ever read or wrote anything after I left school. The only thing I remembered was to read numbers."[26] During the peak years of emigration from southern Italy to the United States, illiteracy south of Naples remained high. Moreover, schooling for children up to age nine, though compulsory as early as 1877, was virtually unenforced before the 1920s.[27] Several factors conspired against the realization of universal elementary schooling, even though this had been an important aim of the newly unified Italian government from its inception in 1861.[28]

In northern Italy, which had chafed under foreign domination for years, a festering political radicalism nurtured literacy and a popular appreciation for education.[29] The South, by contrast, suffered from remoteness and neglect. The establishment of a centralist regime under the Risorgimento Nazionale affected the South in only the most superficial way. The South was generally regarded as a problem region by the other provinces, which exercised far greater control than the South in the Unification government. But the "Southern Question," as it was known, was an expression of contempt for the peoples of the southern provinces rather than a challenge to be addressed by the nation's leaders. Thus it was a question without an answer to the problems of illiteracy, popular schooling, and other infrastructural services monopolized by the North for decades after the unification occurred.[30] As late as 1910, for instance, the government in Rome devoted an annual average of five lire per capita for education in northern Italy, as compared with just 1.8 lire in the South. In the late 1860s the illiteracy rate in the North ranged from 31 percent to 56 percent, whereas in the South 88 percent to 98 percent of all men were illiterate; and women, according to Covello, were not even enumerated because, "with the exception of the *galantuomo* class [shop keepers, landlords, and government officials], all southern Italian women were illiterate."[31] In the North from 1860 to 1920 illiteracy declined steadily even in the more rural areas, whereas in the South in almost every province it stood at around 70 percent for men and was even higher for women (roughly 90 percent in the region of Basilicata in 1911). In the contadini villages, moreover, illiteracy was higher still: nearly 100 percent among peasants (men included) "in some villages as late as 1913."[32]

Yet perhaps more significant than the relative failure of the central government to stimulate school attendance in southern Italy was the way local forces conspired to reinforce the contadini's entrenched resistance to schooling. The galantuomo harbored a long-standing hostility toward the contadini. What elementary schools there were had been established largely to aid the children of the propertied and professional classes in passing the examinations necessary for their admission to higher schools. The "number of schools and the character of instruction in a given community was often determined first by the needs of the local galantuomo class and only secondarily by the interests and requirements of the peasant class." Indeed, the contadini children, according to widely prevalent opinion, "had no business in school at all; they were supposed to work in the fields and help their parents at home."[33] One New York City school teacher who had spent his childhood in Sicily recalled, "I distinctly remember a case when a peasant's son came to our school and the outcry of the parents, 'Per Bacco! [By Heaven!] Things are going too far. We pay the taxes, we rent the building, we support the teacher, so it is up to us to decide whether a . . . [contadino] . . . needs the school.'"[34]

Between the absence of political will in the central government to bring local officials into compliance with compulsory school attendance laws on one hand and the prevalence of taxpayers' attitudes that actively discouraged popular education on the other, compulsory schooling went virtually unenforced in the South.[35] Furthermore, Covello pointed out, the school-year calendar was designed to accommodate the climate and the industry of the North and was therefore too long at either end for farm children in the South. Planting and harvesting occurred a full month earlier in the South than in the North, while schools were officially in session. In the face of these obstacles, village mayors elected by popular vote throughout the South could never gain reelection if they cooperated in enforcing compulsory schooling.[36]

Reinforcing the desire of the middle and upper classes to prevent the children of the common people from rising socially through education were the prejudices of the contadini themselves. The variety of skills required to maintain the status of a peasant, fisherman, or even a craftsman could be learned at an early age in the parental household or by apprenticeship. Moreover, Covello said, such skills and techniques as there were in a peasant economy required only the most straightforward transmission from father to son or from mother to daughter.[37] And the moral code in a relatively homogeneous society was a "reasonably uniform body of rules learned in daily contact and social relations. The moral customs, unshaken for centuries, were effectively transmitted, without any stimulation of a person's logical faculties. . . . [B]eyond a few proverbs, some legends and other bits of generalized wisdom, [formalized] knowledge was at some distance from popular comprehension and consumption."[38]

As a rule, the upper limit of formal schooling for Italian immigrants was about three or four years. Beyond this, a couple of children in a family might receive training in a trade—which, for boys, often depended on the specific skills possessed by older family members. With girls, dressmaking was invariably prized both as a marketable skill and as a money saver in cash-poor households. While the females of all poor households did the finishing work on their family's clothing, the more sophisticated tasks such as pattern-making and cutting were, even in the poorest households, performed by a dressmaker or tailor. Therefore the family that could garner the resources to train one of their daughters in dressmaking would receive a return on their outlay many times over, so this goal was attained if at all possible.[39]

In essence, boys and girls of the contadini underwent a kind of apprenticeship from age seven or eight on. Boys were given a small herd of sheep to tend and helped with the harvest, while girls followed their mothers around the house doing small chores all day long. The children of artisans attended school for a few years because they lived in the towns and could conveniently do so, but concurrently they worked in the shop of a blacksmith, shoemaker, or barber. They did cleaning and other assigned chores for virtually no pay. Moreover, they endured severe discipline and had little time for anything besides their schooling and shop chores. Most often this arrangement was made with a relative, which reinforced the familial aspect of training, discipline, and respect for authority in the eyes of the child. The trade skills acquired could be specifically useful as the child matured, but the most important element of this regime, according to Covello, was the lesson "that he who does not work does not eat."[40]

Play among the contadini children was always directed toward some useful activity such as participating in the harvesting of grapes or making a game out of clearing stones. Stone clearing served two purposes: it cleared a field before it was to be tilled, and the stones themselves could be used to build a wall. The children of the artisan class, however, differed in this respect, for they had recreational activities—like butterfly collecting—which appeared to the contadini as absurdly pointless and even amusing. By the same token, the extent to which boys played ball in America—and the fact that they had so much spare time—stood in stark contrast to the pattern of childhood among southern Italians: "I don't remember [that] we ever played ball, or cops and robbers, or hide-and-seek games," a Sicilian immigrant told Covello. "We were supposed to play only such games as would be of use when we grew up." At an early age—by six, seven, or eight—children were supposed to be occupied with chores and activities that would establish a lifelong sense of responsibility. This "responsible work" meant that "the child (even considering his age) was also a real worker who used real tools, like those of adults except for their size."[41] As noted later in this chapter, contrasting attitudes toward children's play would symbolize for the contadini many of the differences they would encounter in the New World.

The American public school, embodying American conceptions of self and society, was, in the estimation of some Italian immigrants, an alien institution. The school appeared hostile to the immigrant child's sense of self at every level. If in the streets, as one man lamented, children learn that their parents' homeland is despised and their customs are the object of ridicule, in the schools they learn that "the United States is the greatest nation in the world." As a result, "they think that everything Italian is to be thrown away."[42] Covello summed up the feeling of many Italian immigrant parents when he made the following observation about the relative diminution of the home in America: "In Italy, the center of the moral and intellectual life is the home. The Italian home in America crumbles and with it crumbles the morals of the children."[43]

More insidious and far-reaching than the content of the instruction they received in American schools, however, was what immigrant children absorbed in silent observation and what the schools did *not* teach. Irvin L. Child, a social psychologist who lived with an Italian immigrant family in New Haven's Hill section during the 1930s and assessed the assimilating influences on immigrant children, including that of the public schools, has observed that "by plan or not," American language usage, "knowledge of certain American traditions . . . [and] . . . much more of American culture must inevitably be transmitted by the schools."[44] Thus, for example, since few of the public school teachers were of Italian descent, he noted, the immigrant child was "forced to observe how non-Italian adults talk and act, whereas he . . . may not have had any previous opportunity to observe them except at a distance." Moreover, he commented, the immigrant child "is treated by the teachers in the way they have learned as participants in American culture, not in the way his parents have learned as participants in Italian culture."[45]

The stature of the teacher in the eyes of the immigrant child is a powerful theme in Covello's autobiographical work as well. "To be Italian was virtually a faux-pas in our teachers' eyes," wrote Covello in a passage that profoundly evokes the immigrant schoolchild's outlook, "and the genteel American ladies who were our teachers were tactful enough to overlook our error. As a result I can remember a feeling of shame which neighborhood children felt toward their (immigrant) parents and their ways of life."[46] In fact, this sense of shame, which betrayed an embryonic identification with American culture, was bolstered by a growing facility not only in the use of the English language but also in American social norms. As one of Covello's students described the phenomenon: "The child's first difficulty stems from his awkwardness in the use of the English language and his display of ideas and customs brought from home, which make him the object of ridicule at school and instills in him a sense of inferiority. The sense of isolation from his peers intensifies as the child ages. So too do his feelings of embarrassment and shame about his parents' attitudes and language use which isolates him from them as well. Instead of the usual phenomenon of parents interpreting and exemplifying customs to their children the opposite occurs and results in a feeling of contempt by the son for his parents' ignorance and an 'attitude of disrespect of which the parents have become the victims.'"[47]

Another youth characterized the uncomfortable paradox of an educated child in an immigrant home: although his parents, he said, took
great pride in their children's ability to read and write, they "felt hurt
that we . . . were educationally their superiors."[48] In addition, Child
pointed out, Italian immigrant children meet other (non-Italian) children in school and the resultant exposure to American culture "inculcates
in [them] . . . many of its basic traits."[49] As soon as the child begins
school, wrote Covello, "he learns that he has started on the way of
becoming a true American, and it is assured that no greater good fortune
could befall him: All things about America . . . [are] pleasant for the child
to hear about. But when he comes home in the afternoon he feels a
painful contrast between what he sees at home and what he has been
taught during the day. The teacher has said . . . that clean hands, clean
clothing and a tooth brush are essentials; or that plenty of milk should be
taken in the morning. But the father . . . and the mother . . . though they
may not oppose these rules, they do not . . . exemplify them at home."[50]

In the classic sociological formulation of William I. Thomas and
Florian Znaniecki, the emergence of immigrant children as interpreters of
the foreign-host culture to parents subverted power relations within their
families and created the kinds of cultural conflict described by Covello,
Child, and Oscar Handlin. Other scholars deny the existence of such
conflict or believe at least that whatever dissonance resulted was mitigated by the configuration of generational interaction in Italian families.
Sister Mary Fabian Matthews (after Herbert J. Gans), for instance, has
suggested that because Italian families were adult-centered and adults
and children tended to segregate socially, the peer group was much more
influential in children's decision-making than were parents. More important, this separation of generations socially, she concludes, "lessened the
conflict resulting from culture clashes between parents and children."
Outside of the classroom, she argues, school had no effect on children
and did not "disrupt family relations." The experience of such scholars as
Covello, she further suggests, probably exaggerated the impact of formal
education on first-generation immigrants. Strains were more likely to
occur in instances where the child's schooling advanced beyond the minimum compelled by law, developing the by now characteristic alienation
of parent and child in the immigrant family. Covello's extraordinary level

of education made him a rare exception to common experience since most Italian immigrant children of his generation left school soon after the elementary grades. Although there is merit to Mathews' rejoinder, the cases Covello submits as evidence for the experience of a cultural divide between immigrant generations was based on his tenure as a high school principal during the 1930s and 1940s, a time when the high school was commonplace. But ultimately the value of Covello's observations rests upon the kinds of questions he raised and the answers he elicited from immigrant parents and children—the mentalities he describes—rather than the statistical frequency of "cultural conflict." Whether parents and children clashed, the worldview of Italian immigrant parents had been shaped at a time and under circumstances as remote to their children in America as were the villages of southern Italy to East Harlem, or New Haven's "Hill" and Wooster Square.[51]

Even more objectionable than positive pressure to adhere to American standards was what Italian immigrant parents perceived as a kind of moral vacuum in American schooling. In part, this impression stemmed from the contrast between parents' own experience in the elementary schools of southern Italy—however limited—and the range of curriculum in the American schools. Italian immigrant parents commonly referred to American schools as "amoral": "Not in the school . . . do they learn *not* to steal and lie," remarked a parent pointing up the contrast between home life and the school.[52] However disillusioned by the content of their children's learning, which seemed to threaten their authority over their children, uncomprehending parents might still look to school officials to shore up their command of the home. Josephine Patane, a widow, wrote to Covello when he was a high school principal during the 1920s about her adolescent son, Joseph, whom she was raising alone. She had begun to worry about Joseph's personal habits and his apparent disregard for her wishes. At age seventeen, while still in high school, he had started spending a lot of time with a young Jewish man who was two years older. Mrs. Patane had noticed that her son had begun bathing every evening ("a portend of bad things to come," she suggested) before eating and going out. Often he would stay out all night with his friends, only to come home between four and eight o'clock in the morning. He would then drink a glass of milk (a certain sign of his Americanization) and start out for school. Lately, she reported, he had even spoken of converting to Judaism. When she confronted her son about his conduct and his apparent negligence of her own needs, he replied, "I'm my own master. So it should not concern you if I don't return home. . . . At night I wish to enjoy myself with my friends."[53] When the mother threatened to report him to school officials, Joseph warned that he would simply quit school if she did.

In her letter to Covello she pleaded, "I ask you to convince Joseph that nights are made for him to sleep at home." She continued: "Excuse me sir. You seem to be the father of these young people. Perhaps you or others could obligate them to go to church; and to you they should bring a receipt from the priest every Monday. It seems that my son is being advised by bad companions to leave me and to go far away forever. . . . Please make a rule that all high school boys should be faithful to their religion and to respect the church. He scorns priests. This new friendship that keeps him out all night keeps me from sleeping at night. . . . He will come to a bad end. It is a sin that he should go astray. . . . Please show him his duty."[54] Covello cited Mrs. Patane's plea as typical of the southern Italian's view of the schools as part of an interdependent system (including the church and the village) that should together reinforce parents' authority; it seemed natural to her to expect that a high school principal would bolster her authority even as it slipped away.[55]

The absence of extrafamilial support for the prerogatives of parents in the United States galled southern Italian immigrant parents. In Italy the central institutions of social, political, and economic life during the early twentieth century—principally the church and the landowning elite, but even more recent products of egalitarian reform like public schooling and democracy—were organically spun into the web of social relations. Intrusions into the affairs of parents and children were minimal and reinforced, in any case, patriarchal rule and family honor. In the United States, by comparison, the state was an active agent in relations between parents and children; and these mediations appeared to embody all of the cultural differences that immigrant adults experienced in their daily lives. The legal system, social welfare agencies, schools, and the church presented claims on children that seemingly disenfranchised parental authority. The truant officer, factory inspector, and the courts prevented children from contributing to family income. The public schools, settlement houses, and charities taught personal habits and ways of thinking that countermanded those learned at home. Catholic clergy were often ignorant of Italian, not to mention the more common dialects of everyday life in which they conversed. Largely ministered by an Irish- and German-American episcopy hostile to a folk piety grounded in centuries-old agrarian, mystical, and oral Catholic traditions, the American Catholic Church was theirs in name only. The parish schools to which the contadini were instructed to send their children were not only contemptuous of southern Italian religiosity but even less sympathetic to their customs, rituals, and beliefs than the public schools.[56]

Yet the impulse to look to the principal or the teacher in America to buttress their authority remained. Little wonder then that they were baffled by the schools' insistence that they share responsibility for their children's learning. One of the most common parental complaints about the schools in Wooster Square during the 1930s was that they gave too much freedom. Among them were the mother and father of Yolanda Dante, who were in the minority of parents in this neighborhood who expressed the intention of sending their daughter to high school. "The children should be made to study more and do more homework," they complained to a school visitor. Yet it was observed that the Dantes did not offer any help with the children's school work: "At times the older sisters help the younger children but for the most part . . . [they] are left free to shift for themselves." In effect, Italian immigrant parents believed that the schools had failed them by neglecting to reinforce a web of discipline in solidarity with parents.[57]

Another woman, who held even less faith in the value of extended schooling than the Dantes, saw education as a positive evil. She described for Covello the danger that Italian-born parents might adopt the "American" ethic of giving their children an education, allowing them to keep their earnings and getting nothing material in return. A neighbor of hers, she said, sent both of her daughters to college. When one of them married, she stopped giving any of her earnings from her job to her mother. The mother felt she did not need additional help, and since her daughters had worked for the money, it belonged to them. About all this the informant commented: "My idea is that this is all wrong. You raise a daughter, you send her to school, even to college. She earns money and does not give money to her mother. That's breaking down the *mortalità* of the family. Shouldn't the family get some profit from all the *sforzi* [effort] that her family has made? This is a bad American custom. The children owe something to their parents. It was a case of the mother, 'give, give, give,' and the girl 'take, take, take' and no return. How can children be brought up right in this way? And [how] . . . are the girls going to bring up their children? Things will go from bad to worse. *'Ognuna per i Conti Suoi'* ['each one for his own affairs']. Ther[e] is no family, nor anything!"[58]

It is easy to understand how the American schools could seem "amoral" since they failed to encourage children's feelings of respect and devotion to parents. The contadini "don't feel emotionally right—for example—when they become aware of their children being acquainted with social problems" in school, Covello remarked, for such digressions threatened the primacy of parents in their children's moral instruction. At bottom, this vague uneasiness expresses more acutely than the bluntest of their objections to schooling, the conundrum in which they felt themselves ensnared by coming to the United States. Schooling in America undermined the most basic understanding between parents and children: that children owe their parents respect for embodying, by virtue of their age and experience, the legacy of their culture's wisdom; but more than this, they owed their parents—in a most literal way—their very lives and because of this they also owed their parents whatever material comfort they could afford them until they died.[59] "'What good is it if a boy is bright and intelligent,' said one father, 'and then does not know enough to respect his family. Such a boy would be worth nothing! That's the trouble with American kids; they're smart, but the schools don't teach them to respect their families.'"[60]

In addition, then, to challenging a sociocultural tradition in the provinces of southern Italy that viewed education in the most narrowly practical terms, schooling in America implied a conception of children's roles that clashed with Italian immigrants' ideas about age and familial responsibility. The variety of distinctions between age groups in America and the role of the schools in upholding these threatened deeply held convictions about the process of socializing young people. Covello's penetrating appraisal of adolescence as seen through the eyes of Italian immigrants displays impressive acuity about the *constructedness* of childhood, adolescence, and youth in America. "The first reaction to the American school system," Covello remarked, "was based on the immigrant's discovery of a group which, though evidently adult in physical growth, was a child-group since it attended school and indulged in childish activities, such as playing ball. The status of American youth amazed him but also filled him with apprehension. . . . Boys and even girls were compelled to go to school up to a certain age regardless of parental feelings, the child's aptitudes and desires. Below a certain age, work by children was prohibited. And when the child neither goes to school nor attends to useful work, the enforced leisure and idleness detach the child from the orbit of family life and remove him from the wholesome influence of familial tradition."[61]

More familiar to southern Italian immigrant families was a process of incremental, seamless emergence into adult society, "as gradual and uneventful as . . . [the] physical transformation of the infant into an adult." "There were no sharp age divisions, each shaded with the older and the younger." There were, fundamentally, "two groups," said Covello, "children and adults: helpless infants and very old feeble folks (and playful tots, young men and young women) but never what we call [adolescence]."[62] Where the father was sufficiently comfortable and the sole earner in the family, "the parent could indulge a sentimental attitude toward the adolescent and make a concession to the social pattern of America. But most were not in this position." Of greater significance, in any case, he concludes, "The American school system . . . created a group of idle [youths]. . . . The old Italian equilibrium in which adolescents [fit] well and in a useful way into the family struct[ure] and its economy, had entirely broken; youth was hardly [any] longer an integral part of the Italian family institution. From the ages of seven to fourteen years of age, it was said, the Italian boy in American society did nothing but play in the streets."[63] This was not a literal perception of course but rather a projection of the general frustration experienced by many Italian immigrant parents who felt that the indiscriminate compulsion of schooling, *apart* from depriving families of needed income, failed to recognize the variability of children's inclination toward formal learning and forced the same lengthy course of schooling on all.[64]

A woman who came to New Haven during the mid-1910s from the Marches, a northern province, echoed this judgment. She had only disdain for the American schools because, she argued, in educating everyone regardless of their interest or capacity, much time that might otherwise have been spent productively was wasted. She herself had completed only one year of schooling in Italy before she had to "help the family out," but in that short time had learned to read and write Italian. "In Italy," she reported, "except for one brother, we were all crazy to go to school, but we could not go because we were too poor and had to go to work, to earn something. Here, where school is free [and] all our children could go to school as much as they want, they do not care for it and draw any benefit from it."[65]

Although many contadini surely resented the compulsory aspect of American schooling, this woman's evident yearning for education was not widely shared. Moreover, it is important to bear in mind that when southern Italian immigrants, women particularly, spoke of attending school in Italy, their definition was often more broadly conceived than what was meant by schooling in the United States. Phyllis Williams, a social worker whose subjects were drawn from New Haven's large southern Italian community during the 1930s, reported that immigrant women who had stated that they had had some schooling in Italy frequently meant that they had been "enrolled in classes in embroidery in some neighbor's home."[66] Similarly, a woman who had emigrated from Amalfi (in Campania, just south of Naples) in 1918 at the age of twenty-one, related that she had been a teacher in Italy but had decided like so many other young women in this region to leave to improve her chances of marriage.[67] As it happens, what she meant by "teacher" was that she had taught sewing and dressmaking, a highly desirable occupation for a woman in southern Italian villages but a source of confusion for historians attempting to assess the extent of immigrants' schooling upon their arrival in the United States.[68]

The differences in the kinds of education imparted in southern Italy and the United States were discernible even among adult immigrants who had had little formal schooling in Italy. As we have already seen, there was a pronounced continuity in Italy between the moral didacticism promoted by the schools and the stress on respect for parental (and particularly paternal) wishes at home. Schooling in both countries was described by immigrants as "severe" but in different ways: The American schools were unyielding in their insistence on enrollment and attendance, not realizing (or casting an indifferent eye on) the fact that children's absences often meant the difference between family subsistence and privation.[69] The Italian schools, by contrast, were uncompromising in their attention to discipline and outward displays of deference to authority—a concern, in the estimation of immigrant parents, that was in perilously short supply in the American schools.[70]

Dissatisfaction about the relative lack of attention to discipline in American schools translated, further, into a sense that schools were insufficiently serious. One mother, for instance, who faulted the schools for failing to teach her children how to read and write, asserted that "when you pass by a school all you hear is singing or the steps of dancing, or the noise of playing, playing, playing."[71] The frivolousness of American education was further evidenced by the fact that her daughter's teacher had instructed every girl in the classroom to bring a present for a boy classmate at Christmas time. This request seemed to epitomize schooling in America and provoked the mother to remark, "As if there were not enough love-making in the American schools!"[72]

The significant contributions made by children to household and agricultural tasks in Italy—herding sheep, weeding, harvesting, and stone clearing for peasant boys, making and repairing lines and nets in fisherman families, and, for all girls, cleaning, cooking, sewing, spinning, mending, taking care of the younger children, finishing garments, and tending the candles of the family's patron saint—served as fundamental training for children. Taken together, *these* tasks were closer to the sense of "education" held by southern Italian immigrants than was formal schooling in United States.[73]

Historians have remarked upon a tendency among immigrant groups in the United States since the mid-nineteenth century to extend the schooling of younger children at the expense of older ones. One explanation for this pattern is that the younger children simply benefited from the relatively higher income of households that had reached the later phases of the family cycle: as older children entered the workforce, the household reached its peak earning capacity and could afford to keep their younger children in school. In addition, it has been suggested that this trend reflected gradual acculturation. Immigrant groups arriving during the mid-nineteenth century—preeminently the Irish—wished, as soon as they could, to consume like Yankee working-class families. Initially, they accomplished this by sending their children out to work; but later, when male household heads earned a larger income and could reach a certain plane of living without sacrificing their children's education, they reversed the pattern and lengthened schooling to whatever extent feasible for all their children. Birth order rather than gender seems to have been the key determinant within these families in choosing among children to be schooled.[74]

Although birth order was undoubtedly a factor in determining who went to school among Italians in the United States, there seems to have been a stronger bias against schooling girls than was the case in most other ethnic groups.[75] According to Covello, this arose from the conviction that educating girls was "economically disastrous."[76] Although supporting a boy of twelve in school (and thus forgoing his contribution to the household economy) seemed wrong, it was even more absurd in the eyes of Italian immigrant parents that girls should receive anything beyond the most rudimentary education.[77] Therefore, keeping a girl in school until the age of fourteen, Covello observed, was "a source of constant irritation and anger to her parents."[78] Because boys traditionally enjoyed privileges never extended to girls, explained one Sicilian mother, "the idea of [boys] . . . going to school instead of helping us [parents] was only half bad. Boys somehow managed to make a penny or two. . . . But when girls at thirteen and fourteen wasted good time in school, it simply made us regret our coming to America."[79]

Immigrant contadini parents, when they thought they could get away with it, often discouraged girls from attending schools at all. Covello cited an instance in which a ten-year-old girl was forbidden by her father to go to school because he needed her help in running his restaurant. In the father's estimation, "she could read and write, and that was enough for any Italian girl." The father insisted that "she was big enough to give real help to her parents."[80] As more than one parent remarked to Covello, schooling for girls was a "waste of time. . . . 'What's the use of educating them, they will get married and then who will know whether they are educated or not.'"[81]

By removing a girl from her "customary functions of the home," schooling upset the operation of the family economy. Hence the bitter opposition of Italian immigrants to girls' schooling may have also stemmed from the consequent necessity of forcing the mother to work outside the home, a factor noted by Susan Glenn as well in her study of Russian Jewish immigrants in turn-of-the-century New York City.[82] This situation, as Virginia Yans-McLaughlin has emphasized, was viewed as cause for shame in Italian immigrant families.[83]

Another source of "moral" difficulty presented by schooling girls was the perceived danger of rendering a girl unmarriageable by placing her in situations where she might be vulnerable to male improprieties.[84] In southern Italy not only was coeducation unthinkable, it was also feared that simply teaching a girl how to write might afford her access to males beyond family surveillance. Girls' literacy was thought to encourage amorous correspondence between girls and boys—and thus (potentially) to bring shame upon the girl's family and imperil the reputations of her sisters as well. Southern Italian families considered it highly improper for a girl even to be seen on the street with any nonfamily male. Girls and boys were not to speak or communicate in any way with one another. A girl's family was supposed to mediate any interaction she might have with the opposite sex. Above all, a girl and a boy must never be left alone together, because it was believed that the sexual impulse is so potent that it might easily overpower them.[85]

If the potential of literacy to endanger girls' chastity stirred such anxiety, a girl who stayed in school against her parents' wishes represented a much more palpable threat; moreover, it sacrificed whatever leverage and relative autonomy she possessed as a wage-earner in the household. An extreme but instructive example of this is the story of Beppa Giacomini, who left Italy at the age of fourteen to join her father and brothers in New Haven. When she arrived, her brothers, knowing how enthusiastic she had previously been about school, advised her to enroll in New Haven's (free) public school. Yet her father, a compulsive drinker, had habitually promised Beppa in marriage to any man who would buy him the most drinks. As it happened, a man who had known Beppa as a girl in her parents' village arranged to bring her to New Haven in the hope of marrying her. He bought her father so many drinks that eventually he was able to get him to "promise that [Beppa] would be his wife and [without her knowledge] . . . gave her father money for passage to New Haven." After she arrived and was informed of the circumstances of the arrangement her father had made on her behalf, she realized that if she had "stayed home [and attended school] . . . she would have been dependent upon her family and obliged to do as they pleased." By going to work, however, she saw that "she would be independent and if there was to be a fight [about her father's promise] she would be able to support herself. So it was that three days after she arrived in America, she went to work."[86]

"The Italians have the idea that one or two of their sons might become big businessmen while the others should go to work early," remarked a New Haven–born Italian descendant in his twenties during the late 1930s. "Which one [of his sons] is supposed to go into business?" his interviewer inquired. "'Whoever has the most brains.'" "Do they have that idea in your family?" "'Yes . . . but we got in a hole and couldn't do anything about it.'"[87] Covello observed that extended education would have to yield concrete results in order to win parents' approval. Even for Italian immigrant sons, educational prerogatives turned on the demonstration of extraordinary individual intellectual promise in fields certain to yield financial return or valuable service for the family. Therefore, a boy's schooling might extend through high school or beyond only if he aspired to be a physician, attorney, engineer, dentist, or pharmacist. Lacking aptitude or interest in these professions, he might become a school teacher, but teaching was a poor substitute in the eyes of parents and was usually regarded as a choice of last resort.[88]

Should a boy demonstrate strong ability and desire to prepare for a profession, however, his parents would embrace the idea as a potential boon to the family and devote everything to the cause of putting him through law or medical school. Once this process had begun, the same effort that characterized the collective strivings of the family economy would be channeled toward advancing the boy's career. In return, the boy must affect a seriousness of purpose that showed the solemnity of his "bargain" with his family: he was to focus on his preparation to the exclusion of every possible diversion. His family would provide for him financially even to the extent of allotting him an allowance—an unheard of privilege for any other child, boy or girl.[89]

One New Haven man, whose parents had emigrated from Campania in 1911, graduated from Hillhouse High School and Yale College before entering Tufts Medical School during the 1920s. While in medical school, he was spared even the most trivial inconveniences by his family: in addition to receiving their financial support, he sent his laundry by train from Boston to New Haven each week for his mother to clean, press, and return to him by rail the following week.[90]

Not all sons anointed for schooling fared so well, of course, and "bitterness and disillusionment," according to Covello, was the result "when high school education proved a blind alley. . . . No government or city job—no dignified occupation—no status." Much had been sacrificed with nothing gained in recompense. Moreover, the prospect of a son—especially an educated one—who could not support his parents in their old age, but instead looked to his parents for assistance after reaching maturity, was mortifying. Covello noted the case of "D.T.," who wanted to be a writer and dramatist but whose father wanted him to be a doctor. The boy would miss school to go to the library to read dramas and to write. This provoked the father to exclaim, "Am I to spend a fortune in educating this *signorino* so that he can become a *commediante* and bring not only ridicule upon me and my family, but the inevitable of having to support him to the end of my days[?]"[91]

Daughters' educational aspirations were dismissed out of hand. Schooling for girls clearly represented their independence—a radical departure from the expectations commonly held by Italian parents for their daughters and utterly removed from their conception of the purpose of schooling. This choice constricted the latitude of financial and emotional support that a daughter might have counted on had she chosen the more traditional path instead. On the other hand, the case of "Beppa," mentioned earlier, illustrates the alternative: in choosing to go to work, a young woman might purchase a modicum of autonomy from a father's abusive exercise of patriarchal authority. Wage-earning offered immediate leverage, not only by fulfilling parental expectations and "reparation" to parents for nurturing children during their years of dependence, but by offering a tangible basis for renegotiating the implicit contract of reciprocity between parents and children.[92] Beppa's conception of "independence," however, was surely *relative*. Although she reported nothing about the dispensation of her wages, her freedom to exercise control over her own affairs was undoubtedly based on her value to her father as a wage-earner. Still, as Judith Smith has pointed out, even this form of parental control had its limits: if a wage-earning daughter decided that her parents' demands were intolerable, she could resort to withholding all or part of her pay, leaving parents with little choice but to accede to the decision.[93]

Finally, broader differences in parental attitudes toward the schooling of girls and boys stemmed—at least formally—from a very basic material consideration: boys, once married, still "belonged" to the family and could help their parents if necessary; girls, on the other hand, were considered "lost" to their husbands' families once they married.[94] Any material assistance to parents or displays of loyalty were properly directed to a married daughter's husband's family. This factor put added pressure on parents to obtain what material assistance they could from their daughters before they married and therefore discouraged them from supporting girls' education, not to mention any professional ambitions. This disincentive from the parents' perspective was twofold. Time spent in school was wage-earning time taken away from parents; and because women's prospects for professional or even salaried positions were viewed as remote to begin with, parents felt that time spent in school was "wasted."[95]

How do we understand so instrumental a conception of children's duties and ambitions? And what of sentiment? Was there any room in parenting for the unguarded expression of affection and admiration? What of parents' aspirations for their children? We have already seen that among southern Italian immigrant parents, these conformed strictly to long-standing gender norms and family occupational traditions. Chapter 4 explores some connections between the emergence of new consumption patterns after World War I, influences of popular culture, the role of emotions in family life, and the relation of the marriage market to the family wage economy among Italians and their children in New Haven.

4

HANDS TO MOUTHS: THE CHANGING ECONOMY OF GIVING AND TAKING IN ITALIAN IMMIGRANT FAMILIES

Capitalism causes even the poor to be crazy for money and makes the children of respectable people want the wild, depraved life of the rich.
—An Italian immigrant mason in New Haven during the 1930s, quoted in John W. McConnell, *Evolution of Social Classes*

"When the Italians were saying, 'America took from us our children,'" Leonard Covello mused, "they may have [been alluding to] . . . the economic role of the children. But it is more likely that they expressed a cultural conflict."[1] Italian immigrants commonly complained about the loss of their children's earnings in the United States. Their vexation was keen and straightforward in one sense, for the bulk of southern Italians in the United States worked in the most menial of industrial occupations, accepting low wages and hard physical labor in exchange for steady employment.[2] Yet deep dissatisfaction lingered long after they had resigned themselves to constraints on their children's ability to contribute to family earnings. America had "taken" their children from them by compelling boys and girls to go to school, effectively prohibiting them from working until the age of fourteen. Schooling prolonged children's dependence on their parents, lengthening inordinately what was supposed to be a brief phase of growing up—the passage from young child to contributing family member who shouldered steady and ever-increasing responsibilities from about the age of seven. Schooling most palpably embodied the cultural conflict to which Covello referred, for schooling drew the culture of home life into direct confrontation with the "official" culture of the host society over an extended period of children's lives. Respect for age and the authority of men, the sanctity of women, the honor of the family, and the acceptance of ancient platitudes—these were the moral truths of the immigrant southern Italian family economy. More often than not, however, these truths were expressed in what remained unsaid—the proof of their validity resting in the very fact that they did not require articulation but were simply self-evident and so "understood."[3]

The theme of cultural conflict runs through much of the sociological and historical literature on immigrant family life.[4] Indeed, as the "culture concept" gained credibility among American intellectuals after the turn of the century, ultimately subduing Social Darwinist, biological accounts of behavioral diversity, culture became an all-encompassing explanation for attitudinal and behavioral variation in American subgroups.[5] Covello's observations on Italian immigrants and their children fit neatly into the ascending paradigm of mid-twentieth-century interpretive social science.[6] However, while his characterization of the immigrant parental jeremiad rings true, Covello's transposition of culture and economy renders the gnarly roots of family life artificially distinct. It is, in fact, the inseparability of the ideology of family life and its material basis that is its most distinctive feature, for it is impossible to say whether the changing economic role of children in immigrant families (and indeed, across the American working class) reflected a cultural change already in motion or its opposite: that the restricted economic role of children changed the perception of children in the working class and forced them to adopt the middle-class model.

How successful were Italian immigrant youths in shifting the balance of obligations between themselves and their parents? We have already seen how the establishment of compulsory school attendance firmly placed the state between parents and children legally and "morally," and how it recast parents' dependence on children's earnings in the decades before Italians came to New Haven in full force. In subsequent chapters we explore how this interposition ramified through parent-child relations, but here I limit discussion to the drift in relations between parents and children to something resembling a contractual relationship and the precipitating "reversal of wealth flows" that made children the beneficiaries of this reordering.[7]

Many of New Haven's Italian immigrant parents never conquered the feeling that they had made a grave and irreparable error in coming to America. Yet, as each year passed, fewer reasons remained for men and women in their peak earning or child-bearing years to stay behind.[8] For many, then, the prospect of repatriating their homeland dimmed as annual journeys back and forth gradually yielded to permanent, if reluctant, settlement in America's industrial cities.[9] Still, their eventual capitulation did not lessen immigrants' hopes of preserving the folkways and values their ancestors had cultivated for centuries. Living in New Haven's immigrant "colonies" in or near Wooster Square or the Hill, attending nationality parishes such as St. Michael's or St. Anthony's, which commemorated the feast days of their villages' patron saints and whose clergy spoke Italian, buying goods from street vendors and shops that catered to their tastes in the food, clothing, and material culture of the *mezzogiorno* allowed them to feel as though they might forestall the effects of dwelling in a foreign land. Nevertheless, they gradually realized that their children could not live in cultural isolation, even in a city like New Haven, which at the time had an unusually high concentration of Italian immigrants.[10]

Although New Haven's Italians, like its Russian Jews, Poles, and African Americans, felt themselves to be worlds apart from the city's Yankee establishment (or even its socially and politically ascendant Irish Americans), their values were undergoing continual if grudging revision, just as the society in which they dwelled was *itself* in constant flux. It was in this context of purposeful resistance to change in the host culture—change that at once threatened and beckoned—that the notion of legal, institutional protections for children, and of "sentimentalized childhood," were advanced. The absorption of this ideal through American culture, which had begun decades earlier, was an ongoing and open-ended phenomenon rather than a foregone conclusion. The celebration of childhood and the recognition of adolescence that immigrants experienced as an "American" phenomenon was not unique to the United States but manifest throughout industrialized societies.[11] So the prevailing sense that America had *stolen* their children was nourished by their experience with institutions such as schools, which accompanied the growth of cities and mechanized industry across the Western world.

Schooling was the most consistent, active, and visible agent of acculturation in this regard. By daily exposing children of the working class to habits and attitudes that promoted middle-class values like punctuality, regularity, individualism, and meritocracy, schooling ultimately undermined the continuation of the family system of morality. Another important link between changes in attitudes and changes in the material basis of the family wage economy, of course, lay in the changes young people experienced in the kinds of work they performed and the fact that their introduction to the workforce was increasingly a peer-group experience. Previously the child was sent into the workforce without regard for the norms of his or her peers. As school was voluntarily extended beyond the age required by law, however, the forms of work that one's friends aspired to increasingly shaped young people's ideas about the kinds of jobs they themselves might seek. Moreover, the notion of having the opportunity to enjoy the cultural and developmental "space" of adolescence bore down upon their conceptions of themselves as well. This, in turn, began to influence what they felt they owed to their families and it was in this connection especially—what might be termed the "imagined worlds" that young people occupied—that immigrant parents feared American popular culture. However, as this chapter reveals, these parents were usually ill-equipped to protect their children from exposure to the behavior and attitudes of other young people in a city so geographically compact as New Haven.[12]

In the eyes of Italian immigrant parents, the creation of a child bound it literally and permanently to his or her own welfare, establishing a debt to be paid down over the course of the child's lifetime. Obligations between parents and children ran in both directions but were neither finite nor mutual. Thus, for example, an Italian immigrant father complained aloud about his daughter who contributed to family expenses but refused to part with all but a small portion of her earnings each pay day: "But then, why did I make her?" he asked, in a phrase that pronounced a familiar judgment of Italian immigrant parents on the rising generation: "You know how these American children are," he added in disgust, "you cannot talk to them."[13] Under the strain of economic and social change, obligations on both sides were challenged and renegotiated during the 1920s and 1930s.

The compact that governed the family wage economy imbued children with a sense of responsibility for their parents until death. In Italian immigrant families it was presumed that one of the children would shelter, clothe, nurse, and feed aged parents. The idea of having infirm parents cared for in institutions like hospitals or homes for the elderly, in this conception, was considered shameful. Which child provided such caretaking—just as which child was permitted to stay in school rather than quit at the first opportunity—was determined by birth order and gender. The older children normally got short shrift on schooling, as did girls compared with their brothers. A daughter, especially a never-married daughter, would be expected to capitulate silently to a vocation of tending to the needs of declining parents. When all the children were fortunate enough to have married, a daughter (ordinarily) would be expected to make room in her household for parents after their productive years had come to a close. It was during the 1920s and 1930s that this conception of family obligation evolved into the family consumer economy. They were years of *transition* rather than transformation, however, since remnants of time-worn practices and rituals existed side by side with new attitudes about what parents and children owed to one another. Because the collision of ancient and novel ideas about family obligation caused such emotional upheaval, the arising conflicts were captured anecdotally and in abundance by sociologists, ethnographers, economists, and demographers studying household economics, social structure, marriage, religion, and folklife in New Haven between the wars.

Again, although education was one significant vehicle of this change, it is important to bear in mind that Italian immigrant parents' visions of their children's occupational prospects were still only very tenuously connected to schooling during these years. Thus, the model of family reciprocity captured in the notion of "timeliness" that John Modell, Frank F. Furstenberg Jr., and Theodore Hershberg have employed included a range of important life-course decisions: not just how long children should remain in school and at what age they should get a job, but how long they might live at home, when they should marry, and even whom they would marry. To understand changing attitudes toward schooling, then, it is necessary to understand the context in which decisions to prolong children's education were made. That school-leaving is tied to a young person's decision to begin working full-time is obvious, but decisions about spending money and leaving home are inseparable from attitudes toward education; all are linked to notions of family reciprocity and thus merit attention.

If scarcity was the governing principle of the family wage economy, its application was challenged (paradoxically) by the generation that came of age during the twentieth century's most devastating economic depression. All but the poorest children encountered forms of consumption and conceptions of selfhood stemming from new attitudes toward consumption in their leisure time and among their schoolmates that undercut parents' admonitions to hedge against want. The most dramatic sign of change was played out in the contest over youths' wages. But before children could challenge parents over the disposition of their wages, parents determined the parameters of the family wage economy by the number of children they had in the first place. After children reached working age, other issues that threatened parents', and especially fathers', authority, even if only obliquely, fell under the watchful and often jealous eyes of parents who found parts of their children's worlds remote and incomprehensible.[14] Issues such as how much time and money might be spent on things regarded by parents as frivolous, when children might quit school and go to work, what kinds of aspirations sons and daughters harbored, or even the type of friends their children chose all came under parental scrutiny.

Although the high number of children typical among Italian immigrant families in the United States between 1910 and 1930 caused the period's welfare workers and social critics to despair at the Italians' apparent ignorance of contraceptive methods, John W. Briggs has shown that Italian immigrant fertility patterns in fact indicate quite deliberate reproductive behavior, which included contraceptive use.[15] A new tactic was to begin having children at an earlier age and to curtail fertility after a "target" number of children had been reached. The results of this strategy included an early mean age-at-first-marriage for women, conception (on average) at a younger age, and the cessation of reproduction at around age thirty-two, rather than at the biological terminus of a woman's child-bearing years. This new behavior, says Briggs, can be explained by the general elevation of Italians' material standard of living in the United States relative to southern Italy, enabling immigrants to revive a cultural ideal of the homeland—the large family—which had in fact been waning in their own country for decades.[16]

Among the unemployed, E. Wight Bakke has observed that the "sight of men who had children to help when their own earnings failed was too obvious a bit of evidence to miss."[17] Indeed, large-family size was an important component of workers' long-term strategies for weathering the unpredictable if inevitable cycles of joblessness that characterized the career of a wage-earner in the era of industrial capitalism, as Michael Anderson, David Levine, and others have shown.[18] Although fewer than one-third of the workers studied by Bakke "mentioned control of family size as among the conscious attempts made to plan wisely for the future," 14 percent "claimed to have used foresight in limiting their family size."[19] But significantly, another 16 percent "declared with equal emphasis that *large* families were a form of foresight."[20] The idea that fewer children would bring greater material comfort and enduring security was counter-intuitive and seemed to belie experience: although additional hands meant greater and more flexible possibilities for family employment, the accompanying mouths to feed, according to at least one man, merely helped to rein-in "unnecessary" expenditures. A New Haven sheet-metal worker (decidedly not Italian, perhaps an English immigrant, though his ethnicity is unspecified) was asked by Bakke, "Would it not be better to save the money than to have to spend it on children?" to which he replied, "Ah mate, but you don't understand. You wouldn't have saved the money no how. You don't know how you have to go without what you really need if you save. Now if it's for the kids, of course you will do it. But a man's human, you know. Having kids forces you not to spend for nothing foolish—it's funny how you can think a pair of shoes with soles in them is foolish, isn't it, or a new hat or a chair what you can sit in and really rest at night. But in the end the kids is a better investment than such things."[21] This is a penetrating glimpse of the mentality of the family wage economy; it reveals not only the way children represented security but also their importance (real or imagined) as a brake against "excessive" consumption. Moreover, it illuminates the depth of parental resistance to the very different attitudes toward consumption that children would encounter in the world beyond home and neighborhood.

When asked to elaborate on the differences between being raised in Italy and growing up in the United States, one man neatly summarized all the features of the southern Italian family wage economy. One of the most salient differences for him was that in Italy (and contrary to Briggs's retrospective assertions) "all the families are big. . . . [but] Americans don't like this, they [family members] want to think for themselves." He continued: "In big families, . . . the children take care of themselves" as well as their parents. Furthermore, "when the kids are old enough to work, they go to work and they make money so the family can go ahead. They have to bring all the money home and they don't pay board like the Americans or the Polocks and Slovaks. When the kids want something they get it right away when they work. . . . The Italians bring up their children to respect the mother and father. . . . [and] remember that the father and the mother sacrificed a lot of things so that the children could grow up good. My children before they think of anything they want to do they have to ask me, or the mother, if they could do it. The other nationalities don't do this, . . . [the parents] are all for themselves, and that's why their children get to be the same way. Even now many children are trained that when the smaller boys get up in the morning, or when they have to change their clothes, the older children take care of what they want. This way the children get to like everybody in the house just like they have to."[22]

While Bakke reported that by the 1930s in New Haven the family wage economy continued to operate in only the largest of families, it still retained a meaningful symbolic existence in many of the city's immigrant families—especially among Italians and Poles.[23] In Italian immigrant families, according to the testimony of women and men who came of age during the 1920s and 1930s, commitment to the performance of labor for the family's benefit ran so deep that parents expected their sons' and daughters' weekly pay envelopes to be turned over to them unopened each pay day.[24] In most families, it seems, not only the neediest, this custom was observed in some form until World War II. Among Italian immigrants in particular, one of the greatest differences between "early" school-leavers and their peers who continued through high school was the extent to which their families depended on their earnings. Unsurprisingly, although the families of high school graduates relied to a much lesser degree on children's earnings than in families of early school-leavers, the majority of high school graduates made at least nominal contributions to the family purse in recognition of their filial obligations.

In a study of female high school graduates of the class 1930 in New Haven, it was found that of those holding full-time jobs (60 of the 125 women in the study), two-thirds reported that they gave "something at home when I have it left over." Eleven paid a specified amount of their income to their parents each month, and about ten said they "turn[ed] over the pay envelope," meaning that they gave their parents all their earnings.[25] All of the girls and women who worked in New Haven's garment shops, by contrast, turned over the pay envelope to parents.[26] Usually they would get something back for "car" (street car) fare, if they traveled a distance to work, and some spending money. These amounts might range from between $1 and $1.50 per week, out of weekly earnings beginning at between $4 and $5, but were sometimes less.[27] Phyllis Williams wrote that mothers in southern Italy would save youths' earnings for them and return the amount accumulated upon marriage. Daughters received their portion in the form of a dowry, the value of which was roughly known, whereas sons would receive theirs as a "wedding gift," the distinction being that the daughter (and her family by marriage) was entitled to her dowry, while the son's gift was given "freely" but he had no rightful claim to it. It is unclear how long this practice continued in the United States.[28]

Many young people, especially girls in the case of Italian immigrants, experienced the imperatives of the family wage economy as the unimpeachable right of parents to invoke. Parents could command them to quit school to "work for the family" regardless of personal considerations. Certainly some immigrant children preferred the informal give-and-take of the family wage economy while others simply resigned themselves to it as the hand dealt them by life. A woman who grew up in one of the city's Italian immigrant communities during the 1930s and was "sent to work" by her mother when she turned fourteen, said of her mother's decision: "What else can you do with a big family and not much money? I had three brothers and nine sisters. The last two got the education. That seems to be the way things work. The oldest get the rough breaks. They have to help out with the young ones. When you get enough of the kids working and can start saving a few pennies, the last two will get the breaks, if you're lucky and don't need the money for the grocer or the landlord. That's the way it worked with us. The last two got the breaks."[29]

Another woman, "Angela," also from a large family, was presented with the same demand as a thirteen-year-old in 1932. Her father had been out of a job for several months and was on the brink of applying for city relief. However, because he abhorred the prospect of depending on strangers for support, he told Angela that she must find work. Her older brother in the meantime was allowed to continue in school even though he was considered less talented academically and showed little interest in his schoolwork. Angela's sisters, she recalled, told her what a shame it was that she had to quit school because she, more than any of her siblings, had loved school and was the best student in the family. Like so many other Italian immigrant daughters in New Haven during the Depression, she found work in a garment factory. Although Angela dutifully accepted her father's directive, the lost opportunity rankled for the rest of her life.[30]

Irvin L. Child's study of second-generation Italian immigrant men included a questionnaire that illuminates how commonplace it was to turn over the pay envelope. Of the forty-six second-generation Italian men Child interviewed, twenty-eight (61 percent) reported that they contributed all of their earnings to their parents while they lived at home. Seven others said they turned over "most" of their pay, and eleven paid only room and board—an arrangement regarded by many as distinctly "American" because of its implied individualism. Of these eleven, seven reported some conflict with their parents over the expectation that they would hand over their wages.[31] The payment of room and board, by introducing an impersonal, vaguely contractual element, seemed to many parents to alter the nature of the parent-child relationship. One of the men Child interviewed said that his father would have thought that his home had been turned into a "boarding house" if he and his brother had tried to pay room and board. Instead they turned over all their pay to him: "He said that we were assured of security and there was no need for us to keep any money for ourselves."[32]

An Italian immigrant man from nearby Bridgeport stated his opposition to the practice of paying room and board as well, suggesting
that monetizing the parent-child relationship emptied it of meaning.
Remarking upon what to him seemed a grotesque distortion of parent-
child relations under such arrangements, he declared, "I don't believe
this business that my children have to give me board. What will they do if
they are out of work? Then they can't pay no board if they don't work.
So what do I have to do, chase them out of the house? That's why so
many people from the other nationality [sic] chase their children out of
the house, and I don't want any of this thing in my family."[33] While some
youths rebelled against parents' efforts to hold them to what they perceived as an embarrassing remnant of their parents' immigrant past, others appreciated the advantage of family connections: "Don't get too far
from home-base—that's what I say," a second-generation New Haven
Italian bricklayer declared. "It's no use for most men to think they can go
it alone, and to hell with the rest of the family. . . . It may be awful handy
to slide in some day."[34]

Despite the prominence of such attitudes among Italian immigrants
and their children, it would be misleading to suggest that other immigrant groups did not confront the same dilemmas and make similar
choices. Russian- and Polish-born Jews, for instance, who in marked contrast to Italians generally promoted schooling for their children, might
succumb to the necessity (or desire) to establish themselves financially
and press older children into service to bear the burden of meeting the
family's needs. Hymen Lender, one of five children, was the oldest boy in
a family that ultimately established a highly successful bagel bakery in
New Haven, yet he vividly recalls the moment when he was asked to
"help out" the family business even though it ultimately meant giving up
school.[35] Eleven years old when his father moved to the United States
from Poland, Hymen attended school for four years in New Haven until
he quit at the end of his freshman year at Hillhouse High School. He left
school for a combination of reasons: after spending a year in grammar
school learning English, he entered the sixth grade but was quickly promoted to the eighth grade. In retrospect, he felt that this move had
deprived him of skills he would need later to succeed in school. After
graduating from eighth grade, he enrolled at Hillhouse, where he made

the basketball team. However, by this time he was also working in his father's bakery most nights. "It became very hard for me to work in the bakery at night and go to school in the day time. I didn't know what side was up. I didn't know when to sleep and when not to sleep. So it seemed like the easiest thing was to quit school." Although his parents were not entirely happy with his decision to quit school (even though they had implored him to help in the bakery), Hymen reflected, "They needed me, because . . . [my father's] business wasn't the greatest business in the world. It was just a small, little bagel bakery business. And it was like a family thing. As soon as one of the boys grew up a little bit, he had to work in the bakery."[36] One night when his father was desperate for help, he awakened Hymen and said, "'You still have knickers on. You don't have regular long pants like all the other kids do. You come to work, I'll buy you a pair of long pants.' So I went to work." He continued: "And that was the start of my . . . downfall because I did not have a teenage life like most American kids even though it was tough sledding at the time. . . . [T]he bakery was always able to provide food and clothing for the family. But that means that we all had to work. Everybody had to work. . . . I had to drop everything to go work in the bakery. . . . I had not the life of an American young man, and that life evidently was something in America that kids need. To go to proms and to go to basketball games and the dance after the basketball game. Something I couldn't do, because I had to work in the bakery."[37]

Hymen's experience illustrates the fact that even while it is possible to generalize about the reasons and mentality of families who sent their sons and daughters to work, a variety of circumstances, influences, and impulses informed such decisions. Early school-leaving was a response not just to negative economic pressure or a bias against schooling, but also to opportunity framed as necessity and born of a complex of rationalizations, discouragements, and incentives—including the exercise of individual choice. Young people left school for work not solely because they were forced to but because it was at least partly gratifying to do so, and school, aside from a few lucrative professions, as yet did not offer an unequivocal path to affluence.

To the extent that children had been sentimentalized in American culture by the 1930s, it had occurred for the most part "behind the backs" of working-class parents rather than at their instigation. There were major exceptions, of course, but many parents actively fought this sentimentalizing trend, which they experienced as both a challenge to their authority and as a financial impediment. Indeed, the very meaning of "family" was at stake for them and in good part children were often the agents of this change. Accompanying state-imposed protections of childhood and adolescence were signs that young people were beginning to embrace the world of consumer goods and leisure that American culture spread before them.

A 1932 New York City study sheds some light on the kinds of leisure activities popular with second-generation, Italian immigrant adolescents of the day. When asked how they preferred to spend their time, 92 percent of the girls in this study (whose ages ranged from twelve to "seventeen and over," with a mean of 14.5) answered "the movies."[38] The five next most popular activities involved little or no expense: reading was the second favorite leisure activity for 82 percent of these girls; third was to "go down with a girlfriend" (meaning going downstairs to visit a girlfriend on the front stoop to talk and watch people in the street), 24 percent; fourth, "go visiting," 23 percent; fifth, "listen to the Victrola or radio," 19 percent; and sixth, taking walks, 16 percent.[39] Whether they worked or went to school, the girls in this study were unanimous in their insistence that, preferences aside, what they routinely did with their time—after school or after work—was housekeeping, scrubbing, shopping, cooking, mending, and taking care of their younger siblings.[40] Although it is clear that the images generated by mass culture—radio and the movies—promoted consumption, leisure, and the pleasures of personal life, the expectations of these girls and young women were nonetheless very modest.[41] At least one New Haven woman, Antoinette Vecchio, who worked in the garment industry all her life, claimed that she "always had enough," since her parents provided clothing and absorbed other expenses. "We amused ourselves in such different ways that it didn't cost money," Vecchio reminisced, though she did not elaborate on the nature of these amusements.[42] Still, not everyone felt that what their parents returned to them from their pay was sufficient to their needs. Mary Baker, one of the few African-American women to work in New Haven's garment shops during the 1930s, recalled about her

Italian-American coworkers that many would obtain an extra pay envelope and get it signed by their boss, "then take out their pay and give their mother the rest." Tessie Rappa, one of Mary's contemporaries, confirmed this impression, confessing, "I used to try to sneak some of it out, but it wasn't much."[43]

None of these preferences was articulated in a vacuum, of course. It was against the backdrop of the Great Depression that "movies" were chosen over "reading," and among Bernice S. Smith's (New Haven) group, "automobiling" over "visiting." Even though riding in an automobile was out of the question for Italian-American girls of any social class, and reading and visiting surpassed the frequency of visits to the movie theater each week, what was expressed in each survey was often something closer to the gap between desire and its satisfaction than what they actually did.[44] Some portion of these adolescents—especially those from very large families—would have been pressed into work for their parents regardless of the decade's economic cataclysm. Others, it is impossible to know what fraction, were its "victims," since father's unemployment rather than family size abbreviated schooling. But as the crisis ground on, this same group (their younger siblings in effect) were rewarded with more schooling when youth joblessness by mid-decade had discouraged all but the most desperate among them from quitting school for the sake of work not to be found.[45]

Changing attitudes toward consumption can also be discerned in what was perceived both by the older generation and by social observers as a growing attentiveness to personal appearance. John W. McConnell has characterized this as a consequence of the differing experiences of first- and second-generation Italian immigrants. "The Italian heritage," he concluded, "plus the fact that most Italians came here originally with the idea of accumulating money forced this group to adopt a standard of living even lower than they could afford. This is most certainly true of housing. Judging by Italian standards, many of the immigrant families have already made progress toward a better level. Judged by American standards, [however,] the movement is almost imperceptible. The second generation of Italian immigrants, having learned something of the external aspects of 'American' standards, presses the family for a change—specifically for more room, new furniture, good clothes, and a car."[46]

Williams offered a fascinating portrait of young women's concerns with personal appearance, individuation, conceptions of self, and, consequently, notions of what constituted "marriageability." In southern Italy a marriageable woman was one whose industriousness was worn on her hands and fingers. If they bore the marks of hard work, she was sure to be an asset in stretching her family's budget. She would run the household efficiently and be an invaluable help to her husband for the rest of their shared lives. Soft, well-manicured hands, however, were an index of "laziness" and of one "totally unfitted for the sole destiny of the female—marriage and housekeeping."[47]

Although mothers tried to impart these values to their daughters in the United States, many felt that they had failed. "The mother," wrote Williams, "ready for marriage at a younger age than her daughter has reached, sighs, and wonders that the world can change so completely": "School," she continued, "teaches children much, but somehow fails to instill the most important obligations of life—a realization of the necessity of work and a will to do it. Many who do work . . . no longer wish to give their entire earnings to their mother's safekeeping. American girls need at least two hair wavings a month, new clothes, movies, and trips to the shore. 'It is my money,' they assert, and there in [sic] lies the greatest change. Wages used to be used jointly for the common support of the family; now they tend to remain in the possession of the girls and boys who earn them."[48] Whether they remained in school or left for the garment factories, "the American standard of living," in Williams's estimate, "require[d] more time for the embellishment of the person."[49] One manifestation of this trend, she found, was a decline in church attendance among Italian immigrant daughters. In anticipation of a big Sunday meal (an adopted American custom), often preceded by rounds of visiting to nearby kin, young Italian-American women came to "insist upon resting Sunday morning."[50] After having toiled eight to ten hours a day, for six days a week in a garment shop, "Sunday morning . . . [became a time] . . . for manicuring and hair arrangement, for care of the body," rather than for observing the Sabbath or "helping their mothers as they would have done in Italy."[51]

In Italy a girl's status was improved when she stayed home after completing her schooling (however brief) because, conventionally, she would then learn homemaking and enhance her desirability as a potential marriage mate. In the United States, however, the daughters of Italian immigrants either stayed in school or entered the factory instead of helping their mothers at home. Therefore, even though most young women expected that homemaking would be their ultimate vocation, they learned only haphazardly (by their mothers' lights) how to keep house and prepare food.[52] While they were in high school, one observer remarked, they were too busy with their studies and extracurricular activities to have time to learn how to cook from their mothers. After they graduated, they usually went right to work, and even if they married immediately after high school, they often worked outside the home before having children and so had little time to spend with their mothers to acquire the "arts of homemaking."[53]

Williams's analysis of the new attention to personal appearance among girls and young women, however perceptive, makes little distinction between factory girls and those who attended high school during the 1930s. Young women who graduated from high school undoubtedly had more leisure time and greater means (even during the Depression) to indulge in both commercial leisure and—in Williams's phrase—"embellishment of the person." For the women in Smith's study (most of whom lived in their parents' homes five years after graduation and were about twenty-three years old at the time) clothing by far surpassed any other expenditure.[54] Although Smith's study doesn't identify women by ethnic group, it makes useful comparisons that correspond roughly to social economic status and reveals interesting differences among female high school graduates in the way they spent their earnings. Among the women in her study, thirty-nine had graduated from the city's Commercial High School (which offered secretarial and clerical training). These women earned on average $13.50 per week. Twenty-six of them spent between $1 and $5 per week on "novelties and cosmetics," twenty-six spent between $5 and $10 per week on clothes, and another eight spent from $2 to $5 per week on clothes. In other words, the mode for clothing expenditures was about 40 percent of weekly pay, and the mode for "novelties and cosmetics" was another 25 percent.[55]

Of the twenty-one fully employed Hillhouse graduates (who earned an average of $10.50 per week), eighteen spent between $2 and $7 per week on clothes, and sixteen spent between $1 and $5 per week on "novelties and cosmetics." The mode for clothing expenditure for this group was also roughly 40 percent, and the mode expended for novelties and cosmetics was also around 25 percent.[56] "Clothing," Smith reported, "is far and away the most significant item in their budgets, 'novelties and cosmetics' a distant second; board an even more distant third."[57] Even within a group that was decidedly more affluent than those who were forced to go to work, expenditures differed in amounts spent for clothing.

Graduates of New Haven's Commercial High School, whose parents were more likely to have been foreign-born than were the parents of graduates of Hillhouse, and whose preparation was overwhelmingly vocational rather than college preparatory, earned more per week, averaged more weeks employed per year, and spent more on average for clothing than did their graduate peers from Hillhouse.[58] Attention to personal appearance even outweighed the importance of nutrition for these women. Of the sixty women in Smith's sample who had been steadily employed during the three-and-a-half years since their graduation, all but four routinely ate their lunches away from home, yet none of them set aside a regular amount of their pay for lunch, preferring to walk or window-shop during their lunch hour. Typically they would eat well on "pay day and the day after," reported Smith, "tapering off to coffee and a cruller [or] 'pop' and a sandwich on the other days, frequently going without any in order to buy" something to enhance their appearances. These women "unanimously rejected" the idea of bringing their lunch to work, wrote Smith. "Others would see it," they worried (that is, and conclude that they could not afford to eat out), and besides "there would be no place to eat it, and it would be extra work to put it up." Two of these women reported that they had "left [their] crowd" because they could not conform to the clothing standards of their friends; and thirteen said that they went without lunch to buy stockings and cosmetics.[59] Despite the fact that all of these young women had been taught to sew in junior high school, none of them considered making their clothes at home, even from commercially produced but thrifty dress patterns. Moreover, many of them managed to purchase suits, coats, or fine dresses that cost a few weeks' wages. This was made possible by installment buying, Smith

discovered. One-third of the women fully employed bought on installment, "even with as little as five dollars cash."[60]

How do expenditures for personal appearance figure into the equation
of deflated consumption during the Great Depression? Food and clothing were the first two items in any family budget to be scrutinized when
unemployment struck. The first category no one could see; hence the
sense of shame that deepened the hardship of joblessness was somewhat
mitigated by doing without. Clothing, on the other hand, like housing,
was the first thing noticed about others' material well-being. Just as families were loath to move into a lesser rental, they also tried to camouflage
the effects of want when the breadwinner's job ran out.[61] Many families
were able to get secondhand clothing from relatives, others from contacts with well-to-do employers.[62] But "most families," according to
Bakke, "felt a strong revulsion against being seen in what they felt sure
would be recognized as 'charity clothes.' One woman was mortified by
the experience of a neighbor's child who "had it flung into her face by a
schoolmate, 'that looks like the coat I gave to the Red Cross,'" and proclaimed, "I'll not let that happen to my Marie." In Bakke's estimation,
parents (mothers in particular) were more concerned about their children's appearance—the "stigma attached to used or worn out clothing—
than they cared about how they themselves were clad." One mother
became "frantic," he reported, when at the approach of a new school
year she had no new clothing for her daughter: "I've patched and let out
the hems, but by no stretch of the imagination can I see Virginia going to
school in the old clothes." She resolved the impending crisis by writing
to a friend who worked for a "rich lady" to ask for discarded clothing.[63]
Another way to stave off the purchase of new clothing, of course, was
to take great care in preserving what one already had. One woman in
Bakke's budget survey "washed and ironed her children's clothing every
night so that they looked good the next day." She herself did her housework in a petticoat rather than in her dress, which she only wore when
she left the house. Occasionally her husband would get an extra and
unexpected day's work, "which meant three or four dollars, so I put that
away for shoes for him or a pair of pants."[64]

Men, according to McConnell, usually had one good suit purchased,
as in the example just mentioned, even at the expense of their wives'

appearance. Ordinarily this was a dark suit because "you don't know when you might have to go to a funeral or a wedding . . . and [with a dark suit] you look dressed no matter where else you wear it."[65] "Work-clothes," noted McConnell, "consist of the cast-off good suit as long as it lasts; after that, odd pants are secured to go with coats which have not worn out as quickly as the pants." Whereas professional people, Bakke found, readily wore "mismatched" pants and sports coats with "re-spectability," in working-class New Haven wearing a coat with a pair of pants not from the same suit for anything but work was the emblem of low-income status.[66] Vittorio Racca, who made little effort to conceal a patronizing bourgeois sensibility and a northerner's contempt for the people of the South in his reports for the Institute of Human Relations, reserved special scorn for the thriftless among New Haven's Italians.[67]

Racca was assigned to accompany a visiting teacher to the home of the De Nuzzo family to investigate the cause of their children's purported poor nutrition. He found the couple constantly at odds over their limited resources but placed most of the blame on Mrs. De Nuzzo (fourteen years old when she came to New Haven from a village in Caserta in 1908, thirty-eight in 1932), who "buys plenty but unwisely," he commented. "There is no question that whether he or she buys things," Racca observed, "there is plenty to eat in the home; but it is not of the right kind, not well cooked; this is probably why the children eat less well than they should. Then too, she saves on home expenses to make her children look like Americans; of course, she does not know what that means, but that is her ambition. While we were there a girl came home dressed in green velvet—for school! on a rainy day! She is extravagant. She does not know how to mend a torn dress, etc.; she throws away things little used. (She does not get relief from any agency, nor does she get clothing for her children from the Red Cross. . . .) Then, though she dresses her children in a showy manner, she does not know how to keep them and their clothes clean."[68]

Bearing in mind Racca's particular prejudices, his sense that southern Italian immigrants were prone to mistake the trappings of consumer culture for personal advancement resonated with others' assessments as well. An Italian immigrant stonemason, for instance, perceived problems that ran deeper than the predictable hurdles of social adjustment and acculturation his countrymen—and indeed, all immigrants—faced in America. This man reversed the blame, however, placing it squarely on the doorstep of the U.S. economic system. "Capitalism," he commented darkly, "causes even the poor to be crazy for money and makes the children of respectable people want the wild, depraved life of the rich. My children smoked and drank and went on wild parties. I talked to them, but they had lost respect for me, and my wife sided with them. I was old—out-of-date. All they wanted from me was a place to sleep and money and when I couldn't give them that they wouldn't take me in. I never drank. I stayed at home and read, and wanted to discuss economic and political questions but they only wanted a good time. I read and I open my eyes. I understand. I tried to tell my children. But they laughed. They are blind—stupid."[69] Improvidence, superficiality, and overdependence on outsiders were values that immigrants were especially vulnerable to in a misreading of their host culture, according to Racca, since the greater part of their contact with American culture came through exposure to radio, movies, and pulp magazines.[70]

Particularly insidious in Racca's view were the child radio stars whose example seems to have inspired local Italian Americans to enroll their children for singing and dancing lessons. This, he says sardonically, would make their children "real" Americans. "Peter," son of the "Croces" (second-generation New Haven Italians, who in Racca's narrative furnish a particularly egregious example of immigrants striving to "fit in"), would receive an "American" education, his parents decided. "The best way to make Peter a real American [they believed] was to make him learn how to dance and sing." But "sing according to the rules of the 'bel canto' made famous by the Italians, to whom, after all, they belong? Not on your life! No Italian singing; crooning—that is American! Dancing—according to the famous rule of the Italian ballet? Never, never—rather the tap dance, the shimmy and other Negro dances. That, again, is really American! Likewise, he was made to sing for the radio in those horrible 'children's hours' everybody knows and hates. In that way their son will be one hundred per cent Americanized. . . . That is the tragedy of it! They have the radio. They might learn it in that way, but no—all you hear on the radio in their house is the squealing of children singing—horrible!"[71]

If the desire to "fit in" with their peers afflicted many children, some parents perceived the impulse as a slide toward Americanization and discouraged it. Williams, for example, described the unraveling of the Pelotti family, whose eldest daughter, "Rosa," asked to take dancing lessons at the neighborhood settlement house. Recognized as a particularly handsome girl and a graceful dancer by one of the settlement house workers, she was encouraged to take special free lessons. Rosa asked her parents' permission and though they initially had strong reservations, they almost consented. But then they consulted Matteo, her younger brother, who objected to the lessons on the grounds that an exercise so public in nature would stain the family's honor.[72] So the parents reversed themselves, denying Rosa's request. A month later, Matteo inexplicably "announced that he was taking dancing lessons, not at the settlement house but from a private teacher to whom he had to pay a fee." To pay for the lessons, however, he had to use some of the money from his weekly earnings, which ordinarily went to his parents for support. This led to a "disastrous quarrel," as Rosa objected that she had been denied only a month earlier for lessons that were to be at no expense. Matteo left home as a result of the quarrel and began living with a friend. Thus, recorded Williams, the family not only lost his earnings but the esteem of their neighbors as well for their apparent inability to control their son.[73]

Other Italian-American households with which Racca came into contact during his residence in New Haven seem to have shared the Croces' and Pelottis' "misdirected" affinity for American popular culture and, even worse, demonstrated for him the unwitting complicity of American schooling in spreading its influence. Pauline Tranquilli, for example, the thirteen-year-old daughter of immigrants who had come to New Haven as youths, was described by Racca as "fairly bright" but "not overly so": She "goes to school because she must, but does not like it. School does not mean a thing to her or her brothers. . . . All she gets out of the knowledge acquired in the schools is to read love stories in cheap magazines and the funnies in the dailies. She knows enough English to do that, but when you ask her to read something else she says she just cannot do it."[74] Pauline, in Racca's estimation, was typical of many Italian-American adolescents in the way the public schools seemed to inspire in her little more than an ability to appreciate and consume the offerings of mass culture. Her family subscribed to three newspapers, a city daily, an Italian socialist weekly, and another local Italian weekly. Yet the mother "never looks at them," the father looks only at the *Register* (the city daily) "to see if there will be work soon," and the children merely read the comics—"that is all the enlightenment they get from the press." They have a radio, Racca pointed out, but it remains invariably tuned to a station that plays little more than "jazz and comedies." They get no information from the radio to speak of, observed Racca.[75]

Whether American schooling shared the blame in the growing preoccupation with individual gratification among immigrant youths, clearly conceptions of selfhood were bending into a new relation with family members that threatened family morality. A generational divide in attitudes toward consumption that became apparent to all observers arose over the significance of self-presentation. To the immigrant generation, it seems to have mattered not only how one appeared in public but that one's self-presentation be genuinely thrifty as well. Improvidence or thoughtless consumption was considered disgraceful. The younger generation, on the other hand, viewed self-presentation as a token for membership in a wider social group—a group that might transcend one's ethnicity—and whether one achieved this by cunning frugality was a matter of indifference. For the allures of leisure, consumption, and enhanced personal appearance were tied to the marriage market and to ideas about whom one might marry, which engaged the young person's evolving identity. However, these allures did so often at the expense of what parents believed was best for the family group. If we think of the family as an economic unit, which it surely is, then the marriage of children, no less than the disposition of children's earnings, their contributions to housekeeping and child-tending, or their stay in school, was a key component of the Italian immigrant family economy in the United States.[76]

5

FROM COURTSHIP TO DATING: THE MARRIAGE MARKET, SCHOOLING, AND THE FAMILY ECONOMY

Why is it that just as soon as you fellows get a little education you stop going with Italian girls?
—John W. McConnell, *Evolution of Social Classes*

Marriage strategies were among the handful of devices that parents could use to promote the economic interests of the family group.[1] Yet families are not simply economic entities. Rather, they embody "moral" or ideological principles as well.[2] They represent to themselves an idea of the collective good of the group, which ordinarily goes unchallenged and is seen by all members as natural and "just so." For families whose margin of subsistence was narrow, what was "good for the family" never strayed very far from its immediate economic needs. Parents defined these and dictated how they would be addressed.[3] The idea of "family morality" was central to the conception of family life among southern Italian immigrants.[4] Acceptance of the group ethos from an early age was the basis for acquiescence to parental authority in realms distinctly in conflict with American urban, middle-class norms and was manifested in a number of ways: the timing of youths' entry into the workforce, the insistence that children turn over their earnings to their parents, and the parental "right" to choose their children's occupations were the most conspicuous, instrumental forms of acquiescence to parental authority. As we have already seen, these aspects of parent-child relations were widely observed among New Haven's Italian immigrants.[5]

Other lesser-known but significant features of the relationship supported the family morality of Italian immigrants. Corporal punishment was endured dutifully by children as springing from the parents' need to exercise the interests of the group over the desires of the individual. The prerogatives of males over females—husbands over wives in public and brothers over sisters in all instances—produced a double standard in the treatment of sons and daughters. Males were encouraged to be more worldly, to venture out beyond the family circle and neighborhood. Females, by contrast, were expected to stay within and around the confines of home, both to preserve their reputations and to learn how to be skillful wives and mothers.[6] Differing attitudes toward boys and girls applied not only to the relative physical and behavioral autonomy of males but to their freedom to experiment sexually before marriage as well. There was no expectation for boys comparable to the strictures on girls to remain sexually chaste before marriage. Finally, the parental right to select a marital partner for daughters and sons was viewed as a significant and necessary discretionary power wielded to promote the family's long-term well-being.

Whether children, but particularly daughters, lived near their parents after marriage determined what kind of practical help they could be to them, especially in parents' declining years. Parents, therefore, naturally desired as future in-laws young people whose worldviews were consonant with their own. Although New Haven ethnographers all recognized the prevalence of this aim among its Italian immigrants, none closely considered the influence of courtship and marriage customs in southern Italy upon the outlook of immigrant parents in their children's marital choices.[7] Among all of New Haven's ethnic groups, Italians appeared unique in the strength of their desire to exercise this power. Both John W. McConnell and Irvin L. Child have observed that although wage-earners of every ethnicity tended to intervene in their children's marital decisions (a trait that formed one of the most marked attitudinal differences between wage-earners and the city's white-collar workers), Italian immigrant parents were the group *most* apt to assert their preferences for eligible mates over the wishes of their children.[8]

In the precarious and unforgiving economy of southern Italian hillside agriculture, an ethos had developed over the centuries among contadini that compensated a lifetime of hard work and inevitable physical frailty with the unqualified support of children. The means of providing such support ranged from child work to ancient inheritance practices, but even within the narrow cultural scope of southern Italy there was surprising variety in the customs that determined how the balance between hands and mouths was to be maintained and how authority was to be transmitted generationally.[9] Household form, norms for marriage age, and traditions of post-nuptial locality diverged from village to countryside, from province to province, and according to the productive bases of local economies. Similarly, traditions governing the dispersal of property, inheritance, and dowries might appear to work at cross purposes—to strengthen the hand of men in most cases but of women in some others. In all instances, however, two principles were served: the "rules" optimized the family group's ability to subsist economically (if they did not, the rules changed over time); and in totality, practices relating to the labor, residence, property, and status of household members made some provision for the future support of aged parents.[10] After the disposition of children's income, the most distinctive feature of the principles governing family and household was the extent to which parents exercised authority over the spousal choices of both daughters and sons. Rules about whom one could marry varied by gender and social status depending on the relative demand for labor. For farmers in general the demand for labor was determined by cycles of scarcity and abundance each harvest, and within individual farming households, by the availability of workers to cultivate the land.[11]

Because the vocational horizons of the majority of southern Italian immigrants had been forever confined in their native land to what could be coaxed from the soil or fetched from the sea, parents' conceptions of what their children could do vocationally were also circumscribed in the United States. Based on their own attempts at finding work in New Haven, parents' ambitions for their children often mirrored that experience and, as in Italy, those dreams differed for boys and girls. Italian immigrant men in New Haven (like southern Italians throughout urban America) readily found work in construction, which suited their capacity and inclination to perform heavy physical labor seasonally and outdoors.[12] They also labored in the city's major manufacturing plants—

notably in Sargent's hardware factory, L. Candee Rubber, Winchester Repeating Arms, and in the city's rail yards.[13] Before the Great Depression girls and young women often found that work came looking for them. While jobs were to be had at L. Candee Rubber alongside brothers, fathers, and uncles, they also found work at the Strouse-Adler Company, the nation's leading corset manufacturer (whose huge plant occupied an entire block near Wooster Square), and by the 1920s in the city's flourishing shirt, dress, and coat factories—many of them sweatshops that had fled New York City's unionization drive during the war years to set up one-room factories up and down the Connecticut coast and across New Jersey. In New Haven these "runaway" shops colonized immigrant neighborhoods branching off of Oak Street and Legion and Congress Avenues. They honeycombed the blocks of inexpensive warehouse space ringing Wooster Square and shaded into Fair Haven expressly to exploit its cheap, abundant, and often experienced immigrant female garment workers.[14]

In the new social climate in which they found themselves and their children, immigrant parents with a marriageable daughter or son were guided by the principle of finding a suitable match within the Italian immigrant community to a young person whose parents had migrated from the same region of Italy. In the absence of customary social markers, family reputation seems to have served as a stand-in for the cultural harmony promised by a prospective son- or daughter-in-law whose parents had migrated from the same region. It was hoped, thereby, that the person would serve the family's long-term interests.[15] Child observed that "most of the Italians live in neighborhoods where either all their immediate neighbors, or a considerable number of close neighbors, are fellow Italians. Most commonly the immediate neighbors will include families who originated in the same town in Italy."[16] The extent to which immigrants or their children actually succeeded in marrying someone from the same village or region as their own family is unknown. Anecdotal evidence clearly enunciates the ideal, but there is no statistical trace of the practice, so it is difficult to know how widespread the phenomenon was. There is good evidence, though, that Italians of the immigrant generation overwhelmingly chose Italians by birth or descent for marriage partners.

A well-known study of marriage patterns in New Haven by Ruby Jo Reeves, which compared immigrant groups from 1870 to 1930, showed that to a greater degree than most other foreign-born peoples in New Haven, Italians married almost exclusively within their own ethnic group.[17] As late as 1930, Italian-born men married within their group at a rate of 91 percent, and Italian-born women married men of Italian birth or parentage at a rate of 98 percent. Reeves attributed the higher rate of in-group marriage among Italian-born women, in part, to the fact that greater sanctions upon marriage to an outsider were placed on females as compared with males, and in addition, that there were fewer opportunities for Italian immigrant women to meet men of other ethnic groups. The strong orientation of Italian-immigrant daughters toward the parental home, Reeves concluded, combined with the fact that "few women engaged in economic pursuits outside the family sphere," reinforced this tendency. Moreover, she said, Italian women "have long been imbued with the idea of subjection and utter lack of self-assertion," which made the notion of "throwing over the old customs" uncomfortable for them.[18]

Parental restrictiveness toward daughters had been the linchpin of a system that prized family honor, a patriarchal power structure, and the preservation of traditional modes of production. Concern for female submissiveness and chastity, the most conspicuous tokens of family reputation, translated into rigorous scrutiny of girls' encounters with males of any age.[19] According to Leonard Covello, a girl who showed the slightest disregard for the exacting conventions of contadini propriety risked social censure. Moreover, gossip that impugned a female's good name cheapened not only her own value in the marriage market but that of her sisters as well. Covello remarked that a girl could not be seen in public with a male to whom she was not directly related without incurring suspicion on her character. In New Haven, as elsewhere, the daughter of Italian immigrants was to be chaperoned by a sibling if she visited with a boy outside her home; and if a boy called upon a girl in her home, his visit could only occur under the watchful eyes of her parents.[20] Because the perception of female purity and strict attention to decorum in male-female relations determined the quality of the match a young woman could make (consistently good matches added up to old-age security for parents, whose retirement might begin as soon as the last adult child married), girls' reputations were fiercely defended by brothers and fathers.[21]

Historian Robert Anthony Orsi has interpreted the Italian immigrant female's upbringing and her place in the household somewhat differently than observers of Italian immigrants before World War II. Women, he says, were to be groomed not just to marry but also to surround themselves with children. Their domesticity was the foundation of their authority at home as well as in the community. The father in southern Italian society, Orsi asserts, was only nominally the figure of force in the family—he was its public face, whereas the mother of his children possessed the real power. In the streets outside of his house, he says, the father routinely boasted about his authority and behaved as though his home was his kingdom. But in fact, the seemingly submissive, silent wife disciplined the children, using her eldest son to serve as her "captain," or alternately, her influence with her husband to shield the children from their father's intemperate outbursts. The father, Orsi finds, actually had only a rough idea about the doings of his household, the activities of his children, and the machinations of their mother. And he was an indistinct figure, too, in the recollections of children who tried to describe their fathers' influence on their lives, since fathers were typically emotionally detached, physically remote (except in instances where they chose to punish children physically), and away from their homes much of the time. The mother, on the other hand, was at once feared and revered. The minutest as well as most important decisions in her children's lives had to pass her approval. Daughters, who were encouraged or commanded to stay around the house, were subjected to their mother's authority daily. The eldest son kept not only his brothers in line in and out of the house but bossed his sisters as well, regardless of their seniority in the family.[22]

Contemporaneous observers of New Haven's Italian immigrants came to conclusions similar to those offered by Reeves, and like her, they apparently failed to pierce the veil of privacy that shrouded Italian family life from the inner workings of relations between men and women, fathers and mothers. The shrewdness of Orsi's insights lie in his understanding that young women had a vested interest in protecting what was a profound source of power for them—mother-hood. Despite that the mother's authority within the family was also a kind of prison, he allows, it was defended as a natural and proper state that guaranteed the perpetuation of the family line and all its resources.

Early in the twentieth century, ethnic institutions in New Haven ranging from fraternal societies to "national" Catholic parishes and everything in between—social clubs, patron-saint societies, and informal neighborhood groups that acted as webs of gossip—played a significant role in promoting a reliance on family reputation to enforce behavioral norms among females and in bolstering in-group marriage. In addition to their many official purposes, church and lodge served as forums for potential matches to be effected by parents for daughters and sons. A young man whose father belonged to the same mutual benefit society as a young woman's father already had much to recommend him to her family. Similarly, members of St. Anthony's Catholic parish in the Hill or St. Michael's in Wooster Square were probably already familiar to one another's kin. In these taut interrelations of people and institutions that both promoted the upwardly mobile and protected the economically vulnerable in America's ethnic communities, families whose reputations were already known to one another could introduce eligible young people to each other with confidence that the family's honor would be sustained by a potential union.[23]

The tradition of "Sunday visiting" after morning mass, for example, in which kin would spend the day stopping in at one another's homes or at those of neighbors, provided just the sort of parent-supervised, familial setting conducive to such introductions.[24] While calling on kin was the most frequent purpose of Sunday visiting, families friendly to one another by some other connection could be gracefully folded into the routine as well.[25] Sunday visiting and other social routines that allowed informal but supervised contact between marriageable young people offered the possibility of reestablishing some predictability and a feeling of familiarity into New World courtship and marriage customs. These were, in conception and for a time, a comfortable arena for all, since the beginnings of a courtship could be conducted in a way that recognized the gravity that attached to the linking of families' fates by matrimony. Unlike Anglo-American middle-class young people, who were encouraged to cultivate casual female-male friendships, there was no room for such interaction among southern Italian immigrant youths. Because other eligible young men might construe any regular visitation by the same male as a discouragement of their marital aims toward a particular woman, great care was taken to be clear about each young man's intentions. It was not uncommon after a male visitor had been to a young woman's house for a second or third time for her father to inquire directly if marriage was the man's aim.[26]

Such vigilance was integral to the overall operation of the family economy, but there was an even more pressing economic consideration at work as well: in southern Italy a young woman's family's social status and its reputation circumscribed the range of potential mates available to her by the time she approached marriage age and so her "place" in the marriage market was well known long before she was ready to marry. In New Haven, however, these influences were upset by the changed circumstances in which southern Italian immigrants found themselves. Definitive, consequential social distinctions in southern Italy that had enabled the parents of marriage-eligible men and women to discern whether a potential match would cause a son or daughter to "marry up" or "marry down" became blurred in the United States because social status was so much in flux in the industrial economy of immigrant America. Apart from the New Haven *prominenti,* northern Italian immigrants who had migrated as early as the 1870s and had very gradually worked their way into the city's commercial and professional ranks, the bulk of Italian immigrants after 1900 were denuded of social status. It would be naive to suggest that social distinctions within the Italian immigrant community ceased to matter to parents in their children's marital choices because, of course, they did. However, the many gradations of social strata in southern Italy that, for example, prohibited the daughter of a townsman from marrying a contadino, or the sharecropper's son from wedding a *consengola,* dissolved into a broad band of young people whose social backgrounds were less clearly connected to current occupations and whose social trajectories were much more open-ended than in the mezzogiorno.[27] The ethos of southern rural village life was weakened by distance in matters involving courtship and marriage, and increasingly parents would face children who resisted their efforts to control such decisions. Nonetheless, because so much was at stake for parents in children's romantic involvements, the courtship and betrothal of children were felt to be far too important to be left to chance.

As the economic bases of family life were transformed by wage work and the rhythms of factory life in the United States, the cultural forms that maintained the southern Italian family economy began to loosen and disengage. As we have seen, the route that brought young women and men to the altar had its own traditions that had to be tested in a new social setting; and parents who continued to press their wishes on their children often experienced the marriage market that their children entered as chaotic and threatening to their way of life.

McConnell, Phyllis Williams, Child, and Reeves each contrasted what they apprehended as archaic courtship customs among New Haven's Italian immigrants with American-style dating. The contadinis' focus on women's chastity and what these observers perceived as a hyper-sexualization of relations between males and females appeared overbearing by the emerging standards of Anglo-American, urban, middle-class society. Furthermore, the calculus of contadini courtship seemed to them both inegalitarian and crassly unromantic in the modern mode. Indeed, the concept of romantic love, while not unknown to southern Italians and certainly not to be denied entirely, was mostly discouraged and regarded with skepticism. As Dino Cinel has pointed out, southerners cultivated a deeply cynical regard for the ideal of romantic love, which was vividly expressed in the Calabrian folk proverb: "Get married and for a short time you will experience the sweetness of honey which will soon turn into poison."[28] Coupled with southern Italians' bias toward male-older matches, immigrant relationships appeared to New Haven social scientists to engender exaggerated inequities between men and women that clashed with the ascending ideal of companionate marriage in American middle-class culture.[29]

It should be remembered, however, that outside America's major cities, the courtship rituals of the Victorian era died a slow death.[30] Clearly, the conventions of contadini courtship bore a stronger resemblance to

the American Victorian practice of "calling" than New Haven's ethnographers might have liked to concede and were neither so exotic nor
incomprehensible as they tended to portray them. Routine in rural
America until well into the twentieth century, "calling" on a young
woman in her family's parlor had the advantage from the family's
perspective of ensuring that a young woman's path to marriage was
monitored by older, experienced women. At the same time, American
courtship norms were changing rapidly across the social spectrum—
especially during the 1920s—and it was against this backdrop that
immigrant youths were growing up. During the interwar years Anglo-
American gender relations and sexuality were redefined. From principles
codified by the Eighteenth Amendment (such as greater legal equality and
enfranchisement for women) to changing courtship rituals, gender relations, and attitudes toward sexuality enacted by growing numbers of
middle-class youths on college campuses nationwide, by the mid-1930s,
"dating" had surpassed "calling" as the avenue to marriage for the majority of Americans.[31]

Still, neither immigrant parents nor their children could readily appreciate the extent or pace of this change. All of it was new to them, exotic
and potentially harmful. Parents, mothers particularly, were the more
perplexed, having been themselves reared in a largely stable set of
courtship and marriage customs. The idea of dating violated immigrant
parents' sense of decorum and undermined their ability to guide daughters and sons through the hazards that stood between them and a successful match.[32] Images of romantic love in American popular culture
seemed to constitute the psycho-emotional world of American adolescents. Immigrant youths, it was feared, might be tempted into this dangerous realm where loyalties to one's parents and family would be
displaced by the ideals of companionate marriage, the nuclear family, and
more relaxed relations with the opposite sex. Dating, moreover, as John
Modell has emphasized, was a peer-regulated system. Not only did dates
occur outside the household (and beyond the family's eyes), but whom
one dated or did not date was determined by criteria that had little to do
with the family's perceived needs.[33]

It is hard to know how insulated Italian-American adolescents were
from broad cultural currents such as dating. Beth L. Bailey has said

about dating before World War II that it was "not about marriage" but "about competition." In the 1920s it "provided a new frontier for public competition through consumption, and in the 1930s it accepted competitive energies denied outlet elsewhere."[34] While the connection of courtship—whether "calling" or "dating"—to consumption and a market of scarcity and abundance (the ratio of women to men in a marriage market in which males were more numerous, for example) was implicitly plain to anyone eligible and desiring to marry, it is not true that it was *not about* marriage, families, and love, as Bailey argues. Competition was certainly a salient aspect of dating, especially in the ways that romance was portrayed between men and women in popular literature, mass circulation magazines, the motion picture industry, as well as radio, magazine, and newspaper advertising: it was a zero-sum game and one's chances to improve one's fortunes in the game was perceived as coming at someone else's expense. The accoutrements of dating and romance, the "embellishment of the person," to invoke Williams's phrase again, were absolutely tied up with consumption. However, it is an exaggeration to say that dating had nothing to do with love or marriage. It was part of an imaginative process of self-presentation that led to marriage, and in the ascendant middle-class scheme of gender relations the role of "love" as a goal of courtship and coupling (whether mythic or not) was privileged over economic considerations in a way that was novel in the lives of immigrants especially.

In general, as second-generation Italian immigrant youths looked ahead to courtship and marriage after World War I, their experiences could be divided into two clusters. First, there were those who entered the workforce (and this was the majority experience until the early1930s) as soon as they could legally do so and enjoyed a degree of independence from family surveillance previously unrealized in the regions of southern Italy from which New Haven's Italians had migrated. Again, the standards of supervision for boys and girls differed greatly, but in the United States going out to work implied a kind of autonomy for youths that did not pertain in southern Italy. Second, there were those who stayed in school and therefore had wider and more sustained exposure to the heightened significance of gender equality and ideals such as companionate marriage than those who entered the workforce before graduating from high school. Second-generation Italian immigrant boys and girls also experienced changes in courtship and gender norms differently. Boys with more schooling expressed and seem to have acted upon the desire to have more casual and more equal relations with girls than boys who quit school early. They were more accepting of dating and the idea that it was important to determine whether one was compatible temperamentally, socially, sexually, and materially with a potential mate. Girls, because they were more scrupulously monitored, did not have the liberty (whether they chose to exercise it or not) to test the dating scene. And girls, who were forced by custom or necessity out of the classroom and onto the factory floor, also unwittingly shrank their social horizons to encompass little more than the people in their neighborhoods, its businesses, their fellow parishioners, family, and kin. They were also, consequently, more eager to defend and embrace "Italian" mores and attitudes about gender, courtship, and marriage.[35]

While women of the immigrant generation may have been sheltered by their lack of experience in the paid labor force in southern Italy, opportunities for waged work abounded for younger, unmarried immigrant women in New Haven during and after World War I. Indeed, Italian immigrant women—but their daughters especially—were prominent in the city's female workforce. Second-generation Italian girls left school earlier than the daughters of any other ethnic group and found ready employment at a short distance from the tenements they inhabited. McConnell has speculated that young women with jobs may have enjoyed more independence from parents than those who stayed in school; and parents, as we have seen, appeared to tread more lightly on daughters' privileges when they were helping to put bread on the family table. But McConnell has also suggested that the relative autonomy enjoyed by these young women fostered a "quick acquaintance with the ways of the world." The unhappy consequence of their removal from family surveillance was "an attitude in which the romantic element in marriage has little significance . . . [and in which it is] hard to have a courtship period that is anything more than a period of dangerous sex experimentation."[36] In large factories that employed men and women together, such as Winchester Repeating Arms or L. Candee Rubber, two of the city's major industrial manufacturers, women were often segregated from men in the workplace by virtue of their tasks and so had less contact with them on the job than they would have had working in smaller enterprises. Moreover, oftentimes women were hired precisely because they already had a male relative working at a particular factory.[37] This was advantageous from the family's point of view because a family member or someone known to them could keep an eye on their daughters. By contrast, the garment shops that surrounded the city's immigrant neighborhoods employed women almost exclusively. While this meant that there were no kindred males to look out for sisters or daughters on the job, the overwhelming presence of women in the shops was a solace to parents, because they felt less worried by the prospect that their daughters would be tempted by men in the workplace into unseemly behavior that could tarnish their reputations.[38]

By the late 1930s the conventions of southern Italian courtship in New Haven were viewed increasingly as outmoded, awkward, and unsuccessful translations of Old World mores by many young people in the city's rising generation of Italian immigrants. Born in New Haven and exposed to the ways of American life, immigrant youths often absorbed very different ideas about relations between men and women than those cherished by their parents. Contadini courtship customs had begun to seem retrograde and impracticable—like clothes that were no longer fashionable or simply did not fit. Some came to object to the setting of courtship—its enactment in the cramped conditions of their families' quarters, with numerous people constantly about, and the sometimes ungainly family encounters that occurred with so much apparently at stake.[39] According to McConnell, these restrictions had become so objectionable to the second generation that as a consequence they only encouraged contact between girls and boys outside the sanctioned sphere of the family home.

Countervailing influences make it difficult to assess the extent to which second-generation Italian immigrant females were affected by the shift from calling to dating. One reason for this is that much depends on perspective: from the point of view of older immigrant women who had come of age in rural Italy, the landscape of courtship had been transformed. "Mrs. L.," for instance, who came to New Haven around 1910, remarked during the late 1930s that "men nowadays consider foreign-born women old-fashioned and want to marry those born in this country."[40] In New Haven added urgency was felt by parents intent upon determining the marital choices of their daughters since every child was schooled at least to age fourteen. The period of time between school-leaving and marriage for many young women was reduced in the United States to but a few years, which meant that the earning capacity of young women was compressed into a much briefer period. Despite their desire to stem the influence of American culture on their children's behavior and aspirations, however, in reality, contadini customs in New Haven already represented a departure from traditional conventions of courtship and marriage in southern Italy. Compared with women in their home villages in Italy, immigrant daughters in New Haven did appear to have enjoyed relative freedom: even if they left school as early as legally permissible, their tenure in school was at least twice as long as was customary in the mezzogiorno and occurred, furthermore, alongside boys, which gave them a degree of familiarity with the opposite sex unheard of in the farming villages from which their families came. If mixing with nonkindred males in the workplace was mitigated by the presence of relatives in many factories, women's experience outside the sphere of family life and their sheer exposure to the realm of paid labor meant that their worldliness often far exceeded what their mothers or even their older sisters had experienced in the rural economy of southern Italy before World War I. As for the lurking "danger of sex experimentation," alluded to by McConnell, sanctions for sexual misconduct were still so punitive that it seems unlikely that its possibility proved any real alternative even to the adulterated contadini mores sanctioned in New Haven.

Yet many of these early school-leavers seem to have felt that they were being left behind by Italian-American males, who were enjoying the freedom of dating and less binding interactions with members of the opposite sex. By the mid-1930s these young women watched anxiously as eligible young men in their circles gravitated toward less restrictive American-style dating practices. Enough boys of the second generation had embraced American attitudes toward courtship and romance in high school to elicit complaints among their sisters that they thought themselves "too good" for the girls in their neighborhood. "Why is it," one young Italian-American woman asked a group of her brothers' friends, "that just as soon as you fellows get a little education you stop going with Italian girls?"[41] Viewed in this way, by virtue of their independence as wage-earners and in their ability to escape the harsh light of parental scrutiny that had characterized their mothers' experiences, these girls were in their own eyes the new defenders of "Italian" traditions. Despite reported concerns about the perils awaiting impulsive factory girls, these more tradition-bound immigrant daughters understood early on the importance of their conduct and continued to parrot the wisdom of the ages in discussing the attributes of the marriageable woman. As one young woman told McConnell during the late 1930s, "You think that the boys like the flashy dresser that's popular. But for marriage they want a good, quiet, domestic woman that will bear them children and won't argue with them."[42]

Child observed a parallel uneasiness about emerging American courtship practices among a subset of the group of young men he interviewed in New Haven's Hill section during the 1930s. These men, whom Child characterized as "non-assimilators," emphasized the importance of maintaining Italian ways in the face of inertia to assimilate. They often communicated with immigrant parents in the dialect of the region of Italy their family came from and internalized its mores along with a preference for regional foods and "traditional" Italian girls. However, this group, which tended to leave school earlier than their more assimilation-conscious peers, was becoming a minority among the second generation. Although it is difficult to locate the tipping point, this mentality constituted the majority view among men in New Haven's Italian immigrant community. However, a wave of change was sweeping across the generations, and what Italian immigrant sons sought increasingly in potential mates changed sometime during the 1930s. While Williams observed that young Italian men largely preferred "old-fashioned wives"—women who resembled their older sisters and mothers—McConnell and Child found that second-generation men appeared to insist less on thrift and industry. For them, sentiment had come to play a much bigger part in the selection of a marriage partner than it had for their parents' generation.[43] Many Italian-American young men, especially the high school educated, began by the 1920s to find that they preferred the custom of dating that had become common among their age peers at Hillhouse or Commercial high schools. It encouraged less self-conscious, more informal, and "friendly" relations between boys and girls and downplayed the significance of boy-girl interactions.

Although there was, otherwise, an overwhelming tendency to marry someone of the same ethnic and socioeconomic background, high school graduates tended to "marry out" of their group at a higher rate: "Italian boys, particularly northern Italians," McConnell noted, "prefer light-complexioned girls, and since marriage to American girls is usually impossible there is some tendency to marry well-educated Slavs."[44] Child's fine-grained study of second-generation males' social and cultural attitudes was the most precise of these in its assessment of men's opinions on women's marriageability. While Child turned up a range of preferences among the men he interviewed, most pervasive was a feeling that the daughters of Italian immigrants were "too serious" about marriage too early. "Americanized" women, such as Irish or Polish Americans, tended to be more "open-minded" than New Haven's Italian women and were less focused on the implications of dating. As already indicated, commonly among Italian immigrant families, a man who visited a woman more than once was assumed to have marriage as his aim. Young women of other ethnic groups did not maintain such expectations, however, and second-generation Italian men had come to appreciate this. By the same token, most of the men in Child's sample still said that they preferred Italian women because they felt that the similarity in their upbringings improved chances that they would get along with one another's families.[45]

In her famous study of ethnic intermarriage in New Haven during the 1920s and 1930s, Ruby Jo Reeves (also known as Ruby Jo Reeves Kennedy) discerned what she called the emergence of the "Triple Melting Pot" in American culture. Amid worries that Southern and Eastern Europeans would not assimilate in the United States (marriage out of one's ethnic group being one important sign of a group's integration into the larger society), she found that Italians in New Haven, though characteristically insular in their marriage behavior, were assimilating relatively rapidly. She also found that those who married out of their group were most likely to choose a co-religionist—someone from the Catholic faith to marry. Reeves concluded that assimilation was a three-step process (or "triple" melting pot) because complete assimilation was indicated by marriage without regard to ethnicity or religion, and that was still a rarity among Italians.[46] But it also meant that the children of Italian immigrants were marrying young people whose parentage was Irish, German, and Polish. The children of Polish immigrants were most likely to marry Italians because they shared the most similar socioeconomic status. In addition to attending the same schools and living in the same neighborhoods, they also worked in the same factories. And unlike the great majority of Irish and German Americans, Poles were recent immigrants and shared similar attitudes toward schooling.[47] Nevertheless, overall, second-generation women *did* manage to reduce both in-group marriage and the age gap between themselves and their grooms.[48] In 1930 *foreign*-born Italian men and women continued decisively to marry within their own ethnic group and to a greater extent than any group except Russian Jewish and Polish Jewish immigrants. Eventually, however, the desire to find a mate among immigrants from the same province in Italy ran up against the reality of a dwindling pool of suitable candidates as immigration from Italy halted during the 1920s. The rate of in-group marriage among both men and women of the second generation sank to 85 percent, markedly lower than their immigrant counterparts.[49]

The predominance of significant age differences between spouses in groom-older marriages, a condition that intuitively would appear to reinforce female submissiveness, was partly eclipsed in the second generation. While Italian-born grooms were, on average, 6.3 years older than their brides in 1930 (Italian-born men averaged 32.1 years of age, their brides, 25.8 years), among second-generation Italians the average age difference was almost halved, to 3.4 (American-born men of Italian parentage averaged 24.2 years of age and their brides averaged 20.4 years of age).[50] Reeves offered an interesting (if perhaps simplistic) economic explanation for declines in average and modal ages at marriage for both men and women in New Haven's ethnic groups. She found that historically the average age-at-first-marriage had risen for all immigrant groups over the course of a few generations. But she also found that between the first and second generations the average age at marriage actually fell. She predicted nonetheless that the average age-at-first-marriage would ultimately rise again as the grandchildren of immigrants assimilated to the higher standard of living experienced in the United States. Their initial response, she surmised, was to marry as soon as they attained an economic plane that allowed them to set up their own households. And since most of them were shut out of the more skilled jobs that would have required them to delay marriage while they acquired the training and experience needed for more highly remunerated work, they were "free" in essence to marry as soon as they found jobs that paid reliable incomes.[51] As a result, they married at comparatively young ages. Once the children and grandchildren of Italian immigrants sought the kind of specialized occupations that required longer periods of training, they too, she predicted, would delay marriage, for "it takes an ambitious, 'Americanized' young man a relatively long time to become what he considers economically independent and able, in his own opinion, to maintain a suitable household."[52]

The real threat to "traditional" attitudes toward courtship and marriage, then, lay not in employment outside the home but in extended schooling, which provided the very type of training for "specialized occupations" that demanded deferred nuptiality. Moreover, the longer period of preparation for employment before marriage was not the only dimension of this experience that eroded the traditional path to marriage. Italian immigrant daughters who attended high school gained much more everyday exposure to boys and to Anglo-American, middle-class conceptions of romance and marriage than their wage-earning sisters who started working when they were fourteen. More than any other group, Italian-American girls represented the "new face" of New Haven's high school student body. Individually and socially, for these girls the impact of high school was more significant than for any other group because, as we have seen, before extended schooling became common, Italian-American girls had had few opportunities to interact with boys in routine, informal, and unsupervised ways.[53] Hillhouse, Commercial, and Boardman high schools permanently altered the way these young women came of age—transforming their vocational choices, the course of their personal development, and their prospects in the marriage market. Exposure to differing styles of family emotional expression and to divergent forms of family economic organization and parental authority, as well as contact with peers whose aspirational horizons were more expansive than their own, all gave rise to a different notion of parent-child relations. Even if most youths did not challenge parents' conceptions of family obligation, authority, discipline, and personal ambition, their own ideas about family life had been recast and would alter the tone of familial relations when they married and raised children of their own.

By contrast, within the frame of modified contadini courtship customs in New Haven, early school-leavers, though more "Americanized" than their mothers, were comparative bulwarks against the kind of cultural change being experienced by younger sisters, who may have benefited from the workings of the family cycle to continue through high school. Schooling disrupted the "education" embodied in the ethos of family morality and permanently (if not wholly) detached the use of children's marriages as tools to promote family interests. It did so by freeing children from dependence on parents for skills needed as adults to survive economically, by reorienting their priorities from the family group to their own interests as individuals, and, incidentally, by hastening the adoption of courtship practices that had little to do with the needs of the family group.[54] By lengthening, yet again, the expected age at which young people would leave school, schooling was a mechanism for reconfiguring the meaning of age in the family economy. An old Italian adage proclaimed, "An old maid at eighteen, and a family liability at twenty."[55] However, as the collapse of the youth job market deferred the entry of young people into the workforce to age eighteen at the earliest, as high school education achieved the status of a cultural norm, the character of work young people might perform broadened, and the age-at-first-marriage for women and men edged downward and stabilized, the number of years they might actually contribute to the family economy were brief indeed.[56] A marriage market once tied to family needs and social status, as well as to gender and birth order, was unraveled by the erection of the dating system that flourished within the teen society created by high school. Not only was a twenty-year-old daughter a "liability" then to the workings of the family wage economy by the end of the 1930s, she was also often for the first time in her life—if evanescently—a family asset.

6

THE LANDSCAPE OF AMBITION: GEOGRAPHY, ETHNICITY, AND CLASS IN CHILDREN'S SCHOOL EXPERIENCES

We hung out with a crowd that was mostly from Westville, an awful lot of Westville people, who had already made it to the degree and the level of that day and that era. So you knew where you wanted to end up. You wanted to end up, if at all possible, with a home in Westville . . . because there were a lot of people that you . . . [knew] . . . who had already achieved that.
—Murray Lender, interview by Susan L. Neitlich

Just as individual neighborhoods experienced cycles of affluence and poverty that shaped their socioeconomic character, so, too, the ethnic composition of New Haven's neighborhoods and its schools changed with them. In the first decade of the twentieth century, when the city's immigration neared its peak, in neighborhoods around New Haven where the population was dense, housing cheap, and work close to hand, semi-skilled and unskilled workers and their families tended to cluster within the orbit of their own ethnic groups. Thus many neighborhoods were the creations of self-segregating groups, like Wooster Square's Italians, Fair Haven's Irish, or Oak Street's Italians, Polish Jews, and Russian Jews. In the midst of their compatriots, immigrants sought to sustain a sense of the familiar: succor from foods unknown locally and regional favorites prepared in traditional ways, forms of worship that honored age-old rituals and the rhythms of the seasons, young men's clubs, women's sodalities, mutual-aid societies, and informal social networks that linked individuals and families to the necessities of life—where to find shelter, steady work, and help when work was intermittent.[1] Some neighborhoods were segregated by racial prejudice. The Lower Dixwell Avenue area, which had been an African-American settlement since free blacks first arrived in New Haven during the eighteenth century, later became the epicenter of a population that had once been widely dispersed throughout the city.[2] The arrival of tens of thousands of southern and Eastern European immigrants within the space of a few decades crowded most of the city's African Americans out of scattered sites across the city and hemmed them into Lower Dixwell and Newhallville, just to the north. But many other neighborhoods were a mix of ethnic groups and social classes.[3] As a result, the city's elementary schools ranged widely in their social makeup by 1908 (see fig. 6.1).

At one extreme were three remarkably diverse schools that were spread across the city from its northern quarter to its southernmost point. In two of these schools, which were located at the lower end of the Hill and just west of the city's central "nine squares," pupil

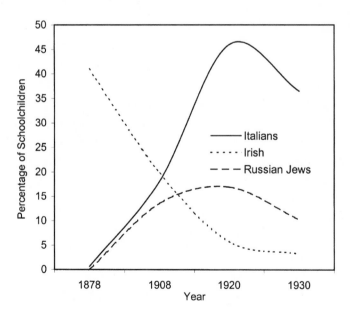

Fig. 6.1 Ethnicity of New Haven schoolchildren, 1878–1930. *Source:* New Haven, *Annual Reports,* 1878–1932

populations were composed of roughly equal proportions of "Americans" (native-born white children of native-born parents), Germans, Irish, "Russians" (Russian and Polish Jews), and Italians. In the third of these three schools, the Winchester school in the Dixwell neighborhood, African Americans were represented in numbers rivaling the other groups.[4]

At the other extreme was the Wallace Street school in Wooster Square, with a city-high 99 percent Italian immigrant student body in 1908. The school had not one "American" student, it was noted in the school census, and there were but two children of Irish descent, one child of Polish parentage. No other school equaled the homogeneity of the Wallace Street school, but similar patterns were revealed in parts of the Hill, whose neighborhoods housed most of the city's Eastern European Jews. The Cedar Street school, in the heart of the Jewish settlement, was 73 percent "Russian." The Zunder school, nearby on Oak Street, was virtually the same: 72 percent of its pupils were children of Eastern European Jews; and the Welch and Webster schools, each within a half-dozen blocks of the Cedar Street and Zunder schools, had shares of 58 percent and 51 percent "Russian" pupils respectively, at a time when the children of Eastern European Jews in New Haven represented 13.6 percent of all school-age children.[5] The children of Italian-born parents by 1908 were the most numerous immigrant population in the city schools, constituting 18.2 percent of all school-age children. Their residence throughout the Hill meant that even in schools like Cedar Street and Zunder, where the children of Eastern European Jews predominated, Italian immigrant children were represented in proportions reflecting their overall presence in the city.[6] In five of the city's forty-five elementary schools, in fact, more than half of the pupils were of Italian parentage; four of the five were in the Wooster Square area. These configurations changed, often dramatically, over the course of the three decades that the board of education tracked the distribution of pupil nationality (from 1908 to 1935).

The history of the West Street school best illustrates the mutability of neighborhood ethnic composition during these years. Before Oak Street rose to commercial prominence at the end of the nineteenth century, the Hill's center of gravity listed toward Oyster Point, its southern tip, maintaining vestigial links to the triangle's maritime past. In 1908 the West Street school bore the Hill's stamp as the most eclectic area of a dynamic and still growing industrial city. By 1915, however, the roughly uniform distribution of ethnic groups earlier present in the school had ebbed as remnants of the nineteenth-century Yankee, German, and Irish settlements removed to the edges and suburbs of the city. Both Eastern European Jews and Italians began to spill out from the Hill as well, but Italians did so only gradually and reluctantly. New Haven's Jewish immigrants moved mainly west up Whalley Avenue toward Westville. The Italians, with some exceptions, moved east, following the Irish into Fair Haven and up the shoreline as well.[7] Despite this easterly migration, however, the concentration of Italian immigrants and their children in the Hill grew every year. In 1915, for example, 45 percent of the children in the West Street school were sons or daughters of Italian immigrants, and 27 percent of the school's pupils were the children of Eastern European Jews. The rest were a smattering of other groups but none in numbers sufficient to challenge the increasing bulk of these two groups. By 1930, 60 percent of the school's pupils were Italian and 17 percent were "Russian," a change encapsulating a broader demographic dynamic throughout the city: even as immigration slowed to a trickle after World War I, the Italian immigrant population increased prodigiously as the immigrant generation revived birth rates customary in the preindustrial hinterlands of southern Italy. Slow to abandon a fertility strategy that had served them well in their homeland—an environment of high mortality and laborious, unchanging agricultural techniques practiced on disparate patches of rocky, unfertile soil, where an abundance of human labor power was essential to survival—large families and a standard of living for most that teetered between subsistence and poverty were the norm. By 1920 the city's population of first- and second-generation Italian immigrants dwarfed every other subgroup.[8] They were also slow to leave the neighborhoods they first inhabited in New Haven. New Haven's Jews, by contrast, were both socially and geographically mobile. Typically they had smaller families, moving up and out of the slums of Oak Street within one or two generations after they arrived.[9]

Yankees formed the third element of this post–World War I demographic dynamic: the largest subgroup in New Haven until 1920, they also declined relative to Italians as they initiated a move to the city's suburbs during the 1920s that continued until they themselves became a minority in the city they had founded three centuries earlier.[10] Each of these trends contributed in its own way to the increasing homogenization of the city's neighborhood elementary schools. Not only were twice as many schools more apt to have greater concentrations of one ethnic group in attendance in 1930 than had been the case in 1908, but half as many schools in 1930 had diverse student populations as in 1908 and no single school had maintained heterogeneity over this period.[11]

Even in neighborhoods of great ethnic diversity the socioeconomic status of a child's neighbors and schoolmates usually bore greater similarities than differences. Elementary schools in most parts of the city drew their students from a radius of two or three blocks, on average, in each direction.[12] This fostered continuity by limiting school size and maximizing the possibility of familiarity between teachers and neighborhood families. If it is the habit of immigrants to cling to whatever fragments of the familiar they can husband, then the successes public schools achieved in cities like New Haven owed in part to the willingness of immigrants to look upon the neighborhood elementary school as an inevitable (if sometimes incomprehensible) feature of their new world. For groups that used the schools to their advantage—notably Eastern European Jewish immigrants, but others as well—the neighborhood school was a node in the network of "thick trust," Robert D. Putman's phrase to describe "trust embedded in personal relations that are strong, frequent, and nested in wider networks."[13] This trust, built on face-to-face relations and reputations arising from these relations, joined the neighborhood school to church, temple, barber shop, shoe repairman, baker, and push cart huckster as a distinctly local institution. Even though the majority of things "American" were encountered as alien, to immigrant parents the neighborhood school gradually acquired an aspect of familiarity from its presence within the constricted scope of their transplanted lives. For immigrant children especially the school might serve as a compass to civic life—a guide to the society of strangers whose city they inhabited. Despite that teachers, principals, and guidance counselors could often be remote, strange, or even disdainful, individual teachers and many of their fellow pupils served as exemplars of what they experienced as "American life."

Did the content of the school curriculum do the work of acculturation or were there other forces, subtler perhaps than the blunt instrument of "Americanization," that caused immigrant children to look outside their own families to mold their futures? Certainly the school promoted attitudes and behaviors in the American grain and so its purposes often ran counter to the aims of parents; but schooling posed a dialectic with different outcomes for different children. At times ideals promoted by teachers were outwardly rejected by parents and their children alike. At other times the ideas espoused by teachers challenged and upset the thinking of pupils whose parents' beliefs and teachings differed from the values represented each day in their classrooms.[14] Children sometimes felt conflicted about the contrast and might resolve it by discarding parental opinion as outmoded and useless in the world in which they found themselves, or they might retrench, remaining impervious to the values of the foreign culture embodied by their teachers and "American" classmates. Indeed, the very homogeneity of many schools helped to preserve the "cake of custom" that immigrant parents often hoped to foster in their children. Since the chance of being surrounded by children of the same ethnicity, religious traditions, and social standing remained high in neighborhoods dominated by people of their own kind, parents could take comfort in the fact that the elementary school was a part of the fabric of daily life in the neighborhood. Until average grade attainment surpassed grade nine, the neighborhood school might reinforce social and ethnic insularity as much as it colonized ethnic communities with American attitudes. This was doubly true of Italian immigrant children in New Haven. Because of their numerical presence in the city's population, they tended to come into contact with one another much more often than children of any other ethnic group.[15]

The men interviewed by Irvin L. Child in 1940 showed decided differences among New Haven's Italian Americans in their acceptance of American cultural norms depending on the amount of schooling they received. Those who had ended their schooling at age fourteen during the 1910s and 1920s, for example, were much more likely than peers who continued on to ninth grade to express a desire to court and marry women of Italian parentage, to show exclusive preference for Italian cuisine, to associate primarily with the sons of Italian immigrants like themselves, and to approve of their parents' child-rearing practices. These "in-groupers," as Child referred to them, "display very markedly a tendency to associate with Italians alone. More than half report they have never had any but Italian friends; this is a statement that very rarely occurs among the other [Italian-American] informants. . . . It is true that of some of these informants that they have mostly Italian friends because they have always lived in solidly Italian neighborhoods."[16] Of the more than forty Italian Americans interviewed by Child, those who had completed some or all of high school were more apt to express either neutrality toward, or a positive embrace of, American middle-class attitudes about marriage and family life. Higher levels of education seem to have translated into different attitudes about life choices, and these may be attributable as well to expanded horizons—that is, increased grade attainment meant greater exposure to parts of the city and to people outside their own neighborhoods.

If Wooster Square was the most homogenous of New Haven's neighborhoods ethnically and socioeconomically, the Hill and Oak Street neighborhoods were its most socially complex regions. And while, as we have seen, New Haven's neighborhood schools generally tended toward homogeneity after World War I, much of the richness of this immigrant catchment area remained even as its component parts became striated along class lines.

The experiences of the Lender children in the Hill and Oak Street neighborhoods are apt examples of the rootedness of the neighborhood elementary school in local surroundings. All of the Lender children went to elementary schools that were close to home, where it was likely their neighborhood friends and their school friends would be one and the same and where there was the possibility for siblings to have had the same teachers as they progressed through the ranks. Mitigating this advantage, however, was another fact of immigrant family life: incessant mobility. By virtue of an improvement in, or for many, a deterioration of household financial circumstances, immigrant families moved often. For many immigrants—indeed, for all those who toiled on the margins of the American economy, especially the working poor, whose lack of skill or abundance of misfortune spelled spotty unemployment—movement from rent to rent within the city was a way of life. But for the Lenders each move came because their father's bakery kept expanding and changing locations with the growth of business. Therefore, although the grammar schools the Lenders attended were never more than a half-dozen blocks away from their residence, the family lived in four different homes between 1930 and 1940, so there was not as much continuity in the schooling experience of the older children as there *might* have been—not as much familiarity with their family on the part of their elementary school teachers as there *could* have been had the family stayed at the same address throughout the time the children were young. The two older boys, Hymen and Samuel, who came to New Haven from Poland with their parents at ages eleven and nine, went to the Zunder school before entering the Truman school and then Hillhouse, but only their time at Zunder overlapped and that was for a single year.[17]

Hy and Sam, like all immigrant children whose English was rudimentary or nonexistent, started in the "Greenhorn Room" of Zunder. The Greenhorn Room was a polite phrase for "The Dummy Room," the more common expression for the classroom where older immigrant children were placed during their initial months in New Haven's schools. After spending six months there, Hy and Sam were placed in the sixth grade before eventually moving on to middle school and high school.

Murray, younger than his brothers by a decade, spent much more time in the same elementary school with the same group of children than did Hy or Sam. He attended the Welch school near Oak Street, fewer than five blocks from where the Lenders lived on Baldwin Street during the late 1930s. Murray was born in New Haven and went through Welch before attending Troupe Junior High School and eventually Hillhouse. In many ways his experience was characteristic of most young people in New Haven before World War II. As Murray remembered it, Welch was a "mix" of kids—African Americans and Jews "but . . . primarily Italian[s]."[18] Baldwin, a one-block street between Davenport and Congress Avenues, was a lower-middle-class neighborhood in which many people owned the one-, two- and three-family homes in which they lived. In this way it was a step up socially for the Lender family from the previous two places they had rented, on and near Oak Street. Baldwin Street's residents were of all ethnicities, and Murray recalled that children from up and down the block visited freely in one another's homes: "Everybody knew everybody and everybody talked to everybody. Starting at one end of the street and going to the other, we had Jewish families, Italian families, Polish families. . . . We had Irish, we had German. . . . There was no such thing as not knowing everybody on the street. . . . I spent frequent times . . . in three-quarters of the homes. . . . It was not a matter of were you [a] friend, it was a matter of the degree of friendship, so when I got down to the Cusano family, six, seven, eight doors down and I played pinochle or poker or whatever with Alfie Cusano on the front stoop, more often than not his mom was schlepping me in and feeding me some pasta. I was always stuffing my face with something, as my mother was stuffing everybody else's face too."[19]

Murray's friends at school, he remembered, were his friends from the neighborhood. "To walk over three blocks, four blocks in that era was going into a new *shtetl*," said Lender. "So [my friends] . . . were mostly the kids from around."[20] And because the Welch school was so close by, he could go home for lunch regularly, which enhanced for him the feeling of being "at home" in school. Having received all of his schooling in the same section of New Haven and being promoted through elementary school with roughly the same group of kids, his neighborhood, the Welch school, his home, and his friends' homes constituted a very intimate social world—porous and variegated in texture but physically finite.

To speak of "the school," of course, is to invoke not a monolithic, faceless thing, but rather the people, the teachers, and administrators who operated it. Especially at the elementary level, the school was inseparable in a child's mind from his or her teachers. Overwhelmingly female as a group, teachers served as matriarchs in the classroom and made impressions that lasted a lifetime. The majority of New Haven's teachers up through World War II lived within the city limits, and as Douglas W. Rae has shown, most lived within one mile of the schools where they taught. Invariably their ethnic and socioeconomic backgrounds differed from their pupils', but they were at the very least acquainted with children's neighborhoods and associates.[21]

Teachers ranged from kindly to stern and unforgiving, but the teacher who made the deepest mark on Murray was "Miss Blackall," his sixth-grade teacher at Welch:

> She was really tough, but when she thought you were doing the
> right thing, she in her own way, really got to you. And I got to—

could you love Miss Blackall? I don't think so. But you certainly could admire her, and you certainly could warm up to her and respect her. Oh, the respect was capital R, capital E. . . . And I think she might have helped mold me into "You gotta do the right thing." . . . She was a dramatic influence. All the teachers were, but she, in particular, was. . . . I think I was considered a good student intellectually, but certainly not the greatest thing that ever hit Welch School. But, you know, I could be counted on for not getting into trouble, be counted on for not making huge waves but always making contributions with discussion or whatever was happening in the class. So I always had, you know, pretty much the respect of my teachers. And if I ever heard anything coming back, through Welch, . . . that I wasn't working up to my maximum potential . . . [it was] probably in most cases . . . correct, you know. The truth of the matter was, I think I was always a little lazy, I think intellectually, and never really pushing myself. And my mother and father, who just said, "Get good marks and work hard," left it at that, because they were in no position to follow up intellectually, because my father, you know, he read, but certainly not brilliantly. And my mother could not read at all. So, you know, all they could do was kick you in the tush and hope that you would respond without really doing any detailed follow-up.[22]

Students of the era often describe their teachers as exacting and authoritative but, just as often, as benign and well-intentioned. Principals and teachers alike often conveyed a sense of the solemnity of education, respect for scholarship, and the sanctity of authority.[23] But this, unfortunately, did not inoculate them from indulging in the prejudices of the day.

Without denying the sensitivity and goodwill of some, it must be remembered that educators were subject to the same biases toward ethnic and racial minorities as their contemporaries and inevitably brought these attitudes to their jobs. Well into the 1930s school administrators and teachers in New Haven—themselves mostly Yankees and Irish Americans, respectively—read decades-old prejudices into their assessments of elementary schoolchildren. Even though IQ, aptitude, and developmental testing had been locally in vogue since the early 1920s, principals and teachers continued to rattle off two- and three-word stereotypes when asked about the academic or characterological attributes of city schoolchildren. Yankees were "shrewd and set in their ways"; Poles "slow-witted," "stubborn and phlegmatic"; Jews "ambitious" but "aggressive and loud"; Italians "slow learning," "emotional and temperamental" but musically and artistically inclined; and African Americans were "care-free," "happy," and (like Italian children) considered gifted in music and art.[24]

At times, it appears, these patronizing, cartoonish opinions had sufficient currency to influence teachers' treatment of students. Italian immigrant children often bore the brunt of such insidiousness. As older siblings were promoted through the schools, they passed on to younger brothers and sisters the wisdom they had acquired through the pain of personal encounters with ethnic prejudice. "Don't say how many you got," an older sibling would say to her sister, meaning, "Don't tell the teacher how many siblings you have because they'll treat you with contempt."[25] Another man reported, "We never went anywhere that we weren't . . . called Guineas, called Wops, and that sort of thing. We got to the point that we didn't want to go to school. We were maligned, we were beaten, we were insulted, we were segregated."[26] These biases lasted well beyond the earlier decades of the twentieth century. As late as the 1950s an Italian immigrant man reported of his experience in New Haven's schools that he would have to eat his sandwich each day in a bathroom stall so that no one would see it. Fried onions and peppers between two pieces of Italian bread soaked in olive oil were a treat he looked forward to each day—comfort food in a cold climate—but he couldn't bear the disdain of his classmates if they spied the oil-stained paper bag that concealed this personal delight.[27] Despite widespread prejudice against New Haven's largest and poorest immigrant group, in the arbitrariness by which ethnic and racial bias chooses its victims, Italian Americans might, in certain circumstances, be favored over Jews or African Americans.

In the Scranton Street school in the Hill neighborhood, for instance, where in 1915 half of the school's students were the children of Eastern

European Jews, the Jewish children in the third grade once walked out of class and marched around the school to protest what they perceived as favoritism toward the Italian pupils.[28] Although their "strike" was quickly settled by the principal, it is remarkable that these children would challenge their treatment collectively and with such directness. That they did so is testimony to their sense of empowerment, which emerged, no doubt, from feeling closely bound to a community of interests with very real stakes in the neighborhood school. These interests existed everywhere throughout the city's school system, if in varying degrees.

An important element in a child's relation to the world outside the family—around the neighborhood, at church or temple, in the local shops, as well as in the school—might arise from one's parents' stature in the community. Sam Lender, for instance, retained a keen and growing sense of himself as his father's son wherever he was on Oak Street or the Hill. Even during his first months in school while he struggled with English in the Greenhorn Room, Sam felt buoyed by an awareness of his father's place in the community. Mitigating the feeling of embarrassment he had at being placed in a room for remediation, Sam remarked: "The respect [during the time we were in the Greenhorn Room] was always there because of what my father had done. In politics—he was not a politician—but he knew all the politicians. . . . For a dozen bagels, he made friends. . . . He found a politician, or someone who wasn't Jewish. Doctor Mongillo wasn't. Mayor Fitzsimmons wasn't. But they were friends with him. . . . He used to say, 'Sam, when you're delivering bagels on Sunday morning, drop off a dozen at Doctor Mongillo's house or Fitzsimmons's house or Ralph Blumberg's house.' . . . So these are the things that I guess gave us respect in the community. But we never really lived a ghetto type of life. . . . We've grown up that way. Living with other people, . . . and doing business with other people."[29] The relationships between families and schools are bound to the neighborhoods and the people who inhabit them. If neighborhood evokes a place, "place" is also a psychological site; and for Sam and his siblings, their father's stature in the community furnished a sense of self-regard that enabled each of them to see themselves in relation to others both in the present and in the future.

Where children did not experience these connections between themselves, their parents, and the surrounding community, the consequences could be detrimental; and the distance they had to travel to school made the absence of this connection more profound. Of all the ways that schools have refined children's sensitivity to age distinctions—by age-grading, testing, promotion, demotion, and age-based compulsory attendance laws—the most consequential to the young person's sense of him- or herself as achieving (or being propelled into) "semi-autonomy" or adolescence was the creation of the middle school and, subsequently, the junior high school. What better mechanism than a school site at some distance from the neighborhood to promote in the young person a feeling of being beyond the reach of the familiar confines of home and its environs? Of course, when the junior high school was pioneered, the intention was quite opposite—to ease the transition to high school from the grade school years—but this occurred even before the majority of children attended high school. Over the course of the 1920s, New Haven built four junior high schools, which enrolled about half of its ninth-grade population. (The other half of the city's ninth-graders continued to be sent to one of the downtown high schools.) While the junior high schools were closer to pupils' homes and neighborhoods than the city's two downtown high schools, continuing on to ninth grade made a real difference in young people's spatial experience of the city and to the variety of teens they encountered as they came of age.

When Beatrice Bonifacio and her sister, Margaret, attended middle school in Wooster Square during the mid-1920s, for example, they daily confronted the meaning of the geography of schooling. Because the middle school in their own neighborhood in Fair Haven was overcrowded, Beatrice and her sister were sent to the Columbus Middle School across the Mill River, near Wooster Square, instead. This meant that they had to traverse a drawbridge each morning to get to school. On days when the bridge was pulled up to let boats pass, they had to wait for some time to cross the bridge, which periodically made them late to school. The school's principal, Dr. Diamond, guarded the front door each day to upbraid late arrivers and, according to Beatrice, he carried a "whip" to punish the tardy as they entered the building.[30] This left Beatrice hardened toward whatever opportunities schooling may have held out to her.

She experienced her teachers similarly, as indifferent to anything but the necessity for order and compliance with the school's rules. Observing a parallel between the behavior of one of her teachers and the treatment she later received in the garment factories, Beatrice noted that one of her teachers, "Miss Kelly," would routinely pace up and down the aisles of the classroom to see that the students observed classroom discipline. Her manner was reminiscent, said Beatrice, of the garment boss's wife who patrolled the shop floor in one of the factories in which she later toiled.[31]

Beatrice's experiences, although perhaps unusual, illustrate an important point: as unschooled immigrants, Beatrice's parents may have felt helpless to protest the principal's actions. Their modest social standing and their lack of connection with the community surrounding the Columbus school precluded in their minds any kind of intervention on her behalf. Katherine A. Lebow has reported that the children of southern Italian immigrants commonly expressed anger at the "impotence of . . . parents in the face of . . . school authorities." Their sense of helplessness arose from their parents' conviction that they "couldn't do anything." Because they were immigrants and uneducated themselves, they lacked experience in dealing with school officials, they felt that they "didn't know the rules and regulations here" and therefore "didn't make a big fuss, because that's the way it was."[32]

Murray Lender recalled his own transition from elementary to junior high school as strained, if not the demoralizing ordeal that chased Beatrice Bonifacio out of school at the age of fourteen. Like Bonifacio, Lender's middle grades were spent at a school some remove from his home on Baldwin Street and was a "considerable walk through various neighborhoods." But unlike Bonifacio, the bullies he encountered were neither his school's principal nor its callous teachers but the usual kind of turf toughs that one inevitably crossed on the journey to school. "I always remember one or two bullies on Orchard Street, which is the street I took to get to Troup [Junior High School]." Orchard consumed ten blocks of his more than a mile walk to school; Troup itself, Lender recalled, was formidable—a "huge, huge building."[33]

The school was "more challenging, socially" than elementary school for a variety of reasons. Among his school mates, he recalled, there was an interest in the opposite sex for the first time. The school was more variegated racially, ethnically, and socioeconomically, and the teachers were "much tougher" than in elementary school, Lender reported, "because the kids . . . [were] much tougher." Despite the relative ethnic heterogeneity of the Welch school, the social composition of Troup was even more complex.[34] Lender remembered coming into contact with many more "kids . . . from more disadvantaged homes" than had been the case at Welch. Troup's student body was drawn from all parts of the Hill, which itself ranged socioeconomically from large segments of the working poor to the middle-class proprietor families that ran the businesses up and down Oak Street and out of, or next to their homes, like the Lenders' bagel bakery.[35]

Murray's social orientation was altered as well. Whereas his school friends all lived in his neighborhood around Welch, this changed once he entered junior high school. The size of Troup and the division of the day into subject periods in which students changed classrooms several times a day had made it less likely that his neighborhood chums would be in the same classes together for extended periods or even on the playground during the same time, so there was less continuity between his home and school friendships. Moreover, the lives Murray led between school and home were further partitioned by his tendency to spend what leisure time he had at the Jewish Community Center (JCC) on Legion Avenue, not far from home. He played basketball for the JCC rather than his school, and so found his time increasingly triangulated among home, school, and the JCC. And of course, as he got older, work claimed more of his time as well, but since unlike his older brothers his efforts were not considered imperative to the survival of the family business, Murray could more comfortably balance the division of his time among increasing demands upon it, maintaining proper emphasis on his schoolwork.

If the distance to school was a recurrent theme in Murray Lender's boyhood, it was no less significant in the experience of Reverdy Whitlock, who entered Hillhouse High School in 1926 to pursue the classical course of study. Whitlock embodied as well as anyone the intense desire for social integration mingled with a sense of insurmountable emotional isolation and separateness from the school's social core. In most respects he was the archetypal New England schoolboy. Both of his parents were Connecticut Yankees. He grew up on a farm on the city's western outskirts and was as familiar with horses and hay as he was to become with the streetcars and trolley tracks that carried him to York Square, home of Hillhouse as well as Yale University (which he would attend in four years' time). Whitlock's reminiscences depict a tender adolescent in awe of everything around him—the high school's commanding and austere principal, the high-minded seriousness, idiosyncrasy, and patent devotion of his teachers, and the poised, self-possession that characterized so many of his peers. "To a sensitive and frightened boy," he reflected on his days at Hillhouse, "the microcosm on York Square back in the twenties was a traumatic experience. It was a terrifying place, but not because any one was ever unkind. It was just too much for a country boy from the frontier of Bethany to relate to."[36] Whitlock casts himself in the role of outsider—the boy with his nose pressed to the pane of glass.

Although the social hierarchy governing peer relations in Hillhouse is evident in the architecture of its extracurricular groups and Greek societies, the phenomenology of membership and exclusion is most palpable in the personal testimonies of those who lived them. Whitlock's account of the first time he was smitten in high school with a girl named "Jessica"—an unrequited affair of fantasized possibilities, imagined slights, and eventual heartbreak—situates him in a world all too familiar to anyone who has passed through high school on this side of World War II. For all of the legendary school's claims to scholastic superiority, at Hillhouse, athleticism, personality, and good looks formed the elements of success in this adolescent realm. "Jessica," he recalled, was the object of his yearning:

> Tall and lithe and endowed with a sort of feline grace, she moved with serenity through the daily round of classroom activities and crises. Nothing ruffled her sense of adequacy. She abounded with joy—a happiness welling out of some hidden reservoir inside her—which never seemed diminished . . . The more I contemplated my abysmal inadequacies in this affair with Jessica, the more self-conscious I became. With a growing sense of urgency, I pursued strategies which I might use. Could I follow her down the hall, and open a conversation which would not be forced and strained? . . . All during that first year at Hillhouse Jessica had a

constant companion, a boy whom I shall call Charles. Charles had all the qualities I so sadly lacked. His manner with Jessica had an air of spontaneity about it which I would have given my soul for. Whenever I saw them together I was wholly overcome with despair and feelings of jealousy. . . . What secrets did they share which they could laugh at so easily? What intimacies did they convey in those knowing glances? . . . All through those years at Hillhouse, Jessica and Charles went around town together in a funny old Model T Ford with no top on it. I would see them often—laughing together about things which only they understood and shared.[37]

Whitlock's poignant tale demonstrates the sense of isolation that the majority of boys and girls—not just immigrant youths—carried around with them in their high school years: the feeling that one could never truly penetrate the school's social inner circle, that the "spiritual" core of the high school experience was inaccessible to all but a select few.

It is important as well to bear in mind what kind of a place high school was—or was becoming—for this new group of students entering its corridors. For many it was a dazzling social arena where a peer culture beyond their neighborhoods flourished and beckoned. As noted already, there were some teens who perceived that the social and occupational skills available to them promised more desirable work than what typified their parents' experience. Yet, for adolescents, the social dimension of high school was something highly desirable in itself, and this too shaped their motives and ambitions.

The expansion of young people's horizons was completed for many personally, geographically, and symbolically by the actual journey to the high schools themselves. This impression is graphically conveyed by another man, the son of Italian immigrants, who grew up in New Haven at the same time and also attended Hillhouse High School during the 1930s. The city's streets from Fair Haven to downtown were pathways to his coming of age. Commenting on his physical relationship to the city and his destination each day on the walk to Hillhouse, he said:

[In our neighborhood] . . . around our home on the corner of Poplar and Wolcott Streets [in Fair Haven] . . . [t]here were single and two family homes, as well as tenements. We all had yards, but because there were so few cars, we also played in the streets. The empty lot at the end of Poplar Street was the scene of many ball games. Everything was in walking distance; stores, bakeries, churches, schools, library, movie theatres, post office, and Quinnipiac Park. The exception was when we entered high school [in 1930]. The three high schools were located downtown in proximity to each other, and situated in the middle of Yale University. The New Haven Green was the hub of the city; like a magnet, it attracted us to it where all kinds of stores, offices, city hall, movie houses, theaters, Yale University, and a public library existed. The YMCA and the YWCA were a few blocks beyond the Green. One transferred trolley cars . . . there. We were walkers; we had to [be], we had so little cash. As we started walking towards the high schools, a couple of miles away, we travelled down Grand Avenue picking up other students like a giant carpet sweeper. Although we had car-tickets for the trolley-car, one year, my brother Bob and I walked every day, except two, even in sub-zero weather.[38]

For adolescents, moreover, the social dimension of high school was emerging as an end in itself, and this too shaped their motives and ambitions. Vittorio Racca has testified to the allure of the journey to high school as a site for social display in the example of an Italian-American adolescent named "Libera." After finishing school at the age of thirteen, Libera applied for working papers. When these were denied (because she was underage), according to Racca, she entered high school. At first Libera liked her new experience there and especially the greater freedom it afforded. Since the high school was located some distance from her neighborhood, she had "the chance to parade through the streets of New Haven . . . [to be] looked at and admired." Racca wrote, "Pretty soon, this became a big thing; study was of no importance."

He continued: "As a matter of fact, she didn't study any more, either at home or in school. The principal sent word home that . . . [this] could not continue. Libera remained unmoved [and] went on parading without studying. More protests came from the school. . . . As her parents told her that something had to be done, she replied that they had to keep her at the high school until the end of the school year, whether she was studying or not; such were the rules. The parents believed it and let things go on as before. When I told them that she had told a fib and that at fourteen she was entitled to leave . . . if they wanted, she grew morose, and stayed home. . . . Now she stays home and does nothing but reading novels or visiting friends. . . . living a life of complete laziness.[39]" Libera is, of course, an extreme manifestation, a caricature really, of the social possibilities open to youths in this new world. But she symbolizes nonetheless a new and salient experience of self in the nonfamilial, pan-ethnic, and multiclass society of peership that was high school by the 1930s.[40]

Ethnicity, parents' socioeconomic status, wider kinship relations, neighborhood, relations with peers in and out of school, and relations with teachers coalesced to produce a sense of self with a specific social trajectory for a second-generation Italian immigrant man called "John," whose life history was recorded by Child during the late 1930s. John's "landscape of ambition" was the outcome of influences that combined in ways that were both unique and typical. But these ingredients, whatever their individual outcomes, were present in the lives of all children in New Haven between 1910 and 1940. Thus, Child's life history of John offers an important window on the way schooling, in interaction with other influences, changed parent-child relations during the early and middle decades of the twentieth century.

As a doctoral student in social psychology at Yale's Institute of Human Relations during the late 1930s, Child produced a study that later became known as *Italian or American?* When the dissertation was published in 1943 an entire chapter of the original study was omitted. The unpublished chapter was an in-depth life history of "John," the second-oldest son of the family with whom Child lived. Even though Child's imposition of social-psychological categories of analysis upon John's narrative are now outdated, Child was supremely gifted as an interviewer and a highly perceptive ethnographic interpreter who strove to preserve the qualities of John's autobiographical voice throughout his account of his life history.[41]

John's account of his life is presented by Child as a series of incidents through which he is aroused to keen awareness of his ethnicity and subsequent attempts to assimilate himself. It is in most respects a tale of passage highly familiar in the literatures of sociology and ethnic history during the first half of the twentieth century: an immigrant child's experience of "cultural conflict" and of earnest striving for acceptance, success, and liberation.[42] Throughout the narrative John tacks between an account of his individual development and expanding consciousness, on one hand, and the changing context of his experience on the other.[43]

John describes his relations with his parents in terms that suggest that by the 1930s the cultural dilemma of the second-generation immigrant was already a concept with much popular currency.[44] Accordingly, John's self-fashioning was rendered for Child as the product of two cultural worlds in collision: the world of the family, which embodied Old World attitudes and behaviors; and the social world beyond the family, especially the school—which by most accounts (though curiously, not John's) sought to Americanize immigrant children and integrate them into the new world.[45] John, who was in his early thirties when interviewed by Child, adds to this confrontation of cultures the dimension of generational conflict. "I wasn't aware of myself as a member of a new generation which had to go through this struggle," John said of his attempt as a young adult to distance himself from his parents. "I wasn't aware that it was a struggle between the old world and the new world."[46] Thus he frames his behavior and motives for Child retrospectively as part of a larger social experience that enables him to make sense of, and accommodate, the multitude of conflicting perceptions and feelings that had arisen during his coming of age. In seeing himself as one who personifies a larger "struggle" between generations in his passage from immigrant child to assimilated adult, John momentarily lifts the shroud of complicity between Child's agenda and his own sense of historical agency. And in this we are reminded of the collaborative nature of ethnography— of John's willing participation in Child's presentation of him as an ideal-type.[47]

Two elements of John's life history furnish clues to the relative influences of class and ethnicity in his developing sense of self. First, many of the differences that separate John from others (as well as the slights he attributes to ethnic prejudice) derive from what we would conceive of as socioeconomic or "class" rather than ethnic attributes. At points John himself seems to discern the distinction, but for the most part it is as if the only vocabulary available to name his feelings of difference is that of ethnicity.[48] Second, while the schools were often portrayed as great assimilators of ethnic youth in the United States, they were probably much more effective as organizers of interethnic and interclass contact among youths. As we have already seen, the schools structured the interaction of ethnic and socioeconomic groups in a stepwise fashion. In the primary grades the concentration of children of the same ethnicity and class was strongest. As a child progressed through the schools, however, this pattern was gradually diffused. In high school second-generation immigrant youths were in a distinct minority and felt the full extent of their alienation from both the dominant culture and from their own ethnic communities. In the case of John at least, while he continued to experience his differences from others mostly as a function of his ethnicity, it was in the informal social life of high school that he "discovered" class and first accounted for cultural differences as grounded in something apart from his or others' ethnicity.

There were three primary influences on John's perception of his own and others' social identity as he was growing up: his parents' behavior and attitudes toward him, his siblings, and others; his own interactions with peers; and his school experiences. John describes his childhood as a world tightly circumscribed by family, friends, and neighbors: "I didn't know the way downtown [less than half a mile away] until I was twelve," he told Child. John and his friends played ball and other games around the neighborhood and made trips to the city dump to collect things to sell to the junk man. "I never knew anything more than this little community for three blocks around," he recalled. "I dared go no further. My parents insisted that I always be within calling distance."[49] All of his parents' friends were Italian, as was much of the neighborhood. A few entrenched Irish families along with clusters of Jews and Poles populated this part of the Hill.[50] John's parents and their friends, many of whom had emigrated from the same province in Italy, reported that they helped one another "make wine, take care of the sick, take care of the children [and] . . . lent money to each other freely."[51]

Both of John's parents came from a small town inland from Naples in the province of Benevento. His father came from a family of craftsmen and was himself a skilled worker before emigrating to the United States.[52] While his father had only enough schooling to know how to read and write, his mother had "more than the usual amount," since her family was of slightly higher status and she had been raised by an aunt who had taught school. John's parents came to New Haven at the turn of the century, and his father worked for a time as an unskilled factory worker while continuing "some craft work at night."[53] Eventually he obtained skilled employment, though Child does not mention his particular skills.

In all there were nine children in John's family. He came third in order of birth (1905); one child, his older sister, had been born in Italy, and an older brother, the first of the children born in the United States, also preceded John. Since John's late childhood, his mother had operated a small grocery store and with his parents' two incomes the family was well-off relative to their neighbors. The income from the store was used for savings, for buying and maintaining their house, and for enabling the children to continue in school beyond age fourteen. His mother's desire to see the children educated was a source of tension and difficulty, however. John's father had expected that the children would bring in regular wages as soon as they were of legal working age (fourteen), but his mother "believed that it was more important [that they] . . . get a good education" and operated the store to "bear the extra expense" of having the children continue in school. In this—his mother's commitment to the children's schooling and in her income-earning—John's family was exceptional, but in no other way, according to Child, did the family "live differently from other working-class families in the neighborhood."[54]

Despite this cushion of economic support, John was apprenticed to a barber when he was ten, and after that, to a shoemaker.[55] Any "outside" money earned by the children was given over to the parents, who in turn gave some portion of it back to the children.[56] "This procedure," wrote Child, "was required as a part of . . . [their] training even if the money involved was not enough to make any difference to the family."[57] The routine typified an Italian practice that, above all else, was didactic. It was the inculcation in children of the importance of collaborative effort that mattered most to parents.[58] In addition, John's parents, particularly his father, enforced a strict routine of chores around the house, which, according to John, included "cleaning the yard, feeding the chickens, seeing that the chickens were roosted and were all in at dark, taking in the vegetables from the front of the store at night, scrubbing the floors, cleaning the stove, going to market every Saturday with my mother. . . . I sometimes had to help in washing dishes also. Chopping wood was another of my tasks, and a big one since we only had about one ton of coal for the winter."[59]

John characterized his family—and particularly his father—as "cold" and lacking in affection. Although he felt great warmth for his mother and was cognizant of the high respect accorded her in the neighborhood, "both for her friendliness and helpfulness and because of her unusually good education," he remembered her primarily as "the very busy manager of a large household who was so occupied with cooking, cleaning, taking care of the grocery store, and giving birth to and raising many younger children, that she had little time to devote to any one child."[60] While his mother was devout and "talked of religion and the Bible," his father was, by contrast, "cynical and pessimistic . . . [and] only spoke of religion to criticize it." John described his father as "stern and strict. . . . not very communicative most of the time" and occasionally "given to fits of temper." John continued: "He would yell and bully my mother when meals were not ready on time, or when he thought she was spending too much money. . . . Most of the outbursts were for very trivial things and most of them came on holidays and feast days, perhaps because of overdrinking."[61] John also remembered his father as a severe disciplinarian. According to Child, "John himself was punished physically a great deal by his father" but evidently less than his older brother, who was not as accepting of his father's authority. "After a good licking," recalled John, "[my brother and I] would converse and plan that as soon as we grew up and reached the age of sixteen we would run away and never come back, or else we would get a job and never give a penny of our money over to him."[62]

In Child's estimation, however, John was actually his father's favorite. He "took more of an interest in [John] . . . and was kindlier toward him"—probably (Child surmised) because John was compliant and "gave his father less reason to punish him." But more than this, a shared passion for music brought John and his father together to go to concerts. They also took walks, during which his father would give him advice. Although he recalled his father lecturing him to "study hard so that I wouldn't have to work as hard as he himself had to," John said that such encouragement did not translate into help with his schoolwork: "I never had any help from my father on any school work. In fact, I never expected my father to help and I knew my school work was entirely my own. I worked through terrific difficulties and yet blissfully I did not realize it. I didn't know, for example, that parents ever helped their children with school work. . . . Bringing home report cards didn't really mean anything. Good or bad made no difference. My father would simply sign the card. My mother would ask what the marks meant, and if I said 'bad' in any subject, she would encourage me a little to try and do 'better.'"[63] In John's memory the only interest his father showed in the advancement of any of the children was that they learn music. Thus, despite Child's assessment that John was relatively well-liked by his father, John felt a general coolness toward him and remembered "as a boy feeling abused . . . and deciding that I would give my children more freedom than I was getting."[64]

The family's status in the neighborhood tended to reinforce John's ethnic and class insularity. The Italian custom of Sunday visiting more commonly brought other families into John's parents' home than outings by his own family, which meant that he had "frequent contact without leaving the house."[65] Even his contacts beyond the family were restricted to the immediate community: his mother's grocery, the barbershop, and the shoemaker's store (where he later worked) all served a local, primarily immigrant clientele. Since he played exclusively with the children of other Italian immigrants, whatever sense of ethnic difference and hierarchy John absorbed during this period appears to have grown from his interactions with other pupils in school. Although he (like Murray Lender) recollected that during his childhood all ethnic groups in his community "mixed easily" together, it was in his grade school that a stratified order of New Haven's primary ethnic groups began to take form in his mind. Slowly, he later realized, he began to internalize the ascribed status of his own ethnicity.

Essentially, it seems, there were "Americans" and everyone else, descending in order from the Irish, to the Italians, Poles, and at the bottom, Jews and then African Americans. Although John maintained that it was not until adolescence that the ethnic groups in his neighborhood began to form into gangs, he long knew to stay clear of the Irish, who apparently took every opportunity to remind the Italians and others of their relative inferiority. The Italian children, he recalled, were especially "subject to ridicule by the Irish, with whom they were in most frequent contact." This ethnic pecking order translated into a routine display of deference by the Italian children toward their Irish age-peers. Therefore, for example, when Irish children took over a playing field, the Italian children understood that they could only join in after every Irish boy had been given a place.[66]

John's primary contact with "Americans" was with his teachers, since few if any Yankees attended the elementary school in this overwhelmingly working-class and (increasingly Italian) immigrant community. The "Americans seemed so far above me that I didn't even bother trying to figure them out," said John. Until grade school, with the exception of his aunt, whom his family regarded as "American," his exposure to Americans had been largely incidental—from occasional visits to the nearby train terminal: "I knew that the people I saw in the station were of another social class which we called Americans. . . . I knew that . . . [they] . . . differed from the older people that I knew in their dress, their language, in the fact they always had bags. . . . I would see people going by who were well-dressed, clean, and neat, and I felt that they were far above us. We had no background, I felt like a foreigner."[67] To John, the equation of his own lack of "background" (that is, the absence of cultural sophistication and respectable social status) with a "foreign" feeling defined succinctly what it was *not* to be an American.

John's tendency to conflate ethnicity and class is best expressed by his family's regard for their "American" Aunt Annie. Aunt Annie's family was of even higher prestige in the neighborhood than John's own. Hers was the only other household that his family visited often—the only family, he said, that he "had much relation to in childhood who appeared to him as American rather than as Italian." Aunt Annie had come to the United States as a young girl and, John recalled, "we looked on her as higher and got a lot about American customs from association with her." By "American," Child learned, John meant people who spoke English at home rather than an Italian dialect, people who wore "good clothing," and people who had nicely furnished homes where "lots of American people" visited.[68]

John thought that the fact that Aunt Annie educated her own children was probably an incentive to his mother to keep him and his siblings in school. She was "very charming, had practically no accent and spoke very fluent English." Her home, said John, "did not seem like an Italian home but like an American home, probably because no Italian was spoken there . . . and because of the better taste, like in furniture."[69] Aunt Annie, John reflected, "had associated so much with that class, when we had no opportunity to." He continued: "In mixing with these people as she did, one naturally acquires many ideas such as dress, arrangement of the home and management of the children. For example, her children were very polite and would address her as 'Mother dear.' They would also kiss her on coming into the house or leaving. Also there was no shouting around the house, and I never saw a child physically chastised. In fact, I couldn't make heads or tails of the place and felt very strange whenever I was in their home."[70] If John was perplexed by what he saw in Aunt Annie's house, school was similarly at odds with the emotional tone of his parents' house. According to Child's reports, school life seemed increasingly divorced from home life, as John felt a new allure to, and warmth at, school.[71] According to Child, John remembered his teachers affectionately: "I recall a pretty teacher in grammar school who would come up to me and cup my chin in a nice manner. . . . I loved to go to this room, just to look at her."[72]

Child noted that none of John's recollections of grade school included any details of what he learned about American culture through the curriculum. John "had only vague recollections of elementary and grammar school," reported Child, speculating that this may have been because the "social groupings [within the school] . . . were undifferentiated from those outside the school." There was one specific extracurricular event, however, that proved critical to John's decision to continue his education after grammar school—and that, in turn, would dramatically alter his relations with neighborhood friends and acquaintances. Through sixth grade John had been a mediocre student at best. Yet he had earned his peers' respect both within and outside school by fighting the leader of a clique to which he belonged and then challenging and "licking" the leaders of other neighborhood cliques. In seventh grade (in 1917) his classmates demonstrated their feeling for John by electing him class leader of their school's War Savings Stamps campaign. His teacher, believing that John was not up to the job, called for a reelection, but John won again and took charge of the campaign. Though he admitted feeling inadequate to the task, his position gave him the confidence to prove himself academically. By the end of the next year he was ranked second in his class."[73]

Another seemingly innocuous event combined with this experience to detach John from his neighborhood associations and redirect his academic ambitions. Some time when he was in grammar school, a branch library opened in his neighborhood. One evening, John recalled, he went into the library "out of curiosity." Gradually he became interested in the books he found there and so he returned with regularity. This custom initiated his weaning away from the neighborhood gang, who, he recalled, "kidded me as a 'high brow.'"[74] John applied to high school that year even though he was not at all sure he wanted to go. His older brother had quit school after eighth grade to work in a factory, but his older sister was enrolled in high school. Her example, John believed, and his mother's faith in education probably persuaded him to go to high school, though his parents did not try to influence him directly. His "bookishness" and his efforts to improve his speech invited the ridicule of his friends, and when he finally did decide to enroll in high school, they chided him as a "sissy." In the meantime, he drifted away from neighborhood friends while working and spending his free time at the library.[75]

John's sense of ethnicity sharpened as he moved from his mostly Italian neighborhood grammar school to Hillhouse High School, where fewer than one in ten students was of Italian parentage.[76] He remembered that even by the eighth grade, he had begun to detect in himself, as he put it, feelings of personal inadequacy around non-Italians and had an impression, too, that other Italians "acted inferior towards non-Italians." Moreover, while "Americans" had earlier appeared to John as a category of people who were "vaguely superior," in high school he was in daily contact with them, which only sharpened his sense of inferiority.[77] This contact involved "sitting near them in class" and "seeing them recite . . . or 'hearing a group of them talk in the halls and sometimes himself being a member of the group,' but never having any close friendships with them." He gravitated toward three other Italian boys in school. While each was aware of segregating himself from the "Americans," none of them ever articulated what was occurring. Instead, they envied the others, said John, "wishing we could be like [them]."[78]

Another effect of the high school's distance from his own neighborhood was that John, increasingly, had to develop and assert himself in academic rather than physical ways. This further diminished his standing among his boyhood friends, on one hand, and attuned him to the nuances of affect and attitude among his school peers on the other. Before high school, Child pointed out, John could work out his feelings of inferiority and aggression physically by challenging other boys to fights. Since all the pupils in his grammar school had lived in the same area, they could fight outside of school without getting into trouble with teachers and other school officials. In high school this changed. Because students came from all over the city, any fight would necessarily occur near the school grounds and so possibly under the eyes of school officials. Therefore, John began to avoid the kinds of confrontations that had helped build his confidence in grammar school, relying instead on his academic achievements to bolster his sense of worth.[79]

It was in high school that John's perceptions of others' class-related social attributes began to intermingle with his notions of non-Italians' ethnicity. The "Americans," John observed, contrasted with the Italians in their speech and bearing, in their "feeling of assurance, in their perfect ease, their lack of tenseness, their dress, their manner, their appearance, their non-seriousness, the fact that they were happy and jovial. These were the impressions I got from the way I saw Americans in school, especially in high school, where I began to realize the existence of social classes. Americans to me were anybody but the Italians or Poles."[80] He found incomprehensible, for instance, that some of the students at the high school "were allowed to drive cars to school." He heard conversations among Americans in which someone would say something such as, "'Gee, I got the dickens from my dad last night—he cut out my allowance,' or he was not allowed to ride his bike for two weeks or not allowed to go to the show for two weeks. These were all forms of punishment that I had never heard of before."[81]

During the same period conflicts began within the family as John and his sisters (who were also in high school) appealed to their parents for better clothing, money for books, and other school materials. But these demands met with stiff resistance. For their parents, observed Child, the issue was not an inability to afford such things but rather a determination that their children should meet "the standards of frugality encouraged by Italian culture." The children, on the other hand, wished to conform to the patterns of their high school peers.[82] Although the parents prevailed as long as John and his sisters remained in school, the children each renegotiated their obligations once they were out of school, earning their own incomes. While high school was the most important form of regular exposure to "Americans," another source of contact and influence during adolescence was the movie theater. During high school John got a job at a local cinema taking tickets and sweeping up. Before he entered high school, his parents had objected to him seeing movies at all. They were suspicious of what went on in the darkness of the theater and, moreover, were simply uninterested in the movies, which they did not understand. Yet when John began working at the theater, their objections subsided.[83] In addition to casual social contact with non-Italians at the movie theater, there was the influence of the movies themselves. By his own account, John absorbed a few moral lessons from the films he watched and also learned a great deal about "American" table manners, taste in furniture and design, and etiquette. Discussing the influence of the movies on him, he said, "I remember . . . [once] changing my hairdress because of some current fashion in the movies, or the way that some particular star wore his hair."[84] Child remarked that John spoke of the movies "as a kind of fairyland presenting people who didn't really exist," but added perceptively that his description of people in the movies paralleled John's earlier observations of the strangers he had encountered at the train station as a youngster.[85]

This insight goes to the very heart of John's efforts to fashion an identity for himself. For the fairyland of the cinema and the strangers in the train station were but a step removed from those he encountered—now daily—in his high school and at the movie theater. These people, whom he had always experienced as "Americans" were themselves just a remove from those with whom he had had more familiar interaction, like his grammar school teachers, and paradigmatically his "American" aunt and her family. What bound them all to one another in his mind was their status as "Americans"—an association that amounted to a misreading produced by his cultural distance from them.

Yet this misreading supplied the basis of John's interpretation of others' ethnic differences, which were grounded in what were, for him, palpable nuances in the demonstration of affect, style, and attitude in social and personal interactions. Each was compared against the emotional style and behavior of his own family. Those at the greatest imaginative distance, such as movie characters, were certainly more superficial influences but seem to have represented for John idealized expressions of the kinds of people with whom he now had routine contact: his "American" high school classmates were merely more worldly copies of the actors he saw in the cinema. And the snatches of conversation he overheard among his non-Italian high school acquaintances reflected decidedly different styles of relations between parents and children. These, in turn, served to reinforce his impressions of having been in the midst of another culture when he visited his Aunt Annie's house—his only immediate exposure to a manner of family interaction different from his own. Through the mundane details of his aunt's family life, he seems to have connected a way of being in concrete terms—a mode of intimacy, personal expression, language, and bearing—with a degree of affluence that constructed for him a bridge to an assimilated self.

Soon after John graduated from high school he was offered a job as a teaching assistant in woodworking at one of the public schools. He accepted the job even though he did not feel qualified to take it, attributing the windfall to good luck and a shortage of teachers in the school system. John was one of the first teachers of Italian descent in the city school system. His immediate superior was also an Italian American, and about 80 percent of the pupils in the school to which John was assigned were children of Italian descent. The job did not offer much immediate income but did promise more in the future, and besides, it carried prestige. Meanwhile, his neighborhood friends were incredulous that he would take a job at such low pay and thought it incongruous that others regarded John's work as prestigious. Although John continued to see a good deal of old friends whose educational and professional ambitions approximated his own, most of his neighborhood friendships had grown distant as he began to socialize with people he had met at work.[86]

After his first year of teaching school, at the age of twenty, a split developed between John and his parents. His older brother had died when John was a senior in high school, but his older sister (who was also a teacher) and John continued to live in their parents' house. John and his sisters (including the younger one, who was still in high school and who would also go on to become a teacher) urged their parents to move to a different, ethnically and socioeconomically mixed neighborhood. Child's interpretation of this request was that living in their parents' neighborhood had begun to conflict with their ability to achieve their aspirations, which could only be attained "by becoming independent of the family and . . . mov[ing] away."[87] When their father rejected their urgings, they relented. However, this episode, according to Child, precipitated another "break" between John and his parents.[88]

Throughout the first year of his new job John had continued to give his entire earnings to his parents, but during the second year he announced that he would be contributing just ten dollars a week for board. "John understood well," wrote Child, "that his father felt it was the duty of the children in return for their being brought up by their parents, to turn over all their money until they were married. His father had made it clear that he expected in this way to have some security for himself for old age through the accumulation of money, and to be responsible for the financial needs of his children."[89] John said he knew that when he made the decision to stop turning over all of his pay, it would cause great conflict and hurt: "I knew it would cause hard feelings; but I knew that that was the American way to do things. . . . It did result in quite a scrap. My father just couldn't get over the idea, and he blamed my older sister, of course, because she had previously gone through the struggle and stopped turning over all her income. My father said, 'What kind of a country is this anyway, where the children are so disrespectful to their parents?' Because to him, of course, this was disrespectful."[90]

This event signaled the attenuation of John's emotional attachment to his parents and their neighborhood, a process that would culminate in his marriage to a fourth-generation Irish-American woman. Upon marriage, John moved out of his parents' home to a middle-class, mostly Yankee and Irish neighborhood. The change in his social contacts, he told Child, was "revolutionary." "Always until this time," commented Child, "he had lived and eaten at home in the middle of a working-class community, populated largely by Italian families." But most of his time thereafter was spent among "non-Italian people and things."[91] Although most of John's life was still ahead of him—he was still a young man when Child interviewed him—in an important way he had completed his journey from immigrant child to outwardly assimilated adult.

How much can we generalize from John's experience? In several ways he seems atypical of his ethnic and class peers. His mere presence in high school during the early 1920s made him unusual. During these years in New Haven, between 7 percent and 11 percent of all students enrolled in grades 9 through 12 were of Italian parentage (whereas Italian children comprised fully 40 percent of all children in the city's public schools during the same years). While John's parents were far removed from the city's *prominenti*—the commercial, professional, and intellectual elite of New Haven's Italians—they occupied a higher than average social position in their mostly working-class, immigrant neighborhood. John's father was fortunate to have a skilled job, since most skilled workers emigrating from southern Italy after 1890 were unable to practice their trades in the United States and had to be content with unskilled or semi-skilled labor for the rest of their working lives.[92] John's mother, by the same token, was unusual in owning a store. Having two incomes made his parents more comfortable than most of their neighbors, yet their relative comfort did not alone account for John's continuation in school. John's older brother, after all, had left school for a factory job following eighth grade, like the majority of New Haven's fourteen-year-olds and like the overwhelming number of Italian boys growing up during the 1910s and 1920s, so it was not his example that spurred John on to high school. Rather, it appears that his mother's single-minded devotion to her children's education supported John's late-developing ambition to continue in school. But, paradoxically, this ambition was also nurtured by a growing self-esteem forged, not in school, but in the backyards, playgrounds, and streets of John's neighborhood through his physical confrontations with other boys.

Despite the apparent singularity of his story in its particulars, it is the process of his identity-making that connects John's experience to his ethnic, class, and age peers and makes his life history such a meaningful window on the past. The rough outlines of that process were shared by all

Italian-American children who entered the schools. Although John was unusual among second-generation immigrant children in the extent of his schooling, during the 1930s southern Italian immigrant boys and girls would begin to enter and graduate from high school in significant numbers. By the early 1930s 20 percent of the city's high school students were children of Italian parentage; as the decade drew to a close, high school had become a commonplace, if not yet typical, experience for the city's Italian-American youth.

The relationship between schooling and immigrants' assimilation is more complicated and interesting than historians have tended to assume.[93] As the two dominant settings for child development and identity formation, schools and families have played powerful roles in framing the way children have perceived themselves. The example of John, at one level a straightforward story of assimilation, illustrates a larger, opposite principle operating in the lives of immigrant children historically: that is, that in earlier periods of heavy immigration, schooling might reinforce an ethnic-based conception of self in immigrant children as much or more than it promoted the embrace of things "American." It was not until the age of compulsory school attendance had been raised to sixteen, which virtually assured enrollment in high school for every youth, and the collapse of the youth job market, which so thoroughly discouraged young people from leaving school that schooling unequivocally assisted assimilation. Again, to the degree that this was achieved, it was aided as much by young people's interactions with peers whose own social backgrounds (ethnic and socioeconomic) diverged from their own as it was effected by the schools' efforts to "Americanize" immigrant pupils. Finally, as John's tale so poignantly testifies, ethnic self-consciousness could also effectively obscure the markings of class. In John's case class distinctions became visible to him (and so, distinguishable from ethnic differences) only when high school took him beyond the solidly working-class neighborhood of his grammar school. Let us now consider how the high school promoted social mobility while reinforcing class- and gender-based conceptions of opportunity within an expanding curriculum and the emergence of a student population from across the social spectrum.

7

"TOO GOOD FOR THAT": EFFORT AND OPPORTUNITY IN THE "NEW" HIGH SCHOOL

Did you ever hear what Henry Ford said? A smart guy, Henry. He says, "The only trouble about the University of Hard Knocks is that when you graduate you're too old to do anything."
—New Haven mechanic, ca. 1935, quoted in E. Wight Bakke, *Unemployed Worker*

If its turn-of-the-century iteration was comparatively exclusive, the "new" high school—high school after 1920—was socioeconomically democratic. Its population more nearly approximated that of the community it inhabited than did high school in 1900, and its broad curriculum reflected the needs and interests of a growing and diverse student body.[1] In few places, perhaps, were these changes more evident than at Hillhouse High School, where the appearance of working-class and immigrant youths, at the margins of the student body in 1900, were represented in rough proportion to their share of the city's population by the end of the 1930s. The influx of immigrant working-class youths in New Haven's academic high school corresponded chronologically with the cresting of the school's prominence nationally during the 1920s.[2]

By 1930 virtually every adolescent in New Haven attended high school. Despite the relative diversity of the Hillhouse student body historically, the complexion of secondary schooling in New Haven over all had changed dramatically. Universal attendance deeply affected the shape and substance of the high school curriculum as well as the social experience of teens. Yet the implications of the "new" high school were different and more far-reaching for some groups than for others. "Yankee" girls and boys, numerically preponderant from the founding of the high school in New Haven until the 1930s, represented one extreme: a new and more complex social order had grown up around them but they continued to dominate formal and informal peer-group activities within and outside the high school.[3] Hillhouse, the bastion of the traditional high-schooler in New Haven, was remade by the rising numbers of immigrant boys and girls in its classrooms, on its athletic fields, and in its student organizations (see fig. 7.1).

Somewhat contradictorily, however, the new high school was also more stratified experientially and in the kinds of outcomes it offered its students later in life. Despite (or because of) its selectivity, high school in the twilight of the nineteenth century also functioned more nearly as a meritocracy and better supported the upward social mobility of its graduates than New Haven's high schools in 1940.[4] The comprehensive curriculum and tracking, two major innovations of progressive educational

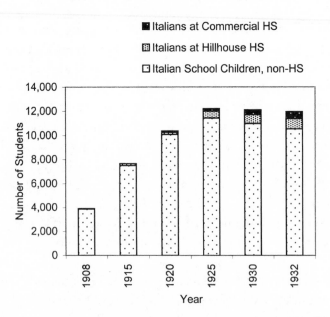

Fig. 7.1 Growth of Italian immigrant enrollments, 1908–32. *Source:* New Haven, *Annual Reports*, 1908–32. Commercial High School did not open until 1920

reform that offered programs of study geared to sustaining pupils' interests throughout their adolescent years, determined, even before boys and girls entered high school, the upper limits of what they could achieve and even encounter through schooling.[5] First-generation high-schoolers sought out, and were encouraged to pursue, practical training that opened avenues of employment that were both dependable and versatile. For the first six decades of the twentieth century having a high school diploma was enough of a credential to assure upward social mobility. The changing occupational structure of the United States from 1900 to 1930 and then a rapidly growing economy between 1940 and 1965 ensured that the high school educated would thrive. But by the end of this period, as higher education expanded under the stimulus of the G.I. Bill after World War II, the diploma, once a ticket to upward social mobility, became a minimum credential, one that a young person had to possess to gain even relatively menial, dead-end, white-collar employment.

The 1930s were pivotal years, when adolescents came to see high school as a means of seizing the chance to gain access to white-collar occupations or, less ambitiously, as a way of keeping up with changing cultural and occupational standards that raised the floor of expected competencies beneath them. As the esteem of "head work" surpassed working with one's hands and high school assumed pride of place over the school of hard knocks, the price paid for nonattendance rose considerably. Nevertheless, for every student in New Haven who had come to believe that he or she was entitled to a high school education, there were three other city youths by the 1930s who felt that their stay in high school was, at best, a way of marking time. The connection of high school to the demands of the workplace remained unclear to many young people despite that the lack of the diploma's credential increasingly arose as a barrier to long-term occupational advancement.[6] The influence of credentialism would only intensify. After World War II even managers who formerly spurned high school–educated workers in favor of those whose skills had been forged on the shop floor had come to regard the diploma as a hurdle that the most desirable of industrial workers would surmount if promotion and security were what they sought.[7]

It would be a mistake, however, to conclude that the popularization of secondary schooling owed strictly to the pressure of market forces. The rise in high school attendance and graduation rates before the onset of the Great Depression indicated profound cultural change beneath a surface of widening acceptance: adolescence, which furnished the psycho-physiological justification for the universalization of high school, had emerged as a "right" even among those for whom the relevance of schooling faded soon after they had mastered the fundamentals of reading, writing, and arithmetic. By the 1920s even early school-leavers expressed regrets at having had their teenage years curtailed by pressures that forced them to put their school days behind them. While the attractions of high school during the 1920s elicited responses from young people ranging from eager engagement to patent indifference, the expectation that a young person would attend at least some high school gathered increasing momentum during the decade. The popularity of high school turned on the naturalization of adolescence as a universal life-stage necessary to healthy human development.

High school could not have been promoted without the spreading belief that the success of one's children relied upon parents' willingness to nurture and provide for them throughout their teenage years, and the growing recognition of adolescence could not have occurred without a means of usefully engaging youths. The collapse of the youth job market in the wake of the economic crisis of 1928–29 instantly transformed what had been a steadily widening social trend into an inescapable social norm.[8] The hardening economic reality was swiftly followed by massive teen unemployment and the elevation, by 1933, of the minimum age of compulsory school attendance in Connecticut from fourteen to sixteen.[9] As with earlier efforts to impose a minimum age for school attendance, the ratcheting up of the age of compulsory schooling to sixteen imposed a social expectation that outstripped the willingness of many young people to comply with it. Nevertheless, the effect was both a rise in the average level of educational attainment and increased concern with those teens who were "dropping out" of school.

The "drop out," of course, implied the high school graduate as the norm. Once an ideal realized by a privileged few, by the 1930s graduating from high school had become a goal to which all might aspire. The social construction of the drop out presumed that most young people desired a high school diploma and that anyone who did not was somehow unfit or insufficiently ambitious. Its evolving pejorative connotation occurred over decades and is reflected in the discursive shift from the use of the phrase "dropping out," which, coined at the end of the nineteenth century, described a behavior—the exercise of a choice among a range of respectable options—to "the drop out," a type who exemplifies a social problem. By the 1930s "the drop out" came to represent not merely an individual rejection of an emerging social norm but a category of social deviance as well. Still, the invention of the drop out had occurred at a time when only about 5 percent of all seventeen-year-olds in the United States remained in high school long enough to graduate (see fig. 7.2).[10]

Educators during the 1890s had begun to think of ways in which to encourage young people to continue on from grammar school to high school and how to keep them there once they had entered.[11] To do so, they sought to understand why young people exited school in the first place. One such attempt was a survey conducted by a New Haven teacher in 1899 polling eighth-grade school-leavers about their reasons for quitting. His respondents volunteered fourteen reasons for not continuing

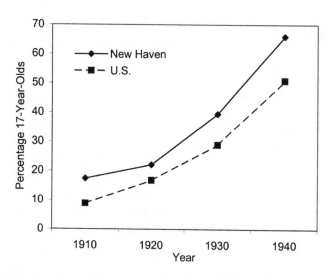

Fig. 7.2 High school graduation rates, 1900–1940. *Sources:* New Haven, *Annual Reports,* 1910–35; U.S. Department of Commerce, Bureau of the Census, *Historical Statistics of the United States,* 214 (Ser. H 383–94); New Haven, *New Haven's Schools,* 26–27

on to high school, ranging from "have to go to work to support the family" and "sick of school" to "grammar school education is sufficient" and "high school too strict." This was at a time when fewer than half of all children entering the first grade in the New Haven public schools would remain in school through the eighth grade, and of these, another one-quarter would not continue on to grade nine.[12]

Thirty years later, when 75 percent of those entering first grade in the city would finish eighth grade and 40 percent of the city's seventeen-year olds graduated from high school, another New Haven study reported that students gave just four reasons for leaving school: "To go to work," "to aid family income," "not interested in school," and "discouraged by low marks." As one would expect, given the worsening economic climate, half of all students interviewed about leaving school either said that they wanted to go to work or they needed to help out their families.[13] But the narrowing of reasons given for not remaining in school between 1899 and 1930 also reflected the degree to which high school had been popularized over the intervening decades. The author of the 1930 study points out that the handful of reasons given by school-leavers were all ones that adolescents knew to be "socially-approved." Because so few people graduated from high school during the 1890s, there had been no shame attached to school-leaving. Therefore, respondents appear to have answered questions about *not* continuing on to high school openly and with little inhibition, whereas by 1930 eighth-grade respondents were more guarded about deviating from what they believed to be acceptable excuses for "dropping out."[14]

Mirror opposites, the drop out and the high school graduate occupied the same culturally sanctioned life-space: adolescence. Increasingly, however, adolescence was positively (and later, exclusively) associated with high school, an arena where this critical stage of human growth could occur under the watchful guidance of adults. It was far preferable, educators believed, for adults to take an active role in shaping this development than to allow young people to fend for themselves. School-leavers, in opting for the world of work, chose not just employment but a social sphere in which, at best, they would come of age under the uneven influence of adults indifferent to their developmental needs. At worst, it was argued, adolescents who left school with no job in view fell under the tutelage of the "street schools" that spawned juvenile delinquency and moral chaos. Schooled or not, there was a spreading awareness in American culture that the salience of adolescence for the individual and his or her social environment was pervasive and real.[15] But the schools, in any case, had paved the way for the acceptance of both high school and its developmental sphere through the practice of age-grading. Age-grading, as we have seen, institutionalized the idea of standard, predictable patterns of intellectual and physiological development. Adopted only haltingly in some cities but zealously and systematically in New Haven (and elsewhere in New England), the effectiveness of age-grading in bringing order to the urban masses was refined by the triumph of the testing and measurement movement. Concepts such as "mental age," achievement, and aptitude legitimized age-grading by lending a scientific aura to the grouping of students by age and measured ability, forever cementing schooling to evolving concepts of human growth and achievement.[16]

The novelty of the idea that every youth should (or should want to) receive some form of post–grammar school education has largely eluded historians. Yet in the formulations of experts, in the realm of popular culture, and in the minds of young people, the idea of adolescence was alive and forming into a consensus. The by-product of this consensus was the "youth problem"—the long lag between school and work that characterized the experience of so many young people throughout the United States, made longer by the agonizing economic crisis of the 1930s. Among historians of education and the New Deal, the Depression is often best remembered for federal efforts to democratize schooling.[17] The Federal Emergency Relief Administration's Emergency Education Program, the Civilian Conservation Corps, and the National Youth Administration were formed expressly to address the "youth problem."[18] These programs and the abolition of child labor represented the first concerted attempt by agencies in the federal government to make schooling more accessible to all children and youths, especially the poor.[19] While chronic parental unemployment during the decade forced many young people to leave school in the face of desperation, for the great majority of youths under eighteen, hard times meant more education, not an early exit from school.[20]

Still, if the national emergency drew attention to the great numbers of young people whose lack of education, in the words of FERA official Hilda Smith, left them "pitifully unequipped . . . to meet the problems of modern life," the rhetoric of crisis also obscured two important long-term trends: average levels of education had been rising steadily since the turn of the century; and the composition of the high school student body and the curricular choices of these new students altered remarkably during the same period.[21] Like other cities in the Northeast and industrial Midwest at the turn of the century, New Haven's high school commercial curriculum and the city's clerical workforce were in the midst of a transformation. Both were feminized between the 1890s and 1930. Before 1900, females pursuing careers in teaching comprised the majority, not only of female high school graduates, but of all girls enrolled in high school. By 1920, however, young women in search of retail and secretarial jobs were preponderant among female secondary students.[22] Furthermore, greater numbers of high school students, but boys especially, were choosing the "general" curricular track, which did not prepare them either for college or for occupations requiring specific technical skills like secretarial work.

While the economic crisis had vividly dramatized the shrunken state of the youth job market during the 1930s, even by the mid-1920s observers in New Haven had detected an increase in the number of students entering into and remaining in high school in response to declining employment opportunities. Average ages per grade level were at an all-time high and still rising, while the number of "over-aged" high school seniors lacking credits sufficient to graduate was growing.[23] By the late 1920s other factors coalesced to extend the average length of schooling. In 1928 the New Haven school board determined that too many pupils were being "eliminated" from the high schools and that something must be done to retain them.[24] Until then it had been the school district's policy to send failing freshmen back to the eighth grade (and thus often to grammar school), a practice that apparently demoralized them and accelerated school-leaving. If the student was beyond the age of compulsory schooling or was certified to work, he or she usually just dropped out. As the economy worsened during 1929 and jobs for young people became scarce, according to one study, "it was felt [by school officials] that the school was falling short of its aim" to keep its students. Thus the practice of demoting freshmen to grammar school was amended "in an attempt to keep all pupils in school for as long as possible." The solution, known as "social promotion," became an indispensable tool in the campaign to popularize secondary schooling.[25]

A variety of forces, then, converged to frame high school as the "normal" teen experience by the 1930s: the rise of the developmental view in psychology and education that offered schooling as an institutional remedy to the unpredictability and storminess of adolescent behavior; the decline and collapse of the youth job market; the adoption of the practice of social promotion to discourage dropping out; curricular changes that promoted life skills and practical learning that made high school graduates more employable; increased emphasis on high school as a credential desirable for most forms of employment; and the feminization of the most popular curriculum in high school—the commercial track—which complemented a corresponding expansion of the clerical workforce at the expense of other sectors of the U.S. occupational structure. High school had been transformed into a mass institution and was remade in the process by the new groups of girls and boys who entered its doors.

If statistics help to reconstruct the skeleton of social life in the past, anecdote and case study make up the flesh and blood of lived experience. Three students—"Frank," "David," and "Evelyn"—succinctly illustrate the ways that young people thought about their schooling in 1940, at a time when the career paths of the high school–educated were becoming more concretely linked to emerging occupations and a conception of students as "appropriately" applying themselves within specified curricular tracks coalesced into achievement norms.[26]

Frank was a fifteen-year-old sophomore in the general course. Both of his parents were native born, and both had finished grammar school. His father worked as a janitor and Frank had two siblings. He carried a "B–" average through his junior year in high school, a grade average surpassed by only two students in the general course and equaled by just nine others; indeed, this record ranked him among the top 20 percent of the students in the general course. Yet Frank "underachieved" in the sense that his aptitude suggested that he should score much higher marks than he did. In this respect—in declining to work up to his tested ability—he typified his male classmates, especially those in the general course.[27] Although in his interview Frank did not agree with those students in the general course of study who felt that a "C" was a desirable grade, he was nonetheless mildly unconcerned about grading. The subject matter of his courses inspired him to work, he said, not a desire for high marks. Frank reported that he would like to join the navy and perhaps attend the Naval Academy. He wanted to be a pilot, but because his poor eyesight precluded that, he said that he would be happy just "to be around airplanes." He felt that his parents had shown "some interest" in his work since elementary school and "on the whole, consider[ed] his work successful." They tended to praise his good work and encouraged reading apart from schoolwork by giving him books on aviation and other subjects that interested him. Frank's primary satisfactions in school came from extracurricular activities ("all of which indicate[d] a strong mechanical ability"), "having many friends," and from "having classmates think well of him."[28]

David was a junior of above average ability in the commercial course, who had maintained an "A" average throughout the first two years of high school. His father was native born, had a grammar school education, and worked as a plumber. His mother had been born in Ireland and had graduated from high school. David had four brothers and sisters. He said that he planned to seek additional schooling after high school and that he had saved money for "college" (by this he meant business college), and he reported that afterward he would "enter the business world." David's parents were very supportive of his schoolwork and especially encouraged his reading in subjects related to business. There is no indication how he chose the commercial, or "business" track, as it was called by the boys. It is evident that his parents gave him wide latitude in matters related to his schoolwork, a liberality probably based on his success in school, for his father hoped but apparently did not insist that David would join him in his plumbing business after completing high school.[29] David's parents, it appears, were content to see where their son's inclinations and talents would take him, offering encouragement whenever possible and allowing him to seek his own level and direction. Yet how supportive David's parents would have been had he enrolled in the academic track—a curriculum without any clear applicability to his father's vocation or to the larger world of business—is a matter of speculation. John W. McConnell has suggested, based on interviews with New Haven parents during the late 1930s, that pressure from children on parents to allow them to continue their schooling often brought positive results where commercial training was concerned. However, it is unclear whether such flexibility extended beyond purely vocational aims of education.[30]

Evelyn had enrolled in the commercial course and was of average ability—yet she had the fourth-highest grade point average in her group during junior year (in 1940).[31] Evelyn's parents were Italian-born, and she had one sibling. Her father was a general laborer, but both of her parents had completed grammar school. Evelyn said that she wanted to be a bookkeeper and attend business college after high school, but she was uncertain whether this would be possible "because of financial conditions." Still, she expressed confidence that her coursework would enable her to get a good job. Her parents were both reportedly "enthusiastic about her plans" and "confident in her ability." She said that they "encouraged her in many ways before and during high school" and "were insistent on her doing her home work." Movies on school nights were forbidden by her parents, who believed that it would interfere with her schoolwork. Although she did not participate in extracurricular activities, Evelyn said that she derived a "great deal of satisfaction in having many friends" and surrounded herself with a group that "regard[ed] good work in school as important."[32]

Evelyn was not unique. One of the most attractive aspects of high school was its social experience, which lent students a feeling of security in "being themselves" and a sense of having things in common with their peers. Thus "making friends," "having many friends," and having "classmates think well of you" were mentioned overwhelmingly (by 70 percent to 79 percent of all students) as being of significant importance among all the attractions of high school.[33] Indeed, apart from the urgings of teachers and parents to perform well in school, this social dimension—which included participation in some out-of-classroom social or friendship group—was cited by many students as an undeniable influence on their decision to attend high school.[34]

Teens like Frank, David, and Evelyn embodied the quiet transformation of American education in the first third of the twentieth century, a transformation that was led in important respects by changes in working-class parents' and children's estimations of the value of extended schooling. This new regard for schooling was perhaps best expressed by a mother, who, pondering why she thought her children should go to high school, remarked, "We all want our children to have the best we are able to give them, because if we don't we'd be afraid we hadn't done what we should for them."[35] While before the 1920s "the best" that working-class parents could offer their children had only exceptionally included a high school education, it would be a mistake to view the incorporation of a high school diploma into working-class family aspirations solely as a symbol of achievement. The establishment of high school education as a realistic aspiration represented aims previously realized within the working class by other means. Ambitions suffocated by the de-skilling of labor and segmentation of work—ambitions such as advancement into a supervisory position, stable employment, and the esteem of one's peers—might be reinvigorated through schooling in a precarious and rapidly changing economy (see fig. 7.3).

Did working-class children and their parents recognize the disjunction between the nature and increasing length of their schooling and their

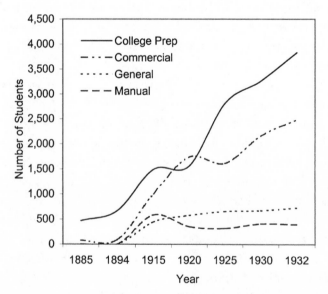

Fig. 7.3 Curriculum of New Haven secondary school students, 1885–1932. *Source:* McConnell, *Evolution of Social Classes,* tables 17 and 18, p. 225

chances to fit themselves into an unpredictable and unmerciful economy? It seems unlikely. As we will see, it appears instead that parents and youths generally absorbed the principle that schooling enlarged individual opportunity without bias; its gender- and class-based contours were either too obscure to perceive or simply ignored as irrelevant to their more limited aims. The idea of prolonged schooling as a key to advancement was a middle-class conception, and it brought the greatest rewards to those who knew how to exploit it. Extended to many working-class Americans during the 1920s and 1930s, this notion was neither well understood nor necessarily welcomed by all working-class parents—immigrant parents in particular.

As we have seen, the number and kinds of students who attended high school by the 1920s and 1930s were inspired to extend their schooling by changes in attitudes toward the utility of education, but they were linked as well to changes in the way that schooling was structured—what it offered vocationally and how this education was organized. The industrial education movement at the turn of the century was one clear source of organizational change. The rise in demand for commercial and business courses furnished the other and ultimately exerted a stronger pressure to reshape secondary schooling. The development of separate schools for these purposes in New Haven has a history both distinct from, and strikingly similar to, those of other northeastern cities, but the eventual unification of the secondary curriculum into a comprehensive offering of all forms of post–grammar school education under one roof reflected most broadly the steadily rising demand for schooling of all types during the years of adolescence.[36]

What came to be known as the comprehensive high school attracted many students into New Haven's high schools who a decade earlier would have joined their kin in New Haven's factories when they turned fourteen. From today's perspective, accustomed as we are to a system of education that transparently reproduces the inequities of class and race, there seems a kind of inevitability about the role of the comprehensive high school in ossifying the social differences latent in American society. Initially, however, the comprehensive high school masked differentiations among students that were explicit and recognizable when secondary schools purposely promoted specialized training for clerical work or for industrial trades. As Jeannie Oakes has suggested, in much of the nation such distinctions were politically unacceptable to various interest groups and contrary to the egalitarian philosophy of public education in the United States. But in New Haven, for a time, both Commercial High School and Boardman Trade School attracted students who regarded some sort of practical education as preferable to none, because the alternative was to follow parents and siblings into the grit, physical exhaustion, and uncertain employment that was the life of a semi-skilled factory worker.

In addition to the real constraints imposed by educators upon students deemed "fit" for one kind of course of study or another, the system often appeared more flexible than it was. Secondary schooling seemed more ready to adjust the curriculum to the needs, ambitions, and abilities of the individual student, more subtle in its effectiveness at distinguishing students from one another, and more encouraging in its capacity to enable them to distinguish among themselves, than in fact it really was. As we have already seen, educators often applied crude, misguided assessments of their students by equating attributes such as socio-economic status, race, or ethnicity with low academic potential or a lack of ambition. And as we will see, school officials also often pre-emptively channeled pupils to Commercial or Hillhouse high schools based on parental socioeconomic status, family size, ethnicity, and the perceived involvement of parents in children's education. Although it is impossible to determine retrospectively the extent to which youths "selected themselves" for Commercial or Hillhouse, decisive differences marked enrollments at each school, and there is sufficient anecdotal evidence to conclude that teachers and administrators played a significant role in sending students to one school or the other (see figs. 7.4 and 7.5).[37]

Their self-confidence in wielding such judgments was matched by the minute discriminations they made in the content of the curriculum across six "tracks" or courses of study. To be sure, as Katherine Lebow has observed, the works of Shakespeare, for instance, were taught to all New Haven high school students except those enrolled in Boardman Trade School. Nonetheless, trivial adjustments were made in the way Shakespeare's plays were combined in the curriculum: "While Classical

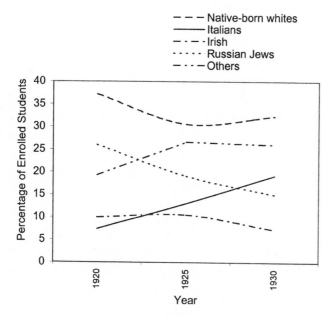

Fig. 7.4 Ethnic composition of Hillhouse High School, 1920–30. *Source:* New Haven, *Annual Reports,* 1920–30

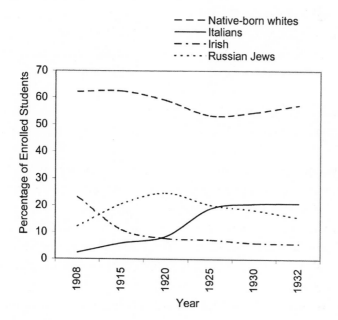

Fig. 7.5 Ethnic composition of Hillhouse High School, 1908–32. *Source:* New Haven, *Annual Reports,* 1908–32

students read *Twelfth Night, Julius Caesar, As You Like It,* and *Macbeth,* Academic students read *A Midsummer Night's Dream, Richard III, Romeo and Juliet,* and *Macbeth.* Students in the Boys' Manual course read only three plays to everyone else's four and so on."[38] As I have already noted, for many students such gradations mattered greatly. Curricular streams refracted the palpable socioeconomic, family, and ethnic differences encountered in their daily lives. Where young people were headed and how they thought about their aspirations shaped the way they perceived themselves and one another, and so curricular choices were consequential both experientially in the present and materially in the future.

Since the inception of high school in the mid-nineteenth century, girls had consistently enrolled in and completed high school at significantly higher rates than boys. However, as high school expanded between 1900 and 1940, and this gap narrowed, curricular choices continued to reflect gender differences. During the first three decades of the twentieth century the proportion of students enrolling in the commercial course of study grew at the expense of all other curricular offerings, and it remained the most popular choice among high school students in New Haven from 1914 through World War II.[39] In 1915 the Commercial track was extended from three years to four, awarding diplomas for the first time in 1916, when it claimed about four of every ten graduates. In 1920 Commercial High School was constructed to accommodate the curriculum's growing popularity.[40]

By 1933 boys' graduation rates began to pull even with that of girls for the first time. But the distribution of girls and boys in New Haven's two high schools significantly affected the tone and content of each school. Throughout the 1930s approximately three-quarters of all Commercial High School students were female, whereas Hillhouse enjoyed a more equal distribution of male and female students.[41] The ethnic composition of each school also varied greatly. Yet working-class boys entering and finishing high school in these years, unlike their sisters, did not generally receive the kind of technical training in high school that could lead directly to a job. A confluence of long-term changes contributed to the elision of any recognizable route to a career in manual trades of working-class boys.

Apprenticeship, the traditional route to skilled employment, had been in decline since at least the mid-nineteenth century.[42] Craft unions had controlled apprenticeships as a way of certifying workmen's skills and instilling proper attitudes toward work but also as a means of restricting the number of entrants in training so that the pool of craftsmen in any given trade would remain below a level that could drive down the price of skilled labor. By the end of the century, however, mechanization and the consequent segmentation of production into discrete tasks had rendered apprenticeship virtually obsolete. Mastery of every aspect of the manufacture of many products was no longer necessary or even possible. Technical competence in specialized parts of the production process became the wave of the future as younger workers increasingly received training offered, not by master craftsmen, but by employers who established their own schools to supply labor to their shops and factories.[43]

City and state boards of education also developed trade schools to counter the demise of apprenticeship, but in practice the trade schools, which were to provide post–grammar school training for adolescents, were kept at arm's length both by the trade unions and by educators.[44] Trade unions disdained the quality of training trade schools offered and viewed them as inimical to controlling the flow of skilled workers into the labor market.[45] Teachers in the secondary schools, on the other hand, often looked upon trade school pupils as those who could not make it at Hillhouse or Commercial High School—and so regarded trade school pupils as "already . . . defeated in social and economic competition."[46] As formal manual skills training was disparaged all around, no viable access to the trades rose up to meet the path of working-class boys comparable to that which greeted their sisters in the working class or the boys and girls of the middle class.

Whatever emerging foundation of faith in schooling lay beneath the rise of high school enrollment during the 1920s and 1930s, then, should be considered in view of a lingering wariness among working-class parents that extended schooling attenuated youths' taste for getting a living: in addition to the white-collar skills that youths were supposed to learn in high school, to many parents it appeared that young people also learned to shun hard or ill-paying work, physical labor, sacrifice, and family obligation. "I've been wondering this past winter whether an education was a good thing after all," confessed one mother: "My boy has gone through high school and he has been educated above taking low wages, but that's all he can get now so he does nothing. The boys who quit school at the end of the eighth grade are willing to start low down and work up, but high-school graduates are too good for that. They used to say that an education helped you to get ahead, but since this depression I wonder if it doesn't put the brakes on them."[47]

Because the Depression kept many youths in school who, in a healthy economic climate, would have left school to work, the new tendency to continue in school after eighth grade masked a certain amount of latent suspicion about the value of education (see fig. 7.6). This skepticism had two aspects: first, a patent indifference to schooling by youths; second, a positive valuation of the "school of hard knocks" more often expressed by parents. The tendency of youths in the general course, for instance, to passively reject the grading system or to dismiss the content of their coursework as meaningless typified one response.[48] To engage this growing group of youths, educators during the 1920s and 1930s continually

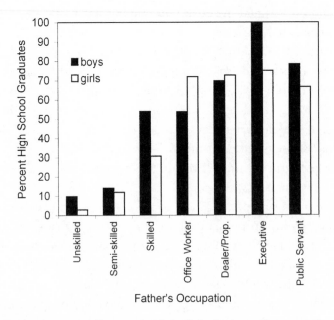

Fig. 7.6 Graduation rates of boys and girls by father's occupation, 1933. *Source:* McConnell, *Evolution of Social Classes,* tables 17 and 18

urged the schools to adopt a more vocationally oriented curriculum: machine shop practice, woodworking, printing, cabinet-making, mechanical and free-hand drawing, applied design, dressmaking, millinery, sewing, cooking, and home economics.[49]

The alternative, positive aspect of this skepticism was recorded by E. Wight Bakke in his rounds among New Haven's workers during the 1930s. "Not all workers had the idea that 'schooling' was the only proper form of education for children," he observed. Among Italians especially, there was a "thorough feeling that schooling was a poor substitute for the educational values of work."[50] A carpenter pointedly advanced this view when he asked rhetorically, "What do you learn when you go to school?" He continued: "Do you learn how to manage people? . . . Do you learn how to work all day? No, of course you don't! When you go to school it's the teacher that manages you. She makes you do what she wants, and as for making money, what you learn in the books won't help you much. I claim my kid is learning more when he is shining shoes than when he is in that brick building there."[51] Such staunch pragmatism, as David Montgomery has shown, had deep roots in the shop culture of artisanal tradition, which, even in the twilight of the apprenticeship system at the end of the nineteenth century, upheld the "superiority of practical training over purely scholastic training."[52] The concern that children, and especially boys, learn to "work all day" is shot through Bakke's surveys of attitudes toward economic relief among New Haven's unemployed families during the mid-1930s. In families in which both parents were unemployed and where there was also a young man living at home, parents commonly expressed a desire that work relief be allotted to the young man. Such sentiments arose, concluded Bakke, "from a recognition of the real danger that young men without work discipline would continue to be an increasing problem in the family as the depression wore on."[53]

Relations between bosses and workers, Montgomery reminds us, were often "intensely personal" during the nineteenth century, when small shops were the rule and even later, after the turn of the century, when inside contracting arose in large manufacturing plants.[54] Much like office workers, manual workers during the 1930s were likely to mention "personal contacts" and "pull" as key to job security and promotion.

A critical instrument in every worker's toolbox, then, was the kind of adroitness in "managing people" to which Bakke's carpenter alluded. Techniques ranging from outright bribery of the foreman or union agent to more subtle personal acts of consideration cultivated informal ties between a worker and his or her boss that could mean the difference between failure and success.[55] And perhaps getting ahead may have depended even more heavily on these means after craft-based criteria for promotion were shouldered aside by mechanization and scientific management.[56] Therefore, while the importance of social skills in manual labor may have been undiminished by changes in the scale and organization of production, the development of such skills was also believed by some to be actively inhibited by formal education. According to the carpenter who so vividly juxtaposed the merits of book-learning and shoe-shining, "learning to work all day" was just half of what working taught. Learning how to manage people was another part of the equation.

Social skills of this nature were more commonly associated by middle-class parents with the less tangible (and often more informal) aspects of secondary and higher education, which points up the distinctiveness of this man's notion of what it was that one "learned-by-doing."[57] Nevertheless, a truck driver who hoped to have his own business one day expressed an arrestingly similar attitude toward his children's schooling: "My kids will probably never get much education, just like me. But I'll see that they learn anyway. I want them to start now, whether it be shining shoes or selling papers, and learn how to manage and meet people. That's what counts."[58] The kinds of social and other skills one acquired in school, then, were at least *perceived* by many working-class parents and youths as only very uneasily transferred to the industrial workplace or even to the running of a small business.

By contrast, the personal attributes that the designers of high school curricula valued and strove to develop—including the types of social and intellectual exercises encouraged through extracurricular activities—were consonant with qualities that white-collar employers were apt to seek out and reward: facility in speech and writing, general knowledgeability, poise, leadership ability, concern for one's appearance, affability, and self-confidence. Asked what criteria determined success in high school, students in a high school in suburban New Haven in 1940 mentioned the following attitudes and behaviors one or more times: good conduct; sincere, helpful, and responsible attitudes; getting along well with teachers and classmates; having a good reputation; securing a high degree of actual learning; developing a "pleasing personality"; demonstrating a high degree of cooperation; success in extracurricular activities; winning teachers' respect; success after high school; enjoying a degree of peer popularity; having valued experiences; preparation for a future career; possessing a degree of self-confidence; good citizenship; and hard work.[59] As high school was expanded, these goals were restricted primarily to the academic and commercial curricular tracks. The general course appeared to serve no one in particular, but it did arise at a time when a high school diploma of any stripe was accepted as certification of a person's ability to learn. In a rapidly changing industrial regime, this aspect of high school training was apparently increasingly desirable to employers, who wanted workers that could be shifted from job to job as needed. For mechanization had created highly specialized tasks that required speedy learners who could master new skills on the job.[60] It is a truism of labor history that employers at the turn of the century required workers with the intelligence to learn quickly, but not so much education that they would become bored and dissatisfied with their work and desert their jobs. By the 1940s this had changed, however. In a study conducted immediately after World War II, Bakke found that employers in New Haven listed a high school education as among nine characteristics they sought in what they considered to be the "ideal" worker. High school had become a kind of guarantor of native intelligence (and so, adaptability) as well as evidence of workers' self-discipline, persistence, and "character."[61]

By the 1930s many working-class parents in New Haven looked to high school as a route to steadier, better-paying jobs for their children than the older path of early school-leaving and on-the-job-training. As one worker remarked about the desirability of sending his children to high school, "You know damned well you're never going to be any great shakes. But you're an important guy, leastwise in your own mind if your kids can go places."[62] Others reasoned that the short-term expense incurred while children were in school was a fair exchange for the enhancement of their income-earning potential and employability. Although episodes of parental pressure on adolescents to earn were common, one man, a meat packer, concluded that once his daughter had begun earning her own paycheck she might be tempted to forgo any further schooling and endanger her chances of finding a good job: "My daughter has another year to go at Commercial [High School]. You can get jobs easier from there. She wanted to work this summer but I'm glad she didn't get [a job]. Her friend got a job and now she doesn't want to leave to go back to school. . . . I guess we can put up with another year's expense so she can get a better job when she gets out."[63]

Even more pronounced than the socioeconomic biases at work in secondary schooling was the expression of gender in what students put into and got out of high school. The rewards of the new high school, as John Modell and J. Trent Alexander have shown, were "intrinsic" for girls and "consequential" for boys: what girls brought to high school in the way of parents' socioeconomic status and good looks, they have found, mattered decidedly more than it did for boys, whose high school experience hinged to a greater degree on what they "took" from it. "For boys, the academic realm offered special possibilities for future payoff and thus posed special challenges." The curricular tracks they chose and how they performed strongly affected whether they were to attend college and how they would fare later in life.[64] But male or female, for many there was no family precedent, no living model from which to fashion the kind of work career that required a high school diploma. Instead, a more nebulous notion of the utility of extended schooling existed in the minds of parents; a conception pieced together from the work experiences of family and friends shaped ideas of how schooling improved their children's life chances. "Get your kids in good jobs—they hear of better jobs for the rest of your kids—and sometimes for you. That's what I says."[65] A munitions worker at Winchester seconded this sentiment: "Lucky is the man who can get his daughter into the office. That takes knowing something, though."[66]

According to McConnell, to varying degrees, parents of all occupations recognized education as "the principal means of rising from one occupational group to another."[67] In 1933 more than 68 percent of the children of office workers, dealers and proprietors, and artisans remained in school beyond eighth grade, continuing a trend established from the inception of public secondary schooling in New Haven during the nineteenth century.[68] Office workers' children surpassed all others. More than three-quarters of them had had some high school and 69 percent received diplomas.[69] By contrast, between 68 percent and 80 percent of the children of "laborers" (which, in McConnell's classification, referred to any unskilled, wage-earning, manual worker) advanced no further than grammar school. Nevertheless, and despite the fact that "many parents questioned the actual value of the things 'children learn in school these days,'" according to McConnell, "only a few [parents] did not realize that education in itself, regardless of specific subject matter, carried great social significance." These "few skeptics" of schooling were most conspicuous among first-generation Italian immigrants and the dealer and proprietor group, generally. While we have already explored the nature of Italian immigrant parents' attitudes toward education, the lack of enthusiasm by small businessmen for their sons' education, according to McConnell, could be explained by a customary reliance on sons to "carry a share of the responsibility" in running their affairs.[70] Yet all parents seem to have expressed at least a desire to "place children on a higher economic plane by means of education." And for some, he wrote, this stride was "sufficiently important . . . to warrant . . . extreme sacrifices," though not all parents were able to help their children realize such aspirations.[71]

Motives for staying in school reflected a high school population more diverse than at any time in the past. Clearly some youths were simply biding their time, while others, as already indicated, directly linked a high school diploma in the commercial course with expanding employment possibilities. Then, of course, there were the traditional consumers of high school: middle- and upper-class college-bound youths. The "well-positioned," as Claudia Goldin has shown, schooled both sons and daughters even though "it is not at all clear that such education enhanced their income." Among those who clearly chose to be in school, opportunities were differently understood and differently exploited.[72] When asked what parents "wanted their children to gain by higher education," wage-earners and dealers and proprietors placed equal emphasis upon the importance of schooling in securing better jobs and a higher standard of living for their children.[73] Just as parents recognized that education bestowed a kind of social status upon their children, they also seem to have believed that a diploma in the academic curricular track without a subsequent college degree had little practical value. The decision to enroll in the commercial or the general course rather than in the academic course was made in light of the odds that a family would not be able to put a daughter or son through college as well.

Office workers, though not unmindful of these considerations, placed more stress on the ability of their children to make "better personal contacts" through schooling.[74] This difference in emphasis was demonstrated as well in the curricular choices of the sons and daughters of these two groups. These choices, even more than boys' and girls' levels of educational attainment, furnish telling examples of how class perceptions of schooling were also gender inflected. While office workers wanted their children to take the academic track, parents in the wage-earning and dealer and proprietor groups continued to emphasize commercial training, an orientation even more pronounced among working-class daughters, who remained in school longer than their male counterparts but enrolled overwhelmingly in commercial courses. Apart from artisans' children, a higher percentage of girls than boys in working-class families received post-secondary education of some kind.

Although, according to McConnell, parents in both the wage-earning and dealer and proprietor groups recognized the advantage of the academic course "from the social point of view," often "economic necessity require[d] that the cultural values of higher education be subordinated to occupational training."[75] However, such "cultural values"—even when wanted—were as yet beyond the means of most working-class youths, many of whom were the first members of their families to finish, or even to enter, high school.[76] As one man, a trucker, said of his daughter, "She's taking Commercial for I guess that's the best when it don't look like she would have a chance to go to college. If things had held out I wanted her to go, and if I get a break even now I might send her. But we have so many debts."[77] Those financially able to support girls' efforts in school were rewarded by steering them toward the more conservative and vocational commercial track. As we have already seen, women who graduated from Commercial High School during the 1930s far surpassed their female peers at Hillhouse in total earnings, number of hours worked, proportion of full-time jobs held, and fewest days involuntarily unemployed.[78]

Even in the face of such apparent good fortune, almost a third of these Commercial High School graduates said they had regretted not having taken the academic course. Some reported that out in the business world the commercial course was considered "not socially acceptable," while others complained of simply feeling "inferior" for having graduated from Commercial High School.[79] Alberta Roseman, who graduated from Hillhouse in 1929, casually expressed the claim to superiority enjoyed by Hillhouse students over their peers at Commercial High School when she remarked sixty years later that "if you were over at Commercial, you were beneath the Hillhouse girls or boys. . . . In other words, you weren't college material." Yet Roseman also conceded the usefulness of the commercial diploma by commenting: "They were the smart ones, . . . We who prepared for the college course really came out unprepared to *do* anything."[80] The consensus among commercial graduates, however, was that they could have done better for themselves had they absorbed the lessons in "culture," "taste," "personality," and "poise" imparted by the academic course and then obtained technical training in a short course after high school.[81] To understand the aspirations of these women, one must read between the lines. Given the blunted career paths confronting educated women of the period, it seems unlikely that the sense of disappointment among these women stemmed from having denied themselves promising careers.[82] Rather, it seems more likely that they felt disadvantaged in the white-collar marriage market. Their technical skills had encouraged fantasies of "marrying up," yet the nuances of middle-class culture—summed up by them in words they used to describe what they felt lacking in themselves, such as "taste," "culture," and "personality"—remained elusive.

A fundamental difference in outlook shaped the expectations of parents whose daughters and sons enrolled in the academic course. For McConnell this difference found succinct expression in the conviction that the academic track in high school, and in turn a college degree, ensured access to the "personal contacts" necessary for success. In the white-collar world, he observed, nothing was "left to chance" where social connections were concerned: "Agents . . . salesmen and junior executives" all asserted that membership in a city social club, political club, fraternal organization, and even the "right" church was "essential to their business success." An insurance agent epitomized this outlook, when commenting that "it doesn't make much difference to God where I worship, and if I can sell more insurance by joining one church rather than another, why not?"[83]

Such concerns reflected more, however, than a simple belief in the efficacy of knowing the right people. After all, as some commercial graduates intimated, an important part of the academic course was schooling in manners, affect, and social ease. Indeed, the "better job" and the "ability to enjoy the better things of life" that parents of commercial students hoped to secure for their children could largely be taken for granted by those enrolled in the academic course. Whereas vocation-minded parents would ask school officials, "Will this education help . . . [my son] get work when he is finished?," white-collar parents would ask, "What class of students do you have here?"[84] What many white-collar parents desired for their children was a winning personal disposition in a professional milieu that appeared at once capricious and manipulable: On one hand, favoritism was believed to figure heavily in personal success, but it also introduced a sense of arbitrariness into the white-collar promotion process. On the other hand, since it was believed that success could be enhanced by judiciously cultivating the interests of one's superiors, a pleasing personality, responsiveness, initiative, and an ability to get along with others could go far toward mitigating caprice, turning favoritism to one's advantage.[85]

Were curricular choices most often imposed by parents? McConnell's and Bakke's interviewees generally assumed so. But how much did youths themselves decide their course of study, and what was the nature of the schools' involvement in shaping these choices? Unfortunately, these questions can be addressed only with scattered, anecdotal evidence; no comprehensive study was ever made of how parents and children arrived at curricular decisions. Clearly, though, some parents held (and articulated) strong opinions about choosing one kind of curriculum over another. Other parents seem to have reached an accord with their children over an appropriate course of study after discussion and negotiation. Still others were entirely indifferent to, or ignorant of, the choices to be exercised. Parents unfamiliar with, or unattuned to, the operation of the schools probably relied upon teachers and school administrators to match their children with a particular course of study. The public schools did so routinely, if often recklessly.

In a grammar school in one of the city's poorest, most crowded, and overwhelmingly Italian communities—a school whose pupils consistently scored 5 percent below the city mean on achievement tests—pupils were described as "apathetic," and their parents so absorbed with the struggle for subsistence that they had little energy or interest left at the end of the day to aid their children in schoolwork. Many parents were said to regard the schoolhouse as little more than a "safe place to send the children to get them out of the home."[86] "Most of the teachers," the same report continued, "seemed to be good sports, and . . . doing their best . . . [but] appeared to consider that, at best, they could not expect to produce results with these children that would be appreciable." Their style of teaching seemed "in general stereotyped and unstimulating," and the teachers themselves were uninspiring and showed little "genuine enthusiasm in their work."[87] Although most of the ten- and eleven-year-olds interviewed at this school expressed an intention to attend high school and aspired to vocations requiring a diploma, few were deemed by teachers as capable of achieving such goals.[88]

In this school, as in grammar schools and junior high schools throughout the city, children were guided into curricular tracks through a combination of formal counseling and teacher assessments of their aptitudes and inclinations. Homeroom teachers in the middle schools were, according to one study, "often able to advise a pupil as to the occupation for which he or she appear[ed] best suited" by recording each pupil's "essential characteristics" and "vocational bent."[89] The same study found that counselors in New Haven's grammar schools advised "low mentality" students to steer clear of the "college" (academic) course at Hillhouse High School so as not to be overmatched scholastically when promoted to grades 9 and 10.[90]

Yet underachievers and students who fell into the below-average range on standardized tests were not the only pupils discouraged by educators from aiming high. At a junior high school in the Fair Haven neighborhood students were systematically discouraged from attempting the academic track when promoted to New Haven's high schools because their parents were typically low-income earners and working class.[91]

Nick Aiello, whose parents were both born in Italy, grew up in Wooster Square, adjacent to Fair Haven. Aiello was one of the younger children in a family of fourteen girls and boys. Seven of his sisters and three brothers quit school at age thirteen or fourteen to work in the Wooster Square shirt shops.[92] His father was on relief periodically throughout the Depression, and his brothers, when unemployed, worked for the Works Progress Administration or Civilian Conservation Corps. Aiello wore "charity shoes," he remembered—shoes given to his family by city relief agencies. Everyone knew their distinctive shape, where they came from, and what they signified. Aiello attended Columbus grammar school and received high marks. He wanted to go to college and dreamed of being a doctor, but both the guidance counselor and the school principal took him aside and told him he "was not academically inclined."[93] When he informed them of his ambitions, they said, "Your family is on . . . [relief] . . . , you'll never go to college. . . . Why waste time on the academic course?" So they placed him in the high school's commercial course when he graduated from Columbus. "They used to have the power to tell you what course you're going to take," reflected Aiello. After receiving honors in the business course (a subset of the commercial track, for boys) during his first year at Hillhouse High, Aiello transferred to the academic course. While wartime military service and family obligations ultimately prevented him from going to college, he was the only one in his family to graduate from high school. In a perverse application of the same logic, African-American students were usually steered toward Hillhouse. Reasoning that no one would hire an African American in sales or clerical occupations (an assumption borne out by occupational statistics during the same period), Hortense Powdermaker and Joseph Semper found that "negroes are discouraged by vocational directors from taking commercial training."[94]

Perhaps the surest sign that high school had become a normative experience—one that any young person could expect to undertake—was the deepening indifference of teens toward their classroom performance on one hand, and a congealing pragmatism in curricular selection on the other. A survey conducted by the New Haven Chamber of Commerce in 1936 revealed that among boys in their senior year in the city's secondary schools, the largest fraction, a little more than one-third, hoped one day to work in some kind of professional occupation, the next largest group of respondents, however, more than one-quarter of all polled, stated that they did not know what kind of occupation or career they hoped to pursue. This survey captures the essence of public high school during the 1930s: partly it served the interests of its traditional constituency and some part of its new adherents had no clear idea what lay beyond schooling for them (see fig. 7.7).[95]

Similarly, a study of high school students in a New Haven suburb at the end of the decade—a district that, until the mid-1930s, had sent its high school–aged pupils to the New Haven school system—offers a revealing glimpse of the kinds of pupils that swelled its commercial and general courses during this period. All 336 subjects of the study were juniors, 55 percent were girls. In each of the three curricular courses offered, boys or girls clearly predominated, which indicated pronounced curricular preferences by gender.[96]

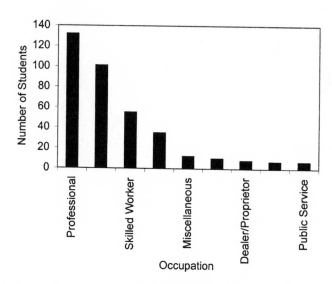

Fig. 7.7 Occupational choices of senior males in New Haven schools, 1936. *Source:* McConnell, *Evolution of Social Classes,* 98. Compiled from a study known as the "Landcraft Survey," conducted by the New Haven Chamber of Commerce in 1936, the survey was a sampling of all male seniors in any of New Haven's public secondary schools

The academic track, which enrolled 48 percent of the junior class, came closest to gender parity with 92 girls (57.5 percent) and 68 boys (42.5 percent). But in the commercial course (one-third of all juniors) girls were nearly three-quarters of all enrollees, 82 out of 112 students. The general course seems to have functioned as the male equivalent of the commercial course: just one-fifth (64 students) of the junior class was enrolled in the general course, but boys outnumbered girls by a ratio of four to one. The commercial and general courses served similar functions in that they certified a student's capacity to learn while providing a curriculum more relevant to job skills than the academic track.

Overall, almost twice as many girls reported working near to "their capacity in school subjects" than did boys; and girls also declared a greater interest in continuing their education beyond high school. Seventy-seven percent of girls said they would go to college, business, nursing, or secretarial school, compared with 66 percent of the boys. In the academic course girls outperformed boys, on average, receiving "decidedly better marks" overall. Among all the groups in the junior class, this one was most sensitive to the stigma of poor or average grades. The girls in this group expressed the deepest dissatisfaction with receiving a grade of "C" for their work. By contrast, girls in the general course (a mere 10 percent of all girls in the junior class) believed more strongly than any other group that grades were an undesirable way of encouraging scholastic performance.[97] Girls in the commercial course marginally outperformed commercial boys, while there was little difference between the scores of girls and boys in the general course.[98] While most commercial students said they would be unhappy with a "C" grade, "more of them [than in the academic course] thought it was not a bad thing . . . , [that] it was at least respectable and was a point of inspiration in working harder for a better grade."[99]

Most striking, however, was the positive attitude general students expressed about average marks, indicating a reluctance to participate wholeheartedly in the reward system of schooling. As one boy said, "'C' is just right because it's not high nor low." Another student stated that an average mark is good "because it's passing and [I] cannot afford to go to college so I'll have to work when I leave school anyway." A third elaborated on this rationale even further, declaring that he could "do better" than a "C" but that he "didn't feel much like it, . . . [because] it doesn't always get you where you want to go. Take college students for example, you see a lot of them just digging didges [*sic*]. You take a high school graduate and he'll have a better job than the other fellow."[100] In other words, working for good grades was pointless if one had no intention of continuing beyond the high school level. A high school diploma itself was deemed desirable but the actual work one did in high school had no intrinsic value and the estimation of one's performance in the classroom, short of failure, was meaningless in the world "outside."[101]

While the 1930s was an era of self-conscious expansion in secondary education, it was also a period in which the aims of high school were stratified to accommodate the new needs of a more diverse student body. High school was shedding its elitism, and in the process its mission began to reflect a constituency more instrumentalist in outlook. At the same time the institution's growing inclusiveness initiated among those previously denied a high school education a quest to exploit the opportunity it presented to cross class boundaries. This was, ironically, more immediately true for girls, who by obtaining clerical skills moved into the margins of white-collar social and commercial spheres. Yet their gender also precluded direct and more meaningful participation in middle-class occupations, which remained the preserve of males. By the same token, while working-class boys (by virtue of their gender) met the minimum criterion for movement into the middle class through occupational mobility, they differed in personal outlook, training, and material resources and thus lacked the disposition necessary to join the ranks of businessmen, managers, bureaucrats, and professionals.

The impressive expansion of secondary education after World War I must be viewed in the context of the general and even more dramatic ascent of the rate of high school graduation among all groups in the United States during the first half of the twentieth century. Between 1900 and 1940 the proportion of seventeen-year-olds graduating from high school shot up from 6.4 percent to 50.8 percent, an eight-fold increase that solidified the belief that high school was within the reach of all youths. Indeed, the fabulous rise of extended schooling in so short a time span made the high school diploma a desirable if not indispensable credential for most occupations in the United States by midcentury. It mattered little that the skills learned in secondary schooling, for many, had not much to do with the actual work performed by graduates after high school. In the new economy of the mid-twentieth century, a high school education certified one's capacity to learn rather than mastery of a particular skill, and in an era of widespread de-skilling in the industrial occupations, adaptability rather than craftsmanship or expertise became the most marketable of assets to those selling their labor.

High school had triumphed where trade schools and scientific management had failed, in that it rewarded the very kind of tractability that employers desired in their workers. Despite ill-defined (or unarticulated) reasons for staying in school, those who did benefited handsomely in the most general way. Gary S. Becker has shown that private rates of return on education after 1939 rewarded high school graduates relatively better than either college graduates or those with fewer than twelve years of school. While private rates of return for college graduates, for instance, remained essentially unchanged from 1940 to 1960, the rate of return for high school graduates rose over the same period by about 75 percent. Although the evidence from before 1939, Becker says, is unreliable, it is believed that the differential rates of return for high school and elementary school graduates widened significantly between the 1920s and the 1950s.[102]

By the 1930s, Viviana A. Zelizer has argued, children were "sacralized" across class lines as they became both "economically useless" and "emotionally priceless." "Children occupied a special and separate world," she finds, "regulated by affection and education, not work or profit."[103] Certainly the elevation of the age of compulsory schooling, a successful national campaign against child labor, and declining opportunities for juvenile labor combined to diminish the instrumental value of children. However, although Zelizer properly locates the direction of change in working-class family relations, she overestimates the swiftness with which this sentimentalizing trend was adopted by working-class parents. A widely shared perplexity and antagonism among parents confronted with children who challenged their sense of generational prerogative calls into question Zelizer's contention that sacralization had penetrated the core utilitarian concerns of working-class parents by the 1930s.

In searching for the origins of our own era, developments that ultimately eclipsed ways of being and thinking that now seem shortsighted and difficult to comprehend, historians tend to overlook the significance of the order that lay beneath the surface of change. As significant as the growth of secondary schooling was, it is also important to underscore the fact that for many of education's new adherents, the link between the credential of high school and avenues to more remunerative or gratifying forms of work was only dimly perceived. For still others—the "unconverted"—formal education continued to bear little or no relation to success in life. One researcher who studied the growing group of young people whose interest in school was tenuous at best tersely summed up the attitude of one student by heading her case study with the following synopsis: "Case VI—Boy . . . Italian Parentage . . . Driving force: None. Family indifferent. Boy felt that since there was no job in sight, he might as well stay in school."[104] To a significant, albeit declining segment of working-class youths, both the coin and content of high school were insubstantial or even appeared as a kind of hoax designed to mislead the unsuspecting. Yet high school and adolescence had become permanently inextricable, an experience that any young person could expect to undergo. Thus, parents whose children were the first in their families to attend high school executed a giant leap of faith when they sent their sons and daughters off to high school.

While for many the future of a high school–educated child was believed to be brighter and more secure than their own lives had been or better than the occupational prospects confronting young people without a diploma, the signposts to that future were not easily apprehended, especially in the midst of the greatest economic disaster in U.S. history. A major unforeseen consequence of the democratization of high school, then, was an implicit exchange: in effect, working-class parents surrendered their faith in the past for the promise of a more affluent future for their children, however obscure the path and indefinite the attainment secured in the bargain. And yet an irony inhered in the exchange. While fathers no longer held the key to their sons' occupational futures as they once had (no longer could they pass along occupational skills to their sons), neither reliably did teachers, to whom responsibility for the transmission of analogous skills had devolved in the new economy. No clear course, then, no concrete sense of the future existed that held out the prospect of greater affluence for high school youths. So the *peer* world became key to defining "self," supplanting the family, and father in particular. As high school became the average experience for youths, families began to relinquish the ability to define the young person's identity, aspirations, obligations, and values in the belief that they were exchanging the power to mold adolescents for the vague prospect of upward social mobility, security, and comfort. But the power that was compromised, even given over, went "nowhere": it did not go to educators; rather, it was effectively yielded up to the peer groups that developed in high school. This was a realm over which parents and educators had little control. It was a realm in which being good-looking, athletic, and popular mattered inordinately to success; but the relation of these attributes to a career path was nevertheless uncertain and abstract. And all of this unfolded in the midst of the Great Depression, when father's unemployment was at its own point of crisis.[105]

CONCLUSION: ELM CITY'S YOUTH

Are you prepared to give up your basketball and your baseball, your parties and your little dances, our summer vacations together? Are you ready to give up all the happy things that young people of your age are entitled to? Now don't you be trapped into being an adult.
—Judge Hardy to son Andy on learning that he has proposed marriage to his high school English teacher, in "Andy Hardy Gets Spring Fever"

"The school as it was envisaged by educators and often imagined by historians," Paula S. Fass has cautioned, "was never as powerful an integrator, equalizer, or socializer as it has been portrayed." Rather, she says, "it was one of many institutions operating consecutively and concurrently in students' lives."[1] It is because our expectations of what schools might do to redress the inequities of American society that reformers and historians have focused so narrowly on schooling, obscuring the significance of other institutions in forming young people's social, intellectual, and economic capacities. Other institutions that played, and continue to play, a role in the formation of children are their families, their jobs, their places of worship, and their participation in recreational and social organizations.

The influence of each of these institutions has its own arc: from the end of the Civil War to about 1900 the labor market for children and youths rose precipitously, and from 1900 to 1930 it fell with equal rapidity. The restriction of children's paid labor from the U.S. economy was prerequisite to the rise of schooling as the major, enduring, nonfamilial influence on their growth and socialization. The removal of children's labor from the marketplace in some instances forced manufacturers to change the way that work was organized and persuaded them to invest in technological improvements that allowed them to operate without the benefit of children's labor. The precise interplay of this relationship varied by industry in the United States and was everywhere complicated by other forces, such as the existence and enforcement of compulsory attendance laws, minimum-age and safety legislation, agitation for child labor reform, the scarcity of labor, and the acceleration of diminishing returns on investments in antiquated forms of mechanized production, which also varied by industry and region, as Hugh D. Hindman has recently shown.[2]

As the birthright of every child came to be defined by freedom from work, however, children's participation in organized recreation and play grew dramatically. The playground movement coalesced at the beginning of the twentieth century to impose order on the potential social problems arising from the "enforced idleness" of childhood. Scouting for boys and girls engaged large numbers of children as well. The Boy Scouts of America and, soon after, the Girl Scouts were established during the first two decades of the twentieth century and later spawned feeder organizations (Cub Scouts and Brownies) to involve younger children. Boys and Girls Clubs promoted physical education and adult-supervised social interaction. Organized sports, such as boxing, football, baseball, and basketball, had their beginnings in late-nineteenth-century high school leagues but spread to younger groups of children as these and other sports gained in popularity over the course of the next century. While it is certain that such adult-supervised recreation has included increasingly large numbers and diverse groups of young people for longer periods of their lives, it is not at all clear what affect this has had on their socialization and development.[3]

Despite the popular perception that religiosity has declined significantly during the twentieth century, historians of religion have shown that when compared with the experience of Europe over the same period, Americans' adherence to formal religion has remained relatively robust, as has religious instruction for children and youths.[4] If adult supervision was the anthem of an emerging juvenile civic life by the late nineteenth century, America's major organized religions joined the chorus by cultivating their own youth programs and activity centers. After the Civil War, Protestants founded Young Men's Christian Associations and Young Women's Christian Associations. Jewish Community Centers, which had their origins in Young Hebrew Men's and Women's Associations of the late nineteenth century, provided athletic facilities and gathering places for social activities for Jewish adolescents. In the 1930s Catholics in cities across the nation established Catholic Youth Organizations, which served comparable needs under the direction of both religious and lay adult coordinators.[5]

The relative and changing significance of each of these institutions for children's development, however, has only begun to be explored by historians and social scientists. While we should expect to find that the economy, religious institutions, adult-supervised recreation, and organized sports affected the course of children's growing up to varying degrees (depending on geography, socioeconomic status, race, ethnicity, religion, and gender), the role of schooling in all children's lives has widened decisively since the late nineteenth century. The expansion of these institutions, but of schooling in particular, has often been experienced by parents as coming at the expense of their own influence over, and aspirations for, their children. Indeed, one of the great social and cultural shifts that occurred between the end of the Civil War and the onset of World War II was the concession of children's supervision to institutions other than their families.

Still, as I suggested at the outset, since the very establishment of European settlements on this continent, children's growing up has consistently occurred in settings that involved adults. Whether it was a "little commonwealth" in which the aims of the "state" (that is, those figures in the settlement who laid down and maintained the laws of the community) and the family were in conspicuous agreement, or the growth of the colony outstripped the ability of the community to police its members' mores, nonfamilial adults have complemented the capacities of parents to socialize and educate children. Churches preached to and disciplined their members, masters supervised the labor and learning of servants and apprentices, and neighbors and kin looked out for, nurtured, and admonished one another's children.

What changed after the establishment of universal schooling in the mid-nineteenth century is that these points of contact between adults and children were amplified, made systematic, and even inescapable. With the adoption of standard methods of instruction, curricular content, and the classification of children's mastery of knowledge and social interaction came the establishment of socially recognized age thresholds. The effective enforcement of compulsory school attendance laws by the end of the nineteenth century essentially ensured that every child under the age of fifteen was attending school. Between the turn of the century and the Great Depression the upper limit of this threshold was raised to include children up to the age of sixteen. But even more significantly, the ratio of young people who chose to continue their education beyond the age of compulsory school attendance rose markedly as well. From 1910 to 1930 the percentage of children who left school between grades 5 and 8 (the period during which a child would reach fourteen years of age) declined from 46 percent to 21 percent. During the same two decades the ratio of adolescents who left school between the ages of fourteen and seventeen declined from 28 percent to 12 percent.[6]

This meant that however circumscribed the influence of high school on young people's lives, it was during the 1920s and 1930s that high school became the principal organizing social experience for virtually all adolescents. Even while the curriculum and the extracurriculum (which was increasingly being brought under the direction of adults) may not have wholly delineated the psychological and social worlds of adolescents, high school became the one institution most likely to be encountered by all people between the ages of fourteen and eighteen. Whether adolescents defined themselves in the high school's terms (that is, as competent, intellectually capable, athletic, or physically and personally appealing), or on the contrary, defined themselves *against* it, it was the fact of high school as a collective experience that enabled youth culture to flourish during the decades before and after World War II. Mass participation in high school forced everything young people encountered outside of high school to refer to it in some way. It became a touchstone in the process of growing up. It came to represent, as the physical psychosocial space in which adolescence was enacted, the site, in Judge Hardy's words, of "all the happy things that young people . . . are entitled to," even if in reality, such "happy things" were unevenly distributed under the cope of high school.

Was the triumph of mass high school attendance tantamount to the internalization by working-class families of a sentimental regard for childhood and "child-centered" attitudes and behaviors, as Zelizer has argued? Not entirely: As we have seen, parents yielded to the slackened market for young workers with the same reluctant resignation they adopted when they found themselves without work. The attitudes of many parents toward their children's continuation in school were an admixture of wariness and the glimmer of possibilities that lay beyond the horizon of their own experience and comprehension. Therefore, extended schooling and its developmental complement, adolescence, were most often viewed, it appears, as an inevitability even while they filled many parents with apprehension.

The opportunity costs of extended schooling were obvious and for some families painful, especially as the United States slid into the Great Depression. Yet the associated "cultural" costs were also evident to most immigrant parents, and especially to southern Italians, whose relations to the official, civic culture of their own land had been tenuous and strained. As we have seen, the dismay that working-class and immigrant parents felt about the attitudes their children encountered in the schools was often expressed in a rhetoric of calamity. Their alarm sprang from a sense that the very foundations of their group life, which dwelled in unspoken codes of reciprocity between parents and children, was being invisibly but surely rubbed out. There was, moreover, a cognitive, developmental dimension to young people's coming of age within the walls of high school that contributed to parents' uneasiness. This was reflected in parents' forebodings about the perplexing connections between the alien (and to them repellently permissive) ways of middle-class child-rearing and the rigors of intellectual discipline on one hand and the uncertain utility of formal education on the other.

Antonio Gramsci once noted that learning how to study well requires a "psycho-physical training" that involves "muscles and nerves as well as intellect. It is a process of adaptation, a habit acquired with effort, tedium and even suffering."[7] Just as the child of an urban, middle-class family absorbs attitudes conducive to this "psycho-physical adaptation" more easily than the child of a manual laborer, observed Gramsci, so the "son of a city worker suffers less when he goes to work in a factory than does a peasant's child." "This is why," he explained, "many people think that the difficulty of study conceals some 'trick' which handicaps them—that is, when they do not simply believe that they are stupid by nature."[8]

Italian immigrant parents who themselves had toiled as farm hands or factory workers often eyed schooling with suspicion. The impression that Gramsci conveys about the seeming deception attending the acquisition of skills needed for success in school was widely shared among southern Italians. And it was a double deception: The first entailed the cultivation of skills that rendered "products" of dubious value—for how could mental aptitudes, whether turned to the interpretation of Shakespeare or the mastery of shorthand to take dictation, really be the same as making an article of clothing that you could wear or food that you could put into your mouth for nourishment? The second was a deception of one's self, that to believe that the skills learned in school amounted to "real" work led, it was feared, to the arrest, rather than the promotion, of growth and resolve in young people. School might interfere with, retard, or undo what children were supposed to learn from the chores they did for their parents or kin, or the modest earnings they brought home from the barber shop or bakery—how to work hard, how to spend and save. Attitudes about getting a living, it was felt, were more critical to the course of their lives than any particular skill or body of knowledge.

Schools, like parents, imparted values in the disciplines they imposed. Parents realized this even if their children might not. The school abstracted concepts such as punctuality, industry, and a concern for the value of time. To children the routines of the school day were as concrete as the asphalt of their playgrounds, as seamless as the blackboards that paved the walls of their classrooms, and in time as startlingly familiar as the bell that told them it was time for recess, lunch, or changing classes. But these routines were grounded in a conception of time that represented a stark departure from their parents' sense of time, which—whether molded by the rhythms of planting season and harvest or the percussion of the production line—was based upon a presumption of availability to meet the needs of one's family—*others'* ability to work, the capacity to earn, the necessity for food, clothing, and shelter, and others' health or infirmity.

Schooling beyond the legal minimum was not new to New Haven's Yankees or Irish, who by the turn of the century were politically and socially preeminent; nor was it altogether foreign to newcomers like New Haven's Italian or Polish immigrants, who understood that high school and even college could lead to a profession that could serve the family interests. What *was* new was the conjoining of extended schooling to adolescence. The notion of development as a set of progressive stages of growth with predictable emotional, cognitive, and social dimensions that were universally experienced and sanctioned by society was a powerful, if almost incomprehensible, cultural force to reckon with.

Adolescence, because it was so strongly allied with voluntary schooling beyond the minimum compelled by the state, was the object of special scorn. It was not that southern Italians lacked a conception of development. Learning of *any* kind implies a notion of development. Rather, it was the prescriptive aspect of adolescence that detached youths' cognitive, emotional, and social growth from the imperatives of family need that so disturbed immigrant parents. The creation of a cultural space for individual and social growth as an entitlement apart from the demands of family and kin was at odds with everything that parents had taught their children about the direction and strength of their loyalties; it asked them to *un*learn most everything that parents had taught them to respect and care about.

NOTES

Introduction

1. Vittorio Racca, "A Few Selected Family Histories Describing the Socio-Economic Background of Italians Who Live in New Haven," TS, Institute of Human Relations Collection, box 37, folder 88, unpag., Manuscripts and Archives, Sterling Memorial Library, Yale University. The typescript from which this story is extracted states that Racca visited the Barone family in 1923; however, the surrounding documents, which form part of the same study, indicate that all of this work was carried out during the early 1930s. According to Racca's résumé, which can be found among the papers of the Institute of Human Relations, Racca was working in New York City during the early 1920s.

2. This kind of cultural dislocation is still commonly experienced by U.S. immigrants from nonindustrialized nations; see, e.g., "A Cultural Reluctance to Spare the Rod: Newcomers Say Americans Spoil Children," *New York Times,* February 29, 1996, B1.

3. See, e.g., William I. Thomas and Florian Znaniecki, *The Polish Peasant in Europe and America: A Monograph of an Immigrant Group,* vol. 2 (New York: Alfred A. Knopf, 1927); and Oscar Handlin, *The Uprooted: The Epic Story of the Great Migrations That Made the American People* (Boston: Little, Brown, 1951).

4. On the rising standard of living for workers in the United States between 1890 and 1930, see David Montgomery, *Fall of the House of Labor: The Workplace, the State, and American Labor Activism, 1865–1925* (New York: Cambridge University Press, 1987); Jeffrey G. Williamson and Peter H. Lindert, *American Inequality: A Macroeconomic History* (New York: Academic Press, 1980); and Claudia Goldin, "Household and Market Production in Families in a Late-Nineteenth-Century American City," *Explorations in Economic History* 16 (1979): 129. But compare with Peter R. Shergold, *Working-Class Life: The "American Standard" in Comparative Perspective, 1899–1913* (Pittsburgh, Pa.: University of Pittsburgh Press, 1982); and Susan

Porter Benson, "Living on the Margin: Working-Class Marriages and Family Survival Strategies in the United States, 1919–1941," in Victoria de Grazia and Ellen Furlough, eds., *The Sex of Things: Gender and Consumption in Historical Perspective* (Berkeley: University of California Press, 1996), 212–43. On the institution of the "breadwinner wage," see Martha May, "The Historical Problem of the Family Wage: The Ford Motor Company and the Five Dollar Day," *Feminist Studies* 8 (Summer 1982): 399–424; Stephen Meyer, *The Five-Dollar Day: Labor Management and Social Control in the Ford Motor Company, 1908–1921* (Albany: SUNY Press, 1981); and Lawrence Glickman, "Inventing the 'American Standard of Living': Gender, Race and Working-Class Identity, 1880–1925," *Labor History* 34 (Spring–Summer 1993): 235.

5. Viviana A. Zelizer, *Pricing the Priceless Child: The Changing Social Value of Children* (New York: Basic Books, 1985).

6. See, e.g., John Modell, *Into One's Own: From Youth to Adulthood in the United States, 1920–1975* (Berkeley: University of California Press, 1989), chaps. 5–7; Elaine Tyler May, *Homeward Bound: American Families in the Cold War Era* (New York: Basic Books, 1988), chaps. 3–7.

7. John C. Caldwell, "Mass Education as a Determinant of the Timing of Fertility Decline," *Population and Development Review* 6 (June 1980): 225–55.

8. Caldwell, "Mass Education," 226.

9. Caldwell, "Mass Education," 226, 235.

10. Even when it means that all children attend school only irregularly, Caldwell observes, schooling erodes children's fidelity to the family system of morality and points them toward an outward-oriented, "community-wide morality"—a widely shared belief that the disinterested promotion of the public good is ultimately linked to the well-being of each individual (Caldwell, "Mass Education," 226). Caldwell's "family morality," which he uses interchangeably with the phrase "family system of morality" could be construed as a version of "amoral familism," Edward C. Banfield's much criticized phrase describing the moral system of the people of Potenza in southern Italy, who were, in his estimation, politically impotent and utter strangers to the notion of public disinterestedness. "Community morality" and "amoral familism," of course, are ideal types occupying opposite points along the spectrum of possible relations between family groups and the social organization of political power; Banfield, *The Moral Basis of a Backward Society* (Glencoe, Ill.: Free Press, 1958), 10–11, 85–104.

11. David Levine, *Reproducing Families: The Political Economy of English Population History* (New York: Cambridge University Press, 1987), 194, 198, 203–4; Levine, of course, concerns himself with England exclusively, where an ideology of "respectability" among the labor aristocracy informed the decision to encourage extended schooling. Moreover, he speaks only to the relationship between schooling and fertility control. Although the mentality of respectability is not without analogy in the United States, the palpability of class in American society is historically much more diffuse than in England, complicated as it is by competing group identities and prejudices arising from religious, ethnic, and racial differences unknown in early-twentieth-century England. The American working-class equivalent to British

working-class "respectability" during these decades is outlined by Glickman in "Inventing the 'American Standard of Living.'"

12. Levine, *Reproducing Families,* 161, 194.

13. Locke in this regard, of course, distinguished between the profound influence of attitudes on the child on one hand and his or her innate capacities and dispositions on the other. Caldwell, however, is concerned with the ideological fissure created by schooling that sets into motion a train of beliefs and behaviors that conflict with those of parents.

14. See Shirley Brice Heath, *Ways with Words: Language, Life, and Work in Communities and Classrooms* (New York: Cambridge University Press, 1983); and John G. Nicholls, *The Competitive Ethos and Democratic Education* (Cambridge, Mass.: Harvard University Press, 1989).

15. Levine, *Reproducing Families,* chap. 4, esp. 202–3.

16. I use the term "voluntary" bearing in mind that the "choice" to continue in school for many working-class youths was increasingly the only alternative to that of unemployment after World War I; thus, to stay in school was voluntary only in the sense that beyond age fourteen, adolescents were not legally compelled to remain in school.

17. New Haven, Conn., New Haven Board of Education, *Annual Report,* 1908–32 (hereafter, New Haven, *Annual Report*); "New Haven School Map," School Volunteers for New Haven, New Haven, 1998; and Maurice R. Davie, "The Pattern of Urban Growth," in G. P. Murdock, ed., *Studies in the Science of Society* (New Haven: Yale University Press, 1937), 132–61. See, for instance, Alfred Kazin's autobiographical account of growing up in the Brownsville section of Brooklyn and the distinct physical boundaries of ethnicity that informed his comprehension of the cultural landscape of his childhood and youth, as well as his sense of the strange and conspicuously Anglo-American character of his grammar school principal and teachers, in *A Walker in the City* (New York: Harcourt, Brace, 1951), 8, 16, 100, 103, 165, 168–70, and 172–73. A similar account is rendered in Leonard Covello (with Guido D'Agostino), *The Heart Is the Teacher* (New York: McGraw-Hill, 1958); and Irvin L. Child, *Italian or American? The Second-Generation in Conflict* (New Haven: Yale University Press, 1943).

18. An obvious counterexample—the exception that proves the rule—are Jewish immigrants from Russia and Poland, who outperformed every subgroup in both their eagerness for schooling and in grade attainment; see Joel Perlmann, *Ethnic Differences: Schooling and Social Structure among the Irish, Italians, Jews, and Blacks in an American City, 1880–1935* (New York: Cambridge University Press, 1988).

19. Enrollments in the elementary schools ranged from 100 to a few hundred pupils and between 1,500 and 2,000 students attending the junior high schools. The enrollment at Hillhouse was 4,261, and enrollment at Commercial High School stood at 2,036. Moreover, since the beginning of the century, Hillhouse was forced to hold "double sessions" to accommodate all of its students—half of whom attended in the mornings and half in the afternoons.

20. *Annual Report,* 1930.

21. Again, see Kazin's reminiscence of intimate "Brunzville" (Brownsville) with the civic greatness of New York and places "beyond"; *Walker in the City,* 18–19, 99–100. For contrast, note Ida Mabel Landcraft's familiarity with and command of New Haven's downtown commercial district during the 1880s, which underscores a distinctly different sense among Yankee middle-class adolescents of comportment and social ease in the city's civic life at a time when high school was still an elite institution; see Jane H. Hunter, *How Young Ladies Became Girls: The Victorian Origins of American Girlhood* (New Haven: Yale University Press, 2003), esp. chap. 8.

22. See, e.g., James S. Coleman, *The Adolescent Society: The Social Life of the Teenager and Its Impact on Education* (New York: Free Press of Glencoe, 1961); and Joseph F. Kett, *Rites of Passage: Adolescence in America, 1790 to the Present* (New York: Basic Books, 1977), esp. chap. 9.

23. See Paula S. Fass's pathbreaking article on this theme, "'Americanizing' the High Schools: New York in the 1930s and '40s," in her *Outside In: Minorities and the Transformation of American Education* (New York: Oxford University Press, 1989), 73–111; see also John Modell and J. Trent Alexander, "High School in Transition: Community, School, and Peer Group in Abilene, Kansas, 1939," *History of Education Quarterly* 37 (Spring 1997): 1–24.

24. Critics of the subfield of the history of family life have long pointed out the conceptual weakness of the notion of "the family," as if families were the same everywhere and for all time. Furthermore, implicit in the nomenclature is a model of family life that aspires to or deviates from structurally and ideologically the urban, middle-class family of societies in the first world; see, e.g., Rayna Rapp, Ellen Ross, and Renate Bridenthal, "Examining Family History," *Feminist Studies* 5 (Spring 1979): 174–200; and Louise Tilly and Miriam Cohen, "Does the Family Have a History?" *Social Science History* 6 (1982): 181–99.

25. Both Bernard Bailyn and Lawrence A. Cremin as early as the 1960s called for increased attention to the historical relationship between schooling and family life in America, and Maris A. Vinovskis underscored the importance of their pleas for a "new and broader interpretation" of the history of education when no such studies had appeared after twenty years, but little has come of it; Bailyn, *Education in the Forming of American Society: Needs and Opportunities for Study* (Chapel Hill: University of North Carolina Press, 1960); Cremin, *The Transformation of the School: Progressivism in American Education, 1876–1957* (New York: Alfred A. Knopf, 1961); and Vinovskis, "Family and Schooling in Colonial and Nineteenth-Century America," *Journal of Family History* 12, nos. 1–3 (1987): 19–37.

26. Bailyn, *Education in the Forming of American Society;* and Cremin, *Transformation of the School.*

27. What is more, they were millenarians who believed that the arrival of their savior on earth was imminent and so they must purify themselves and their community to remain in a constant state of readiness; Sarah Day Woodward, *Early New Haven* (New Haven: Edward P. Judd, 1929), 18–19, 48–49.

28. Quoted by Louise G. Wrinn (with updated spelling) from the *New Haven Colony Records,* vol. 1; Wrinn, "The Development of the Public School System in New Haven, 1639–1930: A Problem in Historical Analysis" (Ph.D. diss., Yale University, 1932), 3.

29. Wrinn, "Development of the Public School System," 10.

30. See Carl F. Kaestle, *Pillars of the Republic: Common Schools and American Society, 1780–1860* (New York: Hill and Wang, 1983), on the role of "charity," "free," "Sunday," and "infant" schools (all forerunners of the common school) in redressing the purported inadequacies of indigent parents. "Charity" schools were denominationally run schools for poor children. "Free" schools were nondenominational and run by voluntary associations. "Sunday" schools were free, nondenominational schools for poor children who were unchurched but willing to attend school on Sundays. They were run by lay people and stressed "rudimentary intellectual skills," "morals," and "nonsectarian religion." Finally, "infant" schools were for children under the age of two and inspired by the conviction that it was critical to catch children "while they were still impressionable and relatively 'unspoiled,'" according to Kaestle; 32–35, 37, 39–40, 45, 47, 55, and 61.

31. Wrinn, "Development of the Public School System," appendix A, 7; Bernard C. Steiner, *The History of Education in Connecticut* (Washington, D.C.: Government Printing Office, 1893), 36; Kaestle says that as many as five hundred students could be supervised by one master in the Lancasterian system, see Kaestle, *Pillars of the Republic,* 40–44.

32. The first two hundred years of education in New Haven have been telescoped here into just a few paragraphs. The rise of the common school in New Haven specifically and Connecticut in general was slow and its story complex, and thus it deserves its own treatment. I mention it here merely to underscore the perceived need to foster cultural consensus in the face of dynamic social and demographic change; on the emergence of the common school in Connecticut, see Steiner, *History of Education,* chap. 3.

33. On the emergence and contradictions of youth culture in the post–World War II years, see William Graebner, *Coming of Age in Buffalo: Youth and Authority in the Postwar Era* (Philadelphia: Temple University Press, 1990).

Chapter 1: Immigrants and Immigrant Neighborhoods

1. See Douglas W. Rae, *City: Urbanism and Its End* (New Haven: Yale University Press, 2003), chap. 4; Elizabeth Mills Brown, *New Haven: A Guide to Architecture and Urban Design* (New Haven: Yale University Press, 1976); and Alan Plattus, "Housing and the Industrial City" (course, "New Haven and the Problem of Urban Change," Yale University, New Haven, March 24, 1998).

2. The most concise yet comprehensive history of the transatlantic migration is Walter Nugent, *Crossings: The Great Transatlantic Migrations, 1870–1914* (Bloomington: Indiana University Press, 1992).

3. Herbert J. Gans, one of the first scholars in the era of urban renewal to recognize that the social cost of slum removal was the irretrievable destruction of effective

community life, coined the phrase "urban villagers" to describe the people, folkways, and group life of Italian Americans in Boston's North End during the late 1950s; Gans, *The Urban Villagers: Group and Class in the Life of Italian-Americans* (New York: Free Press, 1962).

4. Cass Gilbert and Frederick Law Olmstead, "Report of the Civic Improvement Commission" (New Haven: New Haven Civic Improvement Committee, 1910).

5. Originally dubbed "Sodom Hill," because of its early-nineteenth-century reputation for poverty, vice, and crime, eventually it became known simply as "The Hill"; Brown, *New Haven*, 89. In 1701 there were only 142 foreigners in a city of 4,000 people. Fifty years later immigration had begun in earnest as victims of the Irish potato famine began to arrive. The Irish were the city's most numerous immigrant population from 1850 to 1900. In 1850 three of every four immigrants were Irish; by the end of the century Irish immigrants and their descendants were still predominant, but by the next census they were eclipsed by the arrival of thousands of Italians; Neil Hogan, "The Actual Enumeration: New Haven and the U.S. Census," *Journal of the New Haven Colony Historical Society* 38 (Fall 1991): 5, 16.

6. William Porter, "The Farmington Canal: New Haven's Contribution to the 'Canal Epidemic,'" *Journal of the New Haven Colony Historical Society* 20 (October 1971): 55.

7. Originally two separate railroads, the Hartford and New Haven Railroad, running north-south, was completed in 1839 and was the first railroad in Connecticut; the New York and New Haven Railroad, which ran east-west, merged with the former during the 1870s to become the New York, New Haven, and Hartford Railroad; Floyd M. Shumway and Richard Hegel, "New Haven's Two Creeks," *Journal of the New Haven Colony Historical Society* 37 (Fall 1990): 19–22; Brown, *New Haven*, 180.

8. William M. Johnston found that immigrants from every province in northern and central Italy were present in the early settlement; see Johnston, "On the Outside Looking In: Irish, Italian, and Black Ethnic Politics in an American City" (Ph.D. diss., Yale University, 1977).

9. John B. Whitelaw, "The Administration of the Elementary School as the Coordinating Social Factor in the Community" (Ph.D. diss., Yale University, 1935), 111. On early estimates of the city's Italian population, see Vittorio Racca, "Ethnography: The Italians of New Haven," TS, Works Progress Administration, Federal Writers Project, Connecticut Ethnic Survey, box 67, folder 175:3, p. 1, Historical Manuscripts and Archives Division, University of Connecticut Libraries, Storrs. For later figures, see Jerome K. Myers, "The Differential Time Factor in Assimilation" (Ph.D. diss., Yale University, 1950), 25–26. On the socioeconomic status of Italians in New Haven, see Thelma A. Dreis, *A Handbook of Social Statistics of New Haven, Connecticut* (New Haven: Yale University Press, 1936), 70–94.

10. While statistics on return migration from before 1900 are scarce, a 1907 study calculated that 60 percent of Italian immigrants who came to the United States in 1907 returned to Italy during that year; Italians led all other immigrant groups in this respect, and although accurate data is not available during earlier decades, it is

estimated that return migration among Italians was consistently at 50 percent or higher; Nugent, *Crossings*, 95–100, and table 23.

11. Nugent, *Crossings*, 95, 99–100; Dino Cinel, *The National Integration of Italian Return Migration, 1870–1929* (New York: Cambridge University Press, 1991); and Rudolph M. Bell, *Fate and Honor, Family and Village: Demographic and Cultural Change in Rural Italy since 1800* (Chicago: University of Chicago Press, 1979), 198.

12. Cholera and typhus were special dangers on board the slower traveling ships before the 1880s. Nugent estimates that up to the 1840s, "contagions frequently swept away up to 10 percent, and occasionally 25 percent of the passengers during a crossing"; Nugent, *Crossings*, 31–33.

13. An outgrowth of the sponsorship of passage by U.S. companies seeking labor was the "padrone" system. Italian labor bosses would recruit workers, pay their fare for passage by steamship, arrange for their delivery to a factory or mine seeking labor, house and feed them, communicate with their kin back home (including the transmission of some part of their wages), and keep a percentage of their earnings for themselves. Over time, this system gained a reputation for corruption and the exploitation and abuse of Italian workers even if in the short term it served the interests of employee and employer. See Gunther Peck, "Divided Loyalties: Immigrant Padrones and the Evolution of Industrial Paternalism in North America," *International Labor and Working-Class History* 53 (Spring 1998): 49–68; and Peck, "Reinventing Free Labor: Immigrant Padrones and Contract Laborers in North America, 1885–1925," *Journal of American History* 83 (December 1996): 848–71. In New Haven, J. B. Sargent personally recruited workers from Italy for his large hardware manufacturing plant located between Wooster Square and the Long Wharf pier.

14. Nugent, *Crossings*, 96–97; Cinel, *National Integration*, 103–11.

15. Transatlantic migration is often described in terms of "push-pull" factors: until historians began to analyze conditions on both sides of the Atlantic (instead of just U.S. immigration), the reigning metaphor of analysis was the United States as a "magnet" that drew the downtrodden and persecuted to the bounty and freedom of the New World.

16. Nugent, *Crossings*, 95–100.

17. Another smaller group consisting of immigrants from a collection of villages clustered around Benevento gathered on the fringe of the Hill, forming a community that referred to itself as "The Village." Even as of the late 1970s, a neighborhood organization called the "Village Unity League" was maintained in the area; Johnston, "On the Outside," 180. On the Jewish settlement around Oak Street and its subsequent migration up Whalley Avenue, see Susan L. Neitlich, "Here History Is Going," *Jews in New Haven* 6 (1993): 197–221; also see Eli Zimmerman, "What I Remember," *Jews in New Haven* 5 (1992): 39–50; and Fred Ticotsky, "Ticotsky's Bakery and the Legion Avenue Jews," *Jews in New Haven* 3 (1981): 37–49. The Oak Street area's first and foremost industry had been its tanneries, which grew up around the West Creek early during the colonial era and persisted into the twentieth century.

The noxious odors of the tanneries and surrounding marshes made the district one of the least desirable (and cheapest) places to live in all the city; Brown, *New Haven*, 13, 89.

18. New Haven, it is argued, was the first planned city in North America. Laid out in a grid of nine squares, at the center of which lay a town green, it was settled in 1638 by some English Puritan dissenters and capitalists.

19. Brown, *New Haven*, 179–80.

20. Jon E. Purmont, "Sargent Comes to New Haven," *Journal of the New Haven Colony Historical Society* 24 (Spring 1976): 16–30.

21. Douglas Rae, "Capitalism Gathering Steam" (course, "New Haven and the Problem of Urban Change," Yale University, New Haven, January 20, 1997).

22. See Arnold G. Dana, "Carriage Manufacturing in 1900," *New Haven's Problems: Whither the City? Whither All Cities?* (New Haven: Privately published, 1937); and Brown, *New Haven*, 133–52.

23. Whitelaw, "Administration of the Elementary School," 111. The transformation of its ethnic composition is evinced by the square's most prominent architectural feature, St. Michael's Catholic Church, which had been constructed at midcentury as a Congregationalist church. Built in the heyday of early industrialization, it became a Baptist church in 1855 soon after its erection and was purchased, symbolically, in 1899 by the Catholic Diocese of Hartford and turned into a "national" parish for the city's rapidly growing Italian population; Brown, *New Haven*, 178–95.

24. Samuel Koenig, *Immigrant Settlements in Connecticut* (Hartford: State of Connecticut Department of Education, 1938), 27, table 4; Whitelaw, "Administration of the Elementary School," 116.

25. Whitelaw, "Administration of the Elementary School," 117–18.

26. Dreis, *Handbook of Social Statistics*, tables 1, 3–4, 8–9.

27. Whitelaw, "Administration of the Elementary School," 118–19.

28. Whitelaw, "Administration of the Elementary School," 119.

29. On the political history of the Irish in New Haven, see Robert A. Dahl, *Who Governs?: Democracy and Power in an American City* (New Haven: Yale University Press, 1961), chap. 4.

30. Linda Reeder offers one of the most vivid descriptions of *campanalismo* in her rendering of the sentiment among the *Suteresi* of Sicily: "When men from Sutera left their homes, they defined themselves as *Suteresi*. Their identities rooted in their own historical myths of origin and belonging, which differed from the national myths that came down from the north [through the schools]. . . . Fellow *Suteresi* believed they could be distinguished from someone from Campofranco, a town less than two miles away, by their accent and gestures. Being Italian, or even Sicilian, had little meaning in this world where blood and geography still defined a person's place in the world"; Reeder, "Women in the Classroom: Mass Migration, Literacy and the Nationalization of Sicilian Women at the Turn of the Century," *Journal of Social History* 32 (Fall 1998): 111. Michael Johnston describes the social and political consequences of this phenomenon in New Haven; see Johnston, "Italian New Haven: Building an Ethnic Identity," *Journal of the New Haven Colony Historical Society* 26 (Summer 1979): 23–35.

31. See Johnston, "Italian New Haven."

32. Dahl, *Who Governs?* chap. 4.

Chapter 2: Learning and Earning

1. In 1851 in New Haven (the first year for which data are available) there were 4,711 children between the ages of five and sixteen, 3,992 of whom (85 percent) were registered in some school for some part of the year; in 1900 there were 22,741 children ages six through fifteen, 17,954 of whom were in public and nonpublic schools (85 percent). Although the ratio of enrolled to total children enumerated was (remarkably) identical for both years, I argue that the consistency of exposure to the school curriculum was dramatically higher in 1900 than was actually the case at mid-century; New Haven, New Haven Board of Education, *Annual Report,* 1857–1900; and Wrinn, "Development of the Public School System." Specific dates of enactment of compulsory education laws by state can be found in John G. Richardson, "Variation in Date of Enactment of Compulsory School Attendance Laws: An Empirical Inquiry," *Sociology of Education* 53 (July 1980): 157.

2. The classic portrait of this movement is Philippe Ariès, *Centuries of Childhood: A Social History of Family Life,* trans. Robert Baldick (New York: Alfred A. Knopf, 1962).

3. "Life course" refers to the timing of life transitions (such as the passage from childhood to youth, from youth to adulthood, from adulthood to senescence) of individuals in historical time; see Glen H. Elder Jr., "Family History and the Life Course," in Tamara Hareven, ed., *Transitions: The Family and the Life Course in Historical Perspective* (New York: Academic Press, 1978), 17–64. New Haven in 1860 was a medium-size city, comparable in population to Cleveland, Lowell, Richmond, and Troy. Although it was 25 percent larger than Hartford on the eve of the Civil War, by the end of the century Bridgeport, Hartford, and New Haven were all roughly the same size. As a medium-size city in one of the most heavily industrialized states in the nation, New Haven makes a stronger case for representing the "average" social-historical experience than do better studied metropolitan areas like Boston, Chicago, Philadelphia, and New York. On the growth of U.S. urban centers during the mid-nineteenth century, see Allan Pred, *Urban Growth and City-Systems in the United States, 1840–1860* (Cambridge, Mass.: Harvard University Press, 1980), 12–13, table 2.1.

4. See, e.g., Mary P. Ryan, *Cradle of the Middle Class: The Family in Oneida County, New York, 1790–1865* (New York: Cambridge University Press, 1981); Richard Sennett, *Families against the City: Middle Class Homes of Industrial Chicago, 1872–1890* (Cambridge, Mass.: Harvard University Press, 1970); Christopher Lasch, "The Emotions of Family Life," *New York Review of Books* 20 (November 27, 1975): 37–42; Stephanie Coontz, *The Social Origins of Private Life: A History of American Families, 1600–1900* (London: Verso, 1988), chaps. 5–6; and Richard H. Brodhead, "Sparing the Rod: Discipline and Fiction in Antebellum America," *Representations* 21 (Winter 1988): 67–96.

5. E. Anthony Rotundo aptly captures the idea of "semiautonomy" among middle-class boys during the latter half of the nineteenth century in describing the great stretches of time that boys had to roam from the confines of home while their sisters were kept indoors to help around the house. Michael Katz documents the custom of older adolescents and youths letting rooms from middle-class families while working away from home for periods of time. See Rotundo, "Boy Culture: Middle-Class Boyhood in Nineteenth-Century America," in Mark C. Carnes and Clyde Griffen, eds., *Meanings for Manhood: Constructions of Masculinity in Victorian America* (Chicago: University of Chicago Press, 1990), 15–36; and Katz, *The People of Hamilton, Canada West: Family and Class in a Mid-Nineteenth-Century City* (Cambridge, Mass.: Harvard University Press, 1975), chap. 5.

6. Ryan, *Cradle of the Middle Class*, 161–62; "An education appropriate to acquiring the proper sensibility," according to Ryan, "was infused . . . with the spirit of . . . a cautious, prudent small businessman" (161).

7. John Modell, Frank F. Furstenberg Jr., and Theodore Hershberg, "Social Change and Transitions to Adulthood in Historical Perspective," in Theodore Hershberg, ed., *Philadelphia: Work, Space, and Group Experience in the Nineteenth Century* (New York: Oxford University Press, 1981), 336.

8. "Adolescence," which would become a part of the emerging developmental view of children by psychologists and educators, received widespread official recognition only after the turn of the century; see Kett, *Rites of Passage;* on the history of the life course, see Modell et al., "Social Change and Transitions."

9. "Grading," the sorting of children by age and aptitude into grades, ensured a standard, graduated curriculum and thus predictable levels of competence and skill, which in turn certified pupils' employability upon completion of grammar school or, alternatively, preparation for higher levels of schooling. On "sacred" childhood or the "sacralization" of children, see Zelizer, *Pricing the Priceless Child.*

10. Instead, the sentimentalization of children across class has merely been assumed; but see Zelizer, *Pricing the Priceless Child,* who finds traces of its assimilation by the U.S. working class at the end of the nineteenth century.

11. In addition, a public high school was formed in 1856; *Annual Report,* 1857–1932; U.S. Department of Labor, U.S. Children's Bureau, *Administration of Child Labor Laws; Part I: Employment-Certificate System, Connecticut,* Industrial Series No. 2, Part 1, Bureau Publication, No. 12 (Washington, D.C.: Government Printing Office, 1915).

12. The "school age" was defined by the New Haven Board of Education as between the ages of four and sixteen; later this was revised upward to five and sixteen.

13. Even the city's most popular common school was estimated to have only about 66 percent of enrolled children in attendance daily, but that was considered exceptional by school visitors; Wrinn, "Development of the Public School System," 74.

14. Presumably the private schools were better attended, since parents paid for their children's enrollment; nevertheless, it is impossible to know how well they were attended because no attendance records survive. Between 1850 and 1900 the

proportion of private and parochial students in New Haven contracted markedly. From 1851 to 1866 (years for which registration data happen to be available for both public and nonpublic enrollments) nonpublic school enrollment increased by just 5 percent, while public school registrations swelled by 147 percent, translating to a net decline of 34 percent in nonpublic registrations as a share of total enrollment in New Haven. The year before the first of the common schools was graded was 1851, and 1866 was the last year before compulsory schooling for which there is an enumeration of nonpublic school enrollment. Between 1850 and 1870 the city's population increased by 150 percent, while the number of school-age children increased by 70 percent. Even as the city's total population continued to expand (at a rate of between 22 percent and 37 percent a decade until 1920), after 1870 the growth of school-age children outpaced that of the total population, registering increases of between 30 percent and 40 percent in each decade, save the 1890s, which saw the arrival of so many adult immigrants from Italy, Poland, and Russia. Meanwhile, New Haven's ten common schools of 1850 had grown to more than forty schools by 1900. Thereafter, the nonpublic school share of school-age children declined to less than 15 percent, settling at between 11 percent to 14 percent annually until 1930; see Stephen A. Lassonde, "Learning to Forget: Schooling and Family Life in New Haven's Working Class, 1870–1940" (Ph.D. diss., Yale University, 1994), table 1, appendix B; on the problem of estimating private grammar school enrollment and attendance in the nineteenth century, see Lassonde, "Learning to Forget," appendix A.

15. New Haven, Conn., "Report Respecting a High School," *Report of the First School Society of the Special Committee Appointed to Consider the Subject of a High School* (New Haven: Thomas J. Stafford, Printer, 1852), 3–4. The description of the city's common schools as a "public charity" is attributed to Henry Barnard, who also underscored the necessity of middle-class support to a viable public school system; see Barnard, *Connecticut Common School Journal* (1856): 67 (hereafter, *CCSJ*), quoted by Wrinn, "Development of the Public School System," 98. As a consequence of their inferiority, Barnard noted, "The children of the wealthy never saw the inside of a public school" (Wrinn, "Development of the Public School System," 98). The argument for graded schools can be found in New Haven, "Report of the Board of School Visitors," Proceedings of the Board of Education (New Haven: Thomas J. Stafford, Printer, 1856), 3–22.

16. Barnard, *CCSJ* (1854): 106, and Barnard, *CCSJ* (1856): 67, both quoted in Wrinn, "Development of the Public School System," 94, 98; and "Report of the Board of School Visitors," 22.

17. Barnard, *CCSJ* (1854): 106, quoted in Wrinn, "Development of the Public School System," 94. Wrinn comments that before the 1850s, virtually no one in New Haven's common schools remained beyond age twelve: "When scholars reached the age when 'they began to feel the strong promptings of self-respect, and a laudable pride and ambition,'" they entered the city's private schools. After the Webster school was graded, it was pointed out "with some pride" that there were 128 pupils over age twelve, "a larger number of pupils of this age than any other public school in

the city boasted" (Wrinn, "Development of the Public School System," 99); the passage quoted by Wrinn is from *New Haven School Reports, 1850–1860* (1863), 12. Even if Barnard's partisan account was overdrawn, school census figures bear him out.

18. In addition there were three ungraded "African" schools for African-American children that remained ungraded until they were integrated into the city school system during the 1870s.

19. Barnard, *CCSJ* (1854): 106, quoted in Wrinn, "Development of the Public School System," 94; and see Edith Nye MacMullen, *In the Cause of True Education: Henry Barnard and Nineteenth-Century School Reform* (New Haven: Yale University Press, 1991), 123–24.

20. *Annual Report,* 1862, 2.

21. *New Haven School Reports* (1852), 18. Oystering was a major extractive industry in New Haven until the end of the nineteenth century.

22. Quoted in Wrinn, "Development of the Public School System," 88.

23. Quoted by Wrinn, from *New Haven School Reports, 1850–1860* (1850), 10.

24. There is nothing self-evident about the relation between grading and the necessity for a rough continuity of personnel from grade to grade. The relation becomes clear, however, when significant portions of students in any grade fail to be promoted to the next level. Soon they begin to accumulate at the lower levels, become individually demoralized about the prospect of mastering material "appropriate" to their chronological ages, and ultimately become a drag on the system. By glutting classrooms, they reveal the shortcomings of the schools' effort to educate and appear to reflect on the institution's adequacy (or lack thereof).

25. The sequencing and timing of transitions since the early twentieth century is explored by Modell, *Into One's Own;* a broad comparison between the late-nineteenth- and the late-twentieth-century transitions to adulthood is made by Modell et al., "Social Change and Transitions," 311–41; see also Dennis P. Hogan, *Transitions and Social Change: The Early Lives of American Men* (New York: Academic Press, 1981). The degree to which a child was considered "behind" in his or her developmental progression was referred to as grade "retardation": "A 'retarded' pupil . . . is one who is 2 or more years older than the normal age for his grade," U.S. Congress, Senate, *Reports of the Immigration Commission: The Children of Immigrants in Schools,* vol. 29 (reprint of 1911 edition, New York: Arno, 1970), 31. Tyack dates the emergence of "educational science" to about 1911, but he acknowledges the emergence of some of these practices as early as 1890, when he detects "a very rapid increase in the machinery of compulsion and the structural differentiation of the schools." David B. Tyack, "Ways of Seeing: An Essay on the History of Compulsory Schooling," *Harvard Educational Review* 46 (August 1976): 374. If he is correct, the New Haven school system was precocious in this respect, conducting its first school census in 1857.

26. *Annual Report,* 1864, 21.

27. *Annual Report,* 1864, 20.

28. *Annual Report,* 1874, 6–7.

29. *Annual Report,* 1874, 6; for attendance and enrollment statistics for these years, see *Annual Report,* 1860–1870.

30. *Annual Report,* 1871, 10.

31. *Annual Report,* 1871, 20–21.

32. The full text of the 1872 statute is in State of Connecticut, *The General Statutes of the State of Connecticut, Revision of 1875* (Hartford: Case, Lockwood and Brainard, 1874), 126–27. Although it was ruled by amendment in 1885 that a fine was to be levied on any parent or employer in violation of the law, the penalty would not be applied "when it appears that the child is destitute of clothing suitable for attending school, and the parent or person having control of such child is unable to provide such clothing." *Annual Report,* 1886, 22. Further, the original statute stipulated the subjects to be learned and declared that any child under fourteen temporarily out of work should be returned to school until the time he or she could be reemployed. This provision, however, never amounted to more than a stern admonition. Even after more effective monitoring of child labor and education was achieved in 1911, the school districts had great difficulty in reabsorbing children; Helen L. Sumner and Ethel E. Hanks, *Administration of Child Labor Laws, Part I: Administration of the Employment-Certificate Records in Connecticut,* U.S. Department of Labor, U.S. Children's Bureau (Washington, D.C.: Government Printing Office, 1915).

33. *Annual Report,* 1871, 7.

34. *Annual Report,* 1871, 20–21.

35. *Annual Report,* 1872, 8–9.

36. On the relative culpability of parents and businessmen in this respect, see *Annual Report,* 1872, 10–11; and State of Connecticut, Bureau of Labor Statistics, "Education and Employment of Young Persons and Children," *First Annual Report* (Hartford, 1873), 61–62. Apparently this bias persisted even as enforcement of the compulsory education law was intensified. In 1890 the superintendent commented, "Employers don't want to break the law; ignorance and carelessness account for most violations" *Annual Report,* 1890, 25–26.

37. See, e.g., E. P. Thompson, "Time, Work-Discipline, and Industrial Capitalism," *Past and Present* 38 (December 1967): 87; and Daniel T. Rogers, *The Work Ethic in Industrial America, 1850–1920* (Chicago: University of Chicago Press, 1978), introduction, chap. 1.

38. Ryan, *Cradle of the Middle Class,* 161.

39. Since 1856, the superintendent observed, "a long list of studies was named which might be taught, but pupils could never look forward to ascertain . . . when they could take up any particular branches [of study], nor whether they could ever study them, however long they might remain, because no definite, regular course of study had ever been prescribed"; *Annual Report,* 1869, 37.

40. *Annual Report,* 1875, 88.

41. Thompson, "Time, Work-Discipline," 60; U.S. labor historians have fully amplified Thompson's insight. To cite only the most outstanding examples, Herbert G. Gutman, *Work, Society and Culture in Industrializing America: Essays in*

American Working-Class and Social History (New York: Alfred A. Knopf, 1976), chap. 1; and David Montgomery, *Workers' Control in America: Studies in the History of Work, Technology, and Labor Struggles* (New York: Cambridge University Press, 1979). For a useful critique of this literature, see Daniel T. Rogers, "Tradition, Modernity, and the American Industrial Worker: Reflections and Critique," *Journal of Interdisciplinary History* 7 (Spring 1977): 655–81.

42. Tyack, "Ways of Seeing," 382; see also Samuel Bowles and Herbert Gintis, *Schooling in Capitalist America* (New York: Basic Books, 1976), chaps. 2, 4–5, 7, 9; David Nasaw, *Schooled to Order: A Social History of Public Schooling in the United States* (New York: Oxford University Press, 1979); and Ira Katznelson and Margaret Weir, *Schooling for All: Class, Race, and the Decline of the Democratic Ideal* (New York: Basic Books, 1985), chap. 6.

43. *Annual Report*, 1873, 29.

44. It is unclear whether girls or boys in general received more education, although among those who persisted in school, girls predominated: "In a community whose leading industry calls for the work of boys rather than girls," observed the superintendent in 1870, "the latter will be kept at school for a longer period. . . . There is a very great preponderance of girls in the most advanced rooms of the [schools]." *Annual Report*, 1870, 15. The perception of girls' truancy as comparatively innocuous is perhaps best conveyed by the superintendent's description of the difficulty of discerning the occupational status of the city's girls: "The native delicacy of those officers whose duty requires them to question truants and vagrants, in relation to their occupation, when found wandering about the thoroughfares of the city, would naturally restrain them from meddling with the affairs of young misses found on the public walks. Consequently, few if any receive attention in this way; and though they may not appear so frequently on the street as do the boys, they do not all appear in the schools"; *Annual Report*, 1873, 9–10.

45. *Annual Report*, 1873, 28–29.

46. *Annual Report*, 1871, 21.

47. *Annual Report*, 1866, 17.

48. Kett, *Rites of Passage*, 132.

49. "Ungraded classes" should not be confused with "ungraded schools." Once the public schools were thoroughly graded in New Haven (by the mid-1860s), special, ungraded classrooms were set aside to deal with juveniles who went in and out of the schools and could not keep pace with their age peers. This problem, of course, was a direct consequence of grading the schools throughout the system.

50. *Annual Report*, 1871, 8–10, 60.

51. Leonard P. Ayers, *Laggards in Our Schools: A Study of Retardation and Elimination in the City School Systems* (New York: Russell Sage Foundation, 1909), 103–16.

52. After about 1900 much of the "retardation" in the nation's schools was due to the practice of putting children into first grade regardless of their age if their native language was not English; see *Reports of the Immigration Commission*, vol. 29, 31–38.

53. *Annual Report*, 1873, 27; and for an account of the arrest, see Morty Miller, "New Haven: The Italian Community" (senior essay, Department of History, Yale University, 1969), mimeo, 11–12. At the time of the incident only ten Italians appeared in the city census.

54. Hugh Cunningham, "The Employment and Unemployment of Children in England, *c.* 1680–1851," *Past and Present* 126 (February 1990): 121.

55. Again, it is important to bear in mind, as Cunningham has observed, that a certain amount of juvenile unemployment was volitional, because "parents may have had little concern for the structuring of all the time of their children, looking rather to exploit economic opportunities as they arose at particular times of the year, or for ways in which children, by looking after younger siblings . . . could release adults for productive labour." Correspondingly, in New Haven in 1873, two-and-one-half times as many children under sixteen were "out of school without apparent cause" as were those recorded as employed, proportions that suggest a similar lack of rigor by parents in pressing children into full-time school or work; Cunningham, "Employment and Unemployment," 120. Of the 10,666 children accounted for by the school census between the ages of five and sixteen, 881 (8 percent) were reportedly employed and 2,242 (21 percent) were neither "certified" by an employer as working nor attending schools of any kind; *Annual Report*, 1873, 26.

56. On unemployment in the northeastern United States during the nineteenth century, see Alexander Keyssar, *Out of Work: The First Century of Unemployment in Massachusetts* (New York: Cambridge University Press, 1986), chaps. 2–4.

57. Cunningham, "Employment and Unemployment," 148; Keyssar, *Out of Work*, 33–36, 377–78, n. 37; Friedrich Engels, *The Condition of the Working Class in England* [1844], W. O. Henderson and W. H. Chaloner, trans. and eds. (Stanford, Calif.: Stanford University Press, 1968), 97–99.

58. Keyssar, *Out of Work*, quote is from 55; see also 92–93, table 4.6; 95; 393, nn. 37, 39. Although insufficient attention has been paid to the extent to which female workers have fared in episodes of economic depression in the United States, in England, it seems, girls and young women (ages fifteen to nineteen) bore the brunt of unemployment when it struck. This, according to Ellen Jordan, was because work from the early days of industrialism was sex-segmented. Labor was divided in the hierarchy of production along a continuum of greater and lesser skilled tasks: adult males received the more valued and steadier jobs, while women and girls were assigned less "prestigious," more expendable positions. By this logic, presumably, juvenile workers would have received the same treatment as young, unmarried female workers. Jordan, "Female Unemployment in England and Wales, 1851–1911," *Social History* 13 (May 1988): 175–90.

59. On economic crises and unemployment between 1873 and 1900, see Keyssar, *Out of Work*, chap. 3; on the decline in workers' living standards during this period, see Jeffrey G. Williamson and Peter H. Lindert, *American Inequality: A Macroeconomic History* (New York: Academic Press, 1980), chaps. 10–11; and for Connecticut workers' views on the effects of economic conditions on long-term wage

levels in the state, see State of Connecticut, *Bureau of Labor Statistics*, "Receipts and Expenses," in *Annual Reports*, Hartford, Report 4th, 1887/88, 110–19.

60. *Annual Report*, 1872, 10.

61. See, e.g., Cunningham, "Employment and Unemployment"; Neil J. Smelser, *Social Paralysis and Social Change: British Working-Class Education in the Nineteenth Century* (Berkeley: University of California Press, 1991), 257–68.

62. Cunningham, "Employment and Unemployment," 139, 143, 146–50.

63. Connecticut had established a bureau of labor statistics as early as 1873. However, employment and unemployment statistics were not systematically collected until the 1930s, when federal programs were administered in coordination with state governments to aid in unemployment relief. What there is before the Great Depression, then, is haphazard and largely anecdotal. Child labor statistics, moreover, are even harder to come by than are figures on the adult workforce. This changed in 1911, when an employment certificate system was instituted statewide. From 1911 to the 1930s, then, estimates of child employment were much more accurate than those of the workforce as a whole; Sumner and Hanks, *Administration of Child Labor Laws*.

64. For a typical portrayal of urban-rural differences and the seasonality of child labor, see Tyack, "Ways of Seeing," 381; and Pamela Barnhouse Walters and Philip J. O'Connell, "The Family Economy, Work, and Educational Participation in the United States, 1890–1940," *American Journal of Sociology* 93 (March 1988): 1116–52.

65. Indeed, the perception that agricultural work did not impede the education of rural children accounts, at least in part, for the unique exemption of juvenile agricultural labor from child labor legislation even after virtually every other form of child labor in the state had been prohibited in the early 1930s.

66. It was customary for firms to shut down for a couple of weeks during the year, ceasing production altogether; Susan B. Carter and Richard Sutch, "Sticky Wages, Short Weeks, and 'Fairness': The Response of Connecticut Manufacturing Firms to the Depression of 1893–94," Working Paper 2: Historical Labor Statistics Project, University of California, 1991, 7–8, 23. See Susan B. Carter, Roger L. Ransom, and Richard Sutch, "The Historical Labor Statistics Project at the University of California," *Historical Methods* 24 (Spring 1991): 60–62, on hours reductions as a form of savings on labor inputs. Ewan Clague, Walter J. Couper, and E. Wight Bakke determined by examining the employment records of a New Haven factory from the 1880s to 1930 that there were two two-week periods of layoff every year, so that even in the best years, full-time employment meant wages for forty-eight rather than fifty-two weeks; Clague et al., *After the Shutdown* (New Haven: Yale University Press, 1934), 115. This custom was not an innovation by the 1930s but, on the contrary, a holdover from the early years of factory production in New England (Keyssar) and a custom in its twilight, according to Carter and Sutch, as unionization and federal labor legislation disallowed such practices by the end of the Great Depression. Keyssar, *Out of Work*, 15–16; Carter and Sutch, "Sticky Wages," 9.

67. Carter and Sutch, "Sticky Wages," 9–10 and table 5. Peaks and troughs are also reflected in the reports of workers' monthly wages throughout the 1880s in Connecticut, as well as in anecdotal reports by workers on time lost due to annually scheduled (or unscheduled) plant shutdowns and hours reductions; see, e.g., State of Connecticut, "Receipts and Expenses," 110–19. In 1887 a saddler remarked to the state commissioner of labor, "You will see that it is hard to live and support a family on medium wages, when a man is not employed every day during the month. A man ought to have enough wages to make up for all this lost time. I have a record of time worked in 1883, 1884, 1885, and in the whole of the three years there is about twenty four months work at most"; State of Connecticut, "Receipts and Expenses," 119.

68. State of Connecticut, "Receipts and Expenses," 112.

69. A more notable and persistent form of disguised juvenile labor—or "family labor"—was industrial homework. Although take-home garment work was to become more common among Italian immigrant families after the turn of the century, there is no record of its presence in New Haven before then. The classic study of "family labor" in the dawn of factory production is, of course, Neil J. Smelser, *Social Change in the Industrial Revolution, 1770–1840* (Chicago: University of Chicago Press, 1959); but see Jane Mark-Lawson and Anne Witz, "From 'Family Labour' to 'Family Wage'? The Case of Women's Labour in Nineteenth-Century Coalmining," *Social History* 13 (May 1988): 151–74, on the interaction of patriarchy and capitalism within the family economy. For the United States, see Jonathan Prude, *The Coming of Industrial Order* (New York: Cambridge University Press, 1983). On industrial homework in the nineteenth century, see Christine Stansell, *City of Women: Sex and Class in New York, 1789–1860* (Urbana: University of Illinois Press, 1987), chap. 6; and Eileen Boris and Cynthia R. Daniels, eds., *Homework: Historical and Contemporary Perspectives on Paid Labor at Home* (Urbana: University of Illinois Press, 1989). In fact, there was no child labor law in Connecticut during the nineteenth century— indeed, none until the 1930s. However, even while the compulsory education statute was the sole constraint on juvenile labor, the compulsory education law was vague about age as an inhibiting factor in hiring, merely requiring employers to determine that children younger than fourteen demonstrate that they had received the minimum amount of schooling stipulated.

70. *Annual Report*, 1872, 10–11.

71. See, e.g., State of Connecticut, "Education and Employment," 61.

72. During the mid-1870s school officials, after conferring with the state agent of the board of education, ruled that it would be a "cruelty" and contrary to community sentiment to enforce the recently passed compulsory education law in view of economic conditions; *Annual Report*, 1874, 7; the same "concern" for impoverished children by employers is expressed as among the motives of businessmen for violating child labor laws; see *Annual Report*, 1890, 26. Claudia Goldin says that employment-seeking by children was a direct response to fathers' unemployment, see Goldin, "Household and Market Production of Families in a Late Nineteenth Century American City," *Explorations in Economic History* 16 (1979): 125.

73. *Annual Report*, 1873, 27.

74. Between 1865 and 1872 the difference between average and total enrollments ranged from 10 percent to 19 percent.

75. Even these figures may underestimate enrollments: the *Annual Report* of 1889 stated that enumerators over-reported enrollments by 12 percent when they were compared against attendance recorded by teachers for that year; *Annual Report*, 1889, 21. A similar finding had been reported a decade earlier; see *Annual Report*, 1878, 22–23.

76. In the initial phase of the enforcement of compulsory school attendance (1872–82), the law only required that children attend school for sixty full days per year, six weeks of which were to be continuous.

77. *Annual Report*, 1880, 19.

78. *Annual Report*, 1881, 24.

79. This "salutary" action, remarked the superintendent, would chasten negligent parents so that "a few weeks' service by the Agent . . . every year would be a sufficient reminder to all that the laws cannot be violated with impunity." *Annual Report*, 1890, 23–25.

80. *Annual Report*, 1897, 1890–95. In 1902 a second truant officer was added to look for the employment of children in the large manufactories of certain classes of goods and in large dry goods stores. "But . . . [in New Haven] . . . most . . . were found in small stores and manufactories, one child in a place"; *Annual Report*, 1890, 26. Truancy did decline, remaining roughly the same numerically from 1870 to 1890, while declining dramatically (by about 50 percent) as a proportion of the average number of children registered during the year. The number of truants shrank even more—deceptively so, when one compares "cases" of truancy with "truants" from year to year. This was due to a policy change. The courts increasingly dealt with juveniles (and guardians) who had violated the truancy laws, so that even though the frequency of truancy cases remained fairly stable over the period, the number of juveniles listed as "truant" was noticeably smaller.

81. The "family cycle" refers to the entire sequence of stages through which families typically pass: coupling, the establishment of a new household, the birth and rearing of children, and the reversal of the entire process, which ends in the eventual dissolution of the household; see Meyer Fortes, "Introduction," in Jack Goody, ed., *The Developmental Cycle in Domestic Groups* (Cambridge: Cambridge University Press, 1971), 1–14; and Tamara K. Hareven, "The Family as Process: The Historical Study of the Family Cycle," *Journal of Family History* 7 (1973–74): 322–29.

82. *Annual Report*, 1871, 23–24; an agent for the Connecticut Department of Labor, in making his plea for a child labor law to accompany and strengthen the compulsory education statute, noted that children as young as "eight years of age and even younger" in parts of the state "had been known to appear at their factory work in the early morning." Such cases were exceptional, he admitted, but underscored the necessity for greater activism on the state's part; State of Connecticut, "Education and Employment," 1873, 61.

83. *Annual Report*, 1870, 14–15.

84. *Annual Report*, 1909.

85. State of Connecticut, "Receipts and Expenses," 110–19. Again, because of the lack of statistical data on labor in late-nineteenth-century Connecticut, it is hard to gauge the extent of child labor; however, if we look at two examples where the participation of juvenile workers is known, Philadelphia and Massachusetts, we can gain some idea of its range elsewhere in the industrial Northeast. Estimates based on census reports on workforce participation in Philadelphia, whose youths were undeterred from finding work by compulsory education laws until 1901, reveal that the employment of children at thirteen years of age and younger ranged from a low of 16.4 percent for daughters of native-born white Protestant heads of household and up to 48.1 percent for sons of Irish-born fathers. We might think of this figure as representing the "natural" level of labor for children thirteen and younger, since employment for children was abundant and varied in the Philadelphia economy. Claudia Goldin, "Family Strategies and the Family Economy in the Late Nineteenth Century: The Role of Secondary Workers," in T. Hershberg, ed., *Philadelphia: Work, Space, and Group Experience in the Nineteenth Century* (New York: Oxford University Press, 1981), 282–84.

At the other extreme, in Massachusetts, where both child labor and compulsory schooling legislation constrained juvenile employment below age fourteen, child labor below fourteen was evidently rare—roughly 5 percent among children of native-born white Protestant heads of household and about 12 percent among children of Irish household heads with any children at work. (These ratios are derived from Modell's estimates comparing the relative ages at which Yankee and Irish household heads in Massachusetts sent their children to work; Modell, "Patterns of Consumption, Acculturation, and Family Income Strategies in Late Nineteenth-Century America," in Tamara K. Hareven and Maris A. Vinovskis, eds., *Family and Population in Nineteenth-Century America* [Princeton, N.J.: Princeton University Press, 1978], 206–40). On proportions of children working at specified ages, see Goldin, "Family Strategies," 283; and Michael R. Haines, "Poverty, Economic Stress, and the Family in a Late Nineteenth-Century American City: Whites in Philadelphia, 1880," in T. Hershberg, ed., *Philadelphia: Work, Space, and Group Experience in the Nineteenth Century* (New York: Oxford University Press, 1981), 260. Of course, these figures convey only the crudest sense of the spectrum of child labor participation rates. As Modell, Goldin, Haines, Greg A. Hoover, and Jerome M. Clubb, Erik W. Austin, and Gordon W. Kirk each have shown, the rate of child participation in the labor market varied with the child's age, gender, nativity of household head, head's income, household composition, and region; see Goldin, "Family Strategies," 283; and Haines, "Poverty, Economic Stress, and the Family"; Haines, "Industrial Work and the Family Life Cycle, 1889/90," *Research in Economic History* 4 (1979): 289–356; Hoover, "Supplemental Family Income Sources," *Social Science History* 9 (Summer 1985): 293–306; and Clubb et al., *The Process of Historical Inquiry: Everyday Lives of Working Americans* (New York: Columbia University Press, 1989), chaps. 2–4.

86. State of Connecticut, *Bureau of Labor Statistics*, "Extracts from Communications in Monthly Reports," in *Reports, 1873–1946*, Hartford, Report 4th, 1887/88, 113.

87. State of Connecticut, "Extracts from Communications," 117–18.

88. State of Connecticut, "Extracts from Communications," 119.

89. State of Connecticut, "Extracts from Communications," 117–18.

90. Michael Anderson, for instance, sees the best hope for understanding family decision-making in the past as anchored "above all in the context of the economic behavior of . . . [family] members." Anderson, *Approaches to the History of the Western Family, 1500–1914* (London: MacMillan, 1980), 65. The opposite trend, exemplified by Ariès, Lawrence Stone, and Jean-Louis Flandrin, has been to treat attitudinal change as springing entirely from general transformations of ideology. As Anderson incisively observes of these historians' analyses: "Change comes about almost entirely from some combination of a weakening of community and legal constraints and the impact of new religious, philosophical and educational ideas about appropriate relationships between individuals. Change in the economy hardly enters in"; Anderson, *Approaches to the History*, 63. Ariès, *Centuries of Childhood;* Stone, *The Family, Sex, and Marriage in England, 1500–1800* (London: Weidenfeld and Nicholson, 1977); and Flandrin, *Families in Former Times: Kinship, Household and Sexuality*, trans. R. Southern (New York: Cambridge University Press, 1979).

91. "Taylorism" (named for Frederick W. Taylor, pioneer of "scientific management") refers generally to the movement by capitalists to divide the production process into separate parts and time how long it ought to take a worker to complete each task. This allowed managers to establish uniform rates of pay for discrete tasks and significantly, design machines to perform tasks formerly performed by skilled workers. On mechanization, the reorganization of production, and the de-skilling of labor at the turn of the century, see Montgomery, *Workers' Control*, and David F. Noble, *America by Design: Science, Technology, and the Rise of Corporate Capitalism* (New York: Alfred A. Knopf, 1977); on the rise and decline of juvenile employment, see Hugh D. Hindman, *Child Labor: An American History* (New York: M. E. Sharpe, 2002); Stanley Lebergott, *Manpower in Economic Growth: The American Record since 1800* (New York: McGraw-Hill, 1964), 52–56; and Paul Osterman, *Getting Started* (Cambridge, Mass.: MIT Press, 1980), 54. Economic historians have hypothesized that compulsory schooling and child labor legislation essentially ratified an already diminishing demand for juvenile workers in the first three decades of the twentieth century and that the obsolescence of child labor simply transferred to the public schools the responsibility for consuming the time and attention of youngsters rendered "useless" by changes in the organization of production; see especially William Landes and Lewis Solomon, "Compulsory Schooling Legislation: An Economic Analysis of Law and Social Change in the Nineteenth Century," *Journal of Economic History* 32 (March 1972): 54–91; Albert Fishlow, "Levels of Nineteenth Century Investment in Education," *Journal of Economic History* 26 (December 1966): 418–36; and Walters and O'Connell, "Family Economy," 1140. Compare Walter Licht, who finds that in Philadelphia during the same period causes of decline in juvenile employment after

1900 were so complex as to "[preclude] a structuralist kind of explanation" and "may have declined in different decades for different reasons"; Licht, *Getting Work: Philadelphia, 1840–1950* (Cambridge, Mass.: Harvard University Press, 1992), 29–30.

92. Osterman used the term "enclosure" in reference to the combination of three forces beginning at the turn of the twentieth century: declining work opportunities for juveniles, pressure on employers to curtail juvenile employment from 1900 to 1930, and, finally, the institution of federal youth programs during the New Deal. Arguably, however, in Connecticut this process began much earlier and culminated in the prohibition of child labor and the elevation of the minimum age of compulsory schooling to age sixteen in 1932; Osterman, *Getting Started*, 70.

93. Gradgrind, of course, is the schoolmaster character lampooned in Charles Dickens, *Hard Times* (1854), for advocating the regimentation of schoolwork to the complete exclusion of frivolity and leisure time for children. The standardization of grade school curricula throughout the United States in the latter half of the nineteenth and early decades of the twentieth centuries, according to John W. Meyer, David Tyack, Joane Nagel, and Audri Gordon, is a parallel movement connected to "nation-building" and industrialization; see, e.g., Meyer et al., "Public Education as Nation-Building in America: Enrollments and Bureaucratization in the American States, 1870–1930," *American Journal of Sociology* 85 (November 1979): 591–613; Meyer, Francisco O. Ramirez, and Yasemin Nuhoglu Soysal, "World Expansion of Mass Education, 1870–1980," *Sociology of Education* 65 (April 1992): 128–49; and Meyer, David H. Kamens, and Aaron Benavot, *School Knowledge for the Masses: World Models and National Primary Curricular Categories in the Twentieth Century* (Washington, D.C.: Falmer Press, 1992).

Chapter 3: The Painful Contrast

1. Kaestle, *Pillars of the Republic*.

2. In 1877 and 1878 a controversy erupted over the use of the King James Bible in New Haven's public schools. Catholics had protested the use of the King James edition, while school authorities defended it in the name of tradition. The issue was not settled until it was decided that the Bible should not be read aloud in the public schools at all; see *Annual Report*, 1878, 22–32; for an extended discussion defending the tradition, see N. T. Bushnell, Samuel Hemingway, and Patrick Maher, *Views of the Minority of the Board of Education, Concerning the Discontinuance of Religious Exercises in the Public Schools* (New Haven: Tuttle, Morehouse and Taylor, 1878), 31; Diane Y. Choo, "'Dispensing with Devotions': New Haven Public Schooling and the Religious Exercise Question, 1877–1878" (senior essay, Department of History, Yale University, April 2000); and Diane Ravitch, *The Great School Wars: New York City, 1805–1973; A History of the Public Schools as Battlefield of Social Change* (New York: Basic Books, 1974).

3. On the stance of New Haven educators on corporal punishment, see, e.g., *Annual Report*, 1869, 29–31; a discussion of the issue is conducted in the *Annual*

Reports for several years following the Civil War; on twentieth-century working-class disciplinary attitudes, see, e.g., Melvin L. Kohn, *Class and Conformity: A Study in Values*, 2d ed. (Chicago: University of Chicago Press, 1977). Even though corporal punishment was strongly denounced, the practice lingered well into the twentieth century in New Haven. Murray Lender, for instance, recalls having his knuckles rapped by his elementary school teacher during the 1930s; Murray Lender, interview by Susan L. Neitlich, tape recording, July 1996, New Haven.

4. See David W. Galenson, "Ethnic Differences in Neighborhood Effects on the School Attendance of Boys in Early Chicago," *History of Education Quarterly* 38 (Spring 1998): 17–35.

5. *Annual Report*, 1857.

6. Scholars of public schooling in the contemporary United States, however, find virtually no "neighborhood effects" when other factors, such as race and socioeconomic status, are accounted for; see Greg J. Duncan and Stephen W. Raudenbush, "Neighborhoods and Adolescent Development: How Can We Assess the Links?" manuscript presented at the conference "Does It Take a Village? Community Effects on Children, Adolescents, and Families," Pennsylvania State University, University Park, November 5–6, 1998. But see Robert D. Putnam, who emphasizes the crucial role of social capital in children's academic success and its grounding in the interrelationship of families, neighborhoods, and schools; Putnam, *Bowling Alone: The Collapse and Revival of American Community* (New York: Simon and Schuster, 2001).

7. The first "nationality" census in New Haven was conducted in 1878, in apparent response to a controversy over the use of the King James Bible in the public schools. During the last quarter of the nineteenth century, Irish immigrants were the largest immigrant group in New Haven and the second-largest group in the public schools (after native-born whites of native parentage). The next nationality census was in 1908, but there was not another until 1915, when concern over immigrant loyalty arose as an issue in reaction to the outbreak of hostilities in Europe. The census was conducted every year thereafter until the *Annual Report* finally ceased publication in 1935, with a three-year interruption between 1932 and 1935.

8. Covello points out that "illiteracy statistics for the South pertained almost exclusively to men, since, with the exception of women of the *galantuomo* class, all southern Italian women were illiterate." Moreover, he estimates that even these statistics do not indicate the true levels of illiteracy, because they are averages based on the South's larger cities and administrative centers and so do not adequately reflect the extent of illiteracy in the smaller towns and villages, which may have been completely illiterate "as late as 1913"; Covello, *The Social Background of the Italo-American School Child: A Study of the Southern Italian Family Mores and Their Effect on the School Situation in Italy and America* (Leiden, Netherlands: E. J. Brill, 1967), 245–47, 258–59. Reeder's estimates of illiteracy rates for Sicily vary somewhat from Covello's for the South in general. Reeder, drawing from the 1901 data, is less skeptical than Covello was about the reliability of the official census figures. She reports that illiteracy for males

above age six was at 65 percent in 1901 and for females at 77 percent; Reeder, "Women in the Classroom," 110; Banfield's discussion of illiteracy in the South later in the century confirms Covello's findings; see Banfield, *Moral Basis*, 20–22.

9. Whitelaw, "Administration of the Elementary School," appendix C. For more commentary on attitudes toward Italian immigrant children in New Haven schools, see Carl Butts and Joseph Young, "Education in Connecticut," Works Progress Administration, Ethnic Groups Survey, box 37, folder 134:5a, p. 212, Historical Manuscripts and Archives Division, University of Connecticut Libraries, Storrs; and Norma E. Cutts, "The Extent of Bilingualism and Its Effect on Beginning Reading in a Group of First Year Children Largely of Italian Parentage" (Ph.D. diss., Yale University, 1933).

10. U.S. Congress, Senate, *Reports of the Immigration Commission, vol. 30, The Children of Immigrants in Schools*, vol. 4, 61st Cong., 2d sess., S. Doc. 5874 (Washington, D.C.: Government Printing Office, 1911). This multivolume study was known as the "Dillingham Report," after the head of the Immigration Commission. Between 1916 and 1929 seventeen separate studies bearing results from individual tests administered throughout the United States to a total of 3,601 children of Italian-born fathers reconfirmed the singularity of the Italian American schoolchild. During the same period group tests were administered with the same results, according to a sociologist of education who analyzed the effects of bilingualism on the performance of Italian American schoolchildren in New Haven during the 1930s; Cutts, "Extent of Bilingualism," 59–61.

11. Jeannie Oakes, *Keeping Track: How Schools Structure Inequality* (New Haven: Yale University Press, 1985), 35–36.

12. John S. MacDonald and Leatrice D. MacDonald, "Chain Migration: Ethnic Neighborhood Formation and Social Networks," *Milbank Memorial Fund Quarterly* 42 (January 1964): 82–97. Not only did they not speak English, the majority of southern Italian immigrants did not speak Italian either; rather, they spoke the dialect of their region of emigration. Italian was the "national" and official language of Italy, but it had to be acquired in school, which southern Italians typically avoided or were denied.

13. *Annual Report*, 1898, 24.

14. This ended in 1932, when, because of a lack of funds, the board of education ceased publication of its *Annual Report*.

15. On the performance of Italian immigrant children in New Haven's schools, see Cutts, "Extent of Bilingualism"; on truancy, see *Annual Report*, 1900–1932; and on juvenile delinquency (1926–29), see Dreis, *Handboook of Social Statistics*, 112–13.

16. Joel Perlmann, *Ethnic Differences: Schooling and Social Structure among the Irish, Italians, Jews, and Blacks in an American City, 1880–1935* (Cambridge: Cambridge University Press, 1988), 119–21; see also Josef J. Barton, *Peasants and Strangers: Italians, Rumanians, and Slovaks in an American City, 1890–1950* (Cambridge, Mass.: Harvard University Press, 1975).

17. In the area of "economy" versus "sentiment," I do not mean to say that the family functioned purely for economic purposes and that there was no room for the

expression of feeling per se, but rather that it was understood that family members existed for and because of one another and that the family's economic well-being meant that material considerations organize family priorities. Although there is widespread agreement that affection among nonchild family members was suppressed, it should be understood that such feelings were rather assumed than articulated.

18. The *contadino* is an Italian peasant, but the term usually referred specifically to southern Italian small landholders or tenant farmers. It was from this group that most of Italy's immigrants to the United States (and New Haven) came after 1900.

19. From the turn of the century until the passage of immigration restriction legislation in 1924, politicians and intellectuals debated the prospects of assimilating immigrants to the United States. National fear of peoples coming from non-Protestant and non-English-speaking countries peaked in the wake of World War I and the Bolshevik Revolution of 1917. The literature is voluminous but an instance of a sociological work that seeks to understand the workings of assimilation is Robert E. Park and Herbert A. Miller, *Old World Traits Transplanted* (New York: Harper, 1921).

20. His doctoral dissertation, Leonard Covello, "The Social Background of the Italo-American School Child," unpublished until 1967, was submitted for approval to New York University in 1944.

21. See Francesco Cordasco, ed., *Studies in Italian American Social History: Essays in Honor of Leonard Covello* (Totowa, N.J.: Rowman and Littlefield, 1975), ix–xiv, 1–9; and "Preface" to Covello, *Social Background*, vi.

22. Covello (with D'Agostino), *Heart Is the Teacher.*

23. In the 1950s Covello turned his attention to Puerto Rican immigrant children, who were then East Harlem's most recent arrivals.

24. Covello, *Social Background*, 257.

25. Covello, *Social Background*, 261.

26. "Alfano—Brooklyn," interview by Covello, TS, Leonard Covello Papers (hereafter, LCP), MS 40, box 66, folder 18, unpag.

27. In 1904 the minimum age of compulsory schooling was raised to twelve; Covello, *Social Background*, 251.

28. Reeder, "Women in the Classroom."

29. Covello explains the northern affinity for popular education by saying that in the North, "Western European concepts of school education were emulated and adopted by the centralized Ministry of Public Instruction. . . . While the national government . . . regarded illiteracy as an abomination and propagated the concept that book learning had the power to form character, make good citizens, keep family mores pure, elevate morals, cure social vice and disease, and so on. This undoubtedly stimulated book learning as an article of faith." Covello, *Social Background*, 245.

30. On schooling and the "southern problem," see also Cinel, *National Integration*, 89–95; and Christopher Duggan, *A Concise History of Italy* (Cambridge: Cambridge University Press, 1994), 154–55.

31. Covello, *Social Background*, 245.

32. Covello, *Social Background*, 247. In a village in the province of Lucania in southern Italy even as recently as the mid-1950s, Banfield estimated that "nearly 30 percent of those ten to forty years of age were illiterate [as of 1951]." Among people of the outlying areas the rate of illiteracy was as much as 44 percent. Moreover, Banfield observed that poor attendance was still common—especially among farm children—and the tendency for most children of the area was to quit school at age eleven or twelve. "One-third of the men and two-thirds of the women who were twenty-one years of age or over in 1954 had attended fewer than five grades of school. Only 5 percent of the men and fewer than 2 percent of the women had attended more than five grades." Banfield, *Moral Basis*, 20–22.

33. Covello, *Social Background*, 249.

34. Covello, untitled TS, LCP, MS 40, box 66, folder 17, unpag.

35. But see Reeder, "Women in the Classroom."

36. Covello, *Social Background*, 251.

37. Covello, *Social Background*, 268–70.

38. Covello, untitled TS, LCP, MS 40, box 66, folder 17, unpag.

39. Phyllis H. Williams, *South Italian Folkways in Europe and America* (New Haven: Yale University Press, 1938), 27–28.

40. Covello, *Social Background*, 270.

41. Covello, *Social Background*, 265, 269.

42. Covello, Untitled TS, LCP, MS 40, box 66, folder 17, unpag.; school for many contadini children created an intense ambivalence, if not distaste, toward home life. But at the same time this feeling made school something to be endured until they were legally old enough to make their own way in the world.

43. Covello, untitled TS, LCP, MS 40, box 66, folder 17, unpag. Irvin L. Child's interviews with second-generation Italian immigrants in New Haven certainly reinforces this assessment, as does Robert Anthony Orsi, implicitly, in his emphasis on the significance of the "Domus" as the central organizing symbol of contadini group life; Child, "A Psychological Study of Second-Generation Italians" (Ph.D. diss., Yale University, 1939); and Orsi, *The Madonna of 115th Street: Faith and Community in Italian Harlem, 1880–1950* (New Haven: Yale University Press, 1985).

44. Irvin L. Child, *Italian or American? The Second-Generation in Conflict* (New Haven: Yale Unversity Press, 1943), 40.

45. Child, *Italian or American?* 40.

46. Covello, TS, LCP, MS 40, box 66, folder 18, unpag.

47. Stephen Orlando, "Children of Foreign Parentage," theme paper submitted to Prof. Paul G. Cressey, New York University, 1934, LCP, MS 40, box 66, folder 17, p. 22. It is unclear whether the description in the text is autobiographical or derived from the author's research in Italian Harlem. The class referred to was team-taught by Covello and sociologist Cressey.

48. R. Scottino, untitled theme paper, New York University, 1941, LCP, MS 40, box 66, folder 18, unpag.

49. Child, *Italian or American?* 40; see also Marjorie Roberts, "Italian Girls on American Soil," *Mental Hygiene* 13 (October 1929): 761.

50. Covello, untitled TS, LCP, MS 40, box 66, folder 17, unpag.

51. Thomas and Znaniecki, *Polish Peasant in Europe and America*, vol. 1; Child, *Italian or American?* Handlin, *Uprooted;* Sister Mary Fabian Matthews, "The Role of the Public School in the Assimilation of the Italian Immigrant Child in New York City, 1900–1914," in Sylvano M. Tomasi and Madeline H. Engel, eds., *The Italian Immigrant Experience in the United States* (Staten Island, N.Y.: Center for Migration Studies, 1970), 140–41; Gans, *Urban Villagers.* John W. Briggs and Joseph Lopreato support Matthews's contention that no cultural conflict stemmed from the attendance of Italian immigrant children in American schools; see Briggs, *An Italian Passage: Immigrants to Three American Cities, 1890–1930* (New Haven: Yale University Press, 1978), chaps. 3, 9–10; and Lopreato, *Italian Americans* (New York: Random House, 1970), 153–54.

52. Covello, untitled TS, LCP, MS 40, box 66, folder 17, unpag.; emphasis mine.

53. Letter to Leonard Covello from Josephine Patane, December 1942, LCP, MS 40, box 66, folder 17, unpag. Note the rhetoric of the son's characterization of his situation, which is no doubt Covello's rendering rather than his own.

54. Letter to Covello from Patane.

55. Covello, of course, disappointed her by telling her that there was nothing he could do; letter to Covello from Patane.

56. On the state's role in the affairs of Italians in the southern provinces, see Covello, *Social Background*, chaps. 2, 4; on the American Catholic clergy and Italian immigrants, see Rudolph J. Vecoli, "Prelates and Peasants: Italian Immigrants and the Catholic Church," *Journal of Social History* 2 (Spring 1969): 217–68; on Southern Italian immigrant piety, see Orsi, *Madonna of 115th Street;* on relations of Italians to community social welfare agencies, see Virginia Yans-McLaughlin, *Family and Community: Italian Immigrants in Buffalo, 1880–1930* (Ithaca, N.Y.: Cornell University Press, 1977), chap. 5; on immigrants and urban politics in the early twentieth century, see Lizabeth Cohen, *Making a New Deal: Industrial Workers in Chicago, 1919–1939* (New York: Cambridge University Press, 1990); and on Italian immigrants and New Haven politics, see Johnston, "On the Outside."

57. Whitelaw, "Administration of the Elementary School," 325.

58. Covello, "Amorality of American School Education," TS, LCP, MS 40, box 66, folder 17, unpag.

59. Covello, untitled TS, LCP, MS 40, box 66, folder 17, unpag.

60. Covello, untitled TS, LCP, MS 40, box 66, folder 18, unpag.; also quoted in Covello, *Social Background*, 262–63.

61. Covello, *Social Background*, 289.

62. Covello, untitled TS, LCP, MS 40, box 66, folder 17, unpag.; compare the consonance of this view with John Demos's description of coming of age in seventeenth-century New England: "Once the child had begun to assume an adult role and style, around the age of six or seven, the way ahead was fairly straightforward. Development toward full maturity could be accomplished in a gradual, piecemeal, and largely automatic fashion. . . . Here was no 'awkward' age—but rather the steady lengthening of a young person's shadow, and the whole instinctive process through which one generation

yielded imperceptibly to its successor." Demos, *A Little Commonwealth: Family Life in Plymouth Colony* (New York: Oxford University Press, 1970), 150.

63. Covello, untitled TS, LCP, MS 40, box 66, folder 17, p. 5.

64. Covello, *Social Background,* chap. 9, passim, esp. 288, 291.

65. Racca, "Selected Family Histories" (Tranquilli family), 27–28.

66. Williams, *South Italian Folkways,* 81.

67. On this point see Judith E. Smith, *Family Connections: A History of Italian and Jewish Immigrant Lives in Providence, Rhode Island, 1900–1940* (Albany: SUNY Press, 1985), chap. 2.

68. Lucia F., interview by author, tape recording, New Haven, October 5, 1989, Greater New Haven Labor History Association.

69. "Even the small amount [of labor] accomplished by quite young children was frequently so necessary an addition to the family's efforts that they were kept from school for these purposes. The authorities of Southern Italy in particular realized that the enforcement of the so-called compulsory school law might mean the difference between existence and starvation." Williams, *South Italian Folkways,* 21.

70. "Frank G.—118th Street," interview by Leonard Covello, New York, October 20, 1939, TS, LCP, MS 40, box 30, folder 16, p. 11.

71. Racca, "Selected Family Histories" (Tranquilli family), 32.

72. Racca, "Selected Family Histories," 32.

73. Williams, *South Italian Folkways,* 126–27; Covello, *Social Background,* 268–70; and Roberts, "Italian Girls on American Soil," 759.

74. See Modell, "Patterns of Consumption"; John Bodnar, "Immigration, Kinship, and the Rise of Working-Class Realism," *Journal of Social History* 14 (Fall 1980): 45–65; and Susan A. Glenn, *Daughters of the Shtetl: Life and Labor in the Immigrant Generation* (Ithaca, N.Y.: Cornell University Press, 1990), 87.

75. Covello, *Social Background,* 292–97. In almost all ethnic groups, nationally girls tended to have somewhat higher high school graduation rates than boys. Perlmann, however, points out that for "Slavic" groups throughout the United States (Lithuanians, Poles, and Serbs and Croations) a pattern identical to the Italian bias against girls' schooling emerged, but all of these groups had higher overall rates of high school graduation than the Italians. Czechs were the only group with a high school graduation rate comparable to the Italians (at 15 percent to 16 percent in 1915), yet there was no apparent gender bias operating in this group; Perlmann, *Ethnic Differences,* 118–21.

76. Covello, *Social Background,* 292; see also Perlmann, *Ethnic Differences,* 89–90, n. 14, table 3.3; Donna R. Gabaccia, *From Sicily to Elizabeth Street: Housing and Social Change among Italian Immigrants, 1880–1930* (Albany: SUNY Press, 1984), 111–15. Miriam Cohen has shown how this pattern was altered for the children of second-generation Italian immigrants; see Cohen, "Changing Educational Strategies among Immigrant Generations: New York's Italians in Comparative Perspective," *Journal of Social History* 15 (Spring 1982): 443–66.

77. Covello, untitled TS, LCP, MS 40, box 66, folder 17, unpag.

78. Covello, *Social Background,* 292.

79. Covello, *Social Background,* 292.

80. Covello, *Social Background,* 293.

81. Mrs. Apicello, by Leonard Covello, 116th St., New York, November 10, 1930, TS, LCP, MS 40, box 30, folder 16, p. 11.

82. Glenn, *Daughters of the Shtetl,* 66.

83. Yans-McLaughlin, *Family and Community,* chap. 7; Covello, *Social Background,* 292. This was an ideal to be attained only if circumstances permitted, of course. "Lucia F." complained bitterly that because her husband suffered from asthma and could not hold a steady job, she "had to be the man in the family" and work in Wooster Square dress shops while her husband stayed home with their young son. Lucia F., interview by author. A U.S. Bureau of Labor study of five U.S. cities in 1907 through 1908 reported that only 17 percent of Italian women worked outside their homes, yet Russian Jewish women did so even less; Glenn, *Daughters of the Shtetl,* 68–69.

84. See Yans-McLaughlin's discussion of southern Italians' reluctance to permit daughters to work in occupations that might compromise their reputations; Yans-McLaughlin, *Family and Community,* 204–5; see also Roberts, "Italian Girls on American Soil," 759, 763.

85. Covello, *Social Background,* 263–64; Roberts, "Italian Girls on American Soil," 759, 764–66.

86. Racca, "Selected Family Histories" (Tranquilli family), 29.

87. Child, "Psychological Study," 462.

88. One couple with whom Covello had come into contact as principal of Benjamin Franklin High School in New York became very discouraged when they were informed of the obstacles their son would have to surmount to become a doctor, lawyer, or engineer, and, reported Covello, "proclaimed on the spot, that 'if he [can] . . . not become one of these, shall we make him a maestro (teacher)?'" Covello, untitled TS, LCP, MS 40, box 66, folder 17, unpag.

89. See Covello, *Social Background,* 326–27.

90. Maria Betteti, interviews by author, tape recording, New Haven, May 30 and June 20, 1990.

91. Covello, untitled TS, LCP, MS 40, box 66, folder 17, unpag.

92. Roberts, although she does not discuss the consequences of choosing between work and schooling, believed that in going out to work, a young woman incurred even more scrutiny of her social contacts than before; Roberts, "Italian Girls on American Soil," 764.

93. Smith, *Family Connections,* 75–76; although in such an event a young woman ran the risk of expulsion from her parents' household, this seems to have occurred only rarely. For a young woman in particular, this was potentially a very vulnerable position in which to be. While most parents found it difficult to contemplate expulsion (and the shame it would bring upon them), the usual result was an unceasing tension and resentment; see, e.g., Child, "Psychological Study," 135–36, and Williams, *South Italian Folkways,* 98.

94. I say "formally" because, in practice, there were of course many ways in which daughters continued to be of assistance to parents after they married into another family. Moreover, immigration itself might physically foreclose any of the kinds of obligations traditionally associated with patrilocality. Smith in fact shows how, in Providence, many women's parents lived on the floor above or below them in triple-decker houses, often with a married sister in the other flat.

95. Roberts, "Italian Girls on American Soil," 673.

Chapter 4: Hands to Mouths

1. Covello, untitled TS, LCP, MS 40, box 66, folder 17, p. 5; and see Covello, *Social Background*, 296, 403–4.

2. See, e.g., Robert F. Foerster, *The Italian Emigration of Our Times* (Cambridge, Mass.: Harvard University Press, 1919); Yans-McLaughlin, *Family and Community;* and Briggs, *Italian Passage.* On the contrasting experience of Italian immigrants in South America, where the occupational choices and distribution of Italian immigrants across the social structure were much broader, see Samuel L. Baily, *Immigrants in the Lands of Promise: Italians in Buenos Aires and New York City, 1870–1914* (Ithaca, N.Y.: Cornell University Press, 1999).

3. See Pierre Bourdieu's remarks on the "discourse of familiarity," in which he says "the best informed source . . . will not mention those things that are 'understood' because they are selfevident [*sic*]"; Bourdieu, "Marriage Strategies as Strategies of Social Reproduction," Elborg Forster and Patricia M. Ranum, trans., Robert Forster and Orest Ranum, eds., *Family and Society: Selections from the Annales; Economies, Sociétiés, Civilisations* (Baltimore: Johns Hopkins University Press, 1976), 117–18, n. 1.

4. The most exemplary of early-twentieth-century works is, of course, Thomas and Znaniecki, *Polish Peasant in Europe and America;* a good early guide to the sociological literature is Dorothy R. Krall, "The Second-Generation Immigrant in America; with Special Reference to the Problem of Adjustment" (Ph.D. diss., Yale University, 1937). The first significant historical treatment of this topic was Marcus Lee Hansen's *The Problem of the Third Generation Immigrant,* Augustana Historical Society Publication no. 8, pt.1 (Rock Island, Ill.: Augustana Historical Society, 1938); and see the excellent retrospective of the Hansen thesis in Peter Kivisto and Dag Blanck, eds., *American Immigrants and Their Generations: Studies and Commentaries on the Hansen Thesis after Fifty Years* (Urbana: University of Illinois Press, 1980); and see Perlmann's probing notational discussion scattered throughout chapter 3 of his *Ethnic Differences,* 83–121, esp. nn. 5, 8, 9, 49, 55. Finally, the theme of cultural conflict as generational conflict is also a major motif in U.S. immigrant literary production from the 1880s forward; see David M. Fine, *The City, the Immigrant, and American Fiction, 1880–1940* (Metuchen, N.J.: Scarecrow Press, 1977). The bald nationalism exhibited by the public schools in the name of "Americanizing" immigrant children during the years surrounding World War I made the assimilability of non-English-speaking immigrant children a

national issue; see various chapters in Bernard J.Weiss, ed., *American Education and the European Immigrant, 1840–1940* (Urbana: University of Illinois Press, 1981).

5. A classic in the Social Darwinist vein is Madison Grant, *The Passing of the Great Race; or The Racial Basis of European History* (New York: Charles Scribner, 1916); for a history of the relationship of the "culture concept" to conceptions of race, see George W. Stocking Jr., *Race, Culture, and Evolution: Essays in the History of Anthropology* (New York: Free Press, 1968)

6. Stocking, *Race, Culture, and Evolution;* and George W. Stocking, *Victorian Anthropology* (New York: Free Press, 1987).

7. Caldwell, "Mass Education"; and see Levine's commentary on Caldwell in Levine, *Reproducing Families,* 161–62.

8. Cinel, *National Integration;* Nugent, citing Ira A. Glazier, points out that half of the men and women who migrated were between the ages of twenty-five and forty, and men outnumbered women four to one; Nugent, *Crossings,* 99.

9. Cinel, *National Integration.*

10. Samuel Koenig, *Immigrant Settlements in Connecticut* (Hartford: State of Connecticut Department of Education, 1938).

11. John R. Gillis, *Youth and History: Tradition and Change in European Age Relations, 1770–Present* (New York: Academic Press, 1981).

12. See Milton M. Gordon, *Assimilation in American Life: The Role of Race, Religion, and National Origins* (New York: Oxford University Press, 1964), 78; and Richard D. Alba, *Ethnic Identity: The Transformation of White American* (New Haven: Yale University Press, 1991), 185–206.

13. Vittorio Racca, "Selected Family Histories" (Taglieri family). This precise formulation by parents—that children owed their lives to their parents—is so strikingly frequent that one is forced to conclude that this conception underlay children's sense of duty to their parents.

14. See, e.g., Williams, *South Italian Folkways,* 134; Covello, *Social Background,* 289.

15. John W. Briggs estimates that among Italian immigrants in Rochester, the average number of children per completed family was 4.54; Briggs, "Fertility and Cultural Change among Families in Italy and America," *American Historical Review* 91 (December 1986): 1134. Although no comparable data are available for New Haven (i.e., for completed families), the modal family size for Italian heads of household was eight or more persons (17.7 percent of Italian household heads in the 1930 sample, as compared with the "Irish" mode, five persons, and the "United States" mode, three persons), which suggests a similar demographic profile for New Haven; Dreis, *Handboook of Social Statistics,* 123, table 63.

16. Briggs, "Fertility and Cultural Change," 1129–45.

17. E. Wight Bakke, *The Unemployed Worker: A Study of the Task of Making a Living without a Job* (New Haven: Yale University Press, 194), 147.

18. See, e.g., Michael Anderson, *Family Structure in Nineteenth Century Lancashire* (New York: Cambridge University Press, 1971); Flandrin, *Families in Former Times;* and Levine, *Reproducing Families.*

19. This comprises 23 percent of whom were self-identified as "American," 8 percent Italian, and 7 percent "Italian-American"; Bakke, *Unemployed Worker*, 147.

20. Of household heads who informed Bakke that they believed having a large family offered them financial security, 20 percent were "American" (i.e., native-born of native-born parents), 13 percent "Italian," 7 percent Italian American; Bakke, *Unemployed Worker*, 147.

21. Bakke, *Unemployed Worker*, 147.

22. Anonymous Italian immigrant, interview by [first name not given] Frazzetta, Bridgeport, August 26, 1939, TS, pp. 8–9, Peoples of Connecticut Ethnic Heritage Project, Works Progress Administration, Federal Writers' Project, Manuscripts and Archives, University of Connecticut Libraries, Storrs.

23. E. Wight Bakke, *Citizens without Work: A Study of the Effects of Unemployment upon the Workers' Social Relations and Practice* (New Haven: Yale University Press, 1940), 115–17. The continued reliance of large families on children's earnings is certified by investigators for a study by the Women's Bureau of the Connecticut sewing trades as well. A "subsample" was made of younger female workers in the sewing trades, which found that the average size of the thirty-eight families represented in this subsample was 7.5 persons. Of the total persons in these households, half were not wage-earners, one-third of those who were wage-earners in "normal times" were the girls in the subsample, and more than one-fifth of those who were ordinarily wage-earners were unemployed; see U.S. Department of Labor, U.S. Women's Bureau, "The Employment of Women in the Sewing Trades of Connecticut: Preliminary Report." Bulletin of the Women's Bureau, Publication No. 97 (Washington, D.C.: Government Printing Office, 1932), 24.

24. Jenny Alfano and Amelia Spose interview by the Greater New Haven Labor History Association (hereafter, GNHLHA), tape recording, New Haven, November 20, 1988; Frank R. Annunziato, "'Made in New Haven': Unionization and the Shaping of a Clothing Workers' Community," *Labor's Heritage: Quarterly of the George Meany Memorial Archives* 4 (Winter 1992): 30.

25. Smith, *Family Connections*, 96, 186.

26. In oral histories recorded in the late 1980s and early 1990s with surviving members of New Haven's Amalgamated Garment Workers' Union, every woman and man interviewed who had worked in New Haven's garment industry during the 1920s and 1930s confirmed the pervasiveness of the practice of "turning over the pay envelope" through the 1930s; see Annunziato, "'Made in New Haven,'" 30. Pay varied greatly depending on experience, skill, and age, as well as the type of garment, whether it was work paid by the piece or by the hour, whether it was a "contract" shop, and whether the manufacturer was an established or "runaway" shop. Jenny Alfano, for example, reported that she earned between $3.65 and $4.14 per forty-five-hour week as a fourteen-year-old working in a shirt factory, the garment industry's lowest paid sector, in 1928. Investigators for the U.S. Department of Labor, U.S. Women's Bureau found that 53 percent of workers in the shirt factories made less than $10 per week (although they admit that they undercounted younger workers who made decidedly less per

week). Throughout the sewing trades 33 percent of the women earned less than $10 per week, 34 percent earned less than $15 per week, and 21 percent earned between $15 and $20 per week; U.S. Department of Labor, U.S. Women's Bureau, "Employment of Women," 10, table 4; see Alfano, interview, November 20, 1988; Child, "Psychological Study," appendix ("Sample Standard Interviews").

27. See Jennifer Noll, "Italian-American Women in the New Haven Garment Industry" (senior thesis, Department of History, Yale University, April 1994) 15; and Annunziato, "'Made in New Haven,'" 32. According to the U.S. Women's Bureau, a weekly wage of $4 to $5 was typical for girls starting in the dress shops as "cleaners" (those who clipped the threads and trimmed the uneven edges from the garments), but usually a worker would move on to another job in the same shop after a few months, at a higher rate of pay, or change employers if she could not work her way up quickly in the same shop; U.S. Department of Labor, U.S. Women's Bureau, "Employment of Women," 19.

28. Williams, *South Italian Folkways,* 47–48, 77.

29. James S. Davie, "Education and Social Stratification" (Ph.D. diss., Yale University, 1951), chap. 6, 11. This comment echoes Modell's findings on tendencies a half-century earlier among both Yankee and Irish-American working-class families with five or more children to send older children out to work and younger children to school; see Modell, "Patterns of Consumption."

30. "Angela Vecharrio," interview by author, tape recording, New Haven, October 11, 1989, GNHLHA.

31. Child, "Psychological Study," supplement to chap. 5, table 2, and 203.

32. Child, "Psychological Study," 386.

33. Anonymous Italian immigrant, interview by Frazzetta, 8.

34. Bakke, *Unemployed Worker,* 147.

35. Hymen Lender, interview by Susan L. Neitlich, tape recording, New Haven, May 2, 1996.

36. H. Lender, interview by Neitlich, May 2, 1996; see also Fred Ticotsky, "Ticotsky's Bakery and the Legion Avenue Jews," *Jews in New Haven* 3 (1981): 37–49, which corroborates Lender's point about the necessity of all family members contributing to the success of family-owned businesses.

37. H. Lender, interview by Neitlich, May 2, 1996.

38. Dorothy Reed, *Leisure Time of Girls in a "Little Italy"* (Portland, Oreg.: Privately published, 1932), 44, table 14 (Reed's study, incidentally, was conducted in Covello's East Harlem). Curiously, Howard M. Bell's well-known study of youth in Maryland during the late 1930s found that only 12 percent of the girls he surveyed listed movies among their favorite leisure activities. In part, the difference may be due to the older ages of the youths Bell surveyed (sixteen to twenty-four); otherwise, varying regional tastes and the more comprehensive class and ethnic representation in Bell's sample group may explain the disparity. Still, Bernice S. Smith's sample of high school graduates, who fall at the upper end of Bell's "youth" sample, mentioned the following activities in order of desired preference: movies, radio-listening, automobile

riding, and dancing and travel; Bell, *Youth Tell Their Story: A Study of the Conditions and Attitudes of Young People in Maryland between the Ages of Sixteen and Twenty-Four* (Washington, D.C.: American Council on Education, 1938), 162, table 64; Smith, "Depression Graduates: A Follow-Up Study of High School Girls of 1930" (Ph.D. diss., Yale University, 1935), 170.

39. Reed, *Leisure Time of Girls in a "Little Italy,"* 44.

40. Reed, *Leisure Time of Girls in a "Little Italy,"* 43, 52; "Of the six hundred and forty girls only two said they did not have to help at home." All of them, after stating that they had household responsibilities even after coming from work, offered with a hint of resignation, "We have to keep our own houses some day"; Smith, "Depression Graduates," 52; Jenny Alfano, third-born in a New Haven family of seven girls and seven boys, said that before they were even old enough to earn money, "All the older ones had to go home . . . put their other clothes on . . . and each had something to do—throw the dirt away, get the water for the icebox . . . each one had a job, except the last three or four—they were babies"; Jenny Aiello Alfano, interview by Katherine Lebow, tape recording, New Haven, October 19, 1990, GNHLHA, quoted in Noll, "Italian-American Women," 10.

41. May, *Homeward Bound,* chap. 3; Lary May and Stephen Lassonde, "Making the American Way: Moderne Theaters, Audiences, and the Film Industry, 1929–1945," *Prospects: An Annual of American Cultural Studies* 12 (May 1987): 89–124; and Roland Marchand, *Advertising and the American Dream: Making Way for Modernity, 1920–1940* (Berkeley: University of California Press, 1985), chap. 9.

42. Noll, "Italian-American Women," 15.

43. Mary Baker, interview by author, tape recording, New Haven, October 29, 1989, GNHLHA; Baker, interview by Jennifer Noll, tape recording, New Haven, March 1, 1994; Tessie Rappa, interview by Jennifer Noll, tape recording, New Haven, February 25, 1994.

44. "Radio-listening," fifth-ranked among preferences, was a demand realistically satisfied even in New Haven's Italian neighborhoods. In the wards containing the most Italian families (Wards Ten–Twelve), a little more than a quarter owned a radio in 1930; Dreis, *Handbook of Social Statistics,* 93, table 51. Other differences in the preferences expressed by these two groups may be attributed to the higher level of educational attainment and greater ethnic diversity of the New Haven group.

45. Manning and Byrne's (U.S. Department of Labor, U.S. Women's Bureau, "Employment of Women") study of women's employment in Connecticut pointed out that New Haven led the state's cities in issuing "working certificates" in the early years of the Depression, much of the reason for this, they say, is due to the presence of the shirt factories, 20 percent of whose employees were girls under the age of sixteen; U.S. Department of Labor, U.S. Women's Bureau, "Employment of Women," 20. By the same token, however, a Connecticut study in 1934 showed the worsening unemployment for state youths as the number of working certificates dropped by 60 percent between 1928 and 1934; State of Connecticut, *Youths in Search of Jobs!* Connecticut State Employment Service (Hartford, 1934 [FERA Project CPS-F2–87]),

26; nationally in 1933, during the worst year of the decade, unemployment peaked at 24.9 percent. Yet as late as 1938 joblessness among young people between the ages of sixteen and twenty ranged between 56.3 percent and 29.1 percent nationally, the highest rates for any age group in the United States. In the same year, of those employed below the age of twenty-one, between 14 percent and 33 percent could only find part-time work; Bell, *Youth Tell Their Story*, 106, table 34.

46. John W. McConnell, *The Evolution of Social Classes* (Washington, D.C.: American Council on Public Affairs, 1942), 110.

47. Williams, *South Italian Folkways*, 20, 83, 148; see also Covello, *Social Background*, 231; Cinel, *National Integration*, 61.

48. Williams, *South Italian Folkways*, 36.

49. Williams, *South Italian Folkways*, 148.

50. On "visiting," see Reed, *Leisure Time*, 45. For others, especially in the worst years of the Depression, before the garment shops were unionized, not even Sunday was a day of rest. Amelia Spose, who worked at the Max Price Dress factory by the time she was fourteen, recalled that in the early 1930s she had to work a half day on Sunday in addition to working full days the rest of the week. Because work was so scarce, she was told that if she did not come in on Sunday, she "would be fired on Monday when [she] went in"; Amelia Spose, interview by GNHLHA, tape recording, November 20, 1988, GNHLHA; see also U.S. Department of Labor, U.S. Women's Bureau, "The Employment of Women in the Sewing Trades of Connecticut: Hours and Earnings, Employment Fluctuation, and Home Work," *Bulletin of the Women's Bureau*, No. 109 (Washington, D.C.: Government Printing Office, 1935), 1–24.

51. Williams, *South Italian Folkways*, 147–48.

52. Williams, *South Italian Folkways*, 131.

53. Almeda King, "A Study of the Italian Diet in a Group of New Haven Families" (M.A. thesis, Yale University, 1935), 91.

54. Although the author of this study claimed that the families from which these women came (125 of them) were "definitely" representative of the New Haven community, in fact, this was not the case. Fifty-eight percent of them came from families that owned their own homes, as compared with a citywide average of 31 percent; 17.4 percent of their fathers were unemployed, whereas the average for New Haven heads of household was more than 28 percent; and although fully a quarter of New Haven's families received either public or private forms of "welfare" in 1933, just 9.2 percent of the families of these graduates received assistance in 1935; Smith, "Depression Graduates," 74, 83, 92, 100–101. Smith did, however, exercise extreme care in selecting a sample of female graduates that were representative of their graduating class in every respect.

55. "Mode" here refers not to the average expenditure but to the expenditure registered most frequently.

56. Smith, "Depression Graduates," 96.

57. Smith, "Depression Graduates," 97.

58. Smith, "Depression Graduates," 96–99; the ratio of students in 1930 whose parents were foreign-born was 61.2 percent for Commercial and 50.4 percent for New Haven High School (NHHS). The proportion of graduates in Smith's sample group with one or both parents who had been born in Italy was 23 percent (i.e., for graduates of the two high schools combined). The percentage of students of "Italian extraction" enrolled in NHHS, grades 9–12, in 1930 was 18.9; "Italian" students enrolled in Commercial in the same year were 23.1 percent of the total. The ratio of all New Haven schoolchildren whose head of household was of "Italian extraction" in 1930 was 35.7 percent; Smith, "Depression Graduates," 80; *Annual Report*, 1930; Dreis, Handboook of *Social Statistics*, 48, table 26. Amounts spent by Commercial High School graduates on clothing were significantly more than those for graduates of NHHS, but as a proportion of their earnings they were roughly equivalent.

59. Smith, "Depression Graduates," 91, 187.

60. Smith, "Depression Graduates," 99; McConnell noted the expansion of installment buying in New Haven as well, stating that between World War I and the mid-1930s it closely rivaled the older and well-established practice of retail charge accounts; McConnell, *Evolution of Social Classes*, 121.

61. This was Bakke's conclusion, drawn from his analysis of budgets kept by twenty-four unemployed families over the course of six months in New Haven; Bakke, *Unemployed Worker*, appendix, 263, table 14b. Bakke also pointed out, however, that the inability to buy food could have a devastating effect on social life. Italian immigrants insisted on having special foods to serve anyone who visited their homes. If they could not afford to offer something of good quality to eat, they felt they could not invite anyone in. The result, of course, was to greatly inhibit social interaction.

62. Mary Baker, mentioned earlier, was raised solely by her mother, a domestic worker, who she says would only take jobs with families that had children Mary's age so that she could have their used clothing, in effect, boosting her wage; Baker, interview by author, GNHLHA. Although many of the unemployed families whose budgets Bakke scrutinized for six months managed to get by without spending anything on clothing, clothing was, he pointed out, "one of the most frequent forms of outside or family gifts, so that families were often better-clad than expenditures alone might indicate." Bakke, *Unemployed Worker*, 273. Requests for coats, dresses, and shoes were among the most numerically conspicuous items sought by girls and women who wrote letters to Eleanor Roosevelt during the 1930s; see the Eleanor Anna Roosevelt Papers, "Letters to Mrs. Roosevelt," ER 2100–2600, Franklin D. Roosevelt Library, U.S. National Archives and Records Administration, Hyde Park, N.Y.

63. Bakke, *Unemployed Worker*, 272.

64. Bakke, *Unemployed Worker*, 273.

65. McConnell, *Evolution of Social Classes*, 126.

66. McConnell, *Evolution of Social Classes*, 126. Shergold's study of working-class living standards in turn-of-the-century Pittsburgh found that new immigrants in particular seemed to care little about clothing, so intent were they upon saving. By the same token, however, it may be that native-born American workers used clothing to

differentiate themselves from immigrants and the less-skilled among them. This is implied by Shergold and remarked upon by McConnell in the 1930s; Shergold, *Working-Class Life*, 225–26; and McConnell, *Evolution of Social Classes*, 126.

67. Asked to characterize the Italian immigrant population in the Wooster Square district by another researcher, Racca commented that while those living in the "Hill" district (from around Naples and to the north) were "intelligent and accustomed to making a satisfactory living for themselves," another 40 percent—those living around Wooster Square—were from the rugged coastal countryside south of Naples whose principle occupation had been fishing. "For centuries they have lived in poverty," he relayed. "It is the opinion of Dr. Racca," reported Cutts, "that the group in the neighborhood concerned in this investigation represents the lowest group, intellectually, of Italian immigrants that will be found in this country"; Cutts, "Extent of Bilingualism," 164. Racca's contempt for the southerner was rivaled only by his scorn for forms of economic assistance to the unemployed, which he viewed as ensnaring and destructive to traditional forms of Italian social organization and self-reliance; see, e.g., Racca, "Selected Family Histories" (see the "Croce," "De Nuzzo," "Taglieri," "Barone," "Gambardella," and "Tranquilli" families).

68. Racca, "Selected Family Histories" ("De Nuzzo" family), 6–7.

69. An Italian immigrant mason in New Haven during the 1930s, quoted by McConnell, *Evolution of Social Classes*, 110.

70. See Racca, "Selected Family Histories" ("Croce" and "Tranquilli" families in particular).

71. Racca, "Selected Family Histories" ("Croce" family), 23.

72. As Covello points out innumerable times, brothers of almost any age were considered their family's protectors and therefore protectors of their sisters' "honor"; see esp. Covello, *Social Background*, 233, and Williams, *South Italian Folkways*, 78.

73. Williams, *South Italian Folkways*, 90–91.

74. Racca, "Selected Family Histories" ("Tranquilli" family), 30.

75. Racca, "Selected Family Histories" ("Tranquilli" family), 32–33.

76. On the concept and functioning of families as economic units, see Gary S. Becker, *A Treatise on the Family* (Cambridge, Mass.: Harvard University Press, 1981).

Chapter 5: From Courtship to Dating

1. See Bourdieu, "Marriage Strategies."

2. This idea is explored from a variety of perspectives in Diana Tietjens Meyers, Kenneth Kipnis, and Cornelius F. Murphy Jr., eds., *Kindred Matters: Rethinking the Philosophy of the Family* (Ithaca, N.Y.: Cornell University Press, 1993).

3. Caldwell, "Mass Education"; and see Becker, *Treatise on the Family*, 242.

4. Again, as in this book's introduction, I use the phrase "family morality" as a shorthand for Caldwell's phrase "family system of morality," which he uses to describe an ethos that "enjoins children to work hard, demand little, and respect the authority of the old," Caldwell, "Mass Education," 226.

5. Child, "Psychological Study," 56.

6. Orsi, *Madonna of 115th Street,* 136, 139.

7. Covello gave the most detailed rendering of contadini attitudes toward gender, sexuality, courtship, and family life based on his studies of Harlem's southern Italians during the 1920s and 1930s; Covello, *Social Background.* Orsi, who draws much of his material from Covello's interviews and accounts, confirms his claims; Orsi, *Madonna of 115th Street,* esp. chap. 5.

8. Child, "Psychological Study," 56; McConnell, *Evolution of Social Classes,* 178.

9. See David I. Kertzer and Richard P. Saller, eds., *The Family in Italy from Antiquity to the Present* (New Haven: Yale University Press, 1991), part 3, but see esp. Caroline B. Brettel, "Property, Kinship, and Gender: A Mediterranean Perspective," in that volume.

10. Kertzer and Saller, *Family in Italy,* and Brettel, "Property, Kinship, and Gender," passim, and see Bourdieu, "Marriage Strategies," on the broader question of "rules" in contradistinction to "statistical regularity" in customs relating to the transmission of property, grooms, and brides in rural societies.

11. Luigi Tittarelli, "Choosing a Spouse among Nineteenth-Century Central Italian Sharecroppers," in Kertzer and Saller, *Family in Italy,* 282.

12. Innumerable observers have commented on this, but the earliest and most widely cited is Foerster, *Italian Emigration.*

13. Like most immigrants but to an even greater degree, Italians, because of both their great numbers and the habit of American managers and workers to discriminate against them, moved into the least desirable occupations and at the lowest skill levels, regardless of their individual skills. Samuel L. Baily, for example, shows by way of contrast how in Argentina, Italian immigrants were able to find their way into much more diverse occupations than occurred in the United States; see Baily, "Cross-Cultural Comparisons and the Writing of Migration History: Some Thoughts on How to Study Italians in the New World," in Virginia Yans-McLaughlin, ed., *Immigration Reconsidered: History, Sociology, and Politics* (New York: Oxford University Press, 1990), 241–53.

14. The work experience of these women in producing clothing in Italy ordinarily consisted of garment-making at home and by hand. A very good craftswoman would visit other women's homes to cut patterns or do the more difficult detail work of dresses and other more complicated pieces of clothing. On sweatshops in New Haven, see William G. Shepherd, "Robbing the Working Girl," *Collier's* (November 12, 1932): 10–11; 34; and Annunziato, " 'Made in New Haven.' " Even as the Great Depression deepened, garment work remained a source of employment for female workers. In their study of the closing of L. Candee Rubber, Clague et al. reported that between 25 percent and 40 percent of the female workers who lost their jobs at the rubber boot factory found employment during the three years after April 1929 in the garment shops nearby: "The younger women particularly were attracted to this alternative. The presence of the establishments in the neighborhood evidently suggested strongly the possibility of such employment, the heaviest recruiting being from the neighborhoods immediately surrounding them." Clague et al., *After the*

Shutdown, 111, and see 153, table 57, on the expansion of the garment trade in New Haven as the Great Depression deepened.

15. McConnell, *Evolution of Social Classes,* 178.

16. Child, "Psychological Study," 79–80; McConnell makes the same observation in *Evolution of Social Classes,* 178.

17. Only Russian Jews surpassed Italians in this respect (at 96 percent overall); Ruby J. Reeves, "Marriages in New Haven since 1870: Statistically Analyzed and Culturally Interpreted" (Ph.D. diss., Yale University, 1937), chap. 5, p. 16, table 26.

18. Ruby J. Reeves, "Marriage Folkways as Revealed by a Study of Marriage Licenses in New Haven" (M.A. thesis, Yale University, 1934), 51–52.

19. Cinel, *National Integration,* 64, 66; Orsi, *Madonna of 115th Street,* 116, 136–37, 140–41. Jane Schneider and Peter Schneider comment that "female sexuality had to be carefully controlled for women were thought incapable of controlling their own strong impulses toward sexual gratification"; Schneider and Schneider, *Culture and Political Economy in Western Sicily* (New York: Academic Press, 1976), 89.

20. Child, "Psychological Study," 60. One of Child's subjects reported that he thought it was a common Italian attitude to believe that girls should be chaperoned and that they considered it improper for young people to be out past nine or ten o'clock at night. He added that he thought his parents were typical in their disapproval of "the idea of a boy and a girl having a good time together"; Child, "Psychological Study," 475; and see Orsi, *Madonna of 115th Street,* 137, 140–41.

21. See Williams, *South Italian Folkways,* 78; Orsi, *Madonna of 115th Street,* 116, 136–37, 140–41; and Schneider and Schneider, *Culture and Political Economy,* 90–91.

22. Roberts, "Italian Girls on American Soil," 761. Orsi, *Madonna of 115th Street,* chap. 5; see also Constance Cronin, who describes relations between Sicilian men and women in very similar terms in *The Sting of Change: Sicilians in Sicily and Australia* (Chicago: University of Chicago Press, 1970), chaps. 5–6. Schneider and Schneider do not concur entirely in their assessment of gender in Sicilian culture but allow that although it appeared that "women had little individual freedom," this restrictiveness was mitigated by the fact that Sicily, like southern Italy, was sex-segregated, and much of domestic life occurred outdoors and among groups of women. In addition, they say, "Mutual aid and solidarity … plus access to information, combined to make many women formidable figures behind the scenes." Schneider and Schneider, *Culture and Political Economy,* 92–93.

23. See Neitlich's rich, evocative description of the operation of such networks in the Hill section of New Haven, where Jews and Italians predominated; Neitlich, "Here History Is Going."

24. Sunday visiting was spoken about as a "tradition" among Italian Americans, but in fact this custom was innovated in the United States. The reason it was referred to as a "tradition" is because it maintained social ties among extended kin and, as mentioned earlier, reinforced courtship customs practiced in southern Italy. Therefore, it was only traditional in the sense that it served a conservative social function.

25. See Child, *Italian or American?* 79–80; Jessie Ferrucci Palmieri, interview by author, tape recording, New Haven, May 16, 1990.

26. Child, "Psychological Study," 465; Orsi, *Madonna of 115th Street,* 116, 137.

27. Tittarelli, "Choosing a Spouse," 284; a *consengolo* is an agricultural day worker (*consengola,* a female member of a family of such day workers). "The figure of the *consengolo* was subject to long-standing negative prejudice . . . considered lazy and thievish, . . . if a sharecropper needed a farmhand he tended to seek first among other sharecroppers before taking on a *consengolo* lad"; Tittarelli, "Choosing a Spouse," 284.

28. Cinel, *National Integration,* 60 (quoting Vincenzo Padula, *Persone di Calabria* [Milan, 1950], 384).

29. Fifty percent of women whose fathers were in the group McConnell calls "general laborer" were married before the age of twenty; compare this with daughters of fathers in "white-collar" occupations, whose likelihood of being married by age twenty ranged from 34.4 percent down to 6.9 percent (for daughters of "professionals"); McConnell, *Evolution of Social Classes,* table 14, 223. Among unskilled workers, the majority of women married between the ages of fifteen and twenty, whereas their husbands were typically between twenty and twenty-five years of age. Both women and men in white-collar marriages, by contrast, were between the ages of twenty and twenty-five at the time they married; McConnell, *Evolution of Social Classes,* tables 8 and 14.

30. Beth L. Bailey's characterization stresses the leading edge of change and so pronounces "dead" the custom of calling by the mid-1920s, but her evidence is based on middle-class popular literature; Bailey, *From Front Porch to Back Seat: Courtship in Twentieth-Century America* (Baltimore: Johns Hopkins University Press, 1988). Modell, who looks at younger adults and adolescents in small cities and towns rather than metropolitan areas, finds that dating did not supplant calling until the 1930s; Modell, *Into One's Own,* chap. 2.

31. Paula S. Fass has documented the shift in attitudes that ushered in a new era in relations between women and men of the middle class in *The Damned and the Beautiful: American Youth in the 1920s* (New York: Oxford University Press, 1977); and Modell describes the change as the "gendered reconstruction of sexuality" in *Into One's Own,* 97–99; see also Bailey, *From Front Porch to Back Seat,* chap. 2.

32. Orsi's discussion of the involvement of Italian immigrant mothers in children's courtship reminds us that the desire to influence marital choices extended to sons as well as daughters; Orsi, *Madonna of 115th Street,* 125–26, 134.

33. Bailey, *From Front Porch to Back Seat,* 13–24; Fass, *Damned and the Beautiful,* chap. 4; Modell, *Into One's Own,* chap. 3; Ellen K. Rothman, *Hands and Hearts: A History of Courtship in America* (New York: Basic Books, 1984), 285–311.

34. Bailey, *Front Porch to Back Seat,* 25–26.

35. Child, *Italian or American?* Admittedly, men remained more connected than women to wider social contacts by virtue of their participation in the workforce and their greater involvement in social clubs.

36. McConnell, *Evolution of Social Classes*, 178; and see Williams, *South Italian Folkways*, 81, 98–99. On Italian's aversion to sending daughters to work in potentially compromising circumstances, such as domestic service, see Clague et al., *After the Shutdown*, 66. Several historians of southern Italian immigrants in the United States have commented on the dilemma of sending young women out to work in the face of concern for their chastity and family reputation: see Briggs, "Fertility and Cultural Change," 1143–44; Yans-McLaughlin, *Family and Community*, 171, 175, 204; and Gabaccia, *From Sicily to Elizabeth Street*, 47–48, 96–99. Furthermore, according to McConnell, it encouraged a conception of marriage as a pragmatic economic arrangement; McConnell, *Evolution of Social Classes*.

37. In the L. Candee Rubber plant 60 percent of the workers were women, many of whom were married and worked in the factory part-time. Among the younger workers, women "were an overwhelming majority" and the plant, according to one study, was "distinctly a 'family concern' in the sense that many married couples worked there and that many of the younger workers were directly related to the elder"; Clague et al., *After the Shutdown*, 9. A majority of the female workers held semi-skilled jobs that required "hand work" (as opposed to mechanized labor). Sixty percent of the total workforce was either born in Italy or of Italian parentage, and of these, almost 60 percent were the children of Italian immigrants. Finally, the average length of service in the plant was long, a mean of 9.9 years total working time, but the largest clusters of workers were between the ages of fifteen and twenty-nine; Clague et al., *After the Shutdown*, 4, 9–10, 15–16. On the tendency to favor family members in company hiring practices in another city and industry, see Tamara K. Hareven, *Family Time and Industrial Time* (New York: Cambridge University Press, 1981).

38. Worries about daughters' trustworthiness were actually less well founded than the reality of sexual harassment in unorganized garment shops. Before the mid-1930s, when the sewing trades in New Haven were finally unionized, women workers furtively complained to one another about foremen who molested them, but they kept quiet because they were afraid that they would pay for their complaints with their jobs. Women working in the garment shops reported that it was not uncommon for male foremen to try to fondle them while they worked; Baker, interview by author, GNHLHA.

39. McConnell, *Evolution of Social Classes*, 178. Although Orsi highlights the continuing hold of southern Italian customs on second-generation youths, he too describes their restiveness at the crowded conditions of urban courtship; Orsi, *Madonna of 115th Street*, 113.

40. Reeves, "Marriages in New Haven," chap. 5, p. 13.

41. McConnell, *Evolution of Social Classes*, 179.

42. McConnell, *Evolution of Social Classes*, 176–77; Child, "Psychological Study," see his case study of "John."

43. Williams, *South Italian Folkways*, 97–98.

44. McConnell, *Evolution of Social Classes*, 179. Brothers and sisters in the same family, McConnell said, "will have a different cultural background," since the boys

are given more freedom and exposure to "American habits of life," while "the Italian tradition is bred into the girls by their close association with the home," McConnell, *Evolution of Social Classes,* 179.

45. Child, "Psychological Study," appendix ("Sample Standard Interviews," see, e.g., "Henry," "Augie," "Daniel," "Art," and "Nick"), esp. 465.

46. Ruby Jo Reeves Kennedy, "Single or Triple Melting Pot? Intermarriage Trends in New Haven, 1920–1940," *American Journal of Sociology* 1 (1944): 331–39.

47. See Perlmann, *Ethnic Differences,* 118–21.

48. Grooms were older than brides in 75 percent of all marriages; in 13 percent of marriages among Italians spouses' ages were the same; and in 12 percent the female was older than the male.

49. Reeves, "Marriages in New Haven," chap. 5, p. 25a.

50. Reeves, "Marriages in New Haven," chap. 3, pp. 27–28. Three other immigrant groups had greater age disparities: the average age disparity among Polish newlyweds was 6.8 years, Germans were next at 6.6 years, and Irish newlyweds averaged just a bit more than Italians, at 6.4 years. Reeves explained part of the age disparity among all foreign-born marriers by pointing out that a subset of them were second-time marriers—having been widowed or divorced; Reeves, "Marriages in New Haven," table 15, chap. 3, p. 55. Italian-born men, moreover, preferred Italian-born women to women of Italian descent born in the United States. Owing to a surfeit of Italian-born men in New Haven, however, three-quarters of first-generation Italian immigrant women married an Italian-born man, and fewer than half of first-generation Italian men married (or were able to marry) Italian-born women; Reeves, "Marriage Folkways," 47. Incidentally, Reeves's figures for southern Italians in New Haven are almost identical to the immigrants from Abruzzi in Briggs's study of Rochester: the average age-at-first-marriage for men was 24.6, for women it was 20.4; Briggs, "Fertility and Cultural Change," 1139.

51. Again, this anticipates Briggs's explanation for the decline of average age-at-first marriage for southern Italian immigrants in Rochester; Briggs, "Fertility and Cultural Change," 1143–44, n. 29.

52. Reeves, "Marriages in New Haven," chap. 3, pp. 27–28.

53. Many observers of Italian immigrant life in New Haven—Child, McConnell, Reeves, and Williams—came to the same conclusion; and as Bernice Smith aptly put it: "Italian girls rarely feel able to defy the family regulations about late evenings away from home. Camping trips, youth conferences, mixed parties, indeed practically all opportunities to meet a young man, were among the activities . . . [considered] taboo in their families"; Smith, "Depression Graduates," 81.

54. Caldwell attributes these changes to the fact of universal education. However, southern Italians had already been exposed to rudimentary universal schooling by the late nineteenth century without the kinds of effects witnessed in the United States, where schooling was imposed for a much longer period of children's lives; Caldwell, "Mass Education."

55. Covello paraphrases an old southern Italian folk truism: "A girl of nineteen was considered an old maid; at twenty-one, a hopeless spinster"; *Social Background,* 199. Williams refers to the same saying in *South Italian Folkways,* 83; and Briggs quotes Williams to demonstrate that sociologists and historians have mistakenly employed this popular aphorism to draw false conclusions about actual average ages at first marriage for Italian women during the nineteenth and twentieth centuries; Briggs, "Fertility and Cultural Change," 1137.

56. Modell, Frank F. Furstenberg Jr., and Theodore Hershberg support this observation in more general terms in their study of transitions to adulthood in early-twentieth-century America; see Modell et al., "Social Change and Transitions to Adulthood in Historical Perspective," in Theodore Hershberg, ed., *Philadelphia: Work, Space, and Group Experience in the Nineteenth Century* (New York: Oxford University Press, 1981), 322.

Chapter 6: The Landscape of Ambition

1. On Italian immigrant associational life in New Haven, see Racca, "Ethnography," 3. On the Italian settlement in New Haven, see Myers, "Differential Time Factor"; on the history of African Americans in the city to 1940, see Robert A. Warner, *New Haven Negroes: A Social History* (New Haven: Yale University Press, 1940); for an overview of immigrant settlements in New Haven from 1850 to 1950, see Robert A. Dahl, "The New Men," in Dahl, *Who Governs? Democracy and Power in an American City* (New Haven: Yale University Press, 1961).

2. Warner, *New Haven Negroes.*

3. Until the 1940s the African-American population in New Haven never exceeded 5 percent of the total population, yet by 1933, 22.5 percent of household heads in the Dixwell Avenue area were African American. The segregation of African Americans in the Dixwell and Newhallville areas intensified during and after World War II, as the revival of munitions production and wartime manufacturing attracted many more blacks to New Haven than at any time in the past. By the 1960s they would supplant Italian Americans as the majority subgroup in the city; Davie, "Pattern of Urban Growth," 152–53; Dahl, *Who Governs?* chap. 5.

4. In 1908 the West Street school, toward the southern end of the Hill, was still a blend of Yankees as well as old and new immigrants: 21 percent of its pupils were identified as "American" (native-born white of native parentage), 20 percent were Italian, 19 percent were Irish, 18 percent were German, and 14 percent were the children of Eastern European Jewish immigrants. Two other schools approximated the West Street school's heterogeneity in 1908: the Scranton Street school, a couple of blocks north and west of the Hill, had roughly equal proportions of Yankees and Germans (23 and 21 percent respectively), who were about half of the schools' students, along with Irish (12 percent), Italians (11 percent), and Eastern European Jews (13 percent), who made up another third, and a smattering of pupils of other ethnicities. The other was the Winchester Avenue school, in the Dixwell neighborhood.

(The arms manufacturer employed nearby African Americans as custodial workers, saving the desirable factory jobs for white workers, many of whom lived in company-built housing on a corridor that ran south-north alongside the complex.) The Winchester school's student body was 22 percent African American, 26 percent "American," 5 percent Italian, 7 percent "Russian," 13 percent German, and 18 percent Irish; New Haven, *Annual Report*, 1908.

5. Russian and Polish Jews were the second-largest immigrant group in the city at this point; New Haven, *Annual Report*, 1908.

6. Italians were 12 percent of the Webster school student body and 13 percent of students at Welch; New Haven, *Annual Report*, 1908.

7. Dreis, *Handbook of Social Statistics.*

8. The birthrate in Wards Ten and Eleven (Wooster Square), the area with the highest concentration of Italian immigrants in the city, also had the city's highest birthrates (19.2 and 18.2 per thousand, respectively, compared with a citywide mean of 14.7 live births per thousand); Dreis, *Handbook of Social Statistics,* 95–96; and Davie, "Pattern of Urban Growth," 147. On the history of Italian immigrant fertility patterns in the United States during this period, see Briggs, "Fertility and Cultural Change."

9. Davie, "Pattern of Urban Growth."

10. By 1930 the children of Italian immigrants represented an overwhelming 40 percent of all students enrolled in public elementary schools; New Haven, *Annual Report,* 1930. This accelerating trend was remarked upon fifteen years earlier in an analysis of the composition of the schools' ethnicity accompanying the first of seventeen consecutive censuses of pupil "nationality": "A comparison of the nationality situation in our schools at the present time with that of 1908 shows that the Italians and Russians are, and for several years have been, by far the largest of our foreign population. The former are increasing at a more rapid rate than the latter. In 1908 there were 1.34 times as many Italians as Russians; in 1916 there are 1.9 times as many.... [Currently there are a] smaller number of Russians in Welch, Cedar, Zunder, and Webster, and a larger number in the Scranton Street School. The same comparison shows that the number of Italians is increasing in the schools mentioned in which the number of Russians is decreasing. This seems to show that the Russian population is moving toward the western part of the city, and the Italian population, while holding its own in Wooster, Greene Street, and Eaton schools, is also increasing in the Prince Street, Cedar, Zunder, and Webster schools." New Haven, *Annual Report,* 1915, 24.

11. New Haven, *Annual Report,* 1908–32. I thank Avni Gupta for her painstaking work in compiling the school-by-school nationality censuses published in the *Annual Reports* and for her indispensable map of the New Haven public school system in 1928.

12. In the Hill district, for example, in 1928 there were seventeen elementary schools distributed among 108 city blocks—a little more than six blocks per school; "New Haven School Map."

13. Putnam, *Bowling Alone,* 136.

14. Examples abound but even at the most fundamental level the public schools strived to introduce American habits. For example, a study of nutrition among Italian immigrant children revealed a lack of milk products in their diet, so the public schools campaigned (without success) to get Italian immigrant mothers to supplement the family diet with milk. Milk had never been a staple of the southern Italian's diet; goat cheese and fish were favored, and for centuries they had subsisted on a healthy balance of foods available locally. King, "Study of the Italian Diet."

15. Child, *Italian or American?* 45–46.

16. Child, *Italian or American?* 131–32.

17. Their father, Harry, actually preceded the rest of the family in moving to New Haven by a few years, leasing a space for his new business in 1927; M. Lender, interview by Neitlich, August 1996.

18. M. Lender, interview by Neitlich, August 2, 1996; 42 percent of its students were Italian, 21 percent were Jewish, even fewer (18 percent) were "Yankees" (native-born white of native-born white parents), and there were a handful of African Americans, according to the last "census" by the board of education in 1930; New Haven, *Annual Report,* 1930.

19. M. Lender, interview by Neitlich, August 1996.

20. M. Lender, interview by Neitlich, August 1996.

21. Rae, *City,* chap. 5.

22. M. Lender, interview by Neitlich, July 1996.

23. See, e.g., Kazin, *Walker in the City;* and Reverdy Whitlock, "The Hillhouse Papers" (New Haven: Privately published, 1977).

24. Butts and Young, "Education in Connecticut," 264–65. In the upper grades of grammar school, differences were said to be discernible between the children of "old" New Haven's "respectable" and "hard-working" African-American population and those of the city's recent migrants from the Carolinas, who were considered by many to be "lazy," of "low mentality," and, revealingly, in the words of a junior high school principal, "didn't know their place"; Butts and Young, "Education in Connecticut," 264–65. See also Robert A. Warner, *New Haven Negroes: A Social History* (New Haven: Yale University Press, 1940), 122–59.

25. The quotation is from Katherine A. Lebow, "Education and the Immigrant Experience: An Oral History of Working Women and Men of New Haven," *Journal of the Colony Historical Society of New Haven* 40 (Fall 1993): 20. It is easy to dismiss such attitudes today as overdrawn, but they were pervasive and virulent. Just a sample: a real estate agent interviewed by McConnell for his studies of socioeconomic status during the Depression said of New Haven's Italians, "One thing I do know, is that there are too many Italians in this country. They come here and live like animals. God, they work for nothing, live eight or ten in a room and breed like pigs." McConnell, *Evolution of Social Classes,* 107.

26. Anonymous interview quoted in Johnston, "Italian New Haven," 28.

27. Frederico Rosadini, interview by author, tape recording, New Haven, September 18, 1990.

28. Lebow, "Education and the Immigrant Experience," 22.

29. Samuel Lender, interview by Susan L. Neitlich, tape recording, New Haven, August 2, 1996.

30. Lebow, "Education and the Immigrant Experience," 19–20. It's unclear what this implement was, but this was the term used by Beatrice Bonifacio to describe it. Although the long-term academic advantages of the junior high school experience appear to have been negligible, ninth-graders in the junior high schools reported having liked their freshman year better than those attending Hillhouse or Commercial for having been at schools that were smaller, that were closer to home, and where they were senior to the other students in the building. Even so, after the comparative intimacy of their neighborhood elementary schools, junior high school presented social and psychological adjustments to students all the same.

31. Lebow, "Education and the Immigrant Experience," 20–21.

32. Lebow, "Education and the Immigrant Experience," 20–21.

33. M. Lender, interview by Neitlich, August 2, 1996.

34. While Lender remembered Welch as being a "mix" of students, it was heterogeneous only by comparison with other schools in the Hill. For example, the majority of students at both Webster and Scranton elementary schools were Jewish, while Washington and Prince were overwhelmingly Italian in composition.

35. Ethnically Troup was 20 percent Italian, 25 percent Jewish, 30 percent native-born white of native-born parents, and a little fewer than 10 percent African-American students; New Haven, *Annual Report,* 1930. Welch was 18 percent Yankee, 21 percent Italian, 42 percent Jewish, and 1 percent African American.

36. Whitlock, "Hillhouse Papers."

37. Whitlock, "Hillhouse Papers," 5–8.

38. Mario A. Cestaro, "'Just as I Am': Memoir and Musings," TS, September 1992, Manuscripts and Archives, Sterling Memorial Library, Yale University.

39. "This," remarked her parents in response, "is what America makes of our children." Racca, "Selected Family Histories" ("Tranquilli" family), 26–27.

40. There is a small but analytically superb literature on the rise of the extracurriculum and its relation to the retention of students, its social significance, its place in the formation of peer groupings, and its role in defining youths' relation to authority and adult supervision; see Fass, "'Americanizing' the High Schools," 73–111; Thomas W. Gutowski, "Student Initiative and the Origins of the High School Extracurriculum: Chicago, 1880–1915," *History of Education Quarterly* 28 (Spring 1988): 49–72; Modell and Alexander, "High School in Transition"; and William Graebner, "Outlawing Teenage Populism: The Campaign against Secret Societies in the American High School, 1900–1960," *Journal of American History* 74 (1987): 411–35.

41. John was exceptional in becoming only the second male of Italian descent to be hired to teach in the city school system by the mid-1920s. Moreover, among the fifty-three men Child interviewed, only ten, including John, expressed the desire to "achieve complete acceptance by the American group," in Child's phrasing. Child,

Italian or American? 76. Child identified three ideal-typical psychological reactions to the social experience of assimilation as the "in-group" reaction, in which the subject conforms resolutely to the ideals and values of the immigrant community; the "rebel" reaction (exemplified by John), which rejects membership in the immigrant community and attributes identified with it; and the "apathetic" reaction (that characterized the majority of informants), which avoids identification with any group because of a conviction that such affiliations are insidious. Fifty-three men submitted to interviews of any kind by Child, and forty-nine were actually analyzed; Child, *Italian or American?* 69–75, 13.

42. Thomas and Znaniecki's *Polish Peasant* is the leading example of many sociological studies of immigrant group life to address generational conflict. Their work was followed by that of many others, primarily sociologists, but also of social workers during the 1920s and 1930s. Krall's dissertation is a useful survey of the literature up to 1937; Krall, "Second-Generation Immigrant in America." The most notable example in the historical literature, of course, is Hansen, *Problem of the Third Generation Immigrant.* Child's dissertation and John's "life history" in particular conform to Fred H. Matthews's characterization of pre-1950 studies of immigration and ethnicity as reflecting "a pervasive view of life as process and (usually) of progress, as a continuing interaction of individuals in perpetual motion given direction by secular tendencies toward the liberation of the individual from external constraint"; Matthews, "Paradigm Changes in the Interpretations of Ethnicity, 1930–80: From Process to Structure," in Peter Kivisto and Dag Blanck, eds., *American Immigrants and Their Generations: Studies and Commentaries on the Hansen Thesis after Fifty Years* (Urbana: University of Illinois Press, 1990), 167.

43. In an assessment of Child's work that largely concurs with Child's own view of the study, Cordasco has pointed out in his introduction to the 1970 reissue of *Italian or American?* that both Child's and Williams's (*South Italian Folkways,* 1938) studies were "late," meaning that studies inspired by the "social problems" arising from immigration had been around for almost a generation. Williams's study, he suggests, was largely a recycling of older material. Child's, on the other hand, had the merit of bringing a sociopsychological perspective to bear on a well-studied social context. Cordasco, "Introduction," in Child, *Italian or American?* 8, n. 1; and Irvin L. Child, interview by author, telephone, July 8, 1992.

44. That it was familiar among sociologists and social welfare professionals is supported by the number of articles produced on the "problem" of the second-generation immigrant youth during the 1920s and early 1930s. Krall cites seventeen such studies between 1923 and 1935; Krall, "Second-Generation Immigrant." The International Institutes (a branch of the Young Women's Christian Association that concerned itself with the state of immigrant women in the United States) conducted a study from 1928 to 1931 on the "second-generation problem" among young immigrant women in roughly fifty cities across the nation; see the International Institute of Boston, Papers, Immigration History Research Center, University of Minnesota, Twin Cities, St. Paul, box 9, folder 107, esp. 1–3, 18, 21–23, 35–37; on the International

Institutes, see Raymond A. Mohl, "The International Institutes and Immigrant Education, 1910–1940," in Weiss, *American Education and the European Immigrant,* 117–41.

45. The effort to Americanize immigrant children is regarded by many historians as among the most damaging and unfortunate aspects of the treatment of ethnic groups in the United States since the beginning of the century; see, e.g., Cordasco's introduction to the volume he edited, *Studies in Italian American Social History.* The scholarly literature on Americanization is abundant, but see relevant articles collected in Weiss, *American Education and the European Immigrant;* and George E. Pozetta, ed., *Education and the Immigrant* (New York: Garland, 1991). For general treatments, see David B. Tyack, *The One Best System: A History of American Urban Education* (Cambridge, Mass.: Harvard University Press, 1974), part 4; and John Higham, *Strangers in the Land: Patterns of American Nativism, 1860–1925* (New York: Atheneum, 1967), chap. 9. On Americanization efforts in New Haven's high school during the early twentieth century, see Lucy Bernholz, "Education and Assimilation: The Development of the Curriculum at Hillhouse High School, 1880–1930" (senior thesis, Department of History, Yale University), April 1985.

46. Child, "Psychological Study," 135.

47. Child characterized John as particularly "thoughtful," if not especially "sophisticated," compared with the rest of the men interviewed and recalled that John's description of himself as participating in a generational struggle, as well as his evident familiarity with this as a problem typical in the adjustment of immigrant children to the dominant culture, was not at all unusual among this group. By the same token, despite Child's assertion to the contrary, John mentions having read several books on ethnicity during and after adolescence in an effort to overcome his own biases toward others as well as his own sense of inferiority. This, combined with the fact that he was among the minority of interviewees who had graduated from high school, suggests that he was probably better read and more attuned to the issue of assimilation than the rest of Child's subjects. Thus John may have been somewhat more apt than the other men to locate his experience in broader social and historical terms; Child, interview by author, July 8, 1992.

48. For example, John described his life as a three-stage progression to an assimilated self: "I have been learning to take my part as a member of a group which had once seemed [to me] entirely foreign," he remarked upon his self-transformation, which had been achieved by his marriage to a third-generation Irish-American woman, "which I later realized was simply at a different level from my own"; Child, "Psychological Study," 97.

49. Child, "Psychological Study," 100. Some twenty-five years after John entered primary school, a 1933 study of first-grade children in a New Haven neighborhood quite similar to his found that fewer than 20 percent of them had ever taken short trips from New Haven, half had never been on an outing beyond their neighborhood, and only a quarter of them had ever been to the seashore—just three miles from where they lived; Cutts, "Extent of Bilingualism," 196.

50. Child's informants were "mostly descended from the lower and lower-middle classes from the present Campania, around Naples"; Child, *Italian or American?* 20, n. 2. Sixteen informants were obtained through neighborhood contacts, reported Child: three "young men's clubs" with a "majority of second-generation members, located in the solidly Italian district provided twenty; a club of predominantly second-generation Italian membership, at the edge of the solidly Italian district, was the source of an additional five," and five others were contacted by various means, "making a total of fifty-three persons who were interviewed"; Child, *Italian or American?* 13.

51. Child, "Psychological Study," 108.

52. Child does not specify what kind of trade John's father practiced, perhaps to conceal the family's identity.

53. Child, "Psychological Study," 97–99.

54. Child, "Psychological Study," 106, 98.

55. This pattern of apprenticeship was approximated some forty years later by a man who came to New Haven from Naples during the 1950s, when he was eleven years old. He worked first for a tailor, learning to stitch buttons and hems and then, at age fourteen, for a shoemaker until he turned eighteen, when he went to work for his father's construction crew as a carpenter. Later (coincidentally) he became a mathematics teacher in the New Haven area; Rosadini, interview by author, September 18, 1990.

56. John confessed that when he began earning ten cents a week, he would hold back a nickel before giving his parents their share; Child, "Psychological Study," 101.

57. Child, "Psychological Study," 101.

58. Covello exaggerated when he claimed that such income was rarely required for families to subsist; nevertheless, the spirit of his assertion corroborates Child's findings; see Covello, "The Basic Adjustment of Italian Youth to America," TS, LCP, box 66, folder 17, unpag.

59. Child, "Psychological Study," 101. It was common whenever possible for Italian immigrants to keep chickens or, barring that, to buy them live and kill and dress them themselves, for they found "storage chickens" (poultry butchered in advance and preserved) to be inedible; King, "Study of Italian Diet," 99.

60. Child, "Psychological Study," 106–7.

61. Child, "Psychological Study," 107, 104.

62. Child, "Psychological Study," 104.

63. Child, "Psychological Study," 114. Note that John and Murray Lender, whose admiration for his own father was unabashed, say virtually the same thing about the quality of their fathers' involvement in their schoolwork, yet John's recollection is tinged with mild bitterness. This may be attributed to his feelings of emotional remoteness from his father or may stem from his belief as a schoolteacher that parents should take a direct, daily role in their children's schoolwork.

64. Child, "Psychological Study," 104–5.

65. Child, "Psychological Study," 108.

66. Child, "Psychological Study," 111. Somehow, John noted with perplexity, the Jewish children he acquainted seemed impervious to their "position" in the local ethnic hierarchy.

67. More than 80 percent of the school's pupils were children of Italian immigrants; Child, "Psychological Study," 113, 117–18.

68. Child, "Psychological Study," 108.

69. Child, "Psychological Study," 108–9.

70. Child, "Psychological Study," 109.

71. Child, "Psychological Study," 114.

72. Child, "Psychological Study," 115.

73. Child, "Psychological Study," 115; and see "School Children Take Up the Thrift Stamp Movement," *New Haven Register*, January 17, 1918. On the experience of Italian immigrants in New Haven during the war, see Christopher M. Sterba, *Good Americans: Italian and Jewish Immigrants during the First World War* (New York: Oxford University Press, 2003).

74. Child, "Psychological Study," 115.

75. Child, "Psychological Study," 120, 137.

76. From 1919 through 1922, the years during which John attended Hillhouse High School, the ratio of "Italian" students ranged from 6.6 percent to 10.9 percent of the student body; New Haven, *Annual Report*, 1919–22.

77. Child, "Psychological Study," 122

78. Child, "Psychological Study," 122–23.

79. Child, "Psychological Study," 121, 123.

80. Child, "Psychological Study," 122.

81. Child, "Psychological Study," 121.

82. Child, "Psychological Study," 130.

83. Child, "Psychological Study," 126–28. The theater owner, who took an interest in John, was another personal influence. He gave John piano lessons and encouraged him to read more broadly, which, John told Child, initiated his "tendency to learn about the world through reading"; Child, "Psychological Study," 127.

84. Child, "Psychological Study," 127; Child asked all of the participants in his standardized interviews about the effect of movie watching on their own sense of identity and personal affect. On the influence of the movies on mother-daughter relationships in immigrant families, see Sharon Hartmann Strom, "Italian-American Women and Their Daughters in Rhode Island: The Adolescence of Two Generations," in Betty Boyd Caroli, Robert F. Harney, and Lydio F. Tomasi, eds., *The Italian Immigrant Woman in North America* (Toronto: Multicultural History Society of Ontario, 1978), 191–204; and Elizabeth Ewen, "City Lights: Immigrant Women and the Rise of the Movies," *Signs* 5 (Spring 1980): S45–S65. For a thorough and more general discussion of the influence of motion pictures on the emotional and fantasy worlds of adolescents and youths during this period, see Herbert Blumer, *Movies and Conduct* (New York: MacMillan, 1933).

85. Child, "Psychological Study," 128.

86. Child, "Psychological Study," 133, 137.

87. Child, "Psychological Study," 137.

88. John admitted to Child that, in retrospect, such a move could have been devastating to his parents, as it would have cut them off from people in the neighborhood who had emigrated from the same province in Italy; Child, "Psychological Study," 136–37.

89. Child, "Psychological Study," 136.

90. Child, "Psychological Study," 135–36.

91. Child, "Psychological Study," 146.

92. On the difficulty of Italian skilled workers finding comparable employment in the United States, see Smith, *Family Connections*, chap. 2; and Perlmann, *Ethnic Differences*, chap. 3. Compare John's high school experience with that of William V. D'Antonio, whose grandparents came to New Haven during the 1880s and 1890s. D'Antonio's parents were slightly older than John, were both high school educated and placed a high value on schooling their children. Many of D'Antonio's kin found jobs with the postal service (a consequence of the fact that New Haven elected its first Italian mayor during the mid-1940s, opening up many city, state, and federal jobs to Italians in the city for the first time) and secured a foothold in the lower-middle class, while his father rose to postmaster at the Yale University post office. D'Antonio and his older brother both went to Hillhouse High School a generation after John and subsequently won scholarships to Yale College; D'Antonio, "Ethnicity and Assimilation: A Reconsideration," in Cordasco, *Studies in Italian American Social History*, 10–17.

93. Exemplary in its grasp of the subtleties of this question is Fass, "'Americanizing' the High Schools," 73–111.

Chapter 7: "Too Good for That"

1. Modell and Alexander, "High School in Transition."

2. In 1920 pupils who were native-born white of native-born white parents were 44.5 percent of students enrolled in the high school; comparable proportions for other major ethnic groups that year were: children of Italian parentage, 7.2 percent; Irish parentage, 8 percent; and Russian-Jewish parentage, 23.1 percent. By 1930 these proportions had changed particularly in response to the movement of cohorts of the Italian-American pupil population through the school system. In 1930 native-born white of native-born parents comprised 46.1 percent of all students (in Hillhouse, Commercial, and Boardman), while students of Italian parentage increased to 20.2 percent, Irish declined to 6.6 percent, and Russian-Jewish slackened to 17.1 percent of all students enrolled in secondary school. Second-generation Italian and Polish youths were partly siphoned off from Hillhouse, the academic high school, by the opening of Commercial High School in 1920, which helped to sop up the tremendous demand for clerical training. Although Commercial was built next to Hillhouse and Boardman high schools, Hillhouse retained its commercial "track" nonetheless. New Haven, *Annual Report*, 1920–30.

3. Alison Hadjusiewicz found that Yankee girls continued to dominate leadership positions based on either popularity or exclusivity; see Hadjusiewicz, "A Study of Ethnic Social Trends at Hillhouse High School, 1926–1940" (Senior thesis, Department of History, Yale University, 1998). See also Graebner, "Outlawing Teenage Populism."

4. On the social mobility of high school students in the Northeast during the latter part of the nineteenth century, see Reed Ueda, *Avenues to Adulthood: The Origins of the High School and Social Mobility in an American Suburb* (Cambridge: Cambridge University Press, 1987). Modell and Alexander point out that even though public high schools were relatively stratified compared with one another (i.e., some were less so than others), during the 1930s they were characteristically more stratified than they had been thirty years before; Modell and Alexander, "High School in Transition."

5. See David F. Labaree, *How to Succeed in School without Really Learning: The Credentials Race in American Education* (New Haven: Yale University Press, 1997); Oakes, *Keeping Track*, 15–39; and Estelle E. Feldman, "The Dull Child and the Junior High Curriculum" (Ph.D. diss., Yale University, 1936).

6. On the intensification of educational credentialism during the twentieth century, see Labaree, *How to Succeed in School;* on the nineteenth-century origins of credentialism, see Labaree, *Making of an American High School,* and Nancy Beadie, "From Student Markets to Credential Markets: The Creation of the Regents Examination System in New York State, 1864–1890," *History of Education Quarterly* 39 (Spring 1999): 1–30.

7. E. William Noland and E. Wight Bakke, *Workers Wanted: A Study of Employers' Hiring Policies, Preferences and Practices* (New York: Harper and Brothers, 1949), 45, 161.

8. While the Great Depression is popularly remembered as having been initiated by the crash of the stock market in late 1929, in fact unemployment began to rise significantly the previous year; see Margaret H. Hogg, "The Ebb-Tide of Employment," *Survey* (August 1933): 279–80.

9. By the late 1930s the age of compulsory attendance was raised (until World War II) to eighteen.

10. In 1890 the percentage of seventeen-year-olds graduating from high school nationally was 3.5; by 1900 this ratio had reached 6.4; U.S. Department of Commerce, Bureau of the Census, *Historical Statistics of the United States, Colonial Times to 1957: A Statistical Abstract Supplement* (Washington, D.C.: Government Printing Office, 1960), 207.

11. While David Tyack and Elisabeth Hansot state that the term "drop out" began to be used in the first decade of the twentieth century, the New Haven Board of Education's *Annual Report* first employed the term in 1896; Tyack and Hansot, *Learning Together: A History of Coeducation in American Public Schools* (New Haven: Yale University Press, 1990), 174–77. But see Sherman Dorn's history of the "dropout problem," which emerged as a social problem, he says, not until the 1960s. Dorn states that the "dropout problem appeared despite improvements in the proportion of the

population graduating from high school." I suggest that the "dropout problem" appeared instead precisely because of improvements in high school graduation rates rather than despite them. Dorn himself recognizes this phenomenon, but underestimates its effect as well as the extent to which the goal to make high school graduation universal created the dropout as a social problem from the very outset; Dorn, *Creating the Dropout: An Institutional and Social History of School Failure* (Westport, Conn.: Greenwood, 1996), 3, 15–18. There are three excellent histories of the formative period of the public high school in the United States, each quite different in approach, see Ueda, *Avenues to Adulthood;* Labaree, *Making of an American High School;* and. Reese, *Origins of the American High School.* For a sample of the emerging concern among educators toward school-leaving, see Ayers, *Laggards in Our Schools.*

12. New Haven, *Annual Report,* 1901–32. The complete list included: "Have to go to work to support the family," "parents won't let me [continue education]," "would rather go to work than study," "sick of school," "don't like school," "monotony of school life is wearying," "to be free of school duties so as to enjoy . . . [myself]," "grammar school education is sufficient," "high school is of no benefit if one is not going to college," "lessons in high school are too hard," "discouraged by older siblings about the difficulty and disciplinary strictness of high school," "not practical enough," "high school too strict," and "afraid [I] will be dropped"; M. T. Scudder, "A Study of High School Pupils," *School Review* 7 (April 1899): 212.

13. Mabel A. Buckner, "A Study of Pupil Elimination in the New Haven High School" (M.A. thesis, Yale University, 1930), 37, 58–59, table 20.

14. Buckner believed that youths offered a socially approved rationale for leaving when in fact they simply disliked school— attributing school-leaving to the irrelevance of the curriculum to most youths' future occupations and "adolescent fever," by which she meant a general restiveness that accompanies adolescence; Buckner, "Study of Pupil Elimination," 37, 58–59, table 20.

15. One of the quiet cultural transformations of the twentieth century in the United States has been the acceptance in all groups of the meaningfulness of age gradations among children and youths; see, e.g., Howard P. Chudacoff, *How Old Are You? Age Consciousness in American Culture* (Princeton, N.J.: Princeton University Press, 1989). Kett's important book on the history of the idea of adolescence examined the first significant triumph of experts in promoting the concept of human development in American institutional life; Kett, *Rites of Passage;* and also see Jeffrey E. Mirel, "Twentieth-Century America, Adolescence," in R. M. Lerner, A. C. Peterson, and J. Brooks-Gunn, eds., *Encyclopedia of Adolescence,* vol. 2 (New York: Garland, 1991), 1153–67. A recent edition of a popular college psychology textbook identifies the following stages preceding adulthood: early infancy, later infancy, early and middle childhood, and pre-, early, middle, and late adolescence; Michael and Sheila R. Cole, *The Development of Children,* 4th ed. (New York: W. H. Freeman, 2000). Certainly the rise of the expert and the medicalization of "deviance" have contributed significantly to the broad acceptance of age gradations and the developmental perspective. On the increasing popular reliance on the advice of experts, see Loren Baritz, *The Servants of Power:*

A History of the Use of Social Science in American History (Middletown, Conn.: Wesleyan University Press, 1960); and Peter N. Stearns, *American Cool: Constructing a Twentieth-Century Emotional Style* (New York: New York University Press, 1994). On the triumph of the developmental paradigm, see, e.g., Dale B. Harris, "Problems in Formulating a Scientific Concept of Development," in Harris, ed., *The Concept of Development: An Issue in the Study of Human Behavior* (Minneapolis: University of Minnesota Press, 1957), 3–14; Urie Bronfenbrenner, "Developmental Theory in Transition," in Harold W. Stevenson, ed., *Child Psychology,* part 1 (Chicago: University of Chicago Press, 1963), 517–42. On delinquency, see Robert D. Wirt and Peter F. Briggs, "The Meaning of Delinquency," in H. C. Quay, ed., *Juvenile Delinquency: Research and Theory* (Princeton, N.J.: D. Van Nostrand, 1965), 1–26; and Ronald D. Cohen, "*The Delinquents:* Censorship and Youth Culture in Recent U.S. History," *History of Education Quarterly* 37 (Fall 1997): 251–70.

16. On the uneven adoption of age-grading across the nation, see Maris A. Vinovskis with David L. Angus and Jeffrey E. Mirel, "Historical Development of Age Stratification in Schooling," reprinted in Vinovskis, *Education, Society, and Economic Opportunity: A Historical Perspective on Persistent Issues* (New Haven: Yale University Press, 1995), 171–93; on the testing and measurement movement, see Leila Zenderland, *Measuring Minds: Henry Herbert Goddard and the Origins of American Intelligence Testing* (New York: Cambridge University Press, 1998).

17. See discussions in Richard A. Reiman, *The New Deal and American Youth: Ideas and Ideals in a Depression Decade* (Athens: University of Georgia Press, 1992); and David Tyack, Robert Lowe, and Elizabeth Hansot, *Public Schools and Hard Times: The Great Depression and Recent Years* (Cambridge, Mass.: Harvard University Press, 1984).

18. By the late 1930s the perception that there was a "youth problem" was so commonplace that Howard M. Bell's well-known survey of youth's behavior and attitudes could pose the question "[Do you] believe that there is such a thing as a 'youth problem'?" alongside such questions as whether relief is a responsibility of government and "what would be your response if war were declared?"; see Bell, *Youth Tell Their Story: A Study of the Conditions and Attitudes of Young People in Maryland between the Ages of Sixteen and Twenty-Four* (Washington, D.C.: American Council on Education, 1938), chap. 7.

19. The primary perceived danger of such a long idle period for young people was of course delinquency, but as Reiman shows, there was also a degree of serious concern about the ideological appeal of reactionary political forces to unemployed and unschooled youths, which was so evident in Germany and Italy during these years; see Reiman, *New Deal and American Youth.* On education and the definition of the "youth problem" during the Great Depression, see Tyack et al., *Public Schools and Hard Times,* chap. 3 and esp. 136. Two other federal initiatives set precedents for the democratic spirit of New Deal educational reforms, the passage of the Smith-Hughes Act of 1918, which provided federal money for vocational-industrial training (after much controversy), and the abolition of child labor in 1924, the constitutionality of

which was immediately challenged and struck down; Katznelson and Weir, *Schooling for All,* 160–61; and Jane Bernard Powers, *The "Girl Question" in Education: Vocational Education for Young Women in the Progressive Era* (London: Falmer, 1992), chap. 5. On child labor legislation, see Walter I. Trattner, *Crusade for the Children: A History of the National Child Labor Committee and Child Labor Reform in America* (Chicago: Quadrangle Books, 1970); and Hugh D. Hindman, *Child Labor: An American History* (New York: M. E. Sharpe, 2002).

20. Tyack et al., *Public Schools and Hard Times,* chap. 3; and Reiman, *New Deal and American Youth.* As late as 1938, national rates of joblessness among these young people ranged up to 56.3 percent—higher than any other age group. Of those who were employed, almost one-third could only find part-time work; Bell, *Youth Tell Their Story,* 106, table 34. On unemployment among youth in Connecticut, see State of Connecticut, Connecticut State Employment Service, *Youths in Search of Jobs!* FERA Project [CPS-F2-87], Hartford, 1934.

21. Reiman, *New Deal and American Youth,* 82.

22. Ileen A. DeVault has examined the features of this shaping influence in its initial phase in her study of schooling and the class origins of clerical workers in turn-of-the-century Pittsburgh; DeVault, *Sons and Daughters of Labor: Class and Clerical Work in Turn-of-the-Century Pittsburgh* (Ithaca, N.Y.: Cornell University Press, 1990); see also John L. Rury, *Education and Women's Work: Female Schooling and the Division of Labor in Urban America, 1870–1930* (Albany: SUNY Press, 1991); Powers, *"Girl Question";* and Miriam Cohen, *Workshop to Office: Two Generations of Italian Women in New York City, 1900–1950* (Ithaca, N.Y.: Cornell University Press, 1992).

23. On the increasing trend toward "warehousing" youths in New Haven's high schools during the 1920s and early 1930s, see Frederic J. Morton, "A Study of Failures among Hamden Pupils in the New Haven High School" (M.A. thesis, Yale University, 1933), 10; and Helen C. Goodman, "I.Q. in Relation to Graduation after Failure" (M.A. thesis, Yale University, 1933), 41. Labaree discusses the trend toward "over-aged" high school students during the same period in *How to Succeed in School,* chap. 2.

24. Morton, "Study of Failures," 3.

25. Morton, "Study of Failures," 3, and see Labaree's discussion of "social promotion" in *How to Succeed in School,* chap. 2.

26. "Frank" is a fictitious name I have given to William Nordli's case study "F"; "David" and "Evelyn" are, respectively, case studies "D" and "E" in Nordli, "Rewards and Punishments of High School Students" (Ph.D. diss., Yale University, 1942), 123, 246–47, 255–57.

27. Frank's IQ was assessed as 123; Nordli does not provide grade-point averages by curriculum or gender, but I infer that on the whole, students in the general course worked below their potential both because the curriculum was dominated by boys and because students in the general course held the most positive opinion of "average" grades; Nordli, "Rewards and Punishments," 71.

28. Nordli, "Rewards and Punishments," 263.

29. Nordli, "Rewards and Punishments," 246–47.

30. McConnell, *Evolution of Social Classes,* 187, n. 10.

31. Evelyn scored 100 on an IQ test; Nordli, "Rewards and Punishments," 255.

32. Nordli, "Rewards and Punishments," 255–57.

33. Nordli, "Rewards and Punishments,"152; and see Modell and Alexander, "High School in Transition," on the same theme.

34. Nordli, "Rewards and Punishments," 149. In addition, without any means of substantiating the influence of friends, it seems intuitively correct to think that just as friendship groups helped to determine whether youths entered and remained in high school, so they influenced one another's curricular choices in instances where parents did not positively assume authority over children's choices.

35. Bakke, *Unemployed Worker,* 149.

36. See Edward A. Krug, *The Shaping of the American High School,* 2 vols. (New York: Harper and Row, 1964–72).

37. Note, for example, the experience of Nick Aeillo, recounted below, and see case studies "Delogia," "Coviello," "Fontana," and "Gilberti" in appendix B of Whitelaw, "Administration of Elementary School."

38. Lebow, "Education and the Immigrant Experience," 31–32.

39. New Haven, *Annual Report,* 1850–32. An important indicator of the city's recognition of the necessity of adapting the curriculum to the interests of its Italian immigrant population was the decision to introduce Italian language instruction throughout the school system, beginning in the elementary grades, so that the "language could then be continued through high school"; see "Group Urges City Grade Schools Offer Italian Language Course," *New Haven Register,* September 9, 1932.

40. New Haven, *Annual Report,* 1885–1932. The popularity of the commercial course, as DeVault's study shows, can be traced to the 1880s. Of course, if the three "college-bound" tracks are combined, they still form the majority of high school students throughout the period.

41. New Haven High School, *Annual* (New Haven, 1930–40); Commercial High School, *Senior Class Book* (New Haven, 1930–40).

42. Hal Hansen, "Caps and Gowns: Historical Reflections on the Institutions That Shaped Learning for and at Work in Germany and the United States, 1800–1945," *Business and Economic History* 28 (Winter 1999): 19–24. An early important study is Paul H. Douglas, *American Apprenticeship and Industrial Education* (New York: Columbia University Press, 1921). Gillian Hamilton explores the origins of the long decline of apprenticeship in the aftermath of the War of 1812; Hamilton, "The Decline of Apprenticeship in North America: Evidence from Montreal," *Journal of Economic History* 60 (Fall 2000): 627–64. Sean Wilentz discusses the origins of decline during the 1830s and 1840s in *Chants Democratic: New York City and the Rise of the American Working Class, 1788–1850* (New York: Oxford University Press, 1984). Surveys include William J. Rorabough, *The Craft Apprentice: From Franklin to the Machine Age in America* (New York: Oxford University Press, 1986); William Mulligan Jr., "From Artisan to Proletarian: The Family and the Vocational Education of Shoemakers in the

Handicraft Era," in Charles Stephenson and Robert Asher, eds., *Dimensions of American Working-Class History* (Albany: SUNY Press, 1986); Ava Baron examines conceptions of masculinity in the changing relationship of apprenticeship to the printing trade in "Questions of Gender: Deskilling and Demasculinization in the U.S. Printing Trade, 1830–1915," *Gender and History* I (Summer 1989): 178–99; and Montgomery argues that although historians, generally, have believed that apprenticeship by the end of the nineteenth century was "long since dead," in the metal trades it was still considered an important part of the training of the "good workman" as late as the 1890s; see Montgomery, *Fall of the House of Labor*, 184–86.

43. See Ava Baron, "An 'Other' Side of Gender Antagonism at Work: Men, Boys, and the Remasculinization of Printers' Work, 1830–1920," in Baron ed., *Work Engendered: Toward a New History of American Labor* (Ithaca, N.Y.: Cornell University Press, 1991), 63–67, for a summary of these changes in the printing trade. A survey of men applying to Connecticut state unemployment offices during 1933 and 1934 found that for men born between 1908 and 1918, just 4 percent to 5.3 percent had received an apprenticeship of any kind. This may have understated the extensiveness of apprenticeship on one hand, because this was a survey of unemployed men, and skilled workers over the age of twenty-five were most likely of any group to have been employed at this time. On the other hand, since trade school was included as a form of apprenticeship, the ratio reported may have been overstated; State of Connecticut, Connecticut State Employment Service, *Youths in Search of Jobs!* i, table 1.

44. New Haven's first trade school was an industrial arts high school, which opened in 1896. Money for construction of the building was donated by a local philanthropist, but the New Haven school board operated the school.

45. "A leading Chicago unionist," wrote Katznelson and Weir, feared that "vocational schools would turn into 'scab factories' used by employers to crank out cheap labor"; for an outline of the controversy over trade schools, see Katznelson and Weir, *Schooling for All*, 82, 150–77.

46. McConnell, *Evolution of Social Classes*, 134.

47. Bakke, *Unemployed Worker*, 149.

48. See, e.g., Nordli, "Rewards and Punishments," 71; and Feldman, "Dull Child," 117.

49. Morton, "Study of Failures," 39; Feldman, "Dull Child," 12–17; State of Connecticut, Connecticut State Employment Service, *Youths in Search of Jobs!*; Buckner, "Study of Pupil Elimination," 58–59.

50. Bakke, *Unemployed Worker*, 149.

51. Bakke, *Unemployed Worker*, 149.

52. Montgomery, *Fall of the House*, 185.

53. E. Wight Bakke, "The Fifth Winter of Unemployment Relief," TS, Report to the Institute of Human Relations, Yale University, 1935, E. Wight Bakke Papers, Labor-Management Documentation Center, Cornell University, Collection 5522, box 7, folder 34, p. 13.

54. Montgomery, *Fall of the House*, 183.

55. See McConnell, *Evolution of Social Classes,* 134–35.

56. McConnell, *Evolution of Social Classes,* 134–38. In McConnell's estimation, an important consequence of the open shop in New Haven was that union agents, foremen, and shop bosses in the city were themselves more susceptible to corruption and had more influence over their workers individually than would have been the case had organized labor been a more effective force in relations between management and labor.

57. Possibly Bakke's carpenter was speaking directly from his experience in managing a crew of workers on a construction site: coordinating the supply of building materials; ensuring that everyone pulled his own weight so that a sense of equity governed the exertions of his workers; and keeping his men on schedule, yet stretching the job as much as possible both to stabilize his earnings and to keep his crew together. In his control of all facets of the production process, the carpenter comes much closer to the artisanal ideal of the nineteenth-century master craftsman than the average worker in any of New Haven's factories of the 1920s and 1930s. He is a vestige of the past: part worker, part manager, part entrepreneur. Perhaps his experience sheds a little light on how most workers would have thought about the relationship between work and school.

58. McConnell, *Evolution of Social Classes,* 186–87.

59. Nordli, "Rewards and Punishments," 72. The site of Nordli's study, Hamden High School, was identical academically, socioeconomically, and ethnically to Hillhouse High School in 1940.

60. McConnell, *Evolution of Social Classes,* chap. 7.

61. Noland and Bakke, *Workers Wanted,* 45, 161.

62. Bakke, *Unemployed Worker,* 148.

63. Bakke, *Unemployed Worker,* 148.

64. Modell and Alexander, "High School in Transition," 22–23.

65. Bakke, *Unemployed Worker,* 148.

66. Bakke, *Unemployed Worker,* 148. The maxim that by furthering children's prospects one's own climb was aided was surely a faint hope, but it seems to have contained enough of a grain of truth to have been listed among several other methods of obtaining "pull" on the job; Bakke, *Unemployed Worker,* 86.

67. McConnell, *Evolution of Social Classes,* 142. McConnell, a graduate student of Bakke's in the sociology department at Yale during the 1930s, worked for him as a researcher and interviewer for his unemployment studies during the latter half of the decade; see Bakke, "Fifth Winter."

68. McConnell, *Evolution of Social Classes,* appendix, table 17. McConnell's data were based on the Institute of Human Relations's New Haven Sample Family Survey of June 1933. The survey was a one-in-twenty family statistical sample that included 2,007 households; see Dreis, *Handbook of Social Statistics,* part 2. On the occupations of household heads of New Haven High School students soon after it opened in 1860, see Lassonde, "Learning to Forget," table 8, appendix B; and Robert D. Moyer Jr., "'Hurrah for the Sixth of June!'" (senior thesis, Department of History, Yale University, 1992).

69. The "office workers" group consisted of "white-collar" or clerical workers, "business executives," and "public service" workers. Within each of the occupational groupings mentioned by McConnell, gender played an important role in determining the extent of children's schooling, a phenomenon I consider in the next section; McConnell, *Evolution of Social Classes*, appendix, tables 17–18.

70. McConnell, *Evolution of Social Classes*, 187–88. Among "white-collar" household heads, dealers and proprietors were the least educated. Only 15 percent of this group had finished high school by 1933 (as compared with almost 40 percent of "office workers"), and fully 75 percent of them had gone no further than grammar school (appendix, table 15).

71. McConnell, *Evolution of Social Classes*, 142–43.

72. Claudia Goldin, "The Meaning of College in the Lives of American Women: The Past One-Hundred Years," Working Paper No. 4099, National Bureau of Economic Research Working Papers Series, June 1992, 7.

73. "Higher education" in this context refers to secondary schooling.

74. McConnell, *Evolution of Social Classes*, 143.

75. McConnell, *Evolution of Social Classes*, 143.

76. The "cultural values" to which McConnell alluded resemble, collectively, attributes that Pierre Bourdieu would refer to singly as "linguistic," "educational," and "symbolic capital"; see Bourdieu, *Outline of a Theory of Practice*, trans. Richard Nice (Cambridge: Cambridge University Press, 1977), esp. 171–83; Bourdieu, *Distinction: A Social Critique of the Judgement of Taste*, trans. Richard Nice (Cambridge, Mass.: Harvard University Press, 1984), esp. 65–67; and Bourdieu with Jean-Claude Passeron, *Reproduction: In Education, Society and Culture*, trans. Richard Nice (Beverly Hills, Calif.: Sage, 1977), 43–44, 80–89.

77. McConnell, *Evolution of Social Classes*, 143.

78. Smith, "Depression Graduates," 108, table 12, 124–25.

79. Smith, "Depression Graduates," 137.

80. Alberta Roseman, interview by Katherine A. Lebow, tape recording, New Haven, August 1990, GNHLHA, and quoted in Lebow, "Education and the Immigration Experience," 28.

81. Lebow, "Education and the Immigration Experience," 28. On this point I have benefited from many conversations with Erin S. Murphy; see Murphy, "Fur Coats at Sixty Words Per Minute: Female Clerical Workers and the Search for Status" (senior thesis, Department of History, Yale University, 1994).

82. According to Goldin, until after the 1950s half of all women with college degrees engaged in full-time work were employed in one of four vocations: teaching, nursing, librarianship, or social work. Moreover, until the post–World War II period, women were forced to choose between marriage (and child-rearing) and work; Goldin, "Meaning of College," table 2; see also Winifred D. Wandersee, *Women's Work and Family Values, 1920–1940* (Cambridge, Mass.: Harvard University Press, 1981); and Lois Scharf, *To Work and to Wed: Female Employment, Feminism, and the Great Depression* (Westport, Conn.: Greenwood, 1980).

83. McConnell, *Evolution of Social Classes,* 140.

84. McConnell, *Evolution of Social Classes,* 187, n. 10.

85. McConnell, *Evolution of Social Classes,* 133–34.

86. Whitelaw, "Administration of the Elementary School," 196–203. About 85 percent of the children in the schools in this district (Wards Ten–Twelve) were of Italian parentage. One-third of all the families in the area were receiving some kind of "relief funds" during the 1930s; three-quarters of the families were in contact with one or more social agencies; one-third of heads of household were unemployed; the rate of high school graduation for all persons over age eighteen was one-third of that for the city as a whole; average family size was approximately one person more per household than the city average; and the number of families per habitable acre of land was between two and three times that of the rest of the city; Whitelaw, "Administration of the Elementary School," 118–25.

87. Whitelaw, "Administration of the Elementary School," 202–3.

88. Whitelaw, "Administration of the Elementary School," 202–3; see twenty case studies in appendix A.

89. Morton, "Study of Failures," 49.

90. Morton, "Study of Failures," 77.

91. Feldman, "Dull Child."

92. Between grades 6 and 8, according to Whitelaw, registration in the area's grammar schools declined by about 20 percent; the rate for the city as a whole at this time was 11.5 percent; Whitelaw, "Administration of the Elementary School," 138; and see table 4, appendix B.

93. This phrase was used by educators to lump together several groups of children—those of so-called "low mentality," the "dull" child, the "failure," and those of modest means whose capacities appeared so compromised in various ways that college seemed beyond the realm of possibility.

94. Nick Aiello, interview by Jeremy Brecher, New Haven, March 31, 1989; TS, GNHLH, 1–4. Until at least 1930, students were prohibited from transferring out of one course (or school, e.g., from Commercial to Hillhouse) and into another course of study; Smith, "Depression Graduates," 137. Hortense Powdermaker and Joseph Semper, "Education and Occupation among New Haven Negroes," *Journal of Negro History* 23 (April 1938): 209, n.17.

95. McConnell, *Evolution of Social Classes,* 98.

96. Nordli, "Rewards and Punishments."

97. Nordli, "Rewards and Punishments," 207, 174.

98. Nordli, "Rewards and Punishments," 152. According to Nordli, the average IQ of commercial students was 90 percent of that of the academic students. Students in the general curriculum were comparable to the commercial group in mean score, but the range of scores was both higher and lower than commercial students; Nordli, "Rewards and Punishments," 1–3.

99. Nordli, "Rewards and Punishments," 71.

100. Nordli, "Rewards and Punishments," 71.

101. These attitudes accord with the rise of "social promotion" during the same period: that is, the promotion of students from one grade level to the next, "on the grounds that staying with their peers would best serve both the educational and developmental needs of most students." Labaree, who argues that this rationale was most prominent during the 1930s and 1940s, shows that in Philadelphia between 1908 and 1945, the average annual rate of nonpromotion for students in high school declined from 23 percent to 15 percent; Labaree, *How to Succeed*, 54–55.

102. Gary S. Becker, *Human Capital: A Theoretical and Empirical Analysis, with Special Reference to Education* (New York: Columbia University Press, 1975), 206–10, tables 16, 17, and 18. Michael J. Shanahan, Richard A. Miech, and Glen H. Elder Jr. essentially amplify Becker's claim, showing that the "annual mean income of a [high school] graduate in constant dollars . . . increased almost 125% between 1949 and 1968"; Shanahan et al., "Changing Pathways to Attainment in Men's Lives: Historical Patterns of School, Work, and Social Class," *Social Forces* 77 (September 1998): 231–56.

103. Zelizer, *Pricing the Priceless Child*, 209.

104. The subject was a ninth-grade student in Fair Haven Junior High School, from Feldman, "Dull Child," 171.

105. On the effects of the Great Depression on fathers' unemployment and children's development, see Glen H. Elder Jr., *Children of the Great Depression: Social Change in Life Experience* (Chicago: University of Chicago Press, 1974). On peer relations in high school in the interwar era, see Modell and Alexander, "High School in Transition"; on peer relations just after World War II, see Graebner, *Coming of Age in Buffalo*.

Conclusion

Epigraph: Andy Hardy Gets Spring Fever, 1939, directed by W. S. Van Dyke, screenplay by Kay Van Riper (Metro-Goldwyn, Mayer).

1. Fass, "Americanizing the High Schools," 109.

2. See Hindman, *Child Labor*; Hindman's discussion of the bearing of technological change on children's employment is scattered throughout his account but see esp. 135–36, 151, 333–34.

3. Jack W. Berryman, "From the Cradle to the Playing Field: America's Emphasis on Highly Organized Competitive Sports for Preadolescent Boys," *Journal of Sport History* 2 (Spring 1975): 112–131; Allen Guttmann, *A Whole New Ball Game: An Interpretation of American Sports* (Chapel Hill: University of North Carolina Press, 1988); Benjamin G. Rader, *American Sports: From the Age of Folk Games to the Age of Televised Sports* (Englewood Cliffs, N.J.: Prentice Hall, 1999); Shirley Brice Heath and Milbrey W. McLaughlin, eds., *Identity and Inner-City Youth: Beyond Ethnicity and Gender* (New York: Teachers College Press, 1993); and D. A. Kleiber and G. M. Powell, "Historical Change in Leisure Activities during After-School Hours," in Joseph L. Mahoney, Reed W. Larson, and Jacquelynne S. Eccles, eds., *Organized Activities as Contexts of Development: Extracurricular Activities, After School and Community Programs* (New York: Lawrence Erlbaum, forthcoming), chap. 2.

4. Historian Nathan O. Hatch quotes a Gallup poll from the late 1980s reporting that 41 percent of young Americans believed that religion "should be very important" in life. Hatch then boasted that on "any given Sunday morning, over 40 percent of the population in the United States attends religious services" and proclaimed, "statistically, at least, the United States is God's country." Hatch, *The Democratization of American Christianity* (New Haven: Yale University Press, 1989), 210–11. The degree of piety (as measured by church attendance) in the United States both currently and historically is, nonetheless, the subject of intense debate. Much of recent historical evidence on church attendance rests on Gallup, Harris, and Roper polls dating to 1936; see Hazel Gaudet Erskine, "The Polls: Church Attendance," *Public Opinion Quarterly* 28 (Winter 1964): 671–79. Yet since the mid-1990s sociologists have disputed the reliability of these data and even contemporary polling data on church attendance, citing "social desirability" effects that cause respondents to over-report actual attendance. In these critiques over-reporting is thought to double estimates of actual attendance figures. See the series of exchanges on the reliability of statistics on church attendance in 1990s America in Theodore Caplow et al., "A Symposium on Church Attendance in the United States," *American Sociological Review* 63 (February 1998): 111–45; see also C. Kirk Hadaway, Penny Long, and Mark Chaves, "What Polls Don't Show: A Closer Look at U.S. Church Attendance," *American Sociological Review* 58 (December 1993): 741–52.

In England, by comparison, church attendance is estimated to have declined from about 60 percent in 1851 to roughly 10 percent by the end of the twentieth century. On church attendance in England since 1851, see Steve Bruce, "The Social Process of Secularization," in Richard K. Fenn, ed., *The Blackwell Companion to Sociology of Religion* (Oxford: Blackwell, 2001), 249–50. In Europe overall the Catholic countries (excluding the anomalously irreligious France) tend to demonstrate higher church attendance (ranging from 81 percent to 23 percent) than Lutheran countries, which attract from 9 percent to 11 percent of their populations to church each Sunday; on average weekly church attendance in Europe today is estimated at 29 percent; Grace Davie, "Patterns of Religion in Western Europe: An Exceptional Case," in Fenn, ed., *Blackwell Companion,* table 14.1, 267.

5. The Young Men's Hebrew Association was the Jewish "answer" to the Young Men's Christian Association, which excluded Jews from their memberships. See "Beginning of the Jewish Community Center Movement in the West: The First Affair," *Western States Jewish History* 18 (Summer 1986): 218–22; Linda J. Borish, "An Interest in Physical Well-Being among the Feminine Membership: Sporting Activities for Women at Young Men's and Young Women's Hebrew Associations," *American Jewish History* 87 (Winter 1999): 61–93; and Ruth Kelson Rafael, "The YMHA and the YWHA in San Francisco," *Western States Jewish History* 19 (Summer 1987): 208–16. Even less is known about the Catholic equivalent of the JCC, but see Gerald R. Gems, "Sport, Religion, and Americanization: Bishop Sheil and the Catholic Youth Organization," *Journal of the History of Sport* 10 (Spring 1993): 233–41.

6. Stephen Lassonde, "Learning and Earning: Schooling and Family Life in New Haven's Working Class, 1870–1940" (Ph.D. diss., Yale University, 1994), appendix B, tables 5 and 14, pp. 314–15, 327–28.

7. Antonio Gramsci, *Selections from the Prison Notebooks*, ed. and trans. Quintin Hoare and Geoffrey Nowell Smith (New York: International Publishers, 1971), 42.

8. Gramsci, *Selections from the Prison Notebooks*, 42–43.

BIBLIOGRAPHY

Manuscript Sources

Amalgamated Clothing Workers of America Archives. Records. Coll. #6519. Labor-Management Documentation Center, New York State School of Industrial and Labor Relations, Cornell University, Ithaca.

Bakke, E. Wight. Papers, 1932–71. Coll. #5522. Labor-Management Documentation Center, New York State School of Industrial and Labor Relations, Cornell University, Ithaca.

Covello, Leonard. Papers. Research Library of the Balch Institute for Ethnic Studies, Philadelphia.

Dana, Arnold Guyot. "New Haven Old and New, 1641–1947." MS 1. Whitney Library, New Haven Colony Historical Society, New Haven.

Diaries Collection. MS Group 181. Manuscripts and Archives, Sterling Memorial Library, Yale University, New Haven.

Farnam Family Papers. MS Group 203. Manuscripts and Archives, Sterling Memorial Library, Yale University, New Haven.

Hillhouse High School, New Haven. Records, 1859–1984. MS B16. Whitney Library, New Haven Colony Historical Society, New Haven.

Hook, James W. Papers. MS 288. Manuscripts and Archives, Sterling Memorial Library, Yale University, New Haven.

Institute of Human Relations. Yale University, 1929–49. MS Group 37. Manuscripts and Archives, Sterling Memorial Library, Yale University, New Haven.

International Institute of Boston. Papers. Immigration History Research Center, University of Minnesota, Twin Cities, St. Paul.

New Haven. Board of Education. Records, 1799–1970. MS B26. Whitney Library, New Haven Colony Historical Society, New Haven.

New Haven Collection. New Haven Public Library, New Haven.

New Haven Working-Class Oral History Collection. Greater New Haven Labor History Association (GNHLHA). Central Labor Council of New Haven, New Haven.

Peoples of Connecticut Ethnic Heritage Project. Works Progress Administration, Federal Writers' Project. Manuscripts and Archives, University of Connecticut Libraries, Storrs.

Rockefeller Family Archives. RG 2. Rockefeller Archive Center, Rockefeller University, North Tarrytown, N.Y.

Roosevelt, Eleanor Anna. Papers. ER 2100–2600. Franklin D. Roosevelt Library, U.S. National Archives and Records Administration, Hyde Park, N.Y.

School Records, New Haven, Connecticut, 1714–1977. MS 17. Whitney Library, New Haven Colony Historical Society, New Haven.

Interviews

Aiello, Nick. Interview by Jeremy Brecher and Frank Annunziato. New Haven. March 31, 1989. TS. GNHLHA.

Alberti, Josephine Aceto. Interviews by the GNHLHA. Tape recording. New Haven. November 20, 1988, and October 19, 1990. GNHLHA.

Alfano, Jenny Aiello. Interview by Katherine Lebow. Tape recording. New Haven. October 19, 1990. GNHLHA.

Altieri, Eternina. Interview by Katherine Lebow. Tape recording. West Haven. August 25, 1989. GNHLHA.

Baker, Mary. Interview by author. New Haven. October 29, 1989. GNHLHA.

———. Interview by Jennifer Noll. Tape recording. New Haven. March 1, 1994. GNHLHA.

Betteti, Maria. Interviews by author. Tape recording. New Haven. May 30 and June 20, 1990.

Bonito, Maria. Interview by author. Tape recording. New Haven. August 20, 1991.

Bozzuto, Betty. Interview by Mary Johnson and Betty Murray. Tape recording. New Haven. August 10, 1989. GNHLHA.

Buonome, Adeline. Interview by Kate Lebow. Tape recording. New Haven. September 22, 1989. GNHLHA.

Ciarlone, Fred and Marie. Interview by author. Tape recording. North Haven, June 18, 1991.

De Capua, Elvira. Interview by author. Tape recording. New Haven. June 1990.

Ferrigno, Giuseppina. Interview by Deborah Elkin and author. Tape recording. New Haven. November 12, 1989. GNHLHA.

Iacobelli, Jennie. Interview by Frank Annunziato. Tape recording. New Haven. March 30, 1990. GNHLHA.

Iglardi, Jean, Antoinette Izzo, Stella Mattei, and Marie Razzano. Interviews by Deborah Elkin and author. Tape recording. New Haven . November 12, 1989. GNHLHA.

Lender, Hymen. Interview by Susan L. Neitlich. Tape recording. New Haven. May 2, 1996.

Lender, Murray. Interview by Susan L. Neitlich. Tape recording. New Haven. July 1996.

Lender, Samuel. Interview by Susan L. Neitlich. Tape recording. New Haven. August 2, 1996.

Lucia, Francesca. Interview by author. Tape recording. New Haven. October 5, 1989. GNHLHA.

Mordente, Philomena Ciarlone. Interview by author. Tape recording. North Haven. June 18, 1991.

Palmieri, Jessie Ferrucci. Interview by author. Tape recording. New Haven. May 16, 1990.

Raffie, Theresa. Interview by Jennifer Noll. New Haven. February 25, 1994.

Rappa, Tessie. Interview by Jennifer Noll. Tape recording. New Haven. February 25, 1994. GNHLHA.

Rosadini, Frederico. Interview by author. Tape recording. New Haven. September 18, 1990.

Roseman, Alberta. Interview by Katherine A. Lebow. Tape recording. New Haven. August 1990. GNHLHA.

Ruocco, Jennie Marino. Interview by Deborah Elkin. Tape recording. New Haven. June 30, 1989. GNHLHA.

Speranza, Anna. Interview by the GNHLHA. Tape recording. New Haven. November 20, 1988.

Storlazzi, Amelia. Interview by the GNHLHA. Tape recording. New Haven. November 20, 1988. GNHLHA.

Vecharrio, Angela. Interview by author. Tape recording. New Haven. October 11, 1989. GNHLHA.

Federal Documents

U.S. Congress. Senate. *Reports of the Immigration Commission: The Children of Immigrants in Schools,* vols. 29–33. 61st Cong., 3d sess. S. Doc. 749. Washington, D.C.: Government Printing Office, 1911. Reprint, New York: Arno, 1970.

U.S. Department of Commerce. Bureau of the Census. *Census of Population, 1940* [United States]: Public Use Microdata Sample (ICPSR 8236). Ann Arbor, Mich.: Inter-University Consortium for Political and Social Research, 1984.

———. *Historical Statistics of the United States, Colonial Times to 1957: A Statistical Abstract Supplement.* Washington, D.C.: Government Printing Office, 1960.

U.S. Department of Labor. Bureau of Labor Statistics. "Conditions in Connecticut Needle Trades under N.R.A." *Monthly Labor Review* 40 (June 1935): 1499–1504.

———. "Hours and Earnings in the Women's Dress Industry in Connecticut." *Monthly Labor Review* 38 (April 1934): 925–29.

———. "Labor in the Shirt Industry." *Monthly Labor Review* 37 (September 1933): 499–510.

——— . "Minimum-Wage Laws of Connecticut and Ohio." *Monthly Labor Review* 37 (July 1933): 57–63.

U.S. Department of Labor. U.S. Children's Bureau. *Administration of Child Labor Laws; Part I: Employment-Certificate System, Connecticut*. Industrial Series No. 2., Part 1, Bureau Publication No. 12. Washington, D.C.: Government Printing Office, 1915.

——— . *Industrial Instability of Child Workers: A Study of Employment-Certificate Records in Connecticut*. Industrial Series No. 5, Bureau Publication No. 74. Washington, D.C.: Government Printing Office, 1920.

——— . *Standards of Child Welfare: Family Budgets*. Bureau Publication No. 60. Washington, D.C.: Government Printing Office, 1919.

U.S. Department of Labor. U.S. Women's Bureau. *Chronological Development of Labor Legislation for Women in the United States*. Bulletin of the Women's Bureau, Publication No. 66, 157–60. Washington, D.C.: Government Printing Office, 1929.

——— . *The Employment of Women in the Sewing Trades of Connecticut: Hours and Earnings, Employment Fluctuation, and Home Work*. Bulletin of the Women's Bureau, Publication No. 109, 1–45. Washington, D.C.: Government Printing Office, 1935.

——— . *The Employment of Women in the Sewing Trades of Connecticut: Preliminary Report*. Bulletin of the Women's Bureau, Publication No. 97, 1–13. Washington, D.C.: Government Printing Office, 1932.

State and Local Documents

Butts, Carl, and Joseph Young. "Education in Connecticut: A Study of Public, Parochial, and Sunday School Education in Connecticut, with Emphasis on the Ethnic Factors." Peoples of Connecticut Ethnic Heritage Project, Works Progress Administration, Federal Writers' Project. Manuscripts and Archives, University of Connecticut Libraries, Storrs.

Collegiate and Commercial Institute of New Haven. *Collegiate and Commercial Institute Catalogue. 1850–1883*. New Haven.

Commercial High School. *Senior Class Book*. New Haven: New Haven Board of Education, 1930–50.

Hillhouse High School. *The Elm Tree*. New Haven: New Haven Board of Education, 1930–50.

Hopkins Grammar School. *Annual Catalogue of the Officers and Scholars of the New Haven Hopkins Grammar School, 1849–1918*. New Haven.

New Haven, Connecticut. New Haven Board of Education. *Annual Report*, 1856–1935.

——— . *New Haven School Reports*, 1850–60. New Haven: Thomas J. Stafford, Printer.

——— . *New Haven's Schools: An Investment in Your City's Future; Report of a Survey of the Public School System, 1946–47*. New Haven, 1947.

——— . "Report of the Board of School Visitors." *Proceedings of the Board of Education.* New Haven: Thomas J. Stafford, Printer, 1856, 3–22.

——— . "Report Respecting a High School." *Report of the First School Society of the Special Committee Appointed to Consider the Subject of a High School.* New Haven: Thomas J. Stafford, Printer, 1852.

New Haven, Connecticut. New Haven Chamber of Commerce. *Economic and Industrial Survey, New Haven, Connecticut.* New Haven: New Haven Chamber of Commerce, 1939.

Price and Lee Company. *Benham's New Haven City Directory.* New Haven: Price and Lee, 1849–91.

Racca, Vittorio. "Ethnography: The Italians of New Haven." TS. Works Progress Administration, Federal Writers' Project, Connecticut Ethnic Survey. Historical Manuscripts and Archives Division, University of Connecticut Libraries, Storrs.

——— . "A Few Selected Family Histories Describing the Socio-Economic Background of Italians Who Live in New Haven." TS. Institute of Human Relations Collection, Manuscripts and Archives, Sterling Memorial Library, Yale University, New Haven.

State of Connecticut. *The General Statutes of the State of Connecticut, Revision of 1875,* 126–27. Hartford: Case, Lockwood and Brainard, 1874.

——— . *Laws Relating to Labor and Inspection.* Hartford: Aetna Life Insurance, 1908.

State of Connecticut. Bureau of Labor Statistics. *Reports, 1873–1946.* Hartford.

State of Connecticut. Commission on Public Welfare. *Report on Public Welfare.* Hartford, 1919–23.

State of Connecticut. Connecticut State Employment Service. *Community Survey of New Haven, Connecticut.* Hartford, 1934.

——— . "Report of Committee Appointed to Study Possible Plans of Cooperation between the National Youth Administration and Connecticut." Hartford, 1936.

——— . *Youths in Search of Jobs!* FERA Project [C.P.S.-F2-87]. Hartford, 1934.

State of Connecticut. Consumers' League of Connecticut. *Proceedings of the Child Labor Conference.* Hartford, 1908.

State of Connecticut. Department of Labor. Minimum Wage Division. "Hours and Earnings in Connecticut Shirt Factories, 1933, 1934." Mimeo. Hartford, 1935.

——— . "Hours and Earnings in the Women's Dress Industry, 1933, 1934." Mimeo. Hartford, 1935.

State of Connecticut. Department of Labor and Factory Inspection. *Annual Report, 1930–1945.* Hartford.

Books and Articles

Alba, Richard D. *Ethnic Identity: The Transformation of White America.* New Haven: Yale University Press, 1990.

Amalgamated Clothing Workers of America. *The Shirt and Clothing Workers of Connecticut, 1933–1943*. New York: Amalgamated Clothing Workers of America, 1944.

American Youth Commission. *Youth and the Future*. Washington, D.C.: Government Printing Office, 1942.

Anderson, Michael. *Approaches to the History of the Western Family, 1500–1914*. London: MacMillan, 1980.

——— . *Family Structure in Nineteenth Century Lancashire*. Cambridge: Cambridge University Press, 1971.

Angers, David L., and Jeffrey E. Meril. "From Spellers to Spindles: Work-Force Entry by the Children of Textile Workers, 1888–1890." *Social Science History* 9 (Summer 1985): 123–44.

Annunziato, Frank R. "'Made in New Haven': Unionization and the Shaping of a Clothing Workers' Community." *Labor's Heritage: Quarterly of the George Meany Memorial Archives* 4 (Winter 1992): 20–33.

Ariès, Philippe. *Centuries of Childhood: A Social History of Family Life*, trans. Robert Baldick. New York: Alfred A. Knopf, 1962.

——— . *Western Attitudes toward Death: From the Middle Ages to the Present*. Baltimore: Johns Hopkins University Press, 1974.

Ayers, Leonard P. *Laggards in Our Schools: A Study of Retardation and Elimination in the City School Systems*. New York: Russell Sage Foundation, 1909.

Bailey, Beth L. *From Front Porch to Back Seat: Courtship in Twentieth-Century America*. Baltimore: Johns Hopkins University Press, 1988.

Baily, Samuel L. "Cross-Cultural Comparisons and the Writing of Migration History: Some Thoughts on How to Study Italians in the New World." In *Immigration Reconsidered: History, Sociology, and Politics*, ed. Virginia Yans-McLaughlin, 241–53. New York: Oxford University Press, 1990.

——— . *Immigrants in the Lands of Promise: Italians in Buenos Aires and New York City, 1870–1914*. Ithaca, N.Y.: Cornell University Press, 1999.

Bailyn, Bernard. *Education in the Forming of American Society: Needs and Opportunities for Study*. Chapel Hill: University of North Carolina Press, 1960.

Bakke, E. Wight. *Citizens without Work: A Study of the Effects of Unemployment upon the Workers' Social Relations and Practices*. New Haven: Yale University Press, 1940.

——— . *The Unemployed Worker: A Study of the Task of Making a Living without a Job*. New Haven: Yale University Press, 1940.

Banfield, Edward C. *The Moral Basis of a Backward Society*. Glencoe, Ill.: Free Press, 1958.

Barbagli, Marzio, and David I. Kerber, eds. "Italian Family History, 1750–1950: Special Issue." *Journal of Family History* 15 (October 1990).

Baritz, Loren. *The Servants of Power: A History of the Use of Social Science in American History*. Middletown, Conn.: Wesleyan University Press, 1960.

Baron, Ava. "An 'Other' Side of the Gender Antagonism at Work: Men, Boys, and the Remasculinization of Printers' Work, 1830–1920." In *Work Engendered: Towards a New History of American Labor,* ed. Ava Baron, 46–69. Ithaca, N.Y.: Cornell University Press, 1991.

——— . "Questions of Gender: Deskilling and Demasculinization in the U.S. Printing Trade, 1830–1915." *Gender and History* 1 (Summer 1989): 178–99.

Barton, Josef J. *Peasants and Strangers: Italians, Rumanians, and Slovaks in an American City, 1890–1950.* Cambridge, Mass.: Harvard University Press, 1975.

Bass, Paul. "Hidden History: New Haven Finds a New Past." *Progressive* 54 (July 1990): 28–29.

——— . "Sew Many Memories." *New Haven Advocate,* February 12, 1990.

Beadie, Nancy. "From Student Markets to Credential Markets: The Creation of the Regents Examination System in New York State, 1864–1890." *History of Education Quarterly* 39 (Spring 1999): 1–30.

Becker, Gary S. *Human Capital: A Theoretical and Empirical Analysis, with Special Reference to Education.* New York: Columbia University Press, 1975.

——— . *A Treatise on the Family.* Cambridge, Mass.: Harvard University Press, 1981.

"Beginning of the Jewish Community Center Movement in the West: The First Affair." *Western States Jewish History* 18 (Summer 1986): 218–22.

Bell, Daniel. *The Cultural Contradictions of Capitalism.* New York: Basic Books, 1976.

Bell, Howard M. *Youth Tell Their Story: A Study of Conditions and Attitudes of Young People in Maryland between the Ages of Sixteen and Twenty-Four.* Washington, D.C.: American Council on Education, 1938.

Bell, Rudolph M. *Fate and Honor, Family and Village: Demographic and Cultural Change in Rural Italy since 1800.* Chicago: University of Chicago Press, 1979.

Ben-Amos, Ilana Krausman. *Adolescence and Youth in Early Modern England.* New Haven: Yale University Press, 1994.

Benson, Susan. *Counter Cultures: Saleswomen, Managers, and Customers in American Department Stores, 1890–1940.* Urbana: University of Illinois Press, 1986.

——— . "Living on the Margin: Working-Class Marriages and Family Survival Strategies in the United States, 1919–1941." In *The Sex of Things: Gender and Consumption in Historical Perspective,* ed. Victoria de Grazia and Ellen Furlough, 212–43. Berkeley: University of California Press, 1996.

Berger, Peter L., and Thomas Luckmann. *The Social Construction of Reality: A Treatise in the Sociology of Knowledge.* Garden City, N.Y.: Anchor Books, 1967.

Bernard, William S. "Cultural Determinants of Naturalization." *American Sociological Review* 1 (December 1936): 943–53.

Berryman, Jack W. "From the Cradle to the Playing Field: America's Emphasis on Highly Organized Competitive Sports for Preadolescent Boys." *Journal of Sport History* 2 (Spring 1975): 112–31.

Blau, Peter M., and Otis D. Duncan. *The American Occupational Structure.* New York: John Wiley and Sons, 1967.

Blumer, Herbert. *Movies and Conduct.* New York: MacMillan, 1933.

Bodnar, John. "Immigration and Modernization: The Case of Slavic Peasants in Industrial America." *Journal of Social History* 10 (Fall 1976): 47–71.

——— . "Immigration, Kinship, and the Rise of Working-Class Realism." *Journal of Social History* 14 (Fall 1980): 45–65.

——— . "Materialism and Morality: Slavic-American Immigrants and Education, 1890–1940." *Journal of Ethnic Studies* 3 (Winter 1976): 1–19.

——— . *The Transplanted: A History of Immigrants in Urban America.* Bloomington: Indiana University Press, 1985.

Bodnar, John, Roger Simon, and Michael P. Weber. *Lives of Their Own: Blacks, Italians and Poles in Pittsburgh, 1900–1960.* Urbana: University of Illinois Press, 1982.

Boris, Eileen, and Cynthia R. Daniels, eds. *Homework: Historical and Contemporary Perspectives on Paid Labor at Home.* Urbana: University of Illinois Press, 1989.

Borish, Linda J. "An Interest in Physical Well-Being among the Feminine Membership: Sporting Activities for Women at Young Men's and Young Women's Hebrew Associations." *American Jewish History* 87 (Winter 1999): 61–93.

Boswell, John. *The Kindness of Strangers: The Abandonment of Children in Western Europe from Late Antiquity to the Renaissance.* New York: Pantheon, 1988.

Bourdieu, Pierre. *Distinction: A Social Critique of the Judgement of Taste,* trans. Richard Nice. Cambridge, Mass.: Harvard University Press, 1984.

——— . "Marriage Strategies as Strategies of Social Reproduction," trans. Elborg Forster and Patricia M. Ranum. In *Family and Society: Selections from the Annales, Economies, Sociétiés, Civilisations,* ed. Robert Forster and Orest Ranum, 117–44. Baltimore: Johns Hopkins University Press, 1976.

——— . *Outline of a Theory of Practice,* trans. Richard Nice. Cambridge: Cambridge University Press, 1977.

Bourdieu, Pierre, and Loïc J. D. Wacquant. *An Invitation to Reflexive Sociology.* Chicago: University of Chicago Press, 1992.

Bourdieu, Pierre, with Jean-Claude Passeron. *Reproduction: In Education, Society and Culture,* trans. Richard Nice. Beverly Hills, Calif.: Sage, 1977.

Bowles, Samuel, and Herbert Gintis. *Schooling in Capitalist America.* New York: Basic Books, 1976.

Braverman, Harry. *Labor and Monopoly Capital: The Degradation of Work in the Twentieth Century.* New York: Monthly Review Press, 1974.

Brettel, Caroline B. "Property, Kinship, and Gender: A Mediterranean Perspective," In *The Family in Italy from Antiquity to the Present,* ed. David I. Kertzer and Richard P. Saller, 340–53. New Haven: Yale University Press, 1991.

Briggs, John W. *An Italian Passage: Immigrants to Three American Cities, 1890–1930.* New Haven: Yale University Press, 1978.

——— . "Fertility and Cultural Change among Families in Italy and America." *American Historical Review* 91 (December 1986): 1129–45.

Brodhead, Richard H. "Sparing the Rod: Discipline and Fiction in Antebellum America." *Representations* 21 (Winter 1988): 67–96.

Bronfenbrenner, Urie. "Developmental Theory in Transition." In *Child Psychology, Part 1,* ed. Harold W. Stevenson, 517–42. Chicago: University of Chicago Press, 1963.

Brown, Elizabeth Mills. *New Haven: A Guide to Architecture and Urban Design.* New Haven: Yale University Press, 1976.

Bushnell, N. T., Samuel Hemingway, and Patrick Maher. *Views of the Minority of the Board of Education, Concerning the Discontinuance of Religious Exercises in the Public Schools.* New Haven: Tuttle, Morehouse and Taylor, Printers, 1878.

Byington, Margaret F. *Homestead: The Households of a Mill Town.* With an Introduction by Samuel P. Hays. New York: Russell Sage Foundation, 1910.

Caldwell, John C. "Mass Education as a Determinant of the Timing of Fertility Decline." *Population and Development Review* 6 (June 1980): 225–55.

Calhoun, Arthur W. *A Social History of the American Family from Colonial Times to the Present.* 3 vols. Cleveland: Arthur H. Clark, 1917–19.

Campisi, Paul J. "Ethnic Family Patterns: The Italian Family in the United States." *American Journal of Sociology* 53 (1948): 434–47.

Caplow, Theodore, et al. "A Symposium on Church Attendance in the United States." *American Sociological Review* 63 (February 1998): 111–45.

Carter, Susan B., Roger L. Ransom, and Richard Sutch. "The Historical Labor Statistics Project at the University of California." *Historical Methods* 24 (Spring 1991): 60–62.

Carter, Susan B., and Richard Sutch. "Sticky Wages, Short Weeks, and 'Fairness': The Response of Connecticut Manufacturing Firms to the Depression of 1893–94." *Working Paper 2.* Historical Labor Statistics Project. Berkeley: University of California, 1991.

Child, Irvin L. *Italian or American? The Second-Generation in Conflict.* New Haven: Yale University Press, 1941.

——— . *Italian or American? The Second Generation in Conflict.* With an Introduction by Francesco Cordasco. New Haven: Yale Unversity Press, 1941. Reprint, New York: Atheneum , 1970.

Chudacoff, Howard P. *How Old Are You? Age Consciousness in American Culture.* Princeton, N.J.: Princeton University Press, 1989.

Cinel, Dino. *From Italy to San Francisco: The Immigrant Experience.* Stanford, Calif.: Stanford University Press, 1982.

——— . *The National Integration of Italian Return Migration, 1870–1929.* Cambridge: Cambridge University Press, 1991.

Clague, Ewan, Walter J. Couper, and E. Wight Bakke. *After the Shutdown.* New Haven: Yale University Press, 1934.

Clubb, Jerome M., Erik W. Austin, and Gordon W. Kirk Jr. *The Process of Historical Inquiry: Everyday Lives of Working Americans.* New York: Columbia University Press, 1989.

Cohen, Lizabeth. *Making a New Deal: Industrial Workers in Chicago, 1919–1939.* New York: Cambridge University Press, 1990.

Cohen, Miriam. "Changing Educational Strategies among Immigrant Generations: New York Italians in Comparative Perspective." *Journal of Social History* 15 (Spring 1982): 443–66.

——— . "Italian-American Women in New York City, 1900–1950: Work and School." In *Class, Sex, and the Woman Worker,* ed. Milton Cantor and Bruce Laurie. Westport, Conn.: Greenwood, 1977. 120–43.

——— . *Workshop to Office: Two Generations of Italian Women in New York City, 1900–1950.* Ithaca, N.Y.: Cornell University Press, 1992.

Cohen, Ronald D. "*The Delinquents:* Censorship and Youth Culture in Recent U.S. History." *History of Education Quarterly* 37 (Fall 1997): 251–70.

Cole, Michael, and Sheila R. Cole. *The Development of Children.* 4th ed. New York: W. H. Freeman, 2000.

Coleman, James S. *The Adolescent Society: The Social Life of the Teenager and Its Impact on Education.* New York: Free Press of Glencoe, 1961.

Conzen, Kathleen Niels, David A. Gerber, Ewa Morawska, George E. Pozzetta, and Rudolph J. Vecoli. "The Invention of Ethnicity: A Perspective from the U.S.A." *Altreitalie* (April 1990): 37–62.

Coontz, Stephanie. *The Social Origins of Private Life: A History of American Families, 1600–1900.* London: Verso, 1988.

Cordasco, Francesco, ed. *Studies in Italian American Social History: Essays in Honor of Leonard Covello.* Totowa, N.J.: Rowman and Littlefield, 1975.

Cordasco, Francesco, and Eugene Buccioni. *The Italians: Social Background of an American Group.* Clifton, N.J.: Augustus M. Kelley, 1974.

Cornelison, Ann. *Women of the Shadows: The Wives and Mothers of Southern Italy.* New York: Vintage Books, 1976.

Cornell, Laurel L. "Where Can Family Strategies Exist?" *Historical Methods* 20 (Summer 1987): 120–23.

Cott, Nancy F. *The Grounding of Modern Feminism.* New Haven: Yale University Press, 1987.

Covello, Leonard. *The Social Background of the Italo-American School Child: A Study of the Southern Italian Family Mores and Their Effect on the School Situation in Italy and America.* Leiden, Netherlands: E. J. Brill, 1967.

Covello, Leonard, with Guido D'Agostino. *The Heart Is the Teacher.* New York: McGraw-Hill, 1958.

Cremin, Lawrence A. *American Education: The Metropolitan Experience, 1876–1980.* New York: Harper and Row, 1988.

——— . *American Education: The National Experience, 1783–1876.* New York: Harper and Row, 1980.

——— . *The Transformation of the School: Progressivism in American Education, 1876–1957.* New York: Alfred A. Knopf, 1961.

Cronin, Constance. *The Sting of Change: Sicilians in Sicily and Australia.* Chicago: University of Chicago Press, 1970.

"A Cultural Reluctance to Spare the Rod: Newcomers Say Americans Spoil Children." *New York Times,* February 29, 1996, B1.

Cunningham, Hugh. "The Employment and Unemployment of Children in England, c. 1680–1851." *Past and Present* 126 (February 1990): 115–50.

——— . *Children and Childhood in Western Society since 1500*. London: Addison-Wesley, 1995.

Dahl, Robert A. *Who Governs? Democracy and Power in an American City*. New Haven: Yale University Press, 1961.

Dana, Arnold G. *New Haven's Problems: Whither the City? All Cities?* New Haven: Tuttle, Morehouse and Taylor, 1937.

D'Antonio, William V. "Ethnicity and Assimilation: A Reconsideration." In *Studies in Italian American Social History: Essays in Honor of Leonard Covello*, ed. Francesco Cordasco, 10–27. Totowa, N.J.: Rowman and Littlefield, 1975.

Davie, Maurice R. "The Pattern of Urban Growth." In *Studies in the Science of Society*, ed. G. P. Murdock, 132–61. New Haven: Yale University Press, 1937.

Davies, Margery. *Woman's Place Is at the Typewriter: Office Work and Office Workers, 1870–1930*. Philadelphia: Temple University Press, 1982.

Davis, Allison. "American Status Systems and the Socialization of the Child." *American Sociological Review* 6 (June 1941): 345–56.

Davis, Kingsley. "Adolescence and the Social Structure." *Annals of the American Academy of Political and Social Sciences* 236 (November 1944): 8–16.

——— . "The Sociology of Parent-Youth Conflict." *American Sociological Review* 5 (August 1940): 523–35.

——— . "Wives and Work: The Sex Role Revolution and Its Consequences." *Population and Development Review* 10 (September 1984): 397–417.

D'Emilio, John, and Estelle B. Freedman. *Intimate Matters: A History of Sexuality in America*. New York: Harper and Row, 1988.

Demos, John. *A Little Commonwealth: Family Life in Plymouth Colony*. New York: Oxford University Press, 1970.

——— . "Oedipus and America: Historical Perspectives on the Reception of Psychoanalysis in the United States." *Annual of Psychoanalysis* 6 (1978): 23–39.

——— . *Past, Present, and Personal: The Family and the Life Course in American History*. New York: Oxford University Press, 1986.

Demos, John, and Virginia Demos. "Adolescence in Historical Perspective." *Journal of Marriage and the Family* 31 (1969): 632–38.

DeVault, Ileen A. *Sons and Daughters of Labor: Class and Clerical Work in Turn-of-the-Century Pittsburgh*. Ithaca, N.Y.: Cornell University Press, 1990.

Di Leonardo, Micaela. *The Varieties of Ethnic Experience: Kinship, Class and Gender among California Italian-Americans*. Ithaca, N.Y.: Cornell University Press, 1984.

Dore, Grazia. "Some Social and Historical Aspects of Italian Emigration to America." *Journal of Social History* 2 (Winter 1968): 95–122.

Dorn, Sherman. *Creating the Dropout: An Institutional and Social History of School Failure*. Westport, Conn.: Greenwood, 1996.

Douglas, Paul H. *American Apprenticeship and Industrial Education*. New York: Columbia University Press, 1921.

Douglas, William. "The South Italian Family: A Critique." *Journal of Family History* 5 (Winter 1980): 338–59.

Dreis, Thelma A. *A Handboook of Social Statistics of New Haven, Connecticut.* New Haven: Yale University Press, 1936.

Duggan, Christopher. *A Concise History of Italy.* Cambridge: Cambridge University Press, 1994.

Duncan, Beverly. "Dropouts and the Unemployed." *Journal of Political Economy* 73 (April 1965): 121–34.

———. *Family Factors and School Dropout: 1920–1960.* Cooperative Research Project No. 2258. Washington, D.C.: U.S. Department of Health, Education, and Welfare, 1965.

Elder, Glen H., Jr. *Children of the Great Depression: Social Change in Life Experience.* Chicago: University of Chicago Press, 1974.

———. "Family History and the Life Course." In *Transitions: The Family and the Life Course in Historical Perspective,* ed. Tamara Hareven, 17–64. New York: Academic Press, 1978.

Elder, Glen H., Jr., John Modell, and Ross D. Parke. *Children in Time and Place: Developmental and Historical Insights.* New York: Cambridge University Press, 1993.

Engels, Friedrich. *The Condition of the Working Class in England* [1844], trans. and ed. W. O. Henderson and W. H. Chaloner. Stanford, Calif.: Stanford University Press, 1968.

Erenberg, Lewis. *Steppin' Out: New York Nightlife and the Transformation of American Culture, 1890–1930.* Chicago: University of Chicago Press, 1981.

Erikson, Erik H. *Childhood and Society.* New York: W. W. Norton, 1950.

Erskine, Hazel Gaudet. "The Polls: Church Attendance." *Public Opinion Quarterly* 28 (Winter 1964): 671–79.

Ewen, Elizabeth. *Immigrant Women in the Land of Dollars: Life and Culture on the Lower East Side, 1890–1925.* New York: Monthly Review Press, 1985.

———. "City Lights: Immigrant Women and the Rise of the Movies." *Signs* 5 (Spring 1980): S45–S65.

Faires, Nora, et al. "Comment and Debate; John Bodnar's *The Transplanted:* A Roundtable." With an Introduction by Nora Faires. *Social Science History* 12 (Fall 1988): 217–68.

Fass, Paula S. "'Americanizing' the High Schools." In *Outside In: Minorities and the Transformation of American Education,* 73–111. New York: Oxford University Press, 1989.

———. *The Damned and the Beautiful: American Youth in the 1920's.* New York: Oxford University Press, 1977.

———. "New Prospects for American Education History." Review of *Small Victories,* by Samuel G. Freedman, and *Gender and Higher Education in the Progressive Era,* by Lynn D. Gordon. *Journal of Interdisciplinary History* 22 (Winter 1992): 453–64.

Featherman, David L. "Biography, Society, and History: Individual Development as a Population Process." In *Human Development and the Life Course: Multi-disciplinary Perspectives*, ed. Aage B. Sorensen, Franz E. Weinert, and Lonnie R. Sherrod, 99–149. Hillsdale, N.J.: Lawrence Erlbaum, 1986.

Febvre, Lucien. "Sensibility and History: How to Reconstitute the Emotional Life of the Past." In *A New Kind of History: From the Writings of Febvre*, ed. Peter Burke, 12–26. New York: Harper and Row, 1973.

Felt, Jeremy P. *Hostages of Fortune: Child Labor Reform in New York State*. Syracuse, N.Y.: Syracuse University Press, 1965.

Fenn, Richard K., ed. *The Blackwell Companion to Sociology of Religion*. Oxford: Blackwell, 2001.

Ferriss, Abbott L. *Indicators of Trends in American Education*. New York: Russell Sage Foundation, 1969.

Fine, David M. *The City, the Immigrant, and American Fiction, 1880–1940*. Metuchen, N.J.: Scarecrow Press, 1977.

Fishlow, Albert. "Levels of Nineteenth Century Investment in Education." *Journal of Economic History* 26 (December 1966): 418–36.

Flandrin, Jean-Louis. *Families in Former Times: Kinship, Household and Sexuality*. Cambridge: Cambridge University Press, 1977.

Foerster, Robert F. *The Italian Emigration of Our Times*. New York: Russell and Russell, 1919. Reprint, New York: Arno, 1969.

Folbre, Nancy. "Family Strategy, Feminist Strategy." *Historical Methods* 20 (Summer 1987): 115–18.

Folger, John K., and Charles B. Nam. *Education of the American Population: A 1960 Census Monograph*. Washington, D.C.: Government Printing Office, 1967.

Gabaccia, Donna R. *From Sicily to Elizabeth Street: Housing and Social Change among Italian Immigrants, 1880–1930*. Albany: SUNY Press, 1984.

——— . "Immigrant Women: Nowhere at Home?" *Journal of American Ethnic History* 10 (Summer 1991): 61–87.

——— . *Militants and Migrants: Rural Sicilians Become American Workers*. New Brunswick, N.J.: Rutgers University Press, 1988.

Galenson, David W. "Ethnic Differences in Neighborhood Effects on the School Attendance of Boys in Early Chicago." *History of Education Quarterly* 38 (Spring 1998): 17–35.

Gambino, Richard. *Blood of My Blood*. Garden City, N.Y.: Doubleday, 1974.

Gans, Herbert J. "Symbolic Ethnicity: The Future of Ethnic Groups and Cultures in America." In *On the Making of Americans: Essays in Honor of David Reisman*, ed. Herbert J. Gans et al., 193–220. Philadelphia: University of Pennsylvania Press, 1979.

——— . *Urban Villagers: Group and Class in the Life of Italian-Americans*. New York: Free Press, 1962.

Geertz, Clifford. *The Interpretation of Cultures: Selected Essays*. New York: Basic Books, 1973.

———— . *Local Knowledge: Further Essays in Interpretive Anthropology.* New York: Basic Books, 1983.

Gems, Gerald R. "Sport, Religion, and Americanization: Bishop Sheil and the Catholic Youth Organization," *Journal of the History of Sport* 10 (Spring 1993): 233–41.

Gilbert, Cass, and Frederick Law Olmstead. "Report of the Civic Improvement Commission." New Haven: New Haven Civil Improvement Committee, 1910.

Gillette, Jonathon H. "Inside Contracting at the Sargent Hardware Company: A Case Study of a Factory in Transition at the Turn of the Century." *Theory and Society* 17 (March 1988): 159–78.

Gillis, John R. *Youth and History: Tradition and Change in European Age Relations, 1770–Present.* New York: Academic Press, 1981.

Glazer, Nathan, and Daniel P. Moynihan. *Beyond the Melting Pot: The Negroes, Puerto Ricans, Jews, Italians, and Irish of New York City.* 2d ed. Cambridge, Mass.: MIT Press, 1970.

Glazier, Ira A. "Ships and Passengers in Emigration from Italy to the U.S., 1800–1900." In *Emigration from Northern, Central and Southern Europe: Theoretical and Methodological Principles of Research,* ed. Zeszyty Naukowe, 245–76. Kráków: Jagiellonian University, 1984.

Gleason, Philip. *Speaking of Diversity: Language and Ethnicity in Twentieth-Century America.* Baltimore: Johns Hopkins University Press, 1992.

Glenn, Susan A. *Daughters of the Shtetl: Life and Labor in the Immigrant Generation.* Ithaca, N.Y.: Cornell University Press, 1990.

Glickman, Lawrence. "Inventing the 'American Standard of Living': Gender, Race and Working-Class Identity, 1880–1925." *Labor History* 34, nos. 2–3 (Spring–Summer 1993): 221–35.

Goldin, Claudia. "Family Strategies and the Family Economy in the Late Nineteenth Century: The Role of Secondary Workers." In *Philadelphia: Work, Space, and Group Experience in the Nineteenth Century,* ed. T. Hershberg, 277–310. New York: Oxford University Press, 1981.

———— . "Household and Market Production in Families in a Late Nineteenth Century American City." *Explorations in Economic History* 16 (1979): 111–31.

———— . "The Meaning of College in the Lives of American Women: The Past One-Hundred Years." Working Paper No. 4099. National Bureau of Economic Research Working Papers Series, June 1992.

Goldmark, Pauline. *West Side Studies.* New York: Russell Sage Foundation, 1914.

Goody, Jack, ed. *The Developmental Cycle in Domestic Groups.* Introduction by Meyer Fortes. Cambridge: Cambridge University Press, 1971.

Gordon, Linda. *Heroes of Their Own Lives: The Politics and History of Family Violence in Boston, 1880–1960.* New York: Viking Press, 1988.

Gordon, Michael, ed. *The American Family in Socio-Historical Perspective.* New York: St. Martin's, 1973.

Gordon, Milton. *Assimilation in American Life: The Role of Race, Religion and National Origins.* New York: Oxford University Press, 1964.

Graebner, William. *Coming of Age in Buffalo: Youth and Authority in the Postwar Era.* Philadelphia: Temple University Press, 1990.

———— . "Outlawing Teenage Populism: The Campaign against Secret Societies in the American High School, 1900–1960." *Journal of American History* 74 (September 1987): 411–35.

Gramsci, Antonio. *Selections from the Prison Notebooks,* ed. and trans. Quintin Hoare and Geoffrey Nowell Smith. New York: International Publishers, 1971.

Grant, Madison. *The Passing of the Great Race; or The Racial Basis of European History.* New York: Charles Scribner, 1916.

Greven, Philip J., Jr. *Four Generations: Population, Land, and Family in Colonial Andover, Massachusetts.* Ithaca, N.Y.: Cornell University Press, 1970.

———— . *The Protestant Temperament: Patterns of Child-Rearing, Religious Experience, and the Self in Early America.* New York: Alfred A. Knopf, 1977.

———— . *Spare the Child: The Religious Roots of Punishment and the Psychological Impact of Physical Abuse.* New York: Alfred A. Knopf, 1991.

Grossberg, Michael. *Governing the Hearth: Law and the Family in Nineteenth-Century America.* Chapel Hill: University of North Carolina Press, 1985.

Gutman, Herbert. "Work, Culture, and Society in Industrializing America." *American Historical Review* 78 (June 1973): 531–88.

Gutowski, Thomas W. "Student Initiative and the Origins of the High School Extracurriculum: Chicago, 1883–1905." *History of Education Quarterly* 28 (Spring 1988): 49–72.

Guttmann, Allen. *A Whole New Ball Game: An Interpretation of American Sports.* Chapel Hill: University of North Carolina Press, 1988.

Hadaway, C. Kirk, Penny Long, and Mark Chaves. "What Polls Don't Show: A Closer Look at U.S. Church Attendance." *American Sociological Review* 58 (December 1993): 741–52.

Haines, Michael R. "Industrial Work and the Family Life Cycle, 1889/90." *Research in Economic History* 4 (1979): 289–356.

———— . "Poverty, Economic Stress, and the Family in a Late Nineteenth-Century American City: Whites in Philadelphia, 1880." In *Philadelphia: Work, Space, and Group Experience in the Nineteenth Century,* ed. T. Hershberg, 240–76. New York: Oxford University Press, 1981.

Hall, G. Stanley. *Adolescence: Its Psychology and Its Relations to Physiology, Anthropology, Sociology, Sex, Crime, Religion, and Education.* 2 vols. New York: D. Appleton, 1904.

Hamilton, Gillian. "The Decline of Apprenticeship in North America: Evidence from Montreal." *Journal of Economic History* 60 (2000): 627–64.

Handlin, Oscar. *The Uprooted: The Epic Story of the Great Migrations That Made the American People.* Boston: Little, Brown, 1951.

Hansen, Hal. "Caps and Gowns: Historical Reflections on the Institutions That Shaped Learning for and at Work in Germany and the United States, 1800–1945." *Business and Economic History* 28 (Winter 1999): 19–24.

Hansen, Marcus Lee. *The Immigrant in American History.* Cambridge, Mass.: Harvard University Press, 1948.

———. *The Problem of the Third Generation Immigrant.* Augustana Historical Society Publication no. 8, part 1. Rock Island, Ill.: Augustana Historical Society, 1938.

Hareven, Tamara K. "The Family as Process: The Historical Study of the Family Cycle." *Journal of Family History* 7 (1973–74): 322–29.

———. "Family Time and Industrial Time: Family and Work in a Planned Corporation Town, 1900–1924." *Journal of Urban History* 1 (May 1973): 365–89.

———. "Modernization and Family History." *Signs* 2 (Autumn 1976): 190–206.

———, ed. "Symposium Marking the Twenty-Fifth Anniversary of Philippe Ariès' Centuries of Childhood." *Journal of Family History* 12 (October 1987): 343–443.

Hareven, Tamara K., and Maris A. Vinovskis, eds. *Family and Population in Nineteenth-Century America.* Princeton, N.J.: Princeton University Press, 1978.

Harris, Dale B. "Problems in Formulating a Scientific Concept of Development." In *The Concept of Development: An Issue in the Study of Human Behavior,* ed. D. B. Harris, 3–14. Minneapolis: University of Minnesota Press, 1957.

Hartmann, Heidi. "The Family as the Locus of Gender, Class, and Political Struggle: The Example of Housework." *Signs* 6 (Spring 1981): 366–94.

Hatch, Nathan O. *The Democratization of American Christianity.* New Haven: Yale University Press, 1989.

Healy, William, and Augusta F. Bronner. *New Light on Delinquency and Its Treatment: Results of a Research Conducted for the Institute of Human Relations, Yale University.* New Haven: Yale University Press, 1936.

Heath, Shirley Brice. *Ways with Words: Language, Life, and Work in Communities and Classrooms.* New York: Cambridge University Press, 1983.

Heath, Shirley Brice, and Milbrey W. McLaughlin, eds. *Identity and Inner-City Youth: Beyond Ethnicity and Gender.* New York: Teachers College Press, 1993.

Hindman, Hugh D. *Child Labor: An American History.* New York: M. E. Sharpe, 2002.

Hogan, Dennis P. *Transitions and Social Change: The Early Lives of American Men.* New York: Academic Press, 1981.

Hogan, Neil. "The Actual Enumeration: New Haven and the U.S. Census." *Journal of the New Haven Colony Historical Society* 38 (Fall 1991): 5, 16.

Hogg, Margaret H. "The Ebb-Tide of Employment." *Survey* (August 1933): 279–80.

———. *The Incidence of Work Shortage: Report of a Survey by Sample of Families Made in New Haven, Connecticut in May–June, 1931.* New York: Russell Sage Foundation, 1932.

Hollingshead, August B. *Elmtown's Youth: The Impact of Social Classes on Adolescents.* New York: Wiley and Sons, 1949.

Hook, James W. "Industry's Obligation to the Unemployed." *Mechanical Engineering* 53 (October 1931): 707–13.

———. "Preparing for the Next Depression." *The Service Letter on Industrial Relations* 77 (May 30, 1931): 1–8.

———. *The Pros and Cons of Unemployment Reserves for Connecticut Employers.* New Haven: James W. Hook, 1932.

———. *The Unemployed—What Shall We Do with Them? A Complete Plan of Unemployment Relief for the Future.* New Haven: James W. Hook, 1931.

Hoover, Greg A. "Supplemental Family Income Sources." *Social Science History* 9 (Summer 1985): 293–306.

Hughes, Everett C. *French Canada in Transition.* Chicago: University of Chicago Press, 1943.

Hunter, Jane H. *How Young Ladies Became Girls: The Victorian Origins of American Girlhood.* New Haven: Yale University Press, 2003.

Jacobs, Jerry A., and Margaret E. Greene. "Race and Ethnicity, Social Class, and Schooling." In *After Ellis Island: Newcomers and Natives in the 1910 Census,* ed. Susan Cotts Watkins, 209–56. New York: Russell Sage Foundation, 1994.

Jamieson, Lynn. "Theories of Family Development and the Experience of Being Brought Up." *Sociology* 21 (November 1987): 591–607.

Johnston, Michael. "Italian New Haven: Building an Ethnic Identity." *Journal of the New Haven Colony Historical Society* (Summer 1979): 23–35.

Jordan, Ellen. "Female Unemployment in England and Wales, 1851–1911." *Social History* 13 (May 1988): 175–90.

Kaestle, Carl F. *Pillars of the Republic: Common Schools and American Society, 1780–1860.* New York: Hill and Wang, 1983.

Kamarovsky, Mirra. *Blue Collar Marriage.* New York: Random House, 1964.

Kantor, Harvey, and David B. Tyack, eds. *Work, Youth, and Schooling.* Stanford, Calif.: Stanford University Press, 1982.

Kasson, John F. *Amusing the Million: Coney Island at the Turn of the Century.* New York: Hill and Wang, 1978.

Katz, Michael B. *Class, Bureaucracy and the Schools.* New York: Praeger, 1971.

———. *The Irony of Early School Reform.* Cambridge, Mass.: Harvard University Press, 1968.

———. "Occupational Classification in History." *Journal of Interdisciplinary History* 3 (Summer 1972): 63–68.

———. *The People of Hamilton, Canada West: Family and Class in a Mid-Nineteenth-Century City.* Cambridge, Mass.: Harvard University Press, 1975.

Katz, Michael B., Michael Doucet, and Mark J. Stern. *The Social Organization of Early Industrial Capitalism.* Cambridge, Mass.: Harvard University Press, 1982.

Katznelson, Ira, and Margaret Weir. *Schooling for All: Class, Race, and the Decline of the Democratic Ideal.* New York: Basic Books, 1985.

Kazin, Alfred. *A Walker in the City.* New York: Harcourt, Brace, 1951.

Kennedy, Ruby Jo Reeves. "Single or Triple Melting Pot? Intermarriage Trends in New Haven, 1920–1940." *American Journal of Sociology* 1 (1944): 331–39.

Kerber, Linda. "Separate Spheres, Female Worlds, Woman's Place: The Rhetoric of Women's History." *Journal of American History* 75 (June 1988): 9–39.

Kertzer, David I., and Dennis P. Hogan. "Household Organization and Migration in Nineteenth-Century Italy." *Social Science History* 14 (Winter 1990): 483–505.

Kertzer, David I., and Richard P. Saller, eds. *The Family in Italy: From Antiquity to the Present.* New Haven: Yale University Press, 1991.

Kessler-Harris, Alice. *Out to Work: A History of Wage-Earning Women in the United States.* New York: Oxford University Press, 1982.

Kessner, Thomas. *The Golden Door: Italian and Jewish Immigrant Mobility in New York City, 1880–1915.* New York: Oxford University Press, 1977.

Kett, Joseph F. *Rites of Passage: Adolescence in America, 1790 to the Present.* New York: Basic Books, 1977.

Keyssar, Alexander. *Out of Work: The First Century of Unemployment in Massachusetts.* New York: Cambridge University Press, 1986.

Kleiber, D. A., and G. M. Powell. "Historical Change in Leisure Activities during After-School Hours." In *Organized Activities as Contexts of Development: Extracurricular Activities, After School and Community Programs,* ed. Joseph L. Mahoney, Reed W. Larson, and Jacquelynne S. Eccles, chap. 2. New York: Lawrence Erlbaum, forthcoming.

Kleinberg, S. J. *The Shadow of the Mills: Working-Class Families in Pittsburgh, 1870–1907.* Pittsburgh, Pa.: University of Pittsburgh Press, 1989.

Koenig, Samuel. *Immigrant Settlements in Connecticut.* Hartford: State of Connecticut Department of Education, 1938.

Kohn, Melvin L. *Class and Conformity: A Study in Values.* 2d ed. Chicago: University of Chicago Press, 1977.

Krause, Corrine A. "Urbanization without Breakdown: Italian, Jewish and Slavic Immigrant Women in Pittsburgh, 1900–1945." *Journal of Urban History* 4 (May 1978): 291–306.

Krug, Edward A. *The Shaping of the American High School.* 2 vols. New York: Harper and Row, 1964–72.

Labaree, David F. *How to Succeed in School without Really Learning: The Credentials Race in American Education.* New Haven: Yale University Press, 1997.

——— . *The Making of an American High School: The Credentials Market and the Central High School of Philadelphia, 1838–1939.* New Haven: Yale University Press, 1988.

Lamphere, Louise. *From Working Daughter to Working Mother: Immigrant Women in a New England Industrial Community.* Ithaca, N.Y.: Cornell University Press, 1987.

Landes, William M., and Lewis C. Solomon. "Compulsory Schooling Legislation: An Economic Analysis of Law and Social Change in the Nineteenth Century." *Journal of Economic History* 32 (March 1972): 54–91.

Lasch, Christopher. "The Emotions of Family Life." *New York Review of Books* 20 (November 27, 1975): 37–42.

——— . *Haven in a Heartless World: The Family Besieged*. New York: Basic Books, 1977.

Lassonde, Stephen. "Learning and Earning: Schooling, Juvenile Employment, and the Early Life Course in Late Nineteenth-Century New Haven." *Journal of Social History* 29 (Summer 1996): 839–70.

——— . "Should I Go or Should I Stay? School Attainment, Adolescence, and Parent-Child Relations in Italian Immigrant Families of New Haven, 1900–1935." *History of Education Quarterly* 38 (Spring 1998): 37–60.

Lebergott, Stanley. "Annual Estimates of Unemployment in the United States, 1900–1954." In *The Measurement and Behavior of Unemployment: A Conference of the Universities*, ed. National Bureau of Economic Research, 213–39. Princeton, N.J.: Princeton University Press, 1957.

——— . *Manpower in Economic Growth: The American Record since 1800*. New York: McGraw-Hill, 1964.

Lebow, Katherine A. "Education and the Immigrant Experience: An Oral History of Working Women and Men of New Haven." *Journal of the Colony Historical Society of New Haven* 40 (Fall 1993): 14–43.

Levine, David. *Reproducing Families: The Political Economy of English Population History*. New York: Cambridge University Press, 1987.

Licht, Walter. *Getting Work: Philadelphia, 1840–1950*. Cambridge, Mass.: Harvard University Press, 1992.

Lindert, Peter H. *Fertility and Security in America*. Princeton, N.J.: Princeton University Press, 1978.

Liptak, Dolores Ann. *European Immigrants and the Catholic Church in Connecticut, 1870–1920*. Staten Island, N.Y.: Center for Migration Studies, 1987.

Livi-Bacci, Massimo. *A History of Italian Fertility during the Last Two Centuries*. Princeton, N.J.: Princeton University Press, 1977.

Lopreato, Joseph. *Italian Americans*. New York: Random House, 1970.

MacDonald, John S., and Leatrice D. MacDonald, "Chain Migration: Ethnic Neighborhood Formation and Social Networks." *Milbank Memorial Fund Quarterly* 42 (January 1964): 82–97.

MacMullen, Edith Nye. *In the Cause of True Education: Henry Barnard and Nineteenth-Century School Reform*. New Haven: Yale University Press, 1991.

Mark-Lawson, Jane, and Anne Witz. "From 'Family Labour' to 'Family Wage'? The Case of Women's Labour in Nineteenth-Century Coalmining." *Social History* 13 (May 1988): 151–74.

Matthaei, Julie A. *An Economic History of Women in America: Women's Work, the Sexual Division of Labor, and the Development of Capitalism*. New York: Schocken Books, 1982.

Matthews, Fred H. "Paradigm Changes in the Interpretations of Ethnicity, 1930–80: From Process to Structure." In *American Immigrants and Their Generations:*

Studies and Commentaries on the Hansen Thesis after Fifty Years, ed. Peter Kivisto and Dag Blanck, 167–88. Urbana: University of Illinois Press, 1990.

Mauss, Marcel. *The Gift: Forms and Functions of Exchange in Archaic Societies,* trans. Ian Cunnison. Introduction by E. E. Evans-Pritchard. New York: W. W. Norton, 1967.

May, Elaine Tyler. *Homeward Bound: American Families in the Cold War Era.* New York: Basic Books, 1988.

May, Lary. *Screening Out the Past: The Birth of Mass Culture and the Motion Picture Industry, 1896–1929.* New York: Oxford University Press, 1980.

May, Lary, and Stephen Lassonde. "Making the American Way: Moderne Theaters, Audiences, and the Film Industry, 1929–1945." *Prospects: An Annual of American Cultural Studies* 12 (May 1987): 89–124.

May, Martha. "The Historical Problem of the Family Wage: The Ford Motor Company and the Five Dollar Day." *Feminist Studies* 8 (Summer 1982): 399–424.

McConnell, John W. *The Evolution of Social Classes.* Washington, D.C.: American Council on Public Affairs, 1942.

Mead, Margaret. *Coming of Age in Samoa: A Psychological Study of Primitive Youth for Western Civilisation.* Foreword by Franz Boaz. New York: Museum of Natural History, 1932. Reprint, New York: Morrill Quill, 1973.

Medick, Hans, and David Warren Sabean, eds. *Interest and Emotion: Essays on the Study of Family and Kinship.* New York: Cambridge University Press, 1984.

Meyer, John W. "The Social Construction of the Psychology of Childhood: Some Contemporary Processes." In *Child Development in Life-Span Perspective,* ed. E. Mavis Hetherington, Richard Lerner, and Marion Perlmutter, 47–65. Hillsdale, N.J.: Lawrence Erlbaum, 1988.

Meyer, John W., David H. Kamens, and Aaron Benavot. *School Knowledge for the Masses: World Models and National Primary Curricular Categories in the Twentieth Century.* London: Falmer, 1992.

Meyer, John W., Francisco O. Ramirez, and Yasemin Nuhoglu Soysal. "World Expansion of Mass Education, 1870–1980." *Sociology of Education* 65 (April 1992): 128–49.

Meyer, John W., David Tyack, Joane Nage, and Audri Gordon. "Public Education as Nation-Building in America: Enrollments and Bureaucratization in the American States, 1870–1930." *American Journal of Sociology* 85 (November 1979): 591–613.

Meyer, Stephen. *The Five-Dollar Day: Labor Management and Social Control in the Ford Motor Company, 1908–1921.* Albany: SUNY Press, 1981.

Millis, Harry A., and Royal E. Montgomery. *Labor's Progress and Some Basic Labor Problems.* Vol. 1 of *The Economics of Labor.* New York: McGraw-Hill, 1938.

Mirel, Jeffrey E. "Twentieth-Century America, Adolescence." In *Encyclopedia of Adolescence,* ed. R. M. Lerner, A. C. Peterson, and J. Brooks-Gunnm, vol. 2, 1153–67. New York: Garland, 1991.

Modell, John. *Into One's Own: From Youth to Adulthood in the United States, 1920–1975.* Berkeley: University of California Press, 1989.

BIBLIOGRAPHY

———— . "Patterns of Consumption, Acculturation, and Family Income Strategies in Late Nineteenth-Century America." In *Family and Population in Nineteenth-Century America,* ed. Tamara K. Hareven and Maris A. Vinovskis, 206–40. Princeton, N.J.: Princeton University Press, 1978.

Modell, John, and J. Trent Alexander. "High School in Transition: Community, School, and Peer Group in Abilene, Kansas, 1939." *History of Education Quarterly* 37 (Spring 1997): 1–24.

Modell, John, Frank F. Furstenberg Jr., and Theodore Hershberg. "Social Change and Transitions to Adulthood in Historical Perspective." In *Philadelphia: Work, Space, and Group Experience in the Nineteenth Century,* ed. Theodore Hershberg, 311–41. New York: Oxford University Press, 1981.

Montgomery, David. *Citizen Worker: The Experience of Workers in the United States with Democracy and the Free Market during the Nineteenth Century.* New York: Cambridge University Press, 1993.

———— . *Fall of the House of Labor: The Workplace, the State, and American Labor Activism, 1865–1925.* New York: Cambridge University Press, 1987.

———— . *Workers' Control in America: Studies in the History of Work, Technology, and Labor Struggles.* New York: Cambridge University Press, 1979.

Morawska, Ewa. *For Bread with Butter: The Lifeworlds of the East Europeans in Johnstown, Pennsylvania, 1890–1940.* New York: Cambridge University Press, 1985.

Mormimo, Gary Ross. *Immigrants on the Hill: Italian-Americans in St. Louis, 1882–1982.* Urbana: University of Illinois Press, 1986.

Mulligan, William H., Jr. "From Artisan to Proletarian: The Family and the Vocational Education of Shoemakers in the Handicraft Era" In *Life and Labor: Dimensions of American Working-Class History,* ed. Charles Stephenson and Robert Asher, 22–36. Albany: SUNY Press, 1986.

Nasaw, David. *Schooled to Order: A Social History of Public Schooling in the United States.* New York: Oxford University Press, 1979.

Neitlich, Susan L. "Here History Is Going." *Jews in New Haven* 6 (1993): 197–221.

Newcombe, Lydia Bowles. "Some Noted Private Schools of New Haven." *Saturday Chronicle.* New Haven, c. 1910.

"New Haven School Map." School Volunteers for New Haven. New Haven, 1998.

Nicholls, John G. *The Competitive Ethos and Democratic Education.* Cambridge, Mass.: Harvard University Press, 1989.

Noble, David F. *America by Design: Science, Technology, and the Rise of Corporate Capitalism.* New York: Alfred A. Knopf, 1977.

Noland, E. William, and E. Wight Bakke. *Workers Wanted: A Study of Employers' Hiring Policies, Preferences and Practices.* New York: Harper and Brothers, 1949.

Nugent, Walter. *Crossings: The Great Transatlantic Migrations, 1870–1914.* Bloomington: Indiana University Press, 1992.

Oakes, Jeannie. *Keeping Track: How Schools Structure Inequality.* New Haven: Yale University Press, 1985.

Oberdeck, Kathryn. "Women Unionists in 1880s New Haven." *Labor's Legacy* (Summer–Fall 1991): 1–2.

Olneck, Michael R., and Marvin Lazerson. "School Achievement of Immigrant Children, 1900–1930." *History of Education Quarterly* 14 (Winter 1974): 454–82.

Orsi, Robert Anthony. *The Madonna of 115th Street: Faith and Community in Italian Harlem, 1880–1950.* New Haven: Yale University Press, 1985.

Osterman, Paul. *Getting Started: The Youth Labor Market.* Cambridge, Mass.: MIT Press, 1980.

Osterweis, Rollin G. *Three Centuries of New Haven, 1638–1938.* New Haven: Yale University Press, 1953.

Ozment, Steven. *When Fathers Ruled: Family Life in Reformation Europe.* Cambridge, Mass.: Harvard University Press, 1983.

Park, Robert E., and Herbert A. Miller. *Old World Traits Transplanted.* New York: Harper, 1921.

Parsons, Talcott. "Age and Sex in the Social Structure of the United States." *American Sociological Review* 7 (October 1942): 604–17.

——— . *Family, Socialization and Interaction Process.* Glencoe, Ill.: Free Press, 1960.

Peck, Gunther. "Divided Loyalties: Immigrant Padrones and the Evolution of Industrial Paternalism in North America." *International Labor and Working-Class History* 53 (Spring 1998): 49–68.

——— . "Reinventing Free Labor: Immigrant Padrones and Contract Laborers in North America, 1885–1925." *Journal of American History* 83 (December 1996): 848–71.

Peiss, Kathy. *Cheap Amusements: Working Women and Leisure in Turn-of-the-Century New York.* Philadelphia: Temple University Press, 1986.

Perlmann, A. Joel. *Ethnic Differences: Schooling and Social Structure among the Irish, Italians, Jews, and Blacks in an American City, 1880–1935.* New York: Cambridge University Press, 1988.

——— . "The Use of Student Records for the Study of American Educational History." *Historical Methods* 12 (Spring 1979): 66–75.

——— . "Who Stayed in School? Social Structure and Academic Achievement in the Determination of Enrollment Patterns, Providence, Rhode Island, 1880–1925." *Journal of American History* 72 (December 1985): 588–614.

Pleck, Elizabeth H. "A Mother's Wages: A Comparison of Income-Earning among Urban Black and Italian Married Women, 1896–1911." In *The American Family in Socio-Historical Perspective,* ed. Michael Gordon, 490–510. New York: St. Martin's, 1978.

——— . "Two Worlds in One: Work and Family." *Journal of Social History* 10 (Winter 1976): 178–95.

Pollock, Linda A. *Forgotten Children: Parent-Child Relations from 1500 to 1900.* New York: Cambridge University Press, 1983.

Porter, William. "The Farmington Canal: New Haven's Contribution to the 'Canal Epidemic.'" *Journal of the New Haven Colony Historical Society* 20 (October 1971): 55.

Powdermaker, Hortense, and Joseph Semper. "Education and Occupation among New Haven Negroes." *Journal of Negro History* 23 (April 1938): 200–15.

Powers, Jane Bernard. *The "Girl Question" in Education: Vocational Education of Young Women in the Progressive Era*. London: Falmer, 1992.

Pozzetta, George E., ed. *Education and the Immigrant*. New York: Garland, 1991.

Pred, Allan. *Urban Growth and City-Systems in the United States, 1840–1860*. Cambridge, Mass.: Harvard University Press, 1980.

Prude, Jonathan. *The Coming of Industrial Order*. New York: Cambridge University Press, 1983.

Purmont, Jon E. "Sargent Comes to New Haven." *Journal of the New Haven Colony Historical Society* 24 (Spring 1976): 16–30.

Putnam, Robert D. *Bowling Alone: The Collapse and Revival of American Community*. New York: Simon and Schuster, 2001.

Rader, Benjamin G. *American Sports: From the Age of Folk Games to the Age of Televised Sports*. Englewood Cliffs, N.J.: Prentice Hall, 1999.

Rae, Douglas W. *City: Urbanism and Its End*. New Haven: Yale University Press, 2003.

Rafael, Ruth Kelson. "The YMHA and the YWHA in San Francisco." *Western States Jewish History* 19 (Summer 1987): 208–16.

Ralph, John H. "Bias in Historical Enrollment Figures." *Historical Methods* 13 (Fall 1980): 215–21.

Rapp, Rayna, Ellen Ross, and Renate Bridenthal. "Examining Family History." *Feminist Studies* 5 (Spring 1979): 174–200.

Ravitch, Diane. *The Great School Wars: New York City, 1805–1973; A History of the Public Schools as Battlefield of Social Change*. New York: Basic Books, 1974.

Reed, Dorothy. *Leisure Time of Girls in a "Little Italy."* Portland, Oreg.: Privately published, 1932.

Reeder, Linda. "Women in the Classroom: Mass Migration, Literacy and the Nationalization of Sicilian Women at the Turn of the Century." *Journal of Social History* 32 (Fall 1998): 101–24.

Reese, William J. *The Origins of the American High School*. New Haven: Yale University Press, 1995.

Reiman, Richard A. *The New Deal and American Youth: Ideas and Ideals in a Depression Decade*. Athens: University of Georgia Press, 1992.

Richardson, John G. "Variation in Date of Enactment of Compulsory School Attendance Laws: An Empirical Inquiry." *Sociology of Education* 53 (July 1980): 153–63.

Roberts, Marjorie. "Italian Girls on American Soil." *Mental Hygiene* 13 (October 1929): 757–68.

Rodgers, Daniel T. "Tradition, Modernity, and the American Industrial Worker: Reflections and Critique." *Journal of Interdisciplinary History* 7 (Spring 1977): 655–81.

———. *The Work Ethic in Industrial America, 1850–1920*. Chicago: University of Chicago Press, 1978.

Rodnick, David. "Group Frustrations in Connecticut." *American Journal of Sociology* 47 (September 1941): 157–66.

Rorabough, William J. *The Craft Apprentice: From Franklin to the Machine Age in America*. New York: Oxford University Press, 1986.

Rosenholtz, Susan J., and Carl Simpson. "The Formation of Ability Conceptions: Developmental Trend of Social Construction?" *Review of Educational Research* 54 (Spring 1984): 31–63.

Rosenwaike, Ira. "Two Generations of Italians in America: Their Fertility Experience." *International Migration Review* 7 (Fall 1973): 271–80.

Rothman, Ellen K. *Hands and Hearts: A History of Courtship in America*. New York: Basic Books, 1984.

Rotundo, E. Anthony. *American Manhood: Transformations in Masculinity from the Revolution to the Modern Era*. New York: Basic Books, 1993.

———. "Boy Culture: Middle-Class Boyhood in Nineteenth-Century America." In *Meanings for Manhood: Constructions of Masculinity in Victorian America*, ed. Mark C. Carnes and Clyde Griffen, 15–36. Chicago: University of Chicago Press, 1990.

Rozensweig, Roy. *Eight Hours for What We Will: Workers and Leisure in an Industrial City*. New York: Cambridge University Press, 1983.

Rubin, Lillian B. *Worlds of Pain: Life in the Working-Class Family*. New York: Basic Books, 1976.

Rury, John L. *Education and Women's Work: Female Schooling and the Division of Labor in Urban America, 1870–1930*. Albany: SUNY Press, 1991.

Ryan, Mary P. *Cradle of the Middle Class: The Family in Oneida County, New York, 1790–1865*. New York: Cambridge University Press, 1981.

Scharf, Lois. *To Work and to Wed: Female Employment, Feminism, and the Great Depression*. Westport, Conn.: Greenwood, 1980.

Schatz, Ronald W. "Connecticut's Working Class in the 1950s: A Catholic Perspective." *Labor History* 25 (Winter 1984): 83–101.

Schneider, David M. *American Kinship: A Cultural Account*. 2d ed. Chicago: University of Chicago Press, 1980.

Schneider, Jane and Peter. *Culture and Political Economy in Western Sicily*. New York: Academic Press, 1976.

Scott, Joan W., and Louise A. Tilly. *Women, Work and Family*. New York: Holt, Rinehart and Winston, 1978.

Scudder, M. T. "A Study of High School Pupils," *School Review* 7 (April 1899): 212.

Sennett, Richard. *Families against the City: Middle Class Homes of Industrial Chicago, 1872–1890*. Cambridge, Mass.: Harvard University Press, 1970.

Sennett, Richard, and Jonathan Cobb. *The Hidden Injuries of Class.* New York: Alfred A. Knopf, 1972.

Sewell, William H., and Robert M. Hauser. "Causes and Consequences of Higher Education: Models of the Status Attainment Process." In *Schooling and Achievement in American Society,* ed. William H. Sewell, Robert M. Hauser, and David L. Featherman, 9–28. New York: Academic Press, 1976.

Shahar, Shulamith. *Childhood in the Middle Ages.* New York: Routledge, 1990.

Shanahan, Michael J., Richard A. Miech, and Glen H. Elder Jr. "Changing Pathways to Attainment in Men's Lives: Historical Patterns of School, Work, and Social Class." *Social Forces* 77 (September 1998): 231–56.

Shepherd, Jane Bushnell. *Miss Antoinette Turner's Store and Other Reminiscent Sketches.* New Haven: Tuttle, Morehouse, 1939.

Shepherd, William G. "Robbing the Working Girl." *Collier's* (November 12, 1932): 10–11, 34.

Shergold, Peter R. *Working-Class Life: The "American Standard" in Comparative Perspective, 1899–1913.* Pittsburgh: University of Pittsburgh Press, 1982.

Shumway, Floyd M., and Richard Hegel. "New Haven's Two Creeks." *Journal of the New Haven Colony Historical Society* 37 (Fall 1990): 19–22.

Smelser, Neil J. *Social Change in the Industrial Revolution, 1770–1840.* Chicago: University of Chicago Press, 1959.

——— . *Social Paralysis and Social Change: British Working-Class Education in the Nineteenth Century.* Berkeley: University of California Press, 1991.

Smith, Daniel Scott. "Child-Naming Practices, Kinship Ties, and Change in Family Attitudes in Hingham, Massachusetts, 1641 to 1880." *Journal of Social History* 18 (Summer 1985): 541–66.

Smith, Judith E. *Family Connections: A History of Italian and Jewish Immigrant Lives in Providence, Rhode Island, 1900–1940.* Albany: SUNY Press, 1985.

——— . "Our Own Kind: Family and Community Networks in Providence." In *A Heritage of Her Own: Toward a New Social History of American Women,* ed. Nancy F. Cott and Elizabeth H. Pleck, 393–411. New York: Simon and Schuster, 1979.

Sollors, Werner, ed. *The Invention of Ethnicity.* New York: Oxford University Press, 1989.

Stambler, Moses. "The Effect of Compulsory Education and Child Labor Laws on High School Attendance in New York City, 1898–1917." *History of Education Quarterly* 8 (Summer 1968): 189–214.

Stansell, Christine. *City of Women: Sex and Class in New York, 1789–1860.* Urbana: University of Illinois Press, 1987.

Stearns, Peter N. *American Cool: Constructing a Twentieth-Century Emotional Style.* New York: New York University Press, 1994.

Stearns, Peter N., and Carol Z. Stearns. "Emotionology: Clarifying the History of Emotions and Emotional Standards." *American Historical Review* 90 (October 1985): 813–36.

Steinberg, Stephen. *The Ethnic Myth: Race, Ethnicity, and Class in America.* New York: Atheneum, 1981.

Steiner, Bernard C. *The History of Education in Connecticut*. Washington, D.C.: Government Printing Office, 1893.

Sterba, Christopher M. *Good Americans: Italian and Jewish Immigrants during the First World War*. New York: Oxford University Press, 2003.

Stocking, George W., Jr. *Race, Culture, and Evolution: Essays in the History of Anthropology*. New York: Free Press, 1968.

———. *Victorian Anthropology*. New York: Free Press, 1987.

Stone, Lawrence. *The Family, Sex, and Marriage in England, 1500–1800*. London: Weidenfeld and Nicholson, 1977.

Strom, Sharon Hartmann. "Italian-American Women and Their Daughters in Rhode Island: The Adolescence of Two Generations." In *The Italian Immigrant Woman in North America*, ed. Betty Boyd Caroli, Robert F. Harney, and Lydio F. Tomasi, 191–204. Toronto: Multicultural History Society of Ontario, 1978.

Tentler, Leslie Woodcock. *Wage-Earning Women: Industrial Work and Family Life in the United States, 1900–1930*. New York: Oxford University Press, 1979.

Thernstrom, Stephan. *The Other Bostonians: Poverty and Progress in the American Metropolis, 1880–1970*. Cambridge, Mass.: Harvard University Press, 1973.

Thomas, William I., and Florian Znaniecki. *The Polish Peasant in Europe and America: A Monograph of an Immigrant Group*. 2 vols. New York: Alfred A. Knopf, 1927.

Thompson, E. P. "Happy Families." Review of *The Family, Sex, and Marriage*, by Lawrence Stone. *New Society* 41 (September 8, 1977): 499–501.

———. "Time, Work-Discipline, and Industrial Capitalism." *Past and Present* 38 (December 1967): 56–97.

Ticotsky, Fred. "Ticotsky's Bakery and the Legion Avenue Jews." *Jews in New Haven* 3 (1981): 37–49.

Tilly, Louise A. "Beyond Family Strategies, What?" *Historical Methods* 20 (Summer 1987): 123–25.

———. "Comments on the Yans-McLaughlin and Davidoff Papers." *Journal of Social History* 7 (Summer 1974): 452–59.

———. "Individual Lives and Family Strategies in the French Proletariat." *Journal of Family History* 4 (Summer 1979): 137–52.

Tilly, Louise A., and Miriam Cohen. "Does the Family Have a History?: A Review of Theory and Practice in Family History." *Social Science History* 6 (Spring 1982): 131–79.

Tilly, Louise A., Joan Scott, and Miriam Cohen. "Women's Work and European Fertility Patterns." *Journal of Interdisciplinary History* 6 (Winter 1976): 447–76.

Tittarelli, Luigi. "Choosing a Spouse among Nineteenth-Century Central Italian Sharecroppers." In *The Family in Italy from Antiquity to the Present*, ed. David I. Kertzer and Richard P. Saller, 271–85. New Haven: Yale University Press, 1991.

Tomasi, Lydio. *The Italian-American Family: The Southern Italian Family's Process of Adjustment to Urban America*. Staten Island, N.Y.: Center for Migration Studies, 1973.

Tomasi, Sylvano M., and Madeline H. Engel, eds. *The Italian Immigrant Experience in the United States.* Staten Island, N.Y.: Center for Migration Studies, 1970.

Trattner, Walter I. *Crusade for the Children: A History of the National Child Labor Committee and Child Labor Reform in America.* Chicago: Quadrangle Books, 1970.

Troen, Selwyn K. "The Discovery of the Adolescent by American Educational Reformers, 1900–1920: An Economic Perspective." In *Schooling and Society: Studies in the History of Education,* ed. Lawrence Stone, 239–51. Baltimore: Johns Hopkins University Press, 1976.

Tyack, David B. "Ways of Seeing: An Essay on the History of Compulsory Schooling." *Harvard Educational Review* 46 (August 1976): 355–89.

Tyack, David, and Elizabeth Hansot. *Learning Together: A History of Coeducation in American Schools.* New Haven: Yale University Press, 1990.

Tyack, David, Robert Lowe, and Elizabeth Hansot. *Public Schools and Hard Times: The Great Depression and Recent Years.* Cambridge, Mass.: Harvard University Press, 1984.

Ueda, Reed. "American National Identity and Race in Immigrant Generations: Reconsidering Hansen's 'Law.'" Review of *American Immigrants and Their Generations,* ed. Peter Kivisto and Dag Blanck. *Journal of Interdisciplinary History* 22 (Winter 1992): 483–91.

——— . *Avenues to Adulthood: The Origins of the High School and Social Mobility in an American Suburb.* New York: Cambridge University Press, 1987.

Vecoli, Rudolph J. "Contadini in Chicago: A Critique of *The Uprooted.*" *Journal of American History* 51 (December 1964): 404–17.

——— . "Prelates and Peasants: Italian Immigrants and the Catholic Church." *Journal of Social History* 2 (Spring 1969): 217–68.

Vinovskis, Maris A. "Family and Schooling in Colonial and Nineteenth-Century America." *Journal of Family History* 12 (January–April–June 1987): 19–37.

Vinovskis, Maris A., with David L. Angus and Jeffrey E. Mirel. "Historical Development of Age Stratification in Schooling." In Maris A. Vinovskis, *Education, Society, and Economic Opportunity: A Historical Perspective on Persistent Issues,* 171–93. New Haven: Yale University Press, 1995.

Walters, Pamela Barnhouse, and Philip J. O'Connell. "The Family Economy, Work, and Educational Participation in the United States, 1890–1940." *American Journal of Sociology* 93 (March 1988): 1116–52.

Wandersee, Winifred D. *Women's Work and Family Values, 1920–1940.* Cambridge, Mass.: Harvard University Press, 1981.

Warner, Robert A. *New Haven Negroes: A Social History.* New Haven: Yale University Press, 1940.

Warner, W. Lloyd, and Paul S. Lunt. *The Status System of a Modern Community.* Yankee City Series, vol. 2. New Haven: Yale University Press, 1942.

Warner, W. Lloyd, and Leo Srole. *The Social Systems of American Ethnic Groups.* Yankee City Series, vol. 3. New Haven: Yale University Press, 1945.

Watkins, Susan Cotts, ed. *After Ellis Island: Newcomers and Natives in the 1910 Census*. New York: Russell Sage Foundation, 1994.

Weiss, Bernard J., ed. *American Education and the European Immigrant, 1840–1940*. Urbana: University of Illinois Press, 1981.

Weiss, Thomas. "The Industrial Distribution of the Urban and Rural Workforce: Estimates for the United States, 1870–1910." *Journal of Economic History* 32 (December 1972): 919–37.

West, Elliott, and Paula Petrik. *Small Worlds: Children and Adolescents in America, 1850–1950*. Lawrence: University Press of Kansas, 1992.

Whitlock, Reverdy. "The Hillhouse Papers." New Haven: Privately published, 1977.

Whyte, William Foote. *Street Corner Society: The Social Structure of an Italian Slum*. Chicago: University of Chicago Press, 1943. Reprint, 1973.

Wilentz, Sean. *Chants Democratic: New York City and the Rise of the American Working Class, 1788–1850*. New York: Oxford University Press, 1984.

Williams, Phyllis H. *South Italian Folkways in Europe and America: A Handbook for Social Workers, Teachers, Visiting Nurses, School Teachers, and Physicians*. New Haven: Yale University Press, 1938.

Williamson Jeffrey G., and Peter H. Lindert. *American Inequality: A Macroeconomic History*. New York: Academic Press, 1980.

Willis, Paul E. *Learning to Labour: How Working Class Kids Get Working Class Jobs*. Farnborough, England: Saxon House, 1977.

Wirt, Robert D., and Peter F. Briggs. "The Meaning of Delinquency." In *Juvenile Delinquency: Research and Theory*, ed. H. C. Quay, 1–26. Princeton, N.J.: Van Nostrand, 1965.

Wishy, Bernard. *The Child and the Republic: The Dawn of Modern American Child Nurture*. Philadelphia: University of Pennsylvania Press, 1968.

Wood, Reverend S. "Letter from Reverend S. Wood." *Connecticut Common School Journal* 2 (1837): 116.

Woodward, Sarah Day. *Early New Haven*. New Haven: Edward P. Judd, 1929.

Yale Freshman Blue Book; The Class of 1907 Sheffield Blue Book. New Haven, 1904.

Yanagisako, Sylvia Junko. "Captial and Gendered Interest in Italian Family Firms." In *The Family in Italy from Antiquity to the Present*, ed. David I. Kertzer and Richard P. Saller, 321–39. New Haven: Yale University Press, 1991.

Yans-McLauglin, Virginia. *Family and Community: Italian Immigrants in Buffalo, 1880–1930*. Ithaca, N.Y.: Cornell University Press, 1977.

——— . "A Flexible Tradition: Southern Italian Immigrants Confront a New York Experience." *Journal of Social History* 10 (Summer 1974): 429–45.

——— , ed. *Immigration Reconsidered: History, Sociology, and Politics*. New York: Oxford University Press, 1990.

Young, Michael, and Peter Wilmott. *Family and Kinship in East London*. London: Routledge and Kegan Paul, 1957.

Zaretsky, Eli. *Capitalism, the Family and Personal Life*. New York: Harper and Row, 1976.

Zelizer, Viviana A. *Pricing the Priceless Child: The Changing Social Value of Children.* New York: Basic Books, 1985.

Zenderland, Leila. *Measuring Minds: Henry Herbert Goddard and the Origins of American Intelligence Testing.* New York: Cambridge University Press, 1998.

Zimmerman, Eli. "What I Remember." *Jews in New Haven* 5 (1992): 39–50.

Unpublished Papers, Dissertations, and Lectures.

Badgely, Robin F. "Assimilation and Acculturation of the English Immigrant in New Haven." Ph.D. diss., Yale University, 1957.

Bakke, E. Wight. "The Fifth Winter of Unemployment Relief." TS, Yale University, 1935. E. Wight Bakke Papers, Labor-Management Documentation Center, Cornell University.

Barron, Milton L. "Intermarriage in a New England Industrial Community: A Study in Deviation from the Mores of Mate Selection." Ph.D. diss., Yale University, 1945.

Bernard, William S. "Naturalization in Its Social Setting in the United States." Ph.D. diss., Yale University, 1934.

Bernholz, Lucy. "Education and Assimilation: The Development of the Curriculum at Hillhouse High School, 1880–1930." Senior thesis, Department of History, Yale University, 1985.

Buckner, Mabel A. "A Study of Pupil Elimination in the New Haven High School." M.A. thesis, Yale University, 1930.

Buell, Irwin A. "After School Careers of High School Pupils." Ed.D. diss., Yale University, 1925.

Cestaro, Mario A. "'Just As I Am': Memoir and Musings." TS, September 1992, Manuscripts and Archives, Sterling Memorial Library, Yale University, New Haven.

Child, Irvin L. "A Psychological Study of Second-Generation Italians." Ph.D. diss., Yale University, 1939.

Choo, Diane Y. "'Dispensing with Devotions': New Haven Public Schooling and the Religious Exercise Question, 1877–1878." Senior essay, Department of History, Yale University, April 2000.

Clarke, Stephen C. "Progress toward Graduation as a Criterion of Achievement of Junior College Students." Ed.D. diss., Yale University, 1949.

Cohen, Miriam J. "From Workshop to Office: Italian Women and Family Strategies in New York City, 1900–1950." Ph.D. diss., University of Michigan, 1978.

Colucci, Nicholas D. "Connecticut Academy for Females, 1800–1865." Ph.D. diss., University of Connecticut, 1969.

Cutts, Norma E. "The Extent of Bilingualism and Its Effect on Beginning Reading in a Group of First Year Children Largely of Italian Parentage." Ph.D. diss., Yale University, 1933.

Davie, James S. "Education and Social Stratification." Ph.D. diss., Yale University, 1951.

Duncan, Greg J., and Stephen W. Raudenbush. "Neighborhoods and Adolescent Development: How Can We Assess the Links?" MS presented at "Does It Take a

Village? Community Effects on Children, Adolescents, and Families." Pennsylvania State University, University Park, November 5–6, 1998.

Eversull, Frank L. "The Equalization of Certain Secondary School Opportunities in the State of Connecticut." Ed.D. diss., Yale University, 1934.

Feldman, Estelle E. "The Dull Child and the Junior High Curriculum." Ph.D. diss., Yale University, 1936.

Goodman, Helen C. "I.Q. in Relation to Graduation after Failure." M.A. thesis, Yale University, 1933.

Graham, Lloyd S. "Selection and Social Stratification: Factors in the Acceptance or Rejection of Five Innovations by Social Strata in New Haven, Connecticut." Ph.D. diss., Yale University, 1950.

Hadjusiewicz, Alison. "A Study of Ethnic Social Trends at Hillhouse High School, 1926–1940." Senior thesis, Department of History, Yale University, 1998.

Johnston, William M. "On the Outside Looking In: Irish, Italian and Black Ethnic Politics in an American City." Ph.D. diss., Yale University, 1977.

King, Almeda. "A Study of the Italian Diet in a Group of New Haven Families." M.A. thesis, Yale University, 1935.

Knight, Elton E. "A Study of Double Grades in New Haven, Connecticut." Ed.D. diss., Yale University, 1935.

Krall, Dorothy R. "The Second-Generation Immigrant in America; With Special Reference to the Problem of Adjustment." Ph.D. diss., Yale University, 1937.

Lassonde, Stephen A. "Learning to Forget: Schooling and Family Life in New Haven's Working Class, 1870–1940." Ph.D. diss., Yale University, 1994.

MacInnis, Earl C. "Comparative Achievement in Junior High School and Departmentalized Seventh and Eighth Grades." Ed.D. diss., Yale University, 1933.

Matthews, Sister Mary Fabian, S.C.H. "The Role of the Public School in the Assimilation of the Italian Immigrant Child in New York City, 1900–1914." Ph.D. diss., Fordham University, 1966.

McConnell, John W. "The Influence of Occupation upon Social Stratification." Ph.D. diss., Yale University, 1937.

McKee, Frank J. "The Organizational and Educational History of Male High School Graduates." M.A. thesis, Yale University, 1931.

Miller, Morty. "New Haven: The Italian Community." Senior thesis, Department of History, Yale University, 1969.

Miller, T. A., Jr. "Unemployment in Meriden, Connecticut, 1934." M.A. thesis, Yale University, 1934.

Mitchell, Rowland L., Jr. "Social Legislation in Connecticut, 1919–1939." Ph.D. diss., Yale University, 1934.

Morton, Frederic J. "A Study of Failures among Hamden Pupils in the New Haven High School." M.A. thesis, Yale University, 1933.

Moyer, Robert D., Jr., "'Hurrah for the Sixth of June!'" Senior thesis, Department of History, Yale University, 1992.

Murphy, Erin S. "Fur Coats at Sixty Words per Minute: Female Clerical Workers and the Search for Status." Senior thesis, Department of History, Yale University, 1994.

Myers, Jerome K. "The Differential Time Factor in Assimilation." Ph.D. diss., Yale University, 1950.

————. "New Haven Residential Areas by Predominant Characteristics." Research paper, Department of Sociology, Yale University, 1950.

Noll, Jennifer. "Italian-American Women in the New Haven Garment Industry." Senior thesis, Department of History, Yale University, 1994.

Nordli, William. "Rewards and Punishments of High School Students." Ph.D. diss., Yale University, 1942.

Oberdeck, Kathryn J. "Labor's Vicar and the Variety Show: Popular Religion, Popular Theatre, and Cultural Class Conflict in Turn-of-the-Century America." Ph.D. diss., Yale University, 1992.

Oren, Paul, Jr. "Becoming a Mill-Town American." Ph.D. diss., Yale University, 1951.

Plattus, Alan. "Housing and the Industrial City." Lecture, "New Haven and the Problem of Urban Change." Yale University, March 24, 1998.

Psathas, George. "Cultural Factors Related to Adolescents' Independence from Parental Control." Ph.D. diss., Yale University, 1956.

Rae, Douglas. "Capitalism Gathering Steam." Lecture, "New Haven and the Problem of Urban Change." Yale University, January 20, 1997.

Reeves, Ruby J. "Marriage Folkways as Revealed by a Study of Marriage Licenses in New Haven." M.A. thesis, Yale University, 1934.

————. "Marriages in New Haven since 1870: Statistically Analyzed and Culturally Interpreted." Ph.D. diss., Yale University, 1937.

Schwartz, Laura Anker. "Immigrant Voices from Home, Work, and Community: Women and Family in the Migration Process, 1890–1938." Ph.D. diss., State University of New York, College at Old Westbury, 1983.

Sheridan, Marion C. "The Teaching of Reading in Public Schools of New Haven, 1638–1930." Ed.D. diss., Yale University, 1931.

Sims, Werner M. "The Measurement of Socioeconomic Status." Ed.D. diss., Yale University, 1926.

Smith, Bernice S. "Depression Graduates: A Follow-Up Study of High School Girls of 1930." Ph.D. diss., Yale University, 1935.

Sussman, Marvin B. "Family Continuity: A Study of the Factors Which Affect Relationships between Families at Generational Levels." Ph.D. diss., Yale University, 1951.

Vosburgh, William W. "Social Class and Leisure Time." Ph.D. diss., Yale University, 1960.

Waite, Mary G. "A Study of First Grade Promotion and Non-Promotion." Ed.D. diss., Yale University, 1927.

Whitelaw, John B. "The Administration of the Elementary School as the Co-ordinating Social Factor in the Community." Ph.D. diss., Yale University, 1935.

Wrinn, Louise G. "The Development of the Public School System in New Haven, 1639–1930: A Problem in Historical Analysis." Ph.D. diss., Yale University, 1933.

Young, Isabel S. "Behavior Problems of Elementary School Children." Ed.D. diss., Yale University, 1932.

INDEX

Abruzzi, 18, 57

adolescence, 7, 12, 73, 83, 136–39, 160–61, 195, 206n8; high school dropouts, 158–61, 247–48nn11, 12, 14; postwar high school expansion and, 155–88, 192–93, 195, 246–56; "youth problem," 161–62, 249n18

advertising, 7, 113

African Americans, 20, 55, 83, 93–94, 123, 124, 129, 132, 146, 182, 208n18, 238n3, 240n24

age-grading, 26, 27, 28–32, 35–38, 161, 206n9, 208n24

agriculture, 17, 40, 62, 64, 75, 105, 125, 194, 235n27; child labor, 30, 40, 41, 212n65; withdrawal of children from school for, 30

Aiello, Nick, 182

Alexander, J. Trent, 176

Alfano, Jenny, 227n26

Amalfi, 20, 74

American popular culture, 7, 80, 84, 93–102, 113, 149, 150–51, 228n38, 245n84

Anderson, Michael, 87, 216n90

Annual Report, 31, 218n7

"antischool world," 4, 5, 11–12

apprenticeship, 65, 143, 171, 173, 244nn55, 252n42

Apulia, 18, 57

Argentina, 17, 233n13

artisan class, 65, 66, 173, 178, 253n57

Atlantic passage, 16–17, 203n15

Atrani, 20

attendance, school, 23, 27–33, 36–39, 42–52, 54, 75, 82, 154, 198n10, 206–7nn13, 14, 214nn75, 76; compulsory, 23, 27, 32–33, 36–39, 42–52, 75, 82, 154, 158, 190, 192, 214n76; high school, 155–61, 192, 193; late-nineteenth-century, 27–33, 36–39, 42–52, 75; parental compliance, 45–47, 60; problems, 30–32, 36–39, 43–52, 59, 157, 219n44

Avellino, 16

Bailey, Beth L., 112–13, 235n30

Bailyn, Bernard, 10, 200n25; *Education in the Forming of American Society,* 1

Baker, Mary, 93–94

Bakke, E. Wight, 87, 88, 98, 99, 155, 173, 180, 253nn57, 67

Baldwin Street, 129, 135

Barnard, Henry, 28–29, 207n15

Basilicata, 18, 57, 63

basketball, 92, 136, 190

Becker, Gary S., 186

Bell, Howard M., 228n38, 249n18

Benevento, 16, 203n17

Bible, 53–54, 217n2

bilingualism, 58, 67, 219n10

birth order, 47, 121; Italian immigrant roles and schooling, 75–76, 89–90, 143

Boardman Trade School, 120, 168, 246n2

Bonifacio, Beatrice, 134–35, 241n30

Boston, 54, 202n3

boys, 36, 104; exploited as labor, 38–39; favored over girls, 104; high school expansion, 157, 162, 163–65, 170, 176, 182–84; Italian immigrant roles, 65, 66, 73, 75, 78, 98–101, 104, 108–21, 140–54; juvenile employment, 40–44, 48, 49–50, 75–76, 78, 101, 105–6; marriage, 103–21, 127, 232–38; occupational choices of high school seniors, 183; personal appearance, 98–99; schooling, 36–39, 48, 73, 76, 78–79, 114, 162, 170, 176, 210n44, 223n75, 250n27; sexual issues, 104, 111, 114, 116–21, 234; truant and vagrant, 32, 36–39, 43

Boys and Girls Clubs, 190

Boy Scouts, 190

Brazil, 17

breadwinner wage, 2, 4

Bridgeport, 91, 205n3

Briggs, John W., 86–87

Broadway, 6

Calabria, 18, 57

Caldwell, John C., 3–5, 199n13

"calling," 112, 113, 115, 235n30

campanalismo, 21–22

Campania, 16, 18, 57, 74, 79, 244n50

carriage factories, 14

cars, 94, 149, 228n38

Caserta, 16, 99

Catholicism, 54, 71, 109, 119, 191, 204n23, 217n2, 257n4

Cedar Street school, 124

census, 46, 218n7; school, 26, 41–42, 43, 46, 208n25

Center Church, 6

Chapel Street, 6

"charity" schools, 201n30

Chicago, 54

Child, Irvin L., 67, 68, 90, 104, 106, 111, 117, 118, 127–28, 140–52, 221n43, 241–46

"child-centered" family, 3

child labor. See juvenile employment; labor

children and childhood, 21, 23; community and, 133–34, 135, 145; cultural conflicts, 61, 68–80, 81–102, 115–16, 127–28, 141–54, 241–46; economic role, 39–52, 59–60, 62, 64–65, 77, 80, 81–102, 103–21, 160, 175, 189–90, 219n17, 225–38; impact of schooling on parent-child relations, 1–12, 53–80, 81–85, 127–28, 140–54, 158, 165–67, 191–95, 217–25, 242–46; Italian immigrant children at home and at school, 53–80, 217–25; late-nineteenth-century schooling and early life course, 24–52, 205–17; in marriage market and family economy, 103–21, 179, 232–38; middle class views on, 23–29, 35, 47, 82, 83, 103, 110, 111, 120, 128, 147, 167, 174, 193, 206n5; neighborhood ethnicity and schools, 122–54, 238–46; play, 66, 190; sentimentalization of, 24–26, 35, 75, 83–84, 92–93, 186, 193, 206n10; socialization, 24–25, 35, 51, 53, 72–73, 165, 190, 206n10; state-imposed protection of, 70–71, 93; transition to adulthood, 25, 26, 27, 46, 48, 73, 141, 205n3, 208n25, 222n62. See also family; juvenile employment; parent-child relations

Cinel, Dino, 111

City Hall, 6

City Point, 15

Civilian Conservation Corps, 161, 182

Civil War, 19, 31–32, 189, 205n3

clothing, 96–99, 231n66, 233n14

college, 71, 72, 157, 178, 179–80, 184, 186

colonial era, 10–11, 203n17, 204n18

Columbus, Christopher, 22

Columbus Middle School, 134–35, 182

Commercial High School, 6, 96, 97, 118, 120, 156, 199*n*19, 231*n*58, 241*n*30, 246*n*2; postwar expansion, 156, 168, 170, 176, 178–79

common school, rise of, 201*n*32, 207*nn*15, 17

community, 133–34, 135, 145, 191

compulsory education, 7, 11, 23, 74, 116, 186; attendance, 23, 27, 32–33, 36–39, 42–52, 75, 82, 154, 158, 190, 192, 214*n*76; establishment of, 7, 11, 34; late-nineteenth-century New Haven, 24–52; laws, 23, 24, 26, 27, 32–34, 48, 56, 60, 134, 154, 158, 190, 192, 209*n*36, 213*nn*69, 72, 215*n*85, 216*n*91, 223*n*69

Congress Avenue, 106, 129

Connecticut General Assembly, 33

construction, 105, 253*n*57

consumerism, 93, 97

consumption, 80, 93; changing attitudes toward, 93–102, 113; courtship and, 113; post–World War I, 80, 86–88, 93–102, 113, 150

contadini, 60–80, 220*n*18, 221*n*42; marriage and courtship customs, 104–21

contraceptives, 86

corporal punishment, 54, 104, 218*n*3

courtship, 104, 109–21, 232–38

Covello, Leonard, 61–79, 81–82, 107, 218*n*8, 244*n*58; *The Heart Is the Teacher*, 61

craft unions, 171

credentialism, 157, 247*n*6

Cremin, Lawrence, 10, 200*n*25

crime, 37

Cunningham, Hugh, 39, 41

curriculum, school, 127, 147, 154, 205*n*1; academic, 164, 166, 175, 178, 179–82, 184–85; commercial and business, 162, 163, 164–68, 170, 175, 178–80, 183, 184, 251*n*40, 255*n*98; comprehensive, 156–57, 167–68; gender issues, 162, 163, 170, 176, 178–79, 183–85; manual skills, 166, 170–74; parental influences on, 180–81, 187; postwar high school,

155–88, 192–95, 246–56; standardized, 52, 217*n*93

Czechs, 223*n*75

dancing, 100–101

Dante, 22

Dante, Yolanda, 71

D'Antonio, William V., 246*n*92

dating, 111–21, 232–38; competition, 113; shift from "calling" to, 115–16

Davenport Avenue, 129

debt, 49–50

Dillingham Report, 57–58, 219*n*10

discipline, 53, 54, 75, 194; American lack of attention to, 75; classroom, 135

disease, 16, 203*n*12

Dixwell Avenue, 123, 124, 238*n*3

doctors, 78, 79

Dorn, Sherman, 247–48*n*11

dowries, 89, 105

dressmaking and sewing, 65, 74, 227–28*n*26, 233*n*14, 236*n*38. *See also* garment industry

drop outs, high school, 158–61, 247–48*nn*11, 12, 14

early life course, in late-nineteenth-century New Haven, 24–52, 205–17

early school-leaving. *See* drop outs; withdrawal rates

Eastern European immigrants, 14, 15, 57, 58, 118, 123, 124, 125, 126, 132–33, 238*n*4

economy, 2–3, 39, 54; breadwinner wage, 2, 4; depressions and downturns, 40, 42, 44–45, 158, 160, 211*n*58; *1850–1930* changes in, 13–23; family wage, 2–5, 25, 26, 27, 47, 59, 60, 77, 80, 84–102, 103–21; industrial, 13–15, 17–20, 22, 32, 35, 40–41, 45–46, 51, 55, 110, 114–15, 171–74, 189–90, 210–17; Italian immigrant family, 59–60, 62, 64–65, 77, 80, 81–102, 103–21, 160, 175, 219*n*17, 225–38; juvenile employment and, 39–52, 76–80, 81–102, 114–15, 121, 143, 153, 154, 175–76, 189–90, 210–17, 225–32; maritime, 13, 19, 125; marriage market and, 80, 86–87, 95–96, 103–21, 179,

economy (*continued*)
232–38; mercantile, 13; *1928–29* crisis, 158, 162, 247*n*8; of *1930s*, 158, 160–61, 166–67, 173; *1940–65* growth, 157, 186
education. *See* schools and schooling
elementary schools, 6, 29, 31, 36, 38, 39, 64, 69, 142, 199*n*19, 243*n*49; ethnicity and social makeup, 123, 124–30, 135, 142, 146–47, 238–41
Eleventh Ward, 20, 21, 239*n*8
employment. *See* juvenile employment; labor; occupations
England, 39; industrialization, 40; religion, 257*n*4; schooling, 39, 40, 198*n*10
English language skills, 58, 67, 219*n*10
ethnicity, 5, 8, 22, 54, 55, 58, 60, 102, 223*n*75; high school expansion and, 168, 169; intermarriage, 118–19, 152; Italian immigrant children at home and at school, 53–80, 217–25; Italian regional pride, 21–22; neighborhoods, class, and schools, 122–54, 238–46; prejudice, 123, 131–33, 142
extracurricular activities, 7, 96, 147, 164, 165, 174, 192, 241*n*40

factories, 14, 17, 19, 20, 41, 42, 70, 95, 96, 106, 114–15, 153, 167, 168, 171, 212*n*66, 214*n*82, 227*n*26, 236*nn*37, 38, 253*n*57. *See also* industry and manufacturing; *specific factories*
Fair Haven, 18, 106, 122, 134, 138, 139, 181
family, 2–5, 200*n*24, 214*n*81; changing attitudes toward consumption, 93–102, 113; cultural conflicts, 61, 68–80, 81–102, 115–16, 127–28, 141–54, 241–46; impact of schooling on, 1–12, 53–80, 81–85, 127–28, 140–54, 158, 165–67, 191–95, 217–25, 242–46; Italian immigrant children at home and at school, 217–25; Italian immigrant family economy, 59–60, 62, 64–65, 77, 80, 81–102, 103–21, 160, 175, 219*n*17, 225–38; marriage, schooling, and economy, 103–21, 179, 232–38; neighborhood ethnicity and schools,

122–54, 238–46; parent-child roles and obligations, 25–26, 53–80, 81–102, 104–21, 140, 152, 193–94, 225–32; sentimentalized child in, 24–26, 35, 75, 83–84, 92–93, 186, 193, 206*n*10; size, 87–88, 168, 226*n*15, 227*nn*20, 23, 255*n*86. *See also* children and childhood; middle class; parent-child relations; siblings; working class
Farmington Canal, 15, 19
Fass, Paula S., 189
Federal Emergency Relief Administration, 161, 162
fertility patterns, 86–87
"five-dollar day," 2
folk wisdom, 62
food and cooking, 96, 99, 127, 144, 231*n*61, 240*n*14, 244*n*59
fraternal societies, 109
"free" schools, 201*n*30
Furstenberg, Frank F., Jr., 25, 85

G.I. Bill, 157
Galenson, David W., 54
Gans, Herbert J., 68, 201*n*3
garment industry, 74, 93–94, 95, 106, 115, 135, 227*n*26, 228*n*27, 230*n*50, 233*n*14, 236*n*38
gender, 36, 47, 210*n*44, 211*n*58; courtship, dating, and marriage, 103–21; curriculum and, 162, 163, 170, 176, 178–79, 183–85; equality, 113–14; Italian immigrant roles, 59, 76–80, 94–100, 104–21; males favored over females, 104. *See also* boys; girls
German immigrants, 15, 55, 71, 119, 124, 125, 237*n*50, 238*n*4
Giacomini, Beppa, 77–78, 79–80
Gilbert, Cass, "Report of the New Haven Civic Improvement Commission," 13
girls, 36, 104; chastity and sexual issues, 77, 104, 111, 114, 116–21, 234, 236; high school expansion, 157, 162, 163, 165, 170, 176, 178–79, 184; Italian immigrant roles, 65, 74, 75–80, 85, 89, 94–100, 104–21; juvenile employment,

49, 51, 74, 75–76, 79–80, 89–96, 106, 107, 114–15, 211*n*58, 224*nn*83, 84, 93, 227*nn*23, 26, 228*n*27, 229*n*45, 233*n*14, 236*nn*37, 38; literacy, 76, 77; marriage, 77–78, 80, 95–96, 103–21, 179, 225*n*94, 232–38, 254*n*82; parental restrictiveness toward, 107–8, 224; personal appearance, 94–99; schooling, 36, 71–72, 73, 74–80, 95, 114, 120–21, 162, 170, 176, 184, 210*n*44, 223*n*75

Girl Scouts, 190

Glenn, Susan, 77

Goldin, Claudia, 177

graded public schools, 26, 27, 28–32, 35–38, 161, 206*n*9, 208*n*24

Gramsci, Antonio, 193–94

Great Depression, 20, 21, 29, 43, 59, 86, 90, 94, 98, 158, 161–62, 193, 212*n*63, 229*n*45, 230*n*50, 233*n*14; "new" high school and, 158–88, 246–56

Grove Street Cemetery, 19

guidance counselors, 126

Guilford, 11

Handlin, Oscar, 68

Hartford, 11, 18, 205*n*3

Hatch, Nathan O., 257*n*4

Hershberg, Theodore, 25, 85

high schools, 6–7, 69, 89, 96, 118, 120–21, 136–39, 142, 148–54, 155–88, 192–93, 199*n*19; attendance, 155–61, 192, 193; career paths and, 157, 163–88, 246–56; commercial track, 162, 163, 164–68, 170, 175, 178–80, 183, 184; comprehensive, 156–57, 167–68; diploma, 157, 158, 170, 178, 179, 181, 185; drop outs, 158–61, 247–48*nn*11, 12, 14; ethnic composition, 168, 169; graduation rates, 154, 158, 159, 170, 172, 185, 223*n*75, 247*n*10; peers, 136–40, 149–51, 156, 179, 187–88; popularization of, 155–88; postwar expansion of, 155–88, 192–95, 246–56; social promotion, 163, 256*n*101; transition to, 134

Hill district, 15, 16, 18, 20, 67, 69, 83, 117, 123, 124–25, 128, 132, 133, 136, 202*n*5, 203*n*17, 238*n*4, 239*n*12

Hillhouse High School, 6, 23, 79, 91, 96, 97, 118, 120, 129, 136–39, 148–51, 155, 156, 199*n*19, 241*n*30, 246*n*2, 247*n*3; ethnic composition, 169; postwar expansion, 156, 168, 169, 170, 178, 181, 182

Hindman, Hugh D., 190

Hispanics, 20

housekeeping, 96

Howard Avenue, 13

"idleness," 35, 36, 50, 51, 73

illiteracy, 57, 58, 63–64, 218*n*8, 221*n*32

illness, 25

immigrants, 9, 201–5, 220*n*19; Atlantic passage, 16–17, 203*n*15; cultural conflicts, 61, 68–80, 81–102, 115–16, 127–28, 141–54, 241–46; ethnic intermarriage, 118–19; impact of schooling on, 1–12, 53–80, 81–85, 127–28, 140–54, 158, 165–67, 191–95, 217–25, 242–46; Italian immigrant children at home and at school, 53–80, 217–25; labor, 15, 16–17, 20, 105, 113–15; neighborhood ethnicity and schools, 122–54, 238–46; "Old World traits," 61, 82, 83, 105, 141; population, 9, 11, 14–16, 20, 22, 38, 124, 125; postwar high school expansion, 155–88, 192–95, 246–56; prejudice against, 123, 131–33, 142; "return migration," 17, 18, 58, 83, 202–3*n*10. *See also specific nationalities*

income, 21, 143

individualism, 3, 84, 90

industry and manufacturing, 13, 19, 20, 32, 35, 40–41, 93, 105–6, 110, 114–15, 190, 194, 210–17; growth of, 13–15, 17–20, 22, 40–41, 45–46, 51, 55, 189–90; juvenile employment in, 40–46, 93–96, 114–15, 121, 143, 153, 154, 167–68, 175–76, 189–90, 210–17, 225–32; mechanization, 51, 171, 174, 175, 190; of *1930s*, 20–22, 158, 162, 171–74. *See also* factories; *specific industries*

"infant" schools, 201

inflation, 17

inheritance, 105
installment buying, 231*n*60
IQ testing, 57–58, 132, 250*n*27, 255*n*98
Irish immigrants, 15, 16, 18, 20, 21, 22, 38,
 55, 71, 76, 83, 118, 119, 122, 123, 124, 125,
 131, 145, 146, 152, 164, 195, 202*n*5,
 215*n*85, 218*n*7, 228*n*29, 237*n*50, 238*n*4,
 246*n*2; political power, 21
Italian immigrants, 1–2, 8–9, 15, 38,
 53–80, 201–5; acculturation, 76,
 83–102, 115–16, 127–28, 141–54, 241–46;
 birth order issues, 75–76, 89–90,
 143; changing attitudes toward
 consumption, 93–102, 113; chastity and
 sexual issues, 77, 104, 111, 114, 116–21,
 234, 236; children at home and at
 school, 53–80, 217–25; children as
 interpreters of foreign-host culture to
 parents, 68–70; children's play, 66;
 cultural conflicts, 61, 68–80, 81–102,
 115–16, 127–28, 141–54, 241–46;
 1850–1930 economic and residential
 change, 15–23; ethnic intermarriage,
 118–19, 152; family economy and,
 59–60, 62, 64–65, 77, 80, 81–102,
 103–21, 160, 175, 219*n*17, 225–38;
 fertility patterns, 86–87; gender
 roles, 59, 76–80, 104–21; juvenile
 employment, 39–52, 76–80, 81–102,
 114–15, 121, 143, 153, 154, 175–76,
 189–90, 210–17, 224, 225–32;
 marriage and family economy, 80,
 86–87, 95–96, 103–21, 179, 232–38;
 neighborhood ethnicity and schools,
 122–54, 238–46; "Old World traits,"
 61, 82, 83, 105, 141; parent-child
 relations and obligations, 53–80,
 81–102, 104–21, 140, 152, 193–94,
 225–32; politics, 22; population, 20;
 postwar high school expansion and,
 155–88, 192–95, 246–56; regional pride,
 16, 21–22, 106; resistance to schooling,
 57–80, 81–84, 127, 145, 167, 172–73, 177,
 193–94
Italy, 15–17, 18, 21, 202*n*8; marriage
 customs, 104–5, 115–16; Northern,
 63–64, 110, 220*n*29; schooling in,
 62–64, 69, 74–75, 77, 95, 220*n*29,
 221*n*32; Southern, 56–57, 59, 62–64,
 66, 69, 70, 74, 77, 88, 99, 104–5, 110,
 116, 143, 193, 218*n*8, 219*n*12, 221*n*32,
 234*n*22, 237*n*54; Unification
 government, 63–64

Jewish Community Centers, 191, 257*n*5
Jewish immigrants, 15, 16, 18, 69, 70,
 91–92, 119, 122, 123, 124, 125, 126,
 128–30, 132–36, 146, 191, 199*n*18,
 238*n*4, 240*n*18, 241*nn*34, 35, 245*n*66
"John," 140–54, 241–46
junior high schools, 6, 134, 135–36,
 199*n*19, 241*n*30
juvenile delinquency, 37, 59, 161, 249*n*19
juvenile employment, 2, 6, 7, 26, 27, 31,
 35–36, 39–52, 189–90, 210–17;
 courtship and, 114–15; high school
 drop outs and, 158–61; Italian
 American, 39–52, 76–80, 81–102,
 114–15, 121, 143, 153, 154, 175–76,
 189–90, 210–17, 224, 225–32; late-
 nineteenth-century, 39–52, 76–80;
 legislation, 42; post–World War I, 6,
 81–102, 114–15, 121, 143, 153, 154, 158,
 162, 173, 175–76, 225–32; school
 truancy and, 39, 43, 44–52, 210*n*44;
 "working age," 47–48

Katz, Michael, 206*n*5
Kazin, Alfred, 199*n*17
Kett, Joseph F., 37
Keyssar, Alexander, 40

L. Candee Rubber, 106, 114, 233*n*14,
 236*n*37
labor, 2–3, 17, 21, 35, 189–90, 210–17;
 abolition of child labor, 161, 186,
 209*n*32, 212*n*65, 249*n*19; high school
 education and, 157, 163–88, 246–56;
 immigrant, 15, 16–17, 20, 105, 113–15;
 industrial, 13–14, 15, 17, 20, 22, 35,
 40–41, 45–46, 51, 81, 93–96, 105–6,
 114–15, 167–68, 171–74, 189–90,
 210–17; manual, 170–74; movement,
 2; unions, 106, 171, 236*n*38, 253*n*56;

vocation, 105–6, 157–88; wage increases, 2; wartime, 2. *See also* industry and manufacturing; juvenile employment; occupations
Lancasterian school, 11, 201*n*31
Landcraft, Ida Mabel, 200*n*21
Lebow, Katherine A., 135, 168
Legion Avenue, 14, 15, 18, 106
leisure activities, 93–94, 96, 228–29
Lender, Hymen, 91–92, 128–30
Lender, Murray, 122, 128–30, 135, 218*n*3, 244*n*63
Lender, Samuel, 129, 133
Levine, David, 4, 87
Lithuanian immigrants, 10
Locke, John, 4, 199*n*13
Long Island Sound, 19
Lower Dixwell Avenue, 123
Lucania, 221*n*32

Marches, 74
"Marchigiani," 16
maritime commerce, 13, 19, 125
marriage, 74, 76, 77–78, 80, 85, 95, 103–21, 127, 179; age, 105, 119–20, 238*n*55; courtship and dating, 104, 109–21, 232–38; dowry, 89, 105; ethnic intermarriage, 118–19, 152; family economy and, 80, 86–87, 95–96, 103–21, 179, 232–38; Italian American views on, 103–21, 232–38; post–World War I, 103–21; schooling and, 120–21
Massachusetts, 215*n*85
Massachusetts Bay settlement, 10
mass media, 7, 113
Matthews, Sister Mary Fabian, 68, 69
McConnell, John W., 94, 98, 99, 104, 111, 114, 115, 117, 118, 165, 176–80; *Evolution of Social Classes,* 81, 103
mercantilism, 13; decline of, 13
Meriden, 37
meritocracy, 3, 84, 156
middle class, 3, 7, 11–12, 14, 40, 64, 152, 185, 200*nn*21, 24; late-nineteenth-century schooling and early life course, 25–29, 47, 50; sentimentalized child in, 24–26, 35, 75, 83, 92–93, 186,

193, 206*n*10; views on childrearing, 23–29, 35, 47, 82, 83, 103, 110, 111, 120, 128, 147, 167, 174, 193, 206*n*5
middle schools, 6, 129, 134, 147–48, 181–82
Mill River, 18–19, 134
Modell, John, 25, 85, 112, 176
Montgomery, David, 173
morals and manners, 35
movies, 7, 93, 94, 100, 113, 150, 151, 228*n*38, 245*n*84
Murphy, Mayor, 22
mutual-aid societies, 122

Naples, 16, 17, 18, 63, 143
National Youth Administration, 161
neighborhoods, 5, 6–8, 13–23, 54, 83, 114, 122–54, 201–5, 218*n*6; *1850–1930* changes in, 13–23; ethnicity and class, 122–54, 238–46; groups, 109, 122; schooling and, 54–55, 122–54, 238–46. *See also specific neighborhoods and streets*
New Deal, 161–62, 249*n*19
Newhallville, 13, 123
New Haven, 5–12; children at home and at school, 53–80, 217–25; colonial era, 10–11, 203*n*17, 204*n*18; *1850–1930* economic and residential change, 13–23; growth of, 11, 13–23; Italian immigrant family economy, 59–60, 62, 64–65, 77, 80, 81–102, 103–21, 160, 175, 219*n*17, 225–38; juvenile employment, 39–52, 76–80, 81–102, 114–15, 121, 143, 153, 154, 175–76, 189–90, 210–17, 225–32; neighborhood ethnicity and schools, 122–54, 238–46; port of, 11, 15, 19; postwar expansion of high schools, 155–88, 192–95, 246–56; schooling and early life course, 24–52, 205–17. *See also* neighborhoods; schooling; *specific streets*
New Haven Board of Education, 24, 42
New Haven Code, 10
New Haven Green, 6
newspapers, 102, 113
New Testament, 54

New York, 15, 16

New York, New Haven, and Hartford
   Railroad, 15, 19, 202*n*7

New York City, 77, 93, 106

non-English-speaking children, 58, 67,
   210*n*52, 219*n*12

Oakes, Jeannie, 168

Oak Street, 14, 15, 18, 106, 122, 124, 125,
   128, 129, 133, 136, 203*n*17

occupations, 105–6; father's, and high
   school graduation rates of offspring,
   172–78; postwar high school
   expansion and, 157–58, 163–88, 246–56

office workers, 172, 178, 254*n*69

old maids, 238*n*55

Old Testament, 54

Olmstead, Frederick Law, "Report of
   the New Haven Civic Improvement
   Commission," 13

oral culture, peasant society as, 62

Orsi, Robert Anthony, 108–9, 221*n*43

Oyster Point, 124

"padrone" system, 203*n*13

Panic of *1873*, 40, 45

parent-child relations, 1–12, 31, 47,
   82–83; community and, 133–34, 135,
   145; high school expansion and,
   155–88, 192–95, 246–56; immigrant
   children as interpreters of foreign-
   host culture to parents, 68–70; impact
   of schooling on, 1–12, 53–80, 81–85,
   127–28, 140–54, 158, 165–67, 191–95,
   217–25, 242–46; Italian immigrant
   issues and obligations, 53–80, 81–102,
   104–21, 140, 152, 193–94, 225–32;
   marriage strategies and, 103–21;
   postwar, 81–102, 104–21, 140–54,
   155–88, 191–95, 225–38; restrictiveness
   toward daughters, 107–8; role of
   father in, 108, 144–45, 187–88; role of
   mother in, 108–9, 144; state as agent
   in, 70–71, 93. *See also* children; family;
   siblings

parochial schools, 28, 54

Patane, Josephine, 69–70

peers, 5, 11, 84, 121, 142, 146, 147–48, 153,
   154; competition, 40; dating and, 112;
   high school, 136–40, 149–51, 156, 179,
   187–88

Pelotti, Rosa, 101

Perlmann, Joel, 59

personal appearance, 94–99

Philadelphia, 215*n*85, 216*n*91, 256*n*101

play, children's, 66, 190

playground movement, 190

Plymouth colony, 10

police, 60

Polish immigrants, 15, 20, 83, 88, 118, 119,
   195, 223*n*75, 237*n*50; Jewish, 15, 91–92,
   119, 122, 124, 125, 126, 129, 132, 145,
   199*n*18

politics, 21, 22

population, 6; immigrant, 9, 11, 14–16,
   20, 22, 38, 124, 125; school-age, 28,
   124, 153, 154, 156–60, 192, 206*n*12

poverty, 31, 32, 125

Powdermaker, Hortense, 182

"priceless" children, 2–3

principals, 71, 126, 131, 134

private schools, 28, 207*n*17

Prospect Street, 14, 19

Protestantism, 54, 191, 215*n*85,
   257*n*4

psychology, 56, 163

public library, 6

public schools, 8, 22–23; annual
   attrition, 43; *1850–1930* rise of, 11,
   22–23; graded, 26, 27, 28–32, 35–38,
   161, 206*n*9, 208*n*24; impact on
   parent-child relations, 1–12, 53–80,
   81–85, 127–28, 140–54, 158, 165–67,
   191–95, 217–25, 242–46; Italian
   immigrant children in, 53–80, 122–54,
   217–25; late-nineteenth-century New
   Haven, 24–52, 205–17; postwar high
   school expansion, 155–88, 192–95,
   246–56. *See also* compulsory
   education; schools and schooling;
   specific schools

punctuality, 3, 84, 194

Puritans, 10, 204*n*18

Putman, Robert D., 126

Racca, Vittorio, 1–2, 99–102, 139–40, 232*n*67; "Selected Family Histories," 53
race, 54, 167, 168; "mental deficiencies" and, 57–58; prejudice, 123, 131–33, 142. *See also* ethnicity
radio, 7, 93, 100, 102, 113, 228*n*38, 229*n*44
Rae, Douglas W., 130
railroads, 15, 16, 18, 19, 106, 202*n*7
Rappa, Tessie, 94
recreation, 190
Reeder, Linda, 204*n*30
Reeves, Ruby Jo, 107, 111, 118–19, 237*n*50
reform, school, 55
reform schools, 37
religion, 5, 11, 22, 53–54, 85, 127, 144, 190–91, 204*n*23, 217*n*2, 257*nn*4, 5; church groups, 109, 191; in schools, 53–54; southern Italian, 70–71
residential change, of *1850–1930*, 13–23
"retardation," 30, 208*n*25, 210*n*52
"return migration," 17, 18, 58, 83, 202–3*n*10
Revolutionary War, 18
Rome, 16, 63
Roseman, Alberta, 179
Rotundo, E. Anthony, 206*n*5
rural school enrollment, 41
Russian immigrants, 15, 55, 239*n*10; Jewish, 16, 18, 77, 83, 91, 119, 122, 123, 124, 125, 126, 199*n*18, 224*n*83, 246*n*2
Ryan, Mary P., 25

St. Anthony's parish, 109
St. Michael's parish, 109, 204*n*23
Salerno, 20
Scafati, 20
schools and schooling, 3–12, 189–95, 199*n*16; colonial era, 10–11; early-to-mid-nineteenth-century, 11; ethnicity, neighborhoods, and class, 122–54, 238–46; geography of, 134–35, 149; graded, 26, 27, 28–32, 35–38, 161, 206*n*9, 208*n*24; high school expansion, 155–88, 192–95, 246–56; impact on parent-child relations, 1–12, 53–80, 81–85, 127–28, 140–54, 158,

165–67, 191–95, 217–25, 242–46; Italian immigrant children in, 53–80, 122–54, 217–25; late-nineteenth-century New Haven, 7, 11, 24–52, 205–17; marriage, and family economy, 103–21, 179, 232–38; population, 28, 124, 153, 154, 156–60, 192, 206*n*12; postwar, 122–54, 155–88; racism in, 131–33; truancy, 27, 30–33, 36–39, 43, 44–52, 210*n*44. *See also* attendance, school; compulsory education; curriculum; elementary schools; high schools; junior high schools; middle schools; public schools; teachers; withdrawal rates
Scranton Street school, 132–33, 238*n*4, 241*n*34
"second-generation problem," 242*n*44
Semper, Joseph, 182
sentimentalized child, 24–26, 35, 75, 83–84, 92–93, 186, 193, 206*n*10
Shakespeare, William, 168–70, 194
siblings, 5, 8, 121, 132, 142, 144, 148, 152, 211*n*55, 228*n*29, 236*n*44; as chaperones, 107–8. *See also* birth order; family
Sicily, 17, 18, 21, 64, 66, 204*n*30, 234*n*22
skilled employment, 170–71, 172
Slavs, 15, 57, 58, 118, 223*n*75
Smelser, Neil J., 41
Smith, Bernice S., 94, 96–98
Smith, Hilda, 162
Smith, Judith, 80
Smith-Hughes Act of *1918*, 249*n*19
social clubs, 22, 109, 122, 123, 235*n*35
Social Darwinism, 82
social promotion, 163, 256*n*101
social welfare agencies, 21, 56, 70, 86, 230*n*54, 255*n*86
socioeconomic status, 54, 55, 155, 168; neighborhood, ethnicity, and schools, 122–54, 238–46; postwar school expansion and, 155–88. *See also* economy; *specific social classes*
sociologists, 56, 85, 242*n*44
South America, 17
sports, 92, 136, 190

standardized testing, 30, 57–58, 161, 181
State Street, 18
steamships, 16–17
Strouse-Adler Company, 106
suburbs, 126
"Sunday" schools, 201*n*29
Sunday visiting, 109–10, 145, 234*n*24
suspension policy, 32

tardiness, 31, 134
Taylorism, 51, 216*n*91
teachers, 22, 35, 54, 126–27, 130–31, 146,
    147, 181; Italian American, 22, 67, 78,
    151–52; of Italian immigrant children,
    67–68, 71, 130, 132, 146; parental
    attitudes toward, 127, 135
tenements, 14, 15, 19, 20, 114
Tenth Ward, 20, 21, 239*n*8
Thomas, William I., 68
Thompson, E. P., 35
"timelessness," 25–26, 28, 85–86
tracking, 156–57
trade schools, 120, 168, 171, 186, 252*nn*43,
    44, 45
trade skills, 65–66
trade unions, 171
Tranquilli, Pauline, 101
transatlantic migration, 16–17,
    203*n*15
Troupe Junior High School, 129, 135–36,
    241*n*35
truancy, 27, 30–33, 36–39, 43, 44–52, 59,
    210*n*44, 214*n*80; of 1864–1900, 45–46
truant officers, 38, 60, 70, 214*n*80
Truman school, 129
Twelfth Ward, 20, 21

unemployment, 25, 39–40, 41, 42, 44,
    49, 87, 94, 98, 128, 158, 173, 188,
    199*n*16, 211*n*55, 212*n*63, 229–30*nn*45,
    54, 231*nn*61, 62, 232*n*67, 247*n*8,
    249*n*19, 250*n*20, 252*n*43
ungraded schools, 27–30, 210*n*49
Union Station, 15
upper class, 14, 40, 64
urban school enrollment, 41

vagrancy, 27, 36–39, 210*n*44
vandalism, 37
Vecchio, Antoinette, 102
Victorian courtship rituals, 111–12
Vinovskis, Maris A., 200*n*23
vocation. *See* occupations

walk to school, 6, 7
Wallace Street school, 124
Webster school, 28, 124, 207*n*17, 241*n*34
Welch school, 124, 129, 130–31, 133, 136,
    241*n*34
West River, 15
West Street school, 124–25, 238*n*4
Westville, 18, 122
Whalley Avenue, 14
white-collar occupations, 157, 171, 174,
    179–80, 254*n*70
Whitlock, Reverdy, 136–39
Whitney Avenue, 14
Williams, Phyllis, 74, 89, 95, 111, 113, 117
Winchester Repeating Arms, 14, 106, 114
Winchester school, 124, 238*n*4
withdrawal rates, 27, 32, 43, 46, 48–49,
    51, 88, 92, 116, 127, 148, 158–60,
    247–48*nn*11, 12, 14
Wooster Square, 14, 18–21, 69, 71, 83,
    106, 109, 122, 124, 128, 134, 182,
    232*n*67
"working age," 47–48
working class, 2–12, 55; *1850–1930*
    economic and residential changes,
    13–23; Italian American family
    economy, 59–60, 62, 64–65, 77, 80,
    81–102, 103–21, 160, 175, 219*n*17,
    225–38; Italian immigrant children at
    home and at school, 53–80, 217–25;
    late-nineteenth-century schooling
    and early life course, 24–52,
    205–17; marriage market, 103–21;
    neighborhood ethnicity and schools,
    122–54, 238–46; postwar expansion of
    high schools, 155–88, 192–93
Works Progress Administration, 182
World War I, 2, 17, 220*n*19
World War II, 3, 11, 22, 157, 238*n*3

Yale University, 6, 7, 79, 137, 139;
    Institute of Human Relations, 140
Yans-McLaughlin, Virginia, 77
York Square, 137
Young Men's Christian Associations,
    191, 257*n*5
Young Men's Hebrew Association, 191,
    257*n*5

Young Women's Christian Associations,
    191
"youth problem," 161–62, 249*n*18

Zelizer, Viviana A., 186, 193
Znaniecki, Florian, 68
Zunder school, 124, 129